Valgrind 3.11 Reference Manual

A catalogue record for this book is available from the Hong Kong Public Libraries.

Published in Hong Kong by Samurai Media Limited.

Email: info@samuraimedia.org

ISBN 978-988-8381-21-0

Table of Contents

The Valgrind Quick Start Guide

Release 3.11.0 22 September 2015
Copyright © 2000-2015 Valgrind Developers

Email: valgrind@valgrind.org

Table of Contents

The Valgrind Quick Start Guide

1. Introduction

The Valgrind tool suite provides a number of debugging and profiling tools that help you make your programs faster and more correct. The most popular of these tools is called Memcheck. It can detect many memory-related errors that are common in C and C++ programs and that can lead to crashes and unpredictable behaviour.

The rest of this guide gives the minimum information you need to start detecting memory errors in your program with Memcheck. For full documentation of Memcheck and the other tools, please read the User Manual.

2. Preparing your program

Compile your program with -g to include debugging information so that Memcheck's error messages include exact line numbers. Using -O0 is also a good idea, if you can tolerate the slowdown. With -O1 line numbers in error messages can be inaccurate, although generally speaking running Memcheck on code compiled at -O1 works fairly well, and the speed improvement compared to running -O0 is quite significant. Use of -O2 and above is not recommended as Memcheck occasionally reports uninitialised-value errors which don't really exist.

3. Running your program under Memcheck

If you normally run your program like this:
```
myprog arg1 arg2
```

Use this command line:
```
valgrind --leak-check=yes myprog arg1 arg2
```

Memcheck is the default tool. The --leak-check option turns on the detailed memory leak detector.

Your program will run much slower (eg. 20 to 30 times) than normal, and use a lot more memory. Memcheck will issue messages about memory errors and leaks that it detects.

4. Interpreting Memcheck's output

Here's an example C program, in a file called a.c, with a memory error and a memory leak.

```
#include <stdlib.h>

void f(void)
{
   int* x = malloc(10 * sizeof(int));
   x[10] = 0;        // problem 1: heap block overrun
}                    // problem 2: memory leak -- x not freed

int main(void)
{
   f();
   return 0;
}
```

Most error messages look like the following, which describes problem 1, the heap block overrun:

```
==19182== Invalid write of size 4
==19182==    at 0x804838F: f (example.c:6)
==19182==    by 0x80483AB: main (example.c:11)
==19182== Address 0x1BA45050 is 0 bytes after a block of size 40 alloc'd
==19182==    at 0x1B8FF5CD: malloc (vg_replace_malloc.c:130)
==19182==    by 0x8048385: f (example.c:5)
==19182==    by 0x80483AB: main (example.c:11)
```

Things to notice:

- There is a lot of information in each error message; read it carefully.

- The 19182 is the process ID; it's usually unimportant.

- The first line ("Invalid write...") tells you what kind of error it is. Here, the program wrote to some memory it should not have due to a heap block overrun.

- Below the first line is a stack trace telling you where the problem occurred. Stack traces can get quite large, and be confusing, especially if you are using the C++ STL. Reading them from the bottom up can help. If the stack trace is not big enough, use the --num-callers option to make it bigger.

- The code addresses (eg. 0x804838F) are usually unimportant, but occasionally crucial for tracking down weirder bugs.

- Some error messages have a second component which describes the memory address involved. This one shows that the written memory is just past the end of a block allocated with malloc() on line 5 of example.c.

It's worth fixing errors in the order they are reported, as later errors can be caused by earlier errors. Failing to do this is a common cause of difficulty with Memcheck.

Memory leak messages look like this:

```
==19182== 40 bytes in 1 blocks are definitely lost in loss record 1 of 1
==19182==    at 0x1B8FF5CD: malloc (vg_replace_malloc.c:130)
==19182==    by 0x8048385: f (a.c:5)
==19182==    by 0x80483AB: main (a.c:11)
```

The stack trace tells you where the leaked memory was allocated. Memcheck cannot tell you why the memory leaked, unfortunately. (Ignore the "vg_replace_malloc.c", that's an implementation detail.)

There are several kinds of leaks; the two most important categories are:

- "definitely lost": your program is leaking memory -- fix it!

- "probably lost": your program is leaking memory, unless you're doing funny things with pointers (such as moving them to point to the middle of a heap block).

Memcheck also reports uses of uninitialised values, most commonly with the message "Conditional jump or move depends on uninitialised value(s)". It can be difficult to determine the root cause of these errors. Try using the --track-origins=yes to get extra information. This makes Memcheck run slower, but the extra information you get often saves a lot of time figuring out where the uninitialised values are coming from.

If you don't understand an error message, please consult Explanation of error messages from Memcheck in the Valgrind User Manual which has examples of all the error messages Memcheck produces.

5. Caveats

Memcheck is not perfect; it occasionally produces false positives, and there are mechanisms for suppressing these (see Suppressing errors in the Valgrind User Manual). However, it is typically right 99% of the time, so you should be wary of ignoring its error messages. After all, you wouldn't ignore warning messages produced by a compiler, right? The suppression mechanism is also useful if Memcheck is reporting errors in library code that you cannot change. The default suppression set hides a lot of these, but you may come across more.

Memcheck cannot detect every memory error your program has. For example, it can't detect out-of-range reads or writes to arrays that are allocated statically or on the stack. But it should detect many errors that could crash your program (eg. cause a segmentation fault).

Try to make your program so clean that Memcheck reports no errors. Once you achieve this state, it is much easier to see when changes to the program cause Memcheck to report new errors. Experience from several years of Memcheck use shows that it is possible to make even huge programs run Memcheck-clean. For example, large parts of KDE, OpenOffice.org and Firefox are Memcheck-clean, or very close to it.

6. More information

Please consult the Valgrind FAQ and the Valgrind User Manual, which have much more information. Note that the other tools in the Valgrind distribution can be invoked with the --tool option.

Valgrind User Manual

Release 3.11.0 22 September 2015
Copyright © 2000-2015 Valgrind Developers

Email: valgrind@valgrind.org

Table of Contents

1. Introduction

1.1. An Overview of Valgrind

Valgrind is an instrumentation framework for building dynamic analysis tools. It comes with a set of tools each of which performs some kind of debugging, profiling, or similar task that helps you improve your programs. Valgrind's architecture is modular, so new tools can be created easily and without disturbing the existing structure.

A number of useful tools are supplied as standard.

1. **Memcheck** is a memory error detector. It helps you make your programs, particularly those written in C and C++, more correct.

2. **Cachegrind** is a cache and branch-prediction profiler. It helps you make your programs run faster.

3. **Callgrind** is a call-graph generating cache profiler. It has some overlap with Cachegrind, but also gathers some information that Cachegrind does not.

4. **Helgrind** is a thread error detector. It helps you make your multi-threaded programs more correct.

5. **DRD** is also a thread error detector. It is similar to Helgrind but uses different analysis techniques and so may find different problems.

6. **Massif** is a heap profiler. It helps you make your programs use less memory.

7. **DHAT** is a different kind of heap profiler. It helps you understand issues of block lifetimes, block utilisation, and layout inefficiencies.

8. **SGcheck** is an experimental tool that can detect overruns of stack and global arrays. Its functionality is complementary to that of Memcheck: SGcheck finds problems that Memcheck can't, and vice versa..

9. **BBV** is an experimental SimPoint basic block vector generator. It is useful to people doing computer architecture research and development.

There are also a couple of minor tools that aren't useful to most users: **Lackey** is an example tool that illustrates some instrumentation basics; and **Nulgrind** is the minimal Valgrind tool that does no analysis or instrumentation, and is only useful for testing purposes.

Valgrind is closely tied to details of the CPU and operating system, and to a lesser extent, the compiler and basic C libraries. Nonetheless, it supports a number of widely-used platforms, listed in full at http://www.valgrind.org/.

Valgrind is built via the standard Unix ./configure, make, make install process; full details are given in the README file in the distribution.

Valgrind is licensed under the The GNU General Public License, version 2. The valgrind/*.h headers that you may wish to include in your code (eg. valgrind.h, memcheck.h, helgrind.h, etc.) are distributed under a BSD-style license, so you may include them in your code without worrying about license conflicts. Some of the PThreads test cases, pth_*.c, are taken from "Pthreads Programming" by Bradford Nichols, Dick Buttlar & Jacqueline Proulx Farrell, ISBN 1-56592-115-1, published by O'Reilly & Associates, Inc.

If you contribute code to Valgrind, please ensure your contributions are licensed as "GPLv2, or (at your option) any later version." This is so as to allow the possibility of easily upgrading the license to GPLv3 in future. If you want to modify code in the VEX subdirectory, please also see the file VEX/HACKING.README in the distribution.

1.2. How to navigate this manual

This manual's structure reflects the structure of Valgrind itself. First, we describe the Valgrind core, how to use it, and the options it supports. Then, each tool has its own chapter in this manual. You only need to read the documentation for the core and for the tool(s) you actually use, although you may find it helpful to be at least a little bit familiar with what all tools do. If you're new to all this, you probably want to run the Memcheck tool and you might find the The Valgrind Quick Start Guide useful.

Be aware that the core understands some command line options, and the tools have their own options which they know about. This means there is no central place describing all the options that are accepted -- you have to read the options documentation both for Valgrind's core and for the tool you want to use.

2. Using and understanding the Valgrind core

This chapter describes the Valgrind core services, command-line options and behaviours. That means it is relevant regardless of what particular tool you are using. The information should be sufficient for you to make effective day-to-day use of Valgrind. Advanced topics related to the Valgrind core are described in Valgrind's core: advanced topics.

A point of terminology: most references to "Valgrind" in this chapter refer to the Valgrind core services.

2.1. What Valgrind does with your program

Valgrind is designed to be as non-intrusive as possible. It works directly with existing executables. You don't need to recompile, relink, or otherwise modify the program to be checked.

You invoke Valgrind like this:

```
valgrind [valgrind-options] your-prog [your-prog-options]
```

The most important option is `--tool` which dictates which Valgrind tool to run. For example, if want to run the command `ls -l` using the memory-checking tool Memcheck, issue this command:

```
valgrind --tool=memcheck ls -l
```

However, Memcheck is the default, so if you want to use it you can omit the `--tool` option.

Regardless of which tool is in use, Valgrind takes control of your program before it starts. Debugging information is read from the executable and associated libraries, so that error messages and other outputs can be phrased in terms of source code locations, when appropriate.

Your program is then run on a synthetic CPU provided by the Valgrind core. As new code is executed for the first time, the core hands the code to the selected tool. The tool adds its own instrumentation code to this and hands the result back to the core, which coordinates the continued execution of this instrumented code.

The amount of instrumentation code added varies widely between tools. At one end of the scale, Memcheck adds code to check every memory access and every value computed, making it run 10-50 times slower than natively. At the other end of the spectrum, the minimal tool, called Nulgrind, adds no instrumentation at all and causes in total "only" about a 4 times slowdown.

Valgrind simulates every single instruction your program executes. Because of this, the active tool checks, or profiles, not only the code in your application but also in all supporting dynamically-linked libraries, including the C library, graphical libraries, and so on.

If you're using an error-detection tool, Valgrind may detect errors in system libraries, for example the GNU C or X11 libraries, which you have to use. You might not be interested in these errors, since you probably have no control over that code. Therefore, Valgrind allows you to selectively suppress errors, by recording them in a suppressions file which is read when Valgrind starts up. The build mechanism selects default suppressions which give reasonable behaviour for the OS and libraries detected on your machine. To make it easier to write suppressions, you can use the `--gen-suppressions=yes` option. This tells Valgrind to print out a suppression for each reported error, which you can then copy into a suppressions file.

Different error-checking tools report different kinds of errors. The suppression mechanism therefore allows you to say which tool or tool(s) each suppression applies to.

2.2. Getting started

First off, consider whether it might be beneficial to recompile your application and supporting libraries with debugging info enabled (the -g option). Without debugging info, the best Valgrind tools will be able to do is guess which function a particular piece of code belongs to, which makes both error messages and profiling output nearly useless. With -g, you'll get messages which point directly to the relevant source code lines.

Another option you might like to consider, if you are working with C++, is -fno-inline. That makes it easier to see the function-call chain, which can help reduce confusion when navigating around large C++ apps. For example, debugging OpenOffice.org with Memcheck is a bit easier when using this option. You don't have to do this, but doing so helps Valgrind produce more accurate and less confusing error reports. Chances are you're set up like this already, if you intended to debug your program with GNU GDB, or some other debugger. Alternatively, the Valgrind option --read-inline-info=yes instructs Valgrind to read the debug information describing inlining information. With this, function call chain will be properly shown, even when your application is compiled with inlining.

If you are planning to use Memcheck: On rare occasions, compiler optimisations (at -O2 and above, and sometimes -O1) have been observed to generate code which fools Memcheck into wrongly reporting uninitialised value errors, or missing uninitialised value errors. We have looked in detail into fixing this, and unfortunately the result is that doing so would give a further significant slowdown in what is already a slow tool. So the best solution is to turn off optimisation altogether. Since this often makes things unmanageably slow, a reasonable compromise is to use -O. This gets you the majority of the benefits of higher optimisation levels whilst keeping relatively small the chances of false positives or false negatives from Memcheck. Also, you should compile your code with -Wall because it can identify some or all of the problems that Valgrind can miss at the higher optimisation levels. (Using -Wall is also a good idea in general.) All other tools (as far as we know) are unaffected by optimisation level, and for profiling tools like Cachegrind it is better to compile your program at its normal optimisation level.

Valgrind understands the DWARF2/3/4 formats used by GCC 3.1 and later. The reader for "stabs" debugging format (used by GCC versions prior to 3.1) has been disabled in Valgrind 3.9.0.

When you're ready to roll, run Valgrind as described above. Note that you should run the real (machine-code) executable here. If your application is started by, for example, a shell or Perl script, you'll need to modify it to invoke Valgrind on the real executables. Running such scripts directly under Valgrind will result in you getting error reports pertaining to /bin/sh, /usr/bin/perl, or whatever interpreter you're using. This may not be what you want and can be confusing. You can force the issue by giving the option --trace-children=yes, but confusion is still likely.

2.3. The Commentary

Valgrind tools write a commentary, a stream of text, detailing error reports and other significant events. All lines in the commentary have following form:

```
==12345== some-message-from-Valgrind
```

The 12345 is the process ID. This scheme makes it easy to distinguish program output from Valgrind commentary, and also easy to differentiate commentaries from different processes which have become merged together, for whatever reason.

By default, Valgrind tools write only essential messages to the commentary, so as to avoid flooding you with information of secondary importance. If you want more information about what is happening, re-run, passing the `-v` option to Valgrind. A second `-v` gives yet more detail.

You can direct the commentary to three different places:

1. The default: send it to a file descriptor, which is by default 2 (stderr). So, if you give the core no options, it will write commentary to the standard error stream. If you want to send it to some other file descriptor, for example number 9, you can specify `--log-fd=9`.

   This is the simplest and most common arrangement, but can cause problems when Valgrinding entire trees of processes which expect specific file descriptors, particularly stdin/stdout/stderr, to be available for their own use.

2. A less intrusive option is to write the commentary to a file, which you specify by `--log-file=filename`. There are special format specifiers that can be used to use a process ID or an environment variable name in the log file name. These are useful/necessary if your program invokes multiple processes (especially for MPI programs). See the basic options section for more details.

3. The least intrusive option is to send the commentary to a network socket. The socket is specified as an IP address and port number pair, like this: `--log-socket=192.168.0.1:12345` if you want to send the output to host IP 192.168.0.1 port 12345 (note: we have no idea if 12345 is a port of pre-existing significance). You can also omit the port number: `--log-socket=192.168.0.1`, in which case a default port of 1500 is used. This default is defined by the constant `VG_CLO_DEFAULT_LOGPORT` in the sources.

   Note, unfortunately, that you have to use an IP address here, rather than a hostname.

   Writing to a network socket is pointless if you don't have something listening at the other end. We provide a simple listener program, `valgrind-listener`, which accepts connections on the specified port and copies whatever it is sent to stdout. Probably someone will tell us this is a horrible security risk. It seems likely that people will write more sophisticated listeners in the fullness of time.

   `valgrind-listener` can accept simultaneous connections from up to 50 Valgrinded processes. In front of each line of output it prints the current number of active connections in round brackets.

   `valgrind-listener` accepts three command-line options:

   `-e --exit-at-zero`
   When the number of connected processes falls back to zero, exit. Without this, it will run forever, that is, until you send it Control-C.

   `--max-connect=INTEGER`
   By default, the listener can connect to up to 50 processes. Occasionally, that number is too small. Use this option to provide a different limit. E.g. `--max-connect=100`.

`portnumber`
Changes the port it listens on from the default (1500). The specified port must be in the range 1024 to 65535. The same restriction applies to port numbers specified by a `--log-socket` to Valgrind itself.

If a Valgrinded process fails to connect to a listener, for whatever reason (the listener isn't running, invalid or unreachable host or port, etc), Valgrind switches back to writing the commentary to stderr. The same goes for any process which loses an established connection to a listener. In other words, killing the listener doesn't kill the processes sending data to it.

Here is an important point about the relationship between the commentary and profiling output from tools. The commentary contains a mix of messages from the Valgrind core and the selected tool. If the tool reports errors, it will report them to the commentary. However, if the tool does profiling, the profile data will be written to a file of some kind, depending on the tool, and independent of what `--log-*` options are in force. The commentary is intended to be a low-bandwidth, human-readable channel. Profiling data, on the other hand, is usually voluminous and not meaningful without further processing, which is why we have chosen this arrangement.

2.4. Reporting of errors

When an error-checking tool detects something bad happening in the program, an error message is written to the commentary. Here's an example from Memcheck:

```
==25832== Invalid read of size 4
==25832==    at 0x8048724: BandMatrix::ReSize(int, int, int) (bogon.cpp:45)
==25832==    by 0x80487AF: main (bogon.cpp:66)
==25832==  Address 0xBFFFF74C is not stack'd, malloc'd or free'd
```

This message says that the program did an illegal 4-byte read of address 0xBFFFF74C, which, as far as Memcheck can tell, is not a valid stack address, nor corresponds to any current heap blocks or recently freed heap blocks. The read is happening at line 45 of `bogon.cpp`, called from line 66 of the same file, etc. For errors associated with an identified (current or freed) heap block, for example reading freed memory, Valgrind reports not only the location where the error happened, but also where the associated heap block was allocated/freed.

Valgrind remembers all error reports. When an error is detected, it is compared against old reports, to see if it is a duplicate. If so, the error is noted, but no further commentary is emitted. This avoids you being swamped with bazillions of duplicate error reports.

If you want to know how many times each error occurred, run with the `-v` option. When execution finishes, all the reports are printed out, along with, and sorted by, their occurrence counts. This makes it easy to see which errors have occurred most frequently.

Errors are reported before the associated operation actually happens. For example, if you're using Memcheck and your program attempts to read from address zero, Memcheck will emit a message to this effect, and your program will then likely die with a segmentation fault.

In general, you should try and fix errors in the order that they are reported. Not doing so can be confusing. For example, a program which copies uninitialised values to several memory locations, and later uses them, will generate several error messages, when run on Memcheck. The first such error message may well give the most direct clue to the root cause of the problem.

The process of detecting duplicate errors is quite an expensive one and can become a significant performance overhead if your program generates huge quantities of errors. To avoid serious problems, Valgrind will simply stop collecting errors after 1,000 different errors have been seen, or 10,000,000 errors in total have been seen. In this situation you might as well stop your program and fix it, because Valgrind won't tell you anything else useful after this. Note that the 1,000/10,000,000 limits apply after suppressed errors are removed. These limits are defined in `m_errormgr.c` and can be increased if necessary.

To avoid this cutoff you can use the `--error-limit=no` option. Then Valgrind will always show errors, regardless of how many there are. Use this option carefully, since it may have a bad effect on performance.

2.5. Suppressing errors

The error-checking tools detect numerous problems in the system libraries, such as the C library, which come pre-installed with your OS. You can't easily fix these, but you don't want to see these errors (and yes, there are many!) So Valgrind reads a list of errors to suppress at startup. A default suppression file is created by the `./configure` script when the system is built.

You can modify and add to the suppressions file at your leisure, or, better, write your own. Multiple suppression files are allowed. This is useful if part of your project contains errors you can't or don't want to fix, yet you don't want to continuously be reminded of them.

Note: By far the easiest way to add suppressions is to use the `--gen-suppressions=yes` option described in Core Command-line Options. This generates suppressions automatically. For best results, though, you may want to edit the output of `--gen-suppressions=yes` by hand, in which case it would be advisable to read through this section.

Each error to be suppressed is described very specifically, to minimise the possibility that a suppression-directive inadvertently suppresses a bunch of similar errors which you did want to see. The suppression mechanism is designed to allow precise yet flexible specification of errors to suppress.

If you use the `-v` option, at the end of execution, Valgrind prints out one line for each used suppression, giving the number of times it got used, its name and the filename and line number where the suppression is defined. Depending on the suppression kind, the filename and line number are optionally followed by additional information (such as the number of blocks and bytes suppressed by a memcheck leak suppression). Here's the suppressions used by a run of `valgrind -v --tool=memcheck ls -l`:

```
--1610-- used_suppression:     2 dl-hack3-cond-1 /usr/lib/valgrind/default.supp:1234

--1610-- used_suppression:     2 glibc-2.5.x-on-SUSE-10.2-(PPC)-2a /usr/lib/valgrind/d
```

Multiple suppressions files are allowed. Valgrind loads suppression patterns from `$PREFIX/lib/valgrind/default.s` unless `--default-suppressions=no` has been specified. You can ask to add suppressions from additional files by specifying `--suppressions=/path/to/file.supp` one or more times.

If you want to understand more about suppressions, look at an existing suppressions file whilst reading the following documentation. The file `glibc-2.3.supp`, in the source distribution, provides some good examples.

Each suppression has the following components:

- First line: its name. This merely gives a handy name to the suppression, by which it is referred to in the summary of used suppressions printed out when a program finishes. It's not important what the name is; any identifying string will do.

- Second line: name of the tool(s) that the suppression is for (if more than one, comma-separated), and the name of the suppression itself, separated by a colon (n.b.: no spaces are allowed), eg:

```
tool_name1,tool_name2:suppression_name
```

Recall that Valgrind is a modular system, in which different instrumentation tools can observe your program whilst it is running. Since different tools detect different kinds of errors, it is necessary to say which tool(s) the suppression is meaningful to.

Tools will complain, at startup, if a tool does not understand any suppression directed to it. Tools ignore suppressions which are not directed to them. As a result, it is quite practical to put suppressions for all tools into the same suppression file.

- Next line: a small number of suppression types have extra information after the second line (eg. the `Param` suppression for Memcheck)

- Remaining lines: This is the calling context for the error -- the chain of function calls that led to it. There can be up to 24 of these lines.

Locations may be names of either shared objects or functions. They begin `obj:` and `fun:` respectively. Function and object names to match against may use the wildcard characters `*` and `?`.

Important note: C++ function names must be **mangled**. If you are writing suppressions by hand, use the `--demangle=no` option to get the mangled names in your error messages. An example of a mangled C++ name is `_ZN9QListView4showEv`. This is the form that the GNU C++ compiler uses internally, and the form that must be used in suppression files. The equivalent demangled name, `QListView::show()`, is what you see at the C++ source code level.

A location line may also be simply `"..."` (three dots). This is a frame-level wildcard, which matches zero or more frames. Frame level wildcards are useful because they make it easy to ignore varying numbers of uninteresting frames in between frames of interest. That is often important when writing suppressions which are intended to be robust against variations in the amount of function inlining done by compilers.

- Finally, the entire suppression must be between curly braces. Each brace must be the first character on its own line.

A suppression only suppresses an error when the error matches all the details in the suppression. Here's an example:

```
{
  __gconv_transform_ascii_internal/__mbrtowc/mbtowc
  Memcheck:Value4
  fun:__gconv_transform_ascii_internal
  fun:__mbr*toc
  fun:mbtowc
}
```

What it means is: for Memcheck only, suppress a use-of-uninitialised-value error, when the data size is 4, when it occurs in the function `__gconv_transform_ascii_internal`, when that is called from any function of name matching `__mbr*toc`, when that is called from `mbtowc`. It doesn't apply under any other circumstances. The string by which this suppression is identified to the user is `__gconv_transform_ascii_internal/__mbrtowc/mbtowc`.

(See Writing suppression files for more details on the specifics of Memcheck's suppression kinds.)

Another example, again for the Memcheck tool:

```
{
  libX11.so.6.2/libX11.so.6.2/libXaw.so.7.0
  Memcheck:Value4
  obj:/usr/X11R6/lib/libX11.so.6.2
  obj:/usr/X11R6/lib/libX11.so.6.2
  obj:/usr/X11R6/lib/libXaw.so.7.0
}
```

This suppresses any size 4 uninitialised-value error which occurs anywhere in `libX11.so.6.2`, when called from anywhere in the same library, when called from anywhere in `libXaw.so.7.0`. The inexact specification of locations is regrettable, but is about all you can hope for, given that the X11 libraries shipped on the Linux distro on which this example was made have had their symbol tables removed.

Although the above two examples do not make this clear, you can freely mix `obj:` and `fun:` lines in a suppression.

Finally, here's an example using three frame-level wildcards:

```
{
  a-contrived-example
  Memcheck:Leak
  fun:malloc
  ...
  fun:ddd
  ...
  fun:ccc
  ...
  fun:main
}
```

This suppresses Memcheck memory-leak errors, in the case where the allocation was done by `main` calling (though any number of intermediaries, including zero) `ccc`, calling onwards via `ddd` and eventually to `malloc.`.

2.6. Core Command-line Options

As mentioned above, Valgrind's core accepts a common set of options. The tools also accept tool-specific options, which are documented separately for each tool.

Valgrind's default settings succeed in giving reasonable behaviour in most cases. We group the available options by rough categories.

2.6.1. Tool-selection Option

The single most important option.

`--tool=<toolname>` [default: memcheck]
Run the Valgrind tool called `toolname`, e.g. memcheck, cachegrind, callgrind, helgrind, drd, massif, lackey, none, exp-sgcheck, exp-bbv, exp-dhat, etc.

2.6.2. Basic Options

These options work with all tools.

`-h --help`
Show help for all options, both for the core and for the selected tool. If the option is repeated it is equivalent to giving `--help-debug`.

`--help-debug`
Same as `--help`, but also lists debugging options which usually are only of use to Valgrind's developers.

`--version`
Show the version number of the Valgrind core. Tools can have their own version numbers. There is a scheme in place to ensure that tools only execute when the core version is one they are known to work with. This was done to minimise the chances of strange problems arising from tool-vs-core version incompatibilities.

`-q, --quiet`
Run silently, and only print error messages. Useful if you are running regression tests or have some other automated test machinery.

`-v, --verbose`
Be more verbose. Gives extra information on various aspects of your program, such as: the shared objects loaded, the suppressions used, the progress of the instrumentation and execution engines, and warnings about unusual behaviour. Repeating the option increases the verbosity level.

`--trace-children=<yes|no>` [default: no]
When enabled, Valgrind will trace into sub-processes initiated via the `exec` system call. This is necessary for multi-process programs.

Note that Valgrind does trace into the child of a `fork` (it would be difficult not to, since `fork` makes an identical copy of a process), so this option is arguably badly named. However, most children of `fork` calls immediately call `exec` anyway.

`--trace-children-skip=patt1,patt2,...`
This option only has an effect when `--trace-children=yes` is specified. It allows for some children to be skipped. The option takes a comma separated list of patterns for the names of child executables that Valgrind should not trace into. Patterns may include the metacharacters ? and *, which have the usual meaning.

This can be useful for pruning uninteresting branches from a tree of processes being run on Valgrind. But you should be careful when using it. When Valgrind skips tracing into an executable, it doesn't just skip tracing that executable, it also skips tracing any of that executable's child processes. In other words, the flag doesn't merely cause tracing to stop at the specified executables -- it skips tracing of entire process subtrees rooted at any of the specified executables.

`--trace-children-skip-by-arg=patt1,patt2,...`
This is the same as `--trace-children-skip`, with one difference: the decision as to whether to trace into a child process is made by examining the arguments to the child process, rather than the name of its executable.

`--child-silent-after-fork=<yes|no>` [default: no]
When enabled, Valgrind will not show any debugging or logging output for the child process resulting from a `fork` call. This can make the output less confusing (although more misleading) when dealing with processes that create children. It is particularly useful in conjunction with `--trace-children=`. Use of this option is also strongly recommended if you are requesting XML output (`--xml=yes`), since otherwise the XML from child and parent may become mixed up, which usually makes it useless.

`--vgdb=<no|yes|full>` [default: yes]
Valgrind will provide "gdbserver" functionality when `--vgdb=yes` or `--vgdb=full` is specified. This allows an external GNU GDB debugger to control and debug your program when it runs on Valgrind. `--vgdb=full` incurs significant performance overheads, but provides more precise breakpoints and watchpoints. See Debugging your program using Valgrind's gdbserver and GDB for a detailed description.

If the embedded gdbserver is enabled but no gdb is currently being used, the vgdb command line utility can send "monitor commands" to Valgrind from a shell. The Valgrind core provides a set of Valgrind monitor commands. A tool can optionally provide tool specific monitor commands, which are documented in the tool specific chapter.

`--vgdb-error=<number>` [default: 999999999]
Use this option when the Valgrind gdbserver is enabled with `--vgdb=yes` or `--vgdb=full`. Tools that report errors will wait for "`number`" errors to be reported before freezing the program and waiting for you to connect with GDB. It follows that a value of zero will cause the gdbserver to be started before your program is executed. This is typically used to insert GDB breakpoints before execution, and also works with tools that do not report errors, such as Massif.

`--vgdb-stop-at=<set>` [default: none]
Use this option when the Valgrind gdbserver is enabled with `--vgdb=yes` or `--vgdb=full`. The Valgrind gdbserver will be invoked for each error after `--vgdb-error` have been reported. You can additionally ask the Valgrind gdbserver to be invoked for other events, specified in one of the following ways:

• a comma separated list of one or more of `startup exit valgrindabexit`.

  The values `startup exit valgrindabexit` respectively indicate to invoke gdbserver before your program is executed, after the last instruction of your program, on Valgrind abnormal exit (e.g. internal error, out of memory, ...).

  Note: `startup` and `--vgdb-error=0` will both cause Valgrind gdbserver to be invoked before your program is executed. The `--vgdb-error=0` will in addition cause your program to stop on all subsequent errors.

• `all` to specify the complete set. It is equivalent to `--vgdb-stop-at=startup,exit,valgrindabexit`.

• `none` for the empty set.

`--track-fds=<yes|no>` [default: no]
When enabled, Valgrind will print out a list of open file descriptors on exit or on request, via the gdbserver monitor command `v.info open_fds`. Along with each file descriptor is printed a stack backtrace of where the file was opened and any details relating to the file descriptor such as the file name or socket details.

`--time-stamp=<yes|no>` [default: no]
When enabled, each message is preceded with an indication of the elapsed wallclock time since startup, expressed as days, hours, minutes, seconds and milliseconds.

`--log-fd=<number>` [default: 2, stderr]
Specifies that Valgrind should send all of its messages to the specified file descriptor. The default, 2, is the standard error channel (stderr). Note that this may interfere with the client's own use of stderr, as Valgrind's output will be interleaved with any output that the client sends to stderr.

`--log-file=<filename>`

Specifies that Valgrind should send all of its messages to the specified file. If the file name is empty, it causes an abort. There are three special format specifiers that can be used in the file name.

`%p` is replaced with the current process ID. This is very useful for program that invoke multiple processes. WARNING: If you use `--trace-children=yes` and your program invokes multiple processes OR your program forks without calling exec afterwards, and you don't use this specifier (or the `%q` specifier below), the Valgrind output from all those processes will go into one file, possibly jumbled up, and possibly incomplete.

`%q{FOO}` is replaced with the contents of the environment variable `FOO`. If the `{FOO}` part is malformed, it causes an abort. This specifier is rarely needed, but very useful in certain circumstances (eg. when running MPI programs). The idea is that you specify a variable which will be set differently for each process in the job, for example `BPROC_RANK` or whatever is applicable in your MPI setup. If the named environment variable is not set, it causes an abort. Note that in some shells, the { and } characters may need to be escaped with a backslash.

`%%` is replaced with `%`.

If an `%` is followed by any other character, it causes an abort.

If the file name specifies a relative file name, it is put in the program's initial working directory : this is the current directory when the program started its execution after the fork or after the exec. If it specifies an absolute file name (ie. starts with '/') then it is put there.

`--log-socket=<ip-address:port-number>`

Specifies that Valgrind should send all of its messages to the specified port at the specified IP address. The port may be omitted, in which case port 1500 is used. If a connection cannot be made to the specified socket, Valgrind falls back to writing output to the standard error (stderr). This option is intended to be used in conjunction with the `valgrind-listener` program. For further details, see the commentary in the manual.

2.6.3. Error-related Options

These options are used by all tools that can report errors, e.g. Memcheck, but not Cachegrind.

`--xml=<yes|no> [default: no]`

When enabled, the important parts of the output (e.g. tool error messages) will be in XML format rather than plain text. Furthermore, the XML output will be sent to a different output channel than the plain text output. Therefore, you also must use one of `--xml-fd`, `--xml-file` or `--xml-socket` to specify where the XML is to be sent.

Less important messages will still be printed in plain text, but because the XML output and plain text output are sent to different output channels (the destination of the plain text output is still controlled by `--log-fd`, `--log-file` and `--log-socket`) this should not cause problems.

This option is aimed at making life easier for tools that consume Valgrind's output as input, such as GUI front ends. Currently this option works with Memcheck, Helgrind, DRD and SGcheck. The output format is specified in the file `docs/internals/xml-output-protocol4.txt` in the source tree for Valgrind 3.5.0 or later.

The recommended options for a GUI to pass, when requesting XML output, are: `--xml=yes` to enable XML output, `--xml-file` to send the XML output to a (presumably GUI-selected) file, `--log-file` to send the plain text output to a second GUI-selected file, `--child-silent-after-fork=yes`, and `-q` to restrict the plain text output to critical error messages created by Valgrind itself. For example, failure to read a specified suppressions file counts as a critical error message. In this way, for a successful run the text output file will be empty. But if it isn't empty, then it will contain important information which the GUI user should be made aware of.

`--xml-fd=<number>` [default: -1, disabled]
Specifies that Valgrind should send its XML output to the specified file descriptor. It must be used in conjunction with `--xml=yes`.

`--xml-file=<filename>`
Specifies that Valgrind should send its XML output to the specified file. It must be used in conjunction with `--xml=yes`. Any `%p` or `%q` sequences appearing in the filename are expanded in exactly the same way as they are for `--log-file`. See the description of `--log-file` for details.

`--xml-socket=<ip-address:port-number>`
Specifies that Valgrind should send its XML output the specified port at the specified IP address. It must be used in conjunction with `--xml=yes`. The form of the argument is the same as that used by `--log-socket`. See the description of `--log-socket` for further details.

`--xml-user-comment=<string>`
Embeds an extra user comment string at the start of the XML output. Only works when `--xml=yes` is specified; ignored otherwise.

`--demangle=<yes|no>` [default: yes]
Enable/disable automatic demangling (decoding) of C++ names. Enabled by default. When enabled, Valgrind will attempt to translate encoded C++ names back to something approaching the original. The demangler handles symbols mangled by g++ versions 2.X, 3.X and 4.X.

An important fact about demangling is that function names mentioned in suppressions files should be in their mangled form. Valgrind does not demangle function names when searching for applicable suppressions, because to do otherwise would make suppression file contents dependent on the state of Valgrind's demangling machinery, and also slow down suppression matching.

`--num-callers=<number>` [default: 12]
Specifies the maximum number of entries shown in stack traces that identify program locations. Note that errors are commoned up using only the top four function locations (the place in the current function, and that of its three immediate callers). So this doesn't affect the total number of errors reported.

The maximum value for this is 500. Note that higher settings will make Valgrind run a bit more slowly and take a bit more memory, but can be useful when working with programs with deeply-nested call chains.

`--unw-stack-scan-thresh=<number>` [default: 0] , `--unw-stack-scan-frames=<number>` [default: 5]
Stack-scanning support is available only on ARM targets.

These flags enable and control stack unwinding by stack scanning. When the normal stack unwinding mechanisms -- usage of Dwarf CFI records, and frame-pointer following -- fail, stack scanning may be able to recover a stack trace.

Note that stack scanning is an imprecise, heuristic mechanism that may give very misleading results, or none at all. It should be used only in emergencies, when normal unwinding fails, and it is important to nevertheless have stack traces.

Stack scanning is a simple technique: the unwinder reads words from the stack, and tries to guess which of them might be return addresses, by checking to see if they point just after ARM or Thumb call instructions. If so, the word is added to the backtrace.

The main danger occurs when a function call returns, leaving its return address exposed, and a new function is called, but the new function does not overwrite the old address. The result of this is that the backtrace may contain entries for functions which have already returned, and so be very confusing.

A second limitation of this implementation is that it will scan only the page (4KB, normally) containing the starting stack pointer. If the stack frames are large, this may result in only a few (or not even any) being present in the trace. Also, if you are unlucky and have an initial stack pointer near the end of its containing page, the scan may miss all interesting frames.

By default stack scanning is disabled. The normal use case is to ask for it when a stack trace would otherwise be very short. So, to enable it, use `--unw-stack-scan-thresh=number`. This requests Valgrind to try using stack scanning to "extend" stack traces which contain fewer than `number` frames.

If stack scanning does take place, it will only generate at most the number of frames specified by `--unw-stack-scan-frames`. Typically, stack scanning generates so many garbage entries that this value is set to a low value (5) by default. In no case will a stack trace larger than the value specified by `--num-callers` be created.

`--error-limit=<yes|no> [default: yes]`
When enabled, Valgrind stops reporting errors after 10,000,000 in total, or 1,000 different ones, have been seen. This is to stop the error tracking machinery from becoming a huge performance overhead in programs with many errors.

`--error-exitcode=<number> [default: 0]`
Specifies an alternative exit code to return if Valgrind reported any errors in the run. When set to the default value (zero), the return value from Valgrind will always be the return value of the process being simulated. When set to a nonzero value, that value is returned instead, if Valgrind detects any errors. This is useful for using Valgrind as part of an automated test suite, since it makes it easy to detect test cases for which Valgrind has reported errors, just by inspecting return codes.

`--error-markers=<begin>,<end> [default: none]`
When errors are output as plain text (i.e. XML not used), `--error-markers` instructs to output a line containing the `begin` (`end`) string before (after) each error.

Such marker lines facilitate searching for errors and/or extracting errors in an output file that contain valgrind errors mixed with the program output.

Note that empty markers are accepted. So, only using a begin (or an end) marker is possible.

`--sigill-diagnostics=<yes|no> [default: yes]`
Enable/disable printing of illegal instruction diagnostics. Enabled by default, but defaults to disabled when `--quiet` is given. The default can always be explicitly overridden by giving this option.

When enabled, a warning message will be printed, along with some diagnostics, whenever an instruction is encountered that Valgrind cannot decode or translate, before the program is given a SIGILL signal. Often an illegal instruction indicates a bug in the program or missing support for the particular instruction in Valgrind. But some programs do deliberately try to execute an instruction that might be missing and trap the SIGILL signal to detect processor features. Using this flag makes it possible to avoid the diagnostic output that you would otherwise get in such cases.

`--show-below-main=<yes|no> [default: no]`
By default, stack traces for errors do not show any functions that appear beneath `main` because most of the time it's uninteresting C library stuff and/or gobbledygook. Alternatively, if `main` is not present in the stack trace, stack traces will not show any functions below main-like functions such as glibc's `__libc_start_main`. Furthermore, if main-like functions are present in the trace, they are normalised as `(below main)`, in order to make the output more deterministic.

If this option is enabled, all stack trace entries will be shown and `main`-like functions will not be normalised.

`--fullpath-after=<string>` [default: don't show source paths]
By default Valgrind only shows the filenames in stack traces, but not full paths to source files.   When using Valgrind in large projects where the sources reside in multiple different directories, this can be inconvenient. `--fullpath-after` provides a flexible solution to this problem.   When this option is present, the path to each source file is shown, with the following all-important caveat: if `string` is found in the path, then the path up to and including `string` is omitted, else the path is shown unmodified. Note that `string` is not required to be a prefix of the path.

For example, consider a file named `/home/janedoe/blah/src/foo/bar/xyzzy.c`.   Specifying `--fullpath-after=/home/janedoe/blah/src/` will cause Valgrind to show the name as `foo/bar/xyzzy.c`.

Because the string is not required to be a prefix, `--fullpath-after=src/` will produce the same output.   This is useful when the path contains arbitrary machine-generated characters.   For example, the path `/my/build/dir/C32A1B47/blah/src/foo/xyzzy` can be pruned to `foo/xyzzy` using `--fullpath-after=/blah/src/`.

If you simply want to see the full path, just specify an empty string: `--fullpath-after=`. This isn't a special case, merely a logical consequence of the above rules.

Finally, you can use `--fullpath-after` multiple times.   Any appearance of it causes Valgrind to switch to producing full paths and applying the above filtering rule. Each produced path is compared against all the `--fullpath-after`-specified strings, in the order specified.   The first string to match causes the path to be truncated as described above. If none match, the full path is shown. This facilitates chopping off prefixes when the sources are drawn from a number of unrelated directories.

`--extra-debuginfo-path=<path>` [default: undefined and unused]
By default Valgrind searches in several well-known paths for debug objects, such as `/usr/lib/debug/`.

However, there may be scenarios where you may wish to put debug objects at an arbitrary location, such as external storage when running Valgrind on a mobile device with limited local storage. Another example might be a situation where you do not have permission to install debug object packages on the system where you are running Valgrind.

In these scenarios, you may provide an absolute path as an extra, final place for Valgrind to search for debug objects by specifying `--extra-debuginfo-path=/path/to/debug/objects`. The given path will be prepended to the absolute path name of the searched-for object.   For example, if Valgrind is looking for the debuginfo for `/w/x/y/zz.so` and `--extra-debuginfo-path=/a/b/c` is specified, it will look for a debug object at `/a/b/c/w/x/y/zz.so`.

This flag should only be specified once. If it is specified multiple times, only the last instance is honoured.

--debuginfo-server=ipaddr:port [default: undefined and unused]
This is a new, experimental, feature introduced in version 3.9.0.

In some scenarios it may be convenient to read debuginfo from objects stored on a different machine. With this flag, Valgrind will query a debuginfo server running on ipaddr and listening on port port, if it cannot find the debuginfo object in the local filesystem.

The debuginfo server must accept TCP connections on port port. The debuginfo server is contained in the source file auxprogs/valgrind-di-server.c. It will only serve from the directory it is started in. port defaults to 1500 in both client and server if not specified.

If Valgrind looks for the debuginfo for /w/x/y/zz.so by using the debuginfo server, it will strip the pathname components and merely request zz.so on the server. That in turn will look only in its current working directory for a matching debuginfo object.

The debuginfo data is transmitted in small fragments (8 KB) as requested by Valgrind.   Each block is compressed using LZO to reduce transmission time. The implementation has been tuned for best performance over a single-stage 802.11g (WiFi) network link.

Note that checks for matching primary vs debug objects, using GNU debuglink CRC scheme, are performed even when using the debuginfo server.   To disable such checking, you need to also specify --allow-mismatched-debuginfo=yes.

By default the Valgrind build system will build valgrind-di-server for the target platform, which is almost certainly not what you want. So far we have been unable to find out how to get automake/autoconf to build it for the build platform. If you want to use it, you will have to recompile it by hand using the command shown at the top of auxprogs/valgrind-di-server.c.

--allow-mismatched-debuginfo=no|yes [no]
When reading debuginfo from separate debuginfo objects, Valgrind will by default check that the main and debuginfo objects match, using the GNU debuglink mechanism. This guarantees that it does not read debuginfo from out of date debuginfo objects, and also ensures that Valgrind can't crash as a result of mismatches.

This check can be overridden using --allow-mismatched-debuginfo=yes. This may be useful when the debuginfo and main objects have not been split in the proper way. Be careful when using this, though: it disables all consistency checking, and Valgrind has been observed to crash when the main and debuginfo objects don't match.

--suppressions=<filename> [default: $PREFIX/lib/valgrind/default.supp]
Specifies an extra file from which to read descriptions of errors to suppress. You may use up to 100 extra suppression files.

`--gen-suppressions=<yes|no|all> [default: no]`
When set to `yes`, Valgrind will pause after every error shown and print the line:

```
---- Print suppression ? --- [Return/N/n/Y/y/C/c] ----
```

Pressing `Ret`, or `N Ret` or `n Ret`, causes Valgrind continue execution without printing a suppression for this error.

Pressing `Y Ret` or `y Ret` causes Valgrind to write a suppression for this error. You can then cut and paste it into a suppression file if you don't want to hear about the error in the future.

When set to `all`, Valgrind will print a suppression for every reported error, without querying the user.

This option is particularly useful with C++ programs, as it prints out the suppressions with mangled names, as required.

Note that the suppressions printed are as specific as possible. You may want to common up similar ones, by adding wildcards to function names, and by using frame-level wildcards. The wildcarding facilities are powerful yet flexible, and with a bit of careful editing, you may be able to suppress a whole family of related errors with only a few suppressions.

Sometimes two different errors are suppressed by the same suppression, in which case Valgrind will output the suppression more than once, but you only need to have one copy in your suppression file (but having more than one won't cause problems). Also, the suppression name is given as `<insert a suppression name here>`; the name doesn't really matter, it's only used with the `-v` option which prints out all used suppression records.

`--input-fd=<number> [default: 0, stdin]`
When using `--gen-suppressions=yes`, Valgrind will stop so as to read keyboard input from you when each error occurs. By default it reads from the standard input (stdin), which is problematic for programs which close stdin. This option allows you to specify an alternative file descriptor from which to read input.

`--dsymutil=no|yes [yes]`
This option is only relevant when running Valgrind on Mac OS X.

Mac OS X uses a deferred debug information (debuginfo) linking scheme. When object files containing debuginfo are linked into a `.dylib` or an executable, the debuginfo is not copied into the final file. Instead, the debuginfo must be linked manually by running `dsymutil`, a system-provided utility, on the executable or `.dylib`. The resulting combined debuginfo is placed in a directory alongside the executable or `.dylib`, but with the extension `.dSYM`.

With `--dsymutil=no`, Valgrind will detect cases where the `.dSYM` directory is either missing, or is present but does not appear to match the associated executable or `.dylib`, most likely because it is out of date. In these cases, Valgrind will print a warning message but take no further action.

With `--dsymutil=yes`, Valgrind will, in such cases, automatically run `dsymutil` as necessary to bring the debuginfo up to date. For all practical purposes, if you always use `--dsymutil=yes`, then there is never any need to run `dsymutil` manually or as part of your applications's build system, since Valgrind will run it as necessary.

Valgrind will not attempt to run `dsymutil` on any executable or library in `/usr/`, `/bin/`, `/sbin/`, `/opt/`, `/sw/`, `/System/`, `/Library/` or `/Applications/` since `dsymutil` will always fail in such situations. It fails both because the debuginfo for such pre-installed system components is not available anywhere, and also because it would require write privileges in those directories.

Be careful when using `--dsymutil=yes`, since it will cause pre-existing `.dSYM` directories to be silently deleted and re-created. Also note that `dsymutil` is quite slow, sometimes excessively so.

`--max-stackframe=<number>` [default: 2000000]
The maximum size of a stack frame. If the stack pointer moves by more than this amount then Valgrind will assume that the program is switching to a different stack.

You may need to use this option if your program has large stack-allocated arrays. Valgrind keeps track of your program's stack pointer. If it changes by more than the threshold amount, Valgrind assumes your program is switching to a different stack, and Memcheck behaves differently than it would for a stack pointer change smaller than the threshold. Usually this heuristic works well. However, if your program allocates large structures on the stack, this heuristic will be fooled, and Memcheck will subsequently report large numbers of invalid stack accesses. This option allows you to change the threshold to a different value.

You should only consider use of this option if Valgrind's debug output directs you to do so. In that case it will tell you the new threshold you should specify.

In general, allocating large structures on the stack is a bad idea, because you can easily run out of stack space, especially on systems with limited memory or which expect to support large numbers of threads each with a small stack, and also because the error checking performed by Memcheck is more effective for heap-allocated data than for stack-allocated data. If you have to use this option, you may wish to consider rewriting your code to allocate on the heap rather than on the stack.

`--main-stacksize=<number>` [default: use current 'ulimit' value]
Specifies the size of the main thread's stack.

To simplify its memory management, Valgrind reserves all required space for the main thread's stack at startup. That means it needs to know the required stack size at startup.

By default, Valgrind uses the current "ulimit" value for the stack size, or 16 MB, whichever is lower. In many cases this gives a stack size in the range 8 to 16 MB, which almost never overflows for most applications.

If you need a larger total stack size, use `--main-stacksize` to specify it. Only set it as high as you need, since reserving far more space than you need (that is, hundreds of megabytes more than you need) constrains Valgrind's memory allocators and may reduce the total amount of memory that Valgrind can use. This is only really of significance on 32-bit machines.

On Linux, you may request a stack of size up to 2GB. Valgrind will stop with a diagnostic message if the stack cannot be allocated.

`--main-stacksize` only affects the stack size for the program's initial thread. It has no bearing on the size of thread stacks, as Valgrind does not allocate those.

You may need to use both `--main-stacksize` and `--max-stackframe` together. It is important to understand that `--main-stacksize` sets the maximum total stack size, whilst `--max-stackframe` specifies the largest size of any one stack frame. You will have to work out the `--main-stacksize` value for yourself (usually, if your applications segfaults). But Valgrind will tell you the needed `--max-stackframe` size, if necessary.

As discussed further in the description of `--max-stackframe`, a requirement for a large stack is a sign of potential portability problems. You are best advised to place all large data in heap-allocated memory.

`--max-threads=<number> [default:  500]`

By default, Valgrind can handle to up to 500 threads. Occasionally, that number is too small. Use this option to provide a different limit. E.g. `--max-threads=3000`.

2.6.4. malloc-related Options

For tools that use their own version of `malloc` (e.g. Memcheck, Massif, Helgrind, DRD), the following options apply.

`--alignment=<number> [default:  8 or 16, depending on the platform]`

By default Valgrind's `malloc`, `realloc`, etc, return a block whose starting address is 8-byte aligned or 16-byte aligned (the value depends on the platform and matches the platform default). This option allows you to specify a different alignment. The supplied value must be greater than or equal to the default, less than or equal to 4096, and must be a power of two.

`--redzone-size=<number> [default:  depends on the tool]`

Valgrind's `malloc, realloc`, etc, add padding blocks before and after each heap block allocated by the program being run. Such padding blocks are called redzones. The default value for the redzone size depends on the tool. For example, Memcheck adds and protects a minimum of 16 bytes before and after each block allocated by the client. This allows it to detect block underruns or overruns of up to 16 bytes.

Increasing the redzone size makes it possible to detect overruns of larger distances, but increases the amount of memory used by Valgrind. Decreasing the redzone size will reduce the memory needed by Valgrind but also reduces the chances of detecting over/underruns, so is not recommended.

2.6.5. Uncommon Options

These options apply to all tools, as they affect certain obscure workings of the Valgrind core. Most people won't need to use them.

`--smc-check=<none|stack|all|all-non-file>` [default: all-non-file for x86/amd64/s390x, stack for other archs]
This option controls Valgrind's detection of self-modifying code. If no checking is done, when a program executes some code, then overwrites it with new code, and executes the new code, Valgrind will continue to execute the translations it made for the old code. This will likely lead to incorrect behaviour and/or crashes.

For "modern" architectures -- anything that's not x86, amd64 or s390x -- the default is `stack`. This is because a correct program must take explicit action to reestablish D-I cache coherence following code modification. Valgrind observes and honours such actions, with the result that self-modifying code is transparently handled with zero extra cost.

For x86, amd64 and s390x, the program is not required to notify the hardware of required D-I coherence syncing. Hence the default is `all-non-file`, which covers the normal case of generating code into an anonymous (non-file-backed) mmap'd area.

The meanings of the four available settings are as follows. No detection (`none`), detect self-modifying code on the stack (which is used by GCC to implement nested functions) (`stack`), detect self-modifying code everywhere (`all`), and detect self-modifying code everywhere except in file-backed mappings (`all-non-file`).

Running with `all` will slow Valgrind down noticeably. Running with `none` will rarely speed things up, since very little code gets dynamically generated in most programs. The `VALGRIND_DISCARD_TRANSLATIONS` client request is an alternative to `smc check=all` and `--smc-check-all-non-file` that requires more programmer effort but allows Valgrind to run your program faster, by telling it precisely when translations need to be re-made.

`--smc-check=all-non-file` provides a cheaper but more limited version of `--smc-check=all`. It adds checks to any translations that do not originate from file-backed memory mappings. Typical applications that generate code, for example JITs in web browsers, generate code into anonymous mmaped areas, whereas the "fixed" code of the browser always lives in file-backed mappings. `--smc-check=all-non-file` takes advantage of this observation, limiting the overhead of checking to code which is likely to be JIT generated.

`--read-inline-info=<yes|no>` [default: see below]
When enabled, Valgrind will read information about inlined function calls from DWARF3 debug info. This slows Valgrind startup and makes it use more memory (typically for each inlined piece of code, 6 words and space for the function name), but it results in more descriptive stacktraces. For the 3.10.0 release, this functionality is enabled by default only for Linux, Android and Solaris targets and only for the tools Memcheck, Helgrind and DRD. Here is an example of some stacktraces with `--read-inline-info=no`:

```
==15380== Conditional jump or move depends on uninitialised value(s)
==15380==    at 0x80484EA: main (inlinfo.c:6)
==15380==
==15380== Conditional jump or move depends on uninitialised value(s)
==15380==    at 0x8048550: fun_noninline (inlinfo.c:6)
==15380==    by 0x804850E: main (inlinfo.c:34)
==15380==
==15380== Conditional jump or move depends on uninitialised value(s)
==15380==    at 0x8048520: main (inlinfo.c:6)
```

And here are the same errors with `--read-inline-info=yes`:

```
==15377== Conditional jump or move depends on uninitialised value(s)
==15377==    at 0x80484EA: fun_d (inlinfo.c:6)
==15377==    by 0x80484EA: fun_c (inlinfo.c:14)
==15377==    by 0x80484EA: fun_b (inlinfo.c:20)
==15377==    by 0x80484EA: fun_a (inlinfo.c:26)
==15377==    by 0x80484EA: main (inlinfo.c:33)
==15377==
==15377== Conditional jump or move depends on uninitialised value(s)
==15377==    at 0x8048550: fun_d (inlinfo.c:6)
==15377==    by 0x8048550: fun_noninline (inlinfo.c:41)
==15377==    by 0x804850E: main (inlinfo.c:34)
==15377==
==15377== Conditional jump or move depends on uninitialised value(s)
==15377==    at 0x8048520: fun_d (inlinfo.c:6)
==15377==    by 0x8048520: main (inlinfo.c:35)
```

```
--read-var-info=<yes|no> [default:  no]
```
When enabled, Valgrind will read information about variable types and locations from DWARF3 debug info. This slows Valgrind startup significantly and makes it use significantly more memory, but for the tools that can take advantage of it (Memcheck, Helgrind, DRD) it can result in more precise error messages.   For example, here are some standard errors issued by Memcheck:

```
==15363== Uninitialised byte(s) found during client check request
==15363==    at 0x80484A9: croak (varinfo1.c:28)
==15363==    by 0x8048544: main (varinfo1.c:55)
==15363== Address 0x80497f7 is 7 bytes inside data symbol "global_i2"
==15363==
==15363== Uninitialised byte(s) found during client check request
==15363==    at 0x80484A9: croak (varinfo1.c:28)
==15363==    by 0x8048550: main (varinfo1.c:56)
==15363== Address 0xbea0d0cc is on thread 1's stack
==15363==  in frame #1, created by main (varinfo1.c:45)
```

And here are the same errors with `--read-var-info=yes`:

```
==15370== Uninitialised byte(s) found during client check request
==15370==    at 0x80484A9: croak (varinfo1.c:28)
==15370==    by 0x8048544: main (varinfo1.c:55)
==15370== Location 0x80497f7 is 0 bytes inside global_i2[7],
==15370==  a global variable declared at varinfo1.c:41
==15370==
==15370== Uninitialised byte(s) found during client check request
==15370==    at 0x80484A9: croak (varinfo1.c:28)
==15370==    by 0x8048550: main (varinfo1.c:56)
==15370== Location 0xbeb4a0cc is 0 bytes inside local var "local"
==15370==  declared at varinfo1.c:46, in frame #1 of thread 1
```

`--vgdb-poll=<number>` [default: 5000]
As part of its main loop, the Valgrind scheduler will poll to check if some activity (such as an external command or some input from a gdb) has to be handled by gdbserver. This activity poll will be done after having run the given number of basic blocks (or slightly more than the given number of basic blocks). This poll is quite cheap so the default value is set relatively low. You might further decrease this value if vgdb cannot use ptrace system call to interrupt Valgrind if all threads are (most of the time) blocked in a system call.

`--vgdb-shadow-registers=no|yes` [default: no]
When activated, gdbserver will expose the Valgrind shadow registers to GDB. With this, the value of the Valgrind shadow registers can be examined or changed using GDB. Exposing shadow registers only works with GDB version 7.1 or later.

`--vgdb-prefix=<prefix>` [default: /tmp/vgdb-pipe]
To communicate with gdb/vgdb, the Valgrind gdbserver creates 3 files (2 named FIFOs and a mmap shared memory file). The prefix option controls the directory and prefix for the creation of these files.

`--run-libc-freeres=<yes|no>` [default: yes]
This option is only relevant when running Valgrind on Linux.

The GNU C library (`libc.so`), which is used by all programs, may allocate memory for its own uses. Usually it doesn't bother to free that memory when the program ends—there would be no point, since the Linux kernel reclaims all process resources when a process exits anyway, so it would just slow things down.

The glibc authors realised that this behaviour causes leak checkers, such as Valgrind, to falsely report leaks in glibc, when a leak check is done at exit. In order to avoid this, they provided a routine called `__libc_freeres` specifically to make glibc release all memory it has allocated. Memcheck therefore tries to run `__libc_freeres` at exit.

Unfortunately, in some very old versions of glibc, `__libc_freeres` is sufficiently buggy to cause segmentation faults. This was particularly noticeable on Red Hat 7.1. So this option is provided in order to inhibit the run of `__libc_freeres`. If your program seems to run fine on Valgrind, but segfaults at exit, you may find that `--run-libc-freeres=no` fixes that, although at the cost of possibly falsely reporting space leaks in `libc.so`.

`--sim-hints=hint1,hint2,...`
Pass miscellaneous hints to Valgrind which slightly modify the simulated behaviour in nonstandard or dangerous ways, possibly to help the simulation of strange features. By default no hints are enabled. Use with caution! Currently known hints are:

- `lax-ioctls:` Be very lax about ioctl handling; the only assumption is that the size is correct. Doesn't require the full buffer to be initialised when writing. Without this, using some device drivers with a large number of strange ioctl commands becomes very tiresome.

- `fuse-compatible:` Enable special handling for certain system calls that may block in a FUSE file-system. This may be necessary when running Valgrind on a multi-threaded program that uses one thread to manage a FUSE file-system and another thread to access that file-system.

- `enable-outer:` Enable some special magic needed when the program being run is itself Valgrind.

- `no-inner-prefix:` Disable printing a prefix > in front of each stdout or stderr output line in an inner Valgrind being run by an outer Valgrind. This is useful when running Valgrind regression tests in an outer/inner setup. Note that the prefix > will always be printed in front of the inner debug logging lines.

- `no-nptl-pthread-stackcache`:   This hint is only relevant when running Valgrind on Linux.

  The GNU glibc pthread library (`libpthread.so`), which is used by pthread programs, maintains a cache of pthread stacks. When a pthread terminates, the memory used for the pthread stack and some thread local storage related data structure are not always directly released. This memory is kept in a cache (up to a certain size), and is re-used if a new thread is started.

  This cache causes the helgrind tool to report some false positive race condition errors on this cached memory, as helgrind does not understand the internal glibc cache synchronisation primitives. So, when using helgrind, disabling the cache helps to avoid false positive race conditions, in particular when using thread local storage variables (e.g. variables using the `__thread` qualifier).

  When using the memcheck tool, disabling the cache ensures the memory used by glibc to handle __thread variables is directly released when a thread terminates.

  Note: Valgrind disables the cache using some internal knowledge of the glibc stack cache implementation and by examining the debug information of the pthread library. This technique is thus somewhat fragile and might not work for all glibc versions. This has been succesfully tested with various glibc versions (e.g. 2.11, 2.16, 2.18) on various platforms.

- `lax-doors`:   (Solaris only) Be very lax about door syscall handling over unrecognised door file descriptors. Does not require that full buffer is initialised when writing. Without this, programs using libdoor(3LIB) functionality with completely proprietary semantics may report large number of false positives.

`--fair-sched=<no|yes|try>`   [default: no]
The `--fair-sched` option controls the locking mechanism used by Valgrind to serialise thread execution. The locking mechanism controls the way the threads are scheduled, and different settings give different trade-offs between fairness and performance. For more details about the Valgrind thread serialisation scheme and its impact on performance and thread scheduling, see Scheduling and Multi-Thread Performance.

- The value `--fair-sched=yes` activates a fair scheduler. In short, if multiple threads are ready to run, the threads will be scheduled in a round robin fashion. This mechanism is not available on all platforms or Linux versions. If not available, using `--fair-sched=yes` will cause Valgrind to terminate with an error.

  You may find this setting improves overall responsiveness if you are running an interactive multithreaded program, for example a web browser, on Valgrind.

- The value `--fair-sched=try` activates fair scheduling if available on the platform. Otherwise, it will automatically fall back to `--fair-sched=no`.

- The value `--fair-sched=no` activates a scheduler which does not guarantee fairness between threads ready to run, but which in general gives the highest performance.

`--kernel-variant=variant1,variant2,...`
Handle system calls and ioctls arising from minor variants of the default kernel for this platform. This is useful for running on hacked kernels or with kernel modules which support nonstandard ioctls, for example. Use with caution. If you don't understand what this option does then you almost certainly don't need it. Currently known variants are:

- `bproc`: support the `sys_broc` system call on x86. This is for running on BProc, which is a minor variant of standard Linux which is sometimes used for building clusters.

- `android-no-hw-tls`: some versions of the Android emulator for ARM do not provide a hardware TLS (thread-local state) register, and Valgrind crashes at startup. Use this variant to select software support for TLS.

- `android-gpu-sgx5xx`: use this to support handling of proprietary ioctls for the PowerVR SGX 5XX series of GPUs on Android devices. Failure to select this does not cause stability problems, but may cause Memcheck to report false errors after the program performs GPU-specific ioctls.

- `android-gpu-adreno3xx`: similarly, use this to support handling of proprietary ioctls for the Qualcomm Adreno 3XX series of GPUs on Android devices.

`--merge-recursive-frames=<number> [default: 0]`
Some recursive algorithms, for example balanced binary tree implementations, create many different stack traces, each containing cycles of calls. A cycle is defined as two identical program counter values separated by zero or more other program counter values. Valgrind may then use a lot of memory to store all these stack traces. This is a poor use of memory considering that such stack traces contain repeated uninteresting recursive calls instead of more interesting information such as the function that has initiated the recursive call.

The option `--merge-recursive-frames=<number>` instructs Valgrind to detect and merge recursive call cycles having a size of up to `<number>` frames. When such a cycle is detected, Valgrind records the cycle in the stack trace as a unique program counter.

The value 0 (the default) causes no recursive call merging. A value of 1 will cause stack traces of simple recursive algorithms (for example, a factorial implementation) to be collapsed. A value of 2 will usually be needed to collapse stack traces produced by recursive algorithms such as binary trees, quick sort, etc. Higher values might be needed for more complex recursive algorithms.

Note: recursive calls are detected by analysis of program counter values. They are not detected by looking at function names.

`--num-transtab-sectors=<number> [default: 6 for Android platforms, 16 for all others]`
Valgrind translates and instruments your program's machine code in small fragments (basic blocks). The translations are stored in a translation cache that is divided into a number of sections (sectors). If the cache is full, the sector containing the oldest translations is emptied and reused. If these old translations are needed again, Valgrind must re-translate and re-instrument the corresponding machine code, which is expensive. If the "executed instructions" working set of a program is big, increasing the number of sectors may improve performance by reducing the number of re-translations needed. Sectors are allocated on demand. Once allocated, a sector can never be freed, and occupies considerable space, depending on the tool and the value of `--avg-transtab-entry-size` (about 40 MB per sector for Memcheck). Use the option `--stats=yes` to obtain precise information about the memory used by a sector and the allocation and recycling of sectors.

`--avg-transtab-entry-size=<number>` [default: 0, meaning use tool provided default]
Average size of translated basic block. This average size is used to dimension the size of a sector. Each tool provides a default value to be used. If this default value is too small, the translation sectors will become full too quickly. If this default value is too big, a significant part of the translation sector memory will be unused. Note that the average size of a basic block translation depends on the tool, and might depend on tool options. For example, the memcheck option `--track-origins=yes` increases the size of the basic block translations. Use `--avg-transtab-entry-size` to tune the size of the sectors, either to gain memory or to avoid too many retranslations.

`--aspace-minaddr=<address>` [default: depends on the platform]
To avoid potential conflicts with some system libraries, Valgrind does not use the address space below `--aspace-minaddr` value, keeping it reserved in case a library specifically requests memory in this region. So, some "pessimistic" value is guessed by Valgrind depending on the platform. On linux, by default, Valgrind avoids using the first 64MB even if typically there is no conflict in this complete zone. You can use the option `--aspace-minaddr` to have your memory hungry application benefitting from more of this lower memory. On the other hand, if you encounter a conflict, increasing aspace-minaddr value might solve it. Conflicts will typically manifest themselves with mmap failures in the low range of the address space. The provided `address` must be page aligned and must be equal or bigger to 0x1000 (4KB). To find the default value on your platform, do something such as `valgrind -d -d date 2>&1 | grep -i minaddr`. Values lower than 0x10000 (64KB) are known to create problems on some distributions.

`--valgrind-stacksize=<number>` [default: 1MB]
For each thread, Valgrind needs its own 'private' stack. The default size for these stacks is largely dimensioned, and so should be sufficient in most cases. In case the size is too small, Valgrind will segfault. Before segfaulting, a warning might be produced by Valgrind when approaching the limit.

Use the option `--valgrind-stacksize` if such an (unlikely) warning is produced, or Valgrind dies due to a segmentation violation. Such segmentation violations have been seen when demangling huge C++ symbols.

If your application uses many threads and needs a lot of memory, you can gain some memory by reducing the size of these Valgrind stacks using the option `--valgrind-stacksize`.

`--show-emwarns=<yes|no>` [default: no]
When enabled, Valgrind will emit warnings about its CPU emulation in certain cases. These are usually not interesting.

`--require-text-symbol=:sonamepatt:fnnamepatt`
When a shared object whose soname matches `sonamepatt` is loaded into the process, examine all the text symbols it exports. If none of those match `fnnamepatt`, print an error message and abandon the run. This makes it possible to ensure that the run does not continue unless a given shared object contains a particular function name.

Both `sonamepatt` and `fnnamepatt` can be written using the usual `?` and `*` wildcards. For example: `":*libc.so*:foo?bar"`. You may use characters other than a colon to separate the two patterns. It is only important that the first character and the separator character are the same. For example, the above example could also be written `"Q*libc.so*Qfoo?bar"`. Multiple `--require-text-symbol` flags are allowed, in which case shared objects that are loaded into the process will be checked against all of them.

The purpose of this is to support reliable usage of marked-up libraries. For example, suppose we have a version of GCC's `libgomp.so` which has been marked up with annotations to support Helgrind. It is only too easy and confusing to load the wrong, un-annotated `libgomp.so` into the application. So the idea is: add a text symbol in the marked-up library, for example `annotated_for_helgrind_3_6`, and then give the flag `--require-text-symbol=:*libgomp*so*:annotated_for_helgrind_3_6` so that when `libgomp.so` is loaded, Valgrind scans its symbol table, and if the symbol isn't present the run is aborted, rather than continuing silently with the un-marked-up library. Note that you should put the entire flag in quotes to stop shells expanding up the `*` and `?` wildcards.

`--soname-synonyms=syn1=pattern1,syn2=pattern2,...`
When a shared library is loaded, Valgrind checks for functions in the library that must be replaced or wrapped. For example, Memcheck replaces all malloc related functions (malloc, free, calloc, ...) with its own versions. Such replacements are done by default only in shared libraries whose soname matches a predefined soname pattern (e.g. `libc.so*` on linux). By default, no replacement is done for a statically linked library or for alternative libraries such as tcmalloc. In some cases, the replacements allow `--soname-synonyms` to specify one additional synonym pattern, giving flexibility in the replacement.

Currently, this flexibility is only allowed for the malloc related functions, using the synonym `somalloc`. This synonym is usable for all tools doing standard replacement of malloc related functions (e.g. memcheck, massif, drd, helgrind, exp-dhat, exp-sgcheck).

- Alternate malloc library: to replace the malloc related functions in an alternate library with soname `mymalloclib.so`, give the option `--soname-synonyms=somalloc=mymalloclib.so`. A pattern can be used to match multiple libraries sonames. For example, `--soname-synonyms=somalloc=*tcmalloc*` will match the soname of all variants of the tcmalloc library (native, debug, profiled, ... tcmalloc variants).

  Note: the soname of a elf shared library can be retrieved using the readelf utility.

- Replacements in a statically linked library are done by using the `NONE` pattern. For example, if you link with `libtcmalloc.a`, memcheck will properly work when you give the option `--soname-synonyms=somalloc=NONE`. Note that a NONE pattern will match the main executable and any shared library having no soname.

- To run a "default" Firefox build for Linux, in which JEMalloc is linked in to the main executable, use `--soname-synonyms=somalloc=NONE`.

2.6.6. Debugging Options

There are also some options for debugging Valgrind itself. You shouldn't need to use them in the normal run of things. If you wish to see the list, use the `--help-debug` option.

If you wish to debug your program rather than debugging Valgrind itself, then you should use the options `--vgdb=yes` or `--vgdb=full`.

2.6.7. Setting Default Options

Note that Valgrind also reads options from three places:

1. The file `~/.valgrindrc`

2. The environment variable `$VALGRIND_OPTS`

3. The file `./.valgrindrc`

These are processed in the given order, before the command-line options. Options processed later override those processed earlier; for example, options in ./.valgrindrc will take precedence over those in ~/.valgrindrc.

Please note that the ./.valgrindrc file is ignored if it is marked as world writeable or not owned by the current user. This is because the ./.valgrindrc can contain options that are potentially harmful or can be used by a local attacker to execute code under your user account.

Any tool-specific options put in $VALGRIND_OPTS or the .valgrindrc files should be prefixed with the tool name and a colon. For example, if you want Memcheck to always do leak checking, you can put the following entry in ~/.valgrindrc:

--memcheck:leak-check=yes

This will be ignored if any tool other than Memcheck is run. Without the memcheck: part, this will cause problems if you select other tools that don't understand --leak-check=yes.

2.7. Support for Threads

Threaded programs are fully supported.

The main thing to point out with respect to threaded programs is that your program will use the native threading library, but Valgrind serialises execution so that only one (kernel) thread is running at a time. This approach avoids the horrible implementation problems of implementing a truly multithreaded version of Valgrind, but it does mean that threaded apps never use more than one CPU simultaneously, even if you have a multiprocessor or multicore machine.

Valgrind doesn't schedule the threads itself. It merely ensures that only one thread runs at once, using a simple locking scheme. The actual thread scheduling remains under control of the OS kernel. What this does mean, though, is that your program will see very different scheduling when run on Valgrind than it does when running normally. This is both because Valgrind is serialising the threads, and because the code runs so much slower than normal.

This difference in scheduling may cause your program to behave differently, if you have some kind of concurrency, critical race, locking, or similar, bugs. In that case you might consider using the tools Helgrind and/or DRD to track them down.

On Linux, Valgrind also supports direct use of the clone system call, futex and so on. clone is supported where either everything is shared (a thread) or nothing is shared (fork-like); partial sharing will fail.

2.7.1. Scheduling and Multi-Thread Performance

A thread executes code only when it holds the abovementioned lock. After executing some number of instructions, the running thread will release the lock. All threads ready to run will then compete to acquire the lock.

The --fair-sched option controls the locking mechanism used to serialise thread execution.

The default pipe based locking mechanism (--fair-sched=no) is available on all platforms. Pipe based locking does not guarantee fairness between threads: it is quite likely that a thread that has just released the lock reacquires it immediately, even though other threads are ready to run. When using pipe based locking, different runs of the same multithreaded application might give very different thread scheduling.

An alternative locking mechanism, based on futexes, is available on some platforms. If available, it is activated by --fair-sched=yes or --fair-sched=try. Futex based locking ensures fairness (round-robin scheduling) between threads: if multiple threads are ready to run, the lock will be given to the thread which first requested the lock. Note that a thread which is blocked in a system call (e.g. in a blocking read system call) has not (yet) requested the lock: such a thread requests the lock only after the system call is finished.

The fairness of the futex based locking produces better reproducibility of thread scheduling for different executions of a multithreaded application. This better reproducibility is particularly helpful when using Helgrind or DRD.

Valgrind's use of thread serialisation implies that only one thread at a time may run. On a multiprocessor/multicore system, the running thread is assigned to one of the CPUs by the OS kernel scheduler. When a thread acquires the lock, sometimes the thread will be assigned to the same CPU as the thread that just released the lock. Sometimes, the thread will be assigned to another CPU. When using pipe based locking, the thread that just acquired the lock will usually be scheduled on the same CPU as the thread that just released the lock. With the futex based mechanism, the thread that just acquired the lock will more often be scheduled on another CPU.

Valgrind's thread serialisation and CPU assignment by the OS kernel scheduler can interact badly with the CPU frequency scaling available on many modern CPUs. To decrease power consumption, the frequency of a CPU or core is automatically decreased if the CPU/core has not been used recently. If the OS kernel often assigns the thread which just acquired the lock to another CPU/core, it is quite likely that this CPU/core is currently at a low frequency. The frequency of this CPU will be increased after some time. However, during this time, the (only) running thread will have run at the low frequency. Once this thread has run for some time, it will release the lock. Another thread will acquire this lock, and might be scheduled again on another CPU whose clock frequency was decreased in the meantime.

The futex based locking causes threads to change CPUs/cores more often. So, if CPU frequency scaling is activated, the futex based locking might decrease significantly the performance of a multithreaded app running under Valgrind. Performance losses of up to 50% degradation have been observed, as compared to running on a machine for which CPU frequency scaling has been disabled. The pipe based locking locking scheme also interacts badly with CPU frequency scaling, with performance losses in the range 10..20% having been observed.

To avoid such performance degradation, you should indicate to the kernel that all CPUs/cores should always run at maximum clock speed. Depending on your Linux distribution, CPU frequency scaling may be controlled using a graphical interface or using command line such as `cpufreq-selector` or `cpufreq-set`.

An alternative way to avoid these problems is to tell the OS scheduler to tie a Valgrind process to a specific (fixed) CPU using the `taskset` command. This should ensure that the selected CPU does not fall below its maximum frequency setting so long as any thread of the program has work to do.

2.8. Handling of Signals

Valgrind has a fairly complete signal implementation. It should be able to cope with any POSIX-compliant use of signals.

If you're using signals in clever ways (for example, catching SIGSEGV, modifying page state and restarting the instruction), you're probably relying on precise exceptions. In this case, you will need to use `--vex-iropt-register-updates=allregs-at-mem-access` or `--vex-iropt-register-updates=allregs-at-each-insn`.

If your program dies as a result of a fatal core-dumping signal, Valgrind will generate its own core file (`vgcore.NNNNN`) containing your program's state. You may use this core file for post-mortem debugging with GDB or similar. (Note: it will not generate a core if your core dump size limit is 0.) At the time of writing the core dumps do not include all the floating point register information.

In the unlikely event that Valgrind itself crashes, the operating system will create a core dump in the usual way.

2.9. Building and Installing Valgrind

We use the standard Unix `./configure`, `make`, `make install` mechanism. Once you have completed `make install` you may then want to run the regression tests with `make regtest`.

In addition to the usual `--prefix=/path/to/install/tree`, there are three options which affect how Valgrind is built:

- `--enable-inner`

  This builds Valgrind with some special magic hacks which make it possible to run it on a standard build of Valgrind (what the developers call "self-hosting"). Ordinarily you should not use this option as various kinds of safety checks are disabled.

- `--enable-only64bit`

  `--enable-only32bit`

  On 64-bit platforms (amd64-linux, ppc64-linux, amd64-darwin), Valgrind is by default built in such a way that both 32-bit and 64-bit executables can be run. Sometimes this cleverness is a problem for a variety of reasons. These two options allow for single-target builds in this situation. If you issue both, the configure script will complain. Note they are ignored on 32-bit-only platforms (x86-linux, ppc32-linux, arm-linux, x86-darwin).

The `configure` script tests the version of the X server currently indicated by the current `$DISPLAY`. This is a known bug. The intention was to detect the version of the current X client libraries, so that correct suppressions could be selected for them, but instead the test checks the server version. This is just plain wrong.

If you are building a binary package of Valgrind for distribution, please read `README_PACKAGERS` Readme Packagers. It contains some important information.

Apart from that, there's not much excitement here. Let us know if you have build problems.

2.10. If You Have Problems

Contact us at http://www.valgrind.org/.

See Limitations for the known limitations of Valgrind, and for a list of programs which are known not to work on it.

All parts of the system make heavy use of assertions and internal self-checks. They are permanently enabled, and we have no plans to disable them. If one of them breaks, please mail us!

If you get an assertion failure in `m_mallocfree.c`, this may have happened because your program wrote off the end of a heap block, or before its beginning, thus corrupting heap metadata. Valgrind hopefully will have emitted a message to that effect before dying in this way.

Read the Valgrind FAQ for more advice about common problems, crashes, etc.

2.11. Limitations

The following list of limitations seems long. However, most programs actually work fine.

Valgrind will run programs on the supported platforms subject to the following constraints:

- On x86 and amd64, there is no support for 3DNow! instructions. If the translator encounters these, Valgrind will generate a SIGILL when the instruction is executed. Apart from that, on x86 and amd64, essentially all instructions are supported, up to and including AVX and AES in 64-bit mode and SSSE3 in 32-bit mode. 32-bit mode does in fact support the bare minimum SSE4 instructions needed to run programs on MacOSX 10.6 on 32-bit targets.

- On ppc32 and ppc64, almost all integer, floating point and Altivec instructions are supported. Specifically: integer and FP insns that are mandatory for PowerPC, the "General-purpose optional" group (fsqrt, fsqrts, stfiwx), the "Graphics optional" group (fre, fres, frsqrte, frsqrtes), and the Altivec (also known as VMX) SIMD instruction set, are supported. Also, instructions from the Power ISA 2.05 specification, as present in POWER6 CPUs, are supported.

- On ARM, essentially the entire ARMv7-A instruction set is supported, in both ARM and Thumb mode. ThumbEE and Jazelle are not supported. NEON, VFPv3 and ARMv6 media support is fairly complete.

- If your program does its own memory management, rather than using malloc/new/free/delete, it should still work, but Memcheck's error checking won't be so effective. If you describe your program's memory management scheme using "client requests" (see The Client Request mechanism), Memcheck can do better. Nevertheless, using malloc/new and free/delete is still the best approach.

- Valgrind's signal simulation is not as robust as it could be. Basic POSIX-compliant sigaction and sigprocmask functionality is supplied, but it's conceivable that things could go badly awry if you do weird things with signals. Workaround: don't. Programs that do non-POSIX signal tricks are in any case inherently unportable, so should be avoided if possible.

- Machine instructions, and system calls, have been implemented on demand. So it's possible, although unlikely, that a program will fall over with a message to that effect. If this happens, please report all the details printed out, so we can try and implement the missing feature.

- Memory consumption of your program is majorly increased whilst running under Valgrind's Memcheck tool. This is due to the large amount of administrative information maintained behind the scenes. Another cause is that Valgrind dynamically translates the original executable. Translated, instrumented code is 12-18 times larger than the original so you can easily end up with 150+ MB of translations when running (eg) a web browser.

- Valgrind can handle dynamically-generated code just fine. If you regenerate code over the top of old code (ie. at the same memory addresses), if the code is on the stack Valgrind will realise the code has changed, and work correctly. This is necessary to handle the trampolines GCC uses to implemented nested functions. If you regenerate code somewhere other than the stack, and you are running on an 32- or 64-bit x86 CPU, you will need to use the `--smc-check=all` option, and Valgrind will run more slowly than normal. Or you can add client requests that tell Valgrind when your program has overwritten code.

  On other platforms (ARM, PowerPC) Valgrind observes and honours the cache invalidation hints that programs are obliged to emit to notify new code, and so self-modifying-code support should work automatically, without the need for `--smc-check=all`.

- Valgrind has the following limitations in its implementation of x86/AMD64 floating point relative to IEEE754.

  Precision: There is no support for 80 bit arithmetic. Internally, Valgrind represents all such "long double" numbers in 64 bits, and so there may be some differences in results. Whether or not this is critical remains to be seen. Note, the x86/amd64 fldt/fstpt instructions (read/write 80-bit numbers) are correctly simulated, using conversions to/from 64 bits, so that in-memory images of 80-bit numbers look correct if anyone wants to see.

  The impression observed from many FP regression tests is that the accuracy differences aren't significant. Generally speaking, if a program relies on 80-bit precision, there may be difficulties porting it to non x86/amd64 platforms which only support 64-bit FP precision. Even on x86/amd64, the program may get different results depending on whether it is compiled to use SSE2 instructions (64-bits only), or x87 instructions (80-bit). The net effect is to make FP programs behave as if they had been run on a machine with 64-bit IEEE floats, for example PowerPC. On amd64 FP arithmetic is done by default on SSE2, so amd64 looks more like PowerPC than x86 from an FP perspective, and there are far fewer noticeable accuracy differences than with x86.

Rounding: Valgrind does observe the 4 IEEE-mandated rounding modes (to nearest, to +infinity, to -infinity, to zero) for the following conversions: float to integer, integer to float where there is a possibility of loss of precision, and float-to-float rounding. For all other FP operations, only the IEEE default mode (round to nearest) is supported.

Numeric exceptions in FP code: IEEE754 defines five types of numeric exception that can happen: invalid operation (sqrt of negative number, etc), division by zero, overflow, underflow, inexact (loss of precision).

For each exception, two courses of action are defined by IEEE754: either (1) a user-defined exception handler may be called, or (2) a default action is defined, which "fixes things up" and allows the computation to proceed without throwing an exception.

Currently Valgrind only supports the default fixup actions. Again, feedback on the importance of exception support would be appreciated.

When Valgrind detects that the program is trying to exceed any of these limitations (setting exception handlers, rounding mode, or precision control), it can print a message giving a traceback of where this has happened, and continue execution. This behaviour used to be the default, but the messages are annoying and so showing them is now disabled by default. Use --show-emwarns=yes to see them.

The above limitations define precisely the IEEE754 'default' behaviour: default fixup on all exceptions, round-to-nearest operations, and 64-bit precision.

- Valgrind has the following limitations in its implementation of x86/AMD64 SSE2 FP arithmetic, relative to IEEE754.

Essentially the same: no exceptions, and limited observance of rounding mode. Also, SSE2 has control bits which make it treat denormalised numbers as zero (DAZ) and a related action, flush denormals to zero (FTZ). Both of these cause SSE2 arithmetic to be less accurate than IEEE requires. Valgrind detects, ignores, and can warn about, attempts to enable either mode.

- Valgrind has the following limitations in its implementation of ARM VFPv3 arithmetic, relative to IEEE754.

Essentially the same: no exceptions, and limited observance of rounding mode. Also, switching the VFP unit into vector mode will cause Valgrind to abort the program -- it has no way to emulate vector uses of VFP at a reasonable performance level. This is no big deal given that non-scalar uses of VFP instructions are in any case deprecated.

- Valgrind has the following limitations in its implementation of PPC32 and PPC64 floating point arithmetic, relative to IEEE754.

Scalar (non-Altivec): Valgrind provides a bit-exact emulation of all floating point instructions, except for "fre" and "fres", which are done more precisely than required by the PowerPC architecture specification. All floating point operations observe the current rounding mode.

However, fpscr[FPRF] is not set after each operation. That could be done but would give measurable performance overheads, and so far no need for it has been found.

As on x86/AMD64, IEEE754 exceptions are not supported: all floating point exceptions are handled using the default IEEE fixup actions. Valgrind detects, ignores, and can warn about, attempts to unmask the 5 IEEE FP exception kinds by writing to the floating-point status and control register (fpscr).

Vector (Altivec, VMX): essentially as with x86/AMD64 SSE/SSE2: no exceptions, and limited observance of rounding mode. For Altivec, FP arithmetic is done in IEEE/Java mode, which is more accurate than the Linux default setting. "More accurate" means that denormals are handled properly, rather than simply being flushed to zero.

Programs which are known not to work are:

• emacs starts up but immediately concludes it is out of memory and aborts. It may be that Memcheck does not provide a good enough emulation of the `mallinfo` function. Emacs works fine if you build it to use the standard malloc/free routines.

2.12. An Example Run

This is the log for a run of a small program using Memcheck. The program is in fact correct, and the reported error is as the result of a potentially serious code generation bug in GNU g++ (snapshot 20010527).

```
sewardj@phoenix:~/newmat10$ ~/Valgrind-6/valgrind -v ./bogon
==25832== Valgrind 0.10, a memory error detector for x86 RedHat 7.1.
==25832== Copyright (C) 2000-2001, and GNU GPL'd, by Julian Seward.
==25832== Startup, with flags:
==25832== --suppressions=/home/sewardj/Valgrind/redhat71.supp
==25832== reading syms from /lib/ld-linux.so.2
==25832== reading syms from /lib/libc.so.6
==25832== reading syms from /mnt/pima/jrs/Inst/lib/libgcc_s.so.0
==25832== reading syms from /lib/libm.so.6
==25832== reading syms from /mnt/pima/jrs/Inst/lib/libstdc++.so.3
==25832== reading syms from /home/sewardj/Valgrind/valgrind.so
==25832== reading syms from /proc/self/exe
==25832==
==25832== Invalid read of size 4
==25832==    at 0x8048724: BandMatrix::ReSize(int,int,int) (bogon.cpp:45)
==25832==    by 0x80487AF: main (bogon.cpp:66)
==25832==  Address 0xBFFFF74C is not stack'd, malloc'd or free'd
==25832==
==25832== ERROR SUMMARY: 1 errors from 1 contexts (suppressed: 0 from 0)
==25832== malloc/free: in use at exit: 0 bytes in 0 blocks.
==25832== malloc/free: 0 allocs, 0 frees, 0 bytes allocated.
==25832== For a detailed leak analysis, rerun with: --leak-check=yes
```

The GCC folks fixed this about a week before GCC 3.0 shipped.

2.13. Warning Messages You Might See

Some of these only appear if you run in verbose mode (enabled by `-v`):

```
•More than 100 errors detected.    Subsequent errors will still be recorded,
but in less detail than before.
```

After 100 different errors have been shown, Valgrind becomes more conservative about collecting them. It then requires only the program counters in the top two stack frames to match when deciding whether or not two errors are really the same one. Prior to this point, the PCs in the top four frames are required to match. This hack has the effect of slowing down the appearance of new errors after the first 100. The 100 constant can be changed by recompiling Valgrind.

- ```
  More than 1000 errors detected.    I'm not reporting any more.    Final
  error counts may be inaccurate.    Go fix your program!
  ```

After 1000 different errors have been detected, Valgrind ignores any more. It seems unlikely that collecting even more different ones would be of practical help to anybody, and it avoids the danger that Valgrind spends more and more of its time comparing new errors against an ever-growing collection. As above, the 1000 number is a compile-time constant.

- ```
  Warning:   client switching stacks?
  ```

Valgrind spotted such a large change in the stack pointer that it guesses the client is switching to a different stack. At this point it makes a kludgey guess where the base of the new stack is, and sets memory permissions accordingly. At the moment "large change" is defined as a change of more that 2000000 in the value of the stack pointer register. If Valgrind guesses wrong, you may get many bogus error messages following this and/or have crashes in the stack trace recording code. You might avoid these problems by informing Valgrind about the stack bounds using VALGRIND_STACK_REGISTER client request.

- ```
  Warning:   client attempted to close Valgrind's logfile fd <number>
  ```

Valgrind doesn't allow the client to close the logfile, because you'd never see any diagnostic information after that point. If you see this message, you may want to use the --log-fd=<number> option to specify a different logfile file-descriptor number.

- ```
  Warning:   noted but unhandled ioctl <number>
  ```

Valgrind observed a call to one of the vast family of ioctl system calls, but did not modify its memory status info (because nobody has yet written a suitable wrapper). The call will still have gone through, but you may get spurious errors after this as a result of the non-update of the memory info.

- ```
  Warning:   set address range perms:   large range <number>
  ```

Diagnostic message, mostly for benefit of the Valgrind developers, to do with memory permissions.
  ```

3. Using and understanding the Valgrind core: Advanced Topics

This chapter describes advanced aspects of the Valgrind core services, which are mostly of interest to power users who wish to customise and modify Valgrind's default behaviours in certain useful ways. The subjects covered are:

- The "Client Request" mechanism

- Debugging your program using Valgrind's gdbserver and GDB

- Function Wrapping

3.1. The Client Request mechanism

Valgrind has a trapdoor mechanism via which the client program can pass all manner of requests and queries to Valgrind and the current tool. Internally, this is used extensively to make various things work, although that's not visible from the outside.

For your convenience, a subset of these so-called client requests is provided to allow you to tell Valgrind facts about the behaviour of your program, and also to make queries. In particular, your program can tell Valgrind about things that it otherwise would not know, leading to better results.

Clients need to include a header file to make this work. Which header file depends on which client requests you use. Some client requests are handled by the core, and are defined in the header file `valgrind/valgrind.h`. Tool-specific header files are named after the tool, e.g. `valgrind/memcheck.h`. Each tool-specific header file includes `valgrind/valgrind.h` so you don't need to include it in your client if you include a tool-specific header. All header files can be found in the `include/valgrind` directory of wherever Valgrind was installed.

The macros in these header files have the magical property that they generate code in-line which Valgrind can spot. However, the code does nothing when not run on Valgrind, so you are not forced to run your program under Valgrind just because you use the macros in this file. Also, you are not required to link your program with any extra supporting libraries.

The code added to your binary has negligible performance impact: on x86, amd64, ppc32, ppc64 and ARM, the overhead is 6 simple integer instructions and is probably undetectable except in tight loops. However, if you really wish to compile out the client requests, you can compile with `-DNVALGRIND` (analogous to `-DNDEBUG`'s effect on `assert`).

You are encouraged to copy the `valgrind/*.h` headers into your project's include directory, so your program doesn't have a compile-time dependency on Valgrind being installed. The Valgrind headers, unlike most of the rest of the code, are under a BSD-style license so you may include them without worrying about license incompatibility.

Here is a brief description of the macros available in `valgrind.h`, which work with more than one tool (see the tool-specific documentation for explanations of the tool-specific macros).

RUNNING_ON_VALGRIND:
Returns 1 if running on Valgrind, 0 if running on the real CPU. If you are running Valgrind on itself, returns the number of layers of Valgrind emulation you're running on.

VALGRIND_DISCARD_TRANSLATIONS:
Discards translations of code in the specified address range. Useful if you are debugging a JIT compiler or some other dynamic code generation system. After this call, attempts to execute code in the invalidated address range will cause Valgrind to make new translations of that code, which is probably the semantics you want. Note that code invalidations are expensive because finding all the relevant translations quickly is very difficult, so try not to call it often. Note that you can be clever about this: you only need to call it when an area which previously contained code is overwritten with new code. You can choose to write code into fresh memory, and just call this occasionally to discard large chunks of old code all at once.

Alternatively, for transparent self-modifying-code support, use--smc-check=all, or run on ppc32/Linux, ppc64/Linux or ARM/Linux.

VALGRIND_COUNT_ERRORS:
Returns the number of errors found so far by Valgrind. Can be useful in test harness code when combined with the --log-fd=-1 option; this runs Valgrind silently, but the client program can detect when errors occur. Only useful for tools that report errors, e.g. it's useful for Memcheck, but for Cachegrind it will always return zero because Cachegrind doesn't report errors.

VALGRIND_MALLOCLIKE_BLOCK:
If your program manages its own memory instead of using the standard malloc / new / new[], tools that track information about heap blocks will not do nearly as good a job. For example, Memcheck won't detect nearly as many errors, and the error messages won't be as informative. To improve this situation, use this macro just after your custom allocator allocates some new memory. See the comments in valgrind.h for information on how to use it.

VALGRIND_FREELIKE_BLOCK:
This should be used in conjunction with VALGRIND_MALLOCLIKE_BLOCK. Again, see valgrind.h for information on how to use it.

VALGRIND_RESIZEINPLACE_BLOCK:
Informs a Valgrind tool that the size of an allocated block has been modified but not its address. See valgrind.h for more information on how to use it.

VALGRIND_CREATE_MEMPOOL,   VALGRIND_DESTROY_MEMPOOL,   VALGRIND_MEMPOOL_ALLOC, VALGRIND_MEMPOOL_FREE,   VALGRIND_MOVE_MEMPOOL,   VALGRIND_MEMPOOL_CHANGE, VALGRIND_MEMPOOL_EXISTS:
These are similar to VALGRIND_MALLOCLIKE_BLOCK and VALGRIND_FREELIKE_BLOCK but are tailored towards code that uses memory pools. See Memory Pools for a detailed description.

VALGRIND_NON_SIMD_CALL[0123]:
Executes a function in the client program on the *real* CPU, not the virtual CPU that Valgrind normally runs code on. The function must take an integer (holding a thread ID) as the first argument and then 0, 1, 2 or 3 more arguments (depending on which client request is used). These are used in various ways internally to Valgrind. They might be useful to client programs.

Warning: Only use these if you *really* know what you are doing. They aren't entirely reliable, and can cause Valgrind to crash. See valgrind.h for more details.

VALGRIND_PRINTF(format, ...):
Print a printf-style message to the Valgrind log file. The message is prefixed with the PID between a pair of ** markers. (Like all client requests, nothing is output if the client program is not running under Valgrind.) Output is not produced until a newline is encountered, or subsequent Valgrind output is printed; this allows you to build up a single line of output over multiple calls. Returns the number of characters output, excluding the PID prefix.

VALGRIND_PRINTF_BACKTRACE(format, ...):
Like VALGRIND_PRINTF (in particular, the return value is identical), but prints a stack backtrace immediately afterwards.

VALGRIND_MONITOR_COMMAND(command):
Execute the given monitor command (a string). Returns 0 if command is recognised. Returns 1 if command is not recognised. Note that some monitor commands provide access to a functionality also accessible via a specific client request. For example, memcheck leak search can be requested from the client program using VALGRIND_DO_LEAK_CHECK or via the monitor command "leak_search". Note that the syntax of the command string is only verified at run-time. So, if it exists, it is preferrable to use a specific client request to have better compile time verifications of the arguments.

VALGRIND_STACK_REGISTER(start, end):
Registers a new stack. Informs Valgrind that the memory range between start and end is a unique stack. Returns a stack identifier that can be used with other VALGRIND_STACK_* calls.

Valgrind will use this information to determine if a change to the stack pointer is an item pushed onto the stack or a change over to a new stack. Use this if you're using a user-level thread package and are noticing crashes in stack trace recording or spurious errors from Valgrind about uninitialized memory reads.

Warning: Unfortunately, this client request is unreliable and best avoided.

VALGRIND_STACK_DEREGISTER(id):
Deregisters a previously registered stack. Informs Valgrind that previously registered memory range with stack id id is no longer a stack.

Warning: Unfortunately, this client request is unreliable and best avoided.

VALGRIND_STACK_CHANGE(id, start, end):
Changes a previously registered stack. Informs Valgrind that the previously registered stack with stack id id has changed its start and end values. Use this if your user-level thread package implements stack growth.

Warning: Unfortunately, this client request is unreliable and best avoided.

3.2. Debugging your program using Valgrind gdbserver and GDB

A program running under Valgrind is not executed directly by the CPU. Instead it runs on a synthetic CPU provided by Valgrind. This is why a debugger cannot debug your program when it runs on Valgrind.

This section describes how GDB can interact with the Valgrind gdbserver to provide a fully debuggable program under Valgrind. Used in this way, GDB also provides an interactive usage of Valgrind core or tool functionalities, including incremental leak search under Memcheck and on-demand Massif snapshot production.

3.2.1. Quick Start: debugging in 3 steps

The simplest way to get started is to run Valgrind with the flag --vgdb-error=0. Then follow the on-screen directions, which give you the precise commands needed to start GDB and connect it to your program.

Otherwise, here's a slightly more verbose overview.

If you want to debug a program with GDB when using the Memcheck tool, start Valgrind like this:

```
valgrind --vgdb=yes --vgdb-error=0 prog
```

In another shell, start GDB:

```
gdb prog
```

Then give the following command to GDB:

```
(gdb) target remote | vgdb
```

You can now debug your program e.g. by inserting a breakpoint and then using the GDB `continue` command.

This quick start information is enough for basic usage of the Valgrind gdbserver. The sections below describe more advanced functionality provided by the combination of Valgrind and GDB. Note that the command line flag `--vgdb=yes` can be omitted, as this is the default value.

3.2.2. Valgrind gdbserver overall organisation

The GNU GDB debugger is typically used to debug a process running on the same machine. In this mode, GDB uses system calls to control and query the program being debugged. This works well, but only allows GDB to debug a program running on the same computer.

GDB can also debug processes running on a different computer. To achieve this, GDB defines a protocol (that is, a set of query and reply packets) that facilitates fetching the value of memory or registers, setting breakpoints, etc. A gdbserver is an implementation of this "GDB remote debugging" protocol. To debug a process running on a remote computer, a gdbserver (sometimes called a GDB stub) must run at the remote computer side.

The Valgrind core provides a built-in gdbserver implementation, which is activated using `--vgdb=yes` or `--vgdb=full`. This gdbserver allows the process running on Valgrind's synthetic CPU to be debugged remotely. GDB sends protocol query packets (such as "get register contents") to the Valgrind embedded gdbserver. The gdbserver executes the queries (for example, it will get the register values of the synthetic CPU) and gives the results back to GDB.

GDB can use various kinds of channels (TCP/IP, serial line, etc) to communicate with the gdbserver. In the case of Valgrind's gdbserver, communication is done via a pipe and a small helper program called vgdb, which acts as an intermediary. If no GDB is in use, vgdb can also be used to send monitor commands to the Valgrind gdbserver from a shell command line.

3.2.3. Connecting GDB to a Valgrind gdbserver

To debug a program "prog" running under Valgrind, you must ensure that the Valgrind gdbserver is activated by specifying either `--vgdb=yes` or `--vgdb=full`. A secondary command line option, `--vgdb-error=number`, can be used to tell the gdbserver only to become active once the specified number of errors have been shown. A value of zero will therefore cause the gdbserver to become active at startup, which allows you to insert breakpoints before starting the run. For example:

```
valgrind --tool=memcheck --vgdb=yes --vgdb-error=0 ./prog
```

The Valgrind gdbserver is invoked at startup and indicates it is waiting for a connection from a GDB:

```
==2418== Memcheck, a memory error detector
==2418== Copyright (C) 2002-2010, and GNU GPL'd, by Julian Seward et al.
==2418== Using Valgrind-3.7.0.SVN and LibVEX; rerun with -h for copyright info
==2418== Command: ./prog
==2418==
==2418== (action at startup) vgdb me ...
```

GDB (in another shell) can then be connected to the Valgrind gdbserver. For this, GDB must be started on the program prog:

```
gdb ./prog
```

You then indicate to GDB that you want to debug a remote target:

```
(gdb) target remote | vgdb
```

GDB then starts a vgdb relay application to communicate with the Valgrind embedded gdbserver:

```
(gdb) target remote | vgdb
Remote debugging using | vgdb
relaying data between gdb and process 2418
Reading symbols from /lib/ld-linux.so.2...done.
Reading symbols from /usr/lib/debug/lib/ld-2.11.2.so.debug...done.
Loaded symbols for /lib/ld-linux.so.2
[Switching to Thread 2418]
0x001f2850 in _start () from /lib/ld-linux.so.2
(gdb)
```

Note that vgdb is provided as part of the Valgrind distribution. You do not need to install it separately.

If vgdb detects that there are multiple Valgrind gdbservers that can be connected to, it will list all such servers and their PIDs, and then exit. You can then reissue the GDB "target" command, but specifying the PID of the process you want to debug:

```
(gdb) target remote | vgdb
Remote debugging using | vgdb
no --pid= arg given and multiple valgrind pids found:
use --pid=2479 for valgrind --tool=memcheck --vgdb=yes --vgdb-error=0 ./prog
use --pid=2481 for valgrind --tool=memcheck --vgdb=yes --vgdb-error=0 ./prog
use --pid=2483 for valgrind --vgdb=yes --vgdb-error=0 ./another_prog
Remote communication error: Resource temporarily unavailable.
(gdb)  target remote | vgdb --pid=2479
Remote debugging using | vgdb --pid=2479
relaying data between gdb and process 2479
Reading symbols from /lib/ld-linux.so.2...done.
Reading symbols from /usr/lib/debug/lib/ld-2.11.2.so.debug...done.
Loaded symbols for /lib/ld-linux.so.2
[Switching to Thread 2479]
0x001f2850 in _start () from /lib/ld-linux.so.2
(gdb)
```

Once GDB is connected to the Valgrind gdbserver, it can be used in the same way as if you were debugging the program natively:

- Breakpoints can be inserted or deleted.

- Variables and register values can be examined or modified.

- Signal handling can be configured (printing, ignoring).

- Execution can be controlled (continue, step, next, stepi, etc).

- Program execution can be interrupted using Control-C.

And so on. Refer to the GDB user manual for a complete description of GDB's functionality.

3.2.4. Connecting to an Android gdbserver

When developing applications for Android, you will typically use a development system (on which the Android NDK is installed) to compile your application. An Android target system or emulator will be used to run the application. In this setup, Valgrind and vgdb will run on the Android system, while GDB will run on the development system. GDB will connect to the vgdb running on the Android system using the Android NDK 'adb forward' application.

Example: on the Android system, execute the following:

```
valgrind --vgdb-error=0 --vgdb=yes prog
# and then in another shell, run:
vgdb --port=1234
```

On the development system, execute the following commands:

```
adb forward tcp:1234 tcp:1234
gdb prog
(gdb) target remote :1234
```

GDB will use a local tcp/ip connection to connect to the Android adb forwarder. Adb will establish a relay connection between the host system and the Android target system. Be sure to use the GDB delivered in the Android NDK system (typically, arm-linux-androideabi-gdb), as the host GDB is probably not able to debug Android arm applications. Note that the local port nr (used by GDB) must not necessarily be equal to the port number used by vgdb: adb can forward tcp/ip between different port numbers.

In the current release, the GDB server is not enabled by default for Android, due to problems in establishing a suitable directory in which Valgrind can create the necessary FIFOs (named pipes) for communication purposes. You can stil try to use the GDB server, but you will need to explicitly enable it using the flag --vgdb=yes or --vgdb=full.

Additionally, you will need to select a temporary directory which is (a) writable by Valgrind, and (b) supports FIFOs. This is the main difficult point. Often, /sdcard satisfies requirement (a), but fails for (b) because it is a VFAT file system and VFAT does not support pipes. Possibilities you could try are /data/local, /data/local/Inst (if you installed Valgrind there), or /data/data/name.of.my.app, if you are running a specific application and it has its own directory of that form. This last possibility may have the highest probability of success.

You can specify the temporary directory to use either via the --with-tmpdir= configure time flag, or by setting environment variable TMPDIR when running Valgrind (on the Android device, not on the Android NDK development host). Another alternative is to specify the directory for the FIFOs using the --vgdb-prefix= Valgrind command line option.

We hope to have a better story for temporary directory handling on Android in the future. The difficulty is that, unlike in standard Unixes, there is no single temporary file directory that reliably works across all devices and scenarios.

3.2.5. Monitor command handling by the Valgrind gdbserver

The Valgrind gdbserver provides additional Valgrind-specific functionality via "monitor commands". Such monitor commands can be sent from the GDB command line or from the shell command line or requested by the client program using the VALGRIND_MONITOR_COMMAND client request. See Valgrind monitor commands for the list of the Valgrind core monitor commands available regardless of the Valgrind tool selected.

The following tools provide tool-specific monitor commands:

- Memcheck Monitor Commands

- Callgrind Monitor Commands

- Massif Monitor Commands

- Helgrind Monitor Commands

An example of a tool specific monitor command is the Memcheck monitor command `leak_check full reachable any`. This requests a full reporting of the allocated memory blocks. To have this leak check executed, use the GDB command:

```
(gdb) monitor leak_check full reachable any
```

GDB will send the `leak_check` command to the Valgrind gdbserver. The Valgrind gdbserver will execute the monitor command itself, if it recognises it to be a Valgrind core monitor command. If it is not recognised as such, it is assumed to be tool-specific and is handed to the tool for execution. For example:

```
(gdb) monitor leak_check full reachable any
==2418== 100 bytes in 1 blocks are still reachable in loss record 1 of 1
==2418==    at 0x4006E9E: malloc (vg_replace_malloc.c:236)
==2418==    by 0x804884F: main (prog.c:88)
==2418==
==2418== LEAK SUMMARY:
==2418==    definitely lost: 0 bytes in 0 blocks
==2418==    indirectly lost: 0 bytes in 0 blocks
==2418==      possibly lost: 0 bytes in 0 blocks
==2418==    still reachable: 100 bytes in 1 blocks
==2418==         suppressed: 0 bytes in 0 blocks
==2418==
(gdb)
```

As with other GDB commands, the Valgrind gdbserver will accept abbreviated monitor command names and arguments, as long as the given abbreviation is unambiguous. For example, the above `leak_check` command can also be typed as:

```
(gdb) mo l f r a
```

The letters `mo` are recognised by GDB as being an abbreviation for `monitor`. So GDB sends the string `l f r a` to the Valgrind gdbserver. The letters provided in this string are unambiguous for the Valgrind gdbserver. This therefore gives the same output as the unabbreviated command and arguments. If the provided abbreviation is ambiguous, the Valgrind gdbserver will report the list of commands (or argument values) that can match:

```
(gdb) mo v. n
v. can match v.set v.info v.wait v.kill v.translate v.do
(gdb) mo v.i n
n_errs_found 0 n_errs_shown 0 (vgdb-error 0)
(gdb)
```

Instead of sending a monitor command from GDB, you can also send these from a shell command line. For example, the following command lines, when given in a shell, will cause the same leak search to be executed by the process 3145:

```
vgdb --pid=3145 leak_check full reachable any
vgdb --pid=3145 l f r a
```

Note that the Valgrind gdbserver automatically continues the execution of the program after a standalone invocation of vgdb. Monitor commands sent from GDB do not cause the program to continue: the program execution is controlled explicitly using GDB commands such as "continue" or "next".

3.2.6. Valgrind gdbserver thread information

Valgrind's gdbserver enriches the output of the GDB `info threads` command with Valgrind-specific information. The operating system's thread number is followed by Valgrind's internal index for that thread ("tid") and by the Valgrind scheduler thread state:

```
(gdb) info threads
  4 Thread 6239 (tid 4 VgTs_Yielding)  0x001f2832 in _dl_sysinfo_int80 () from /lib/ld-l
* 3 Thread 6238 (tid 3 VgTs_Runnable)  make_error (s=0x8048b76 "called from London") at
  2 Thread 6237 (tid 2 VgTs_WaitSys)  0x001f2832 in _dl_sysinfo_int80 () from /lib/ld-li
  1 Thread 6234 (tid 1 VgTs_Yielding)  main (argc=1, argv=0xbedcc274) at prog.c:105
(gdb)
```

3.2.7. Examining and modifying Valgrind shadow registers

When the option `--vgdb-shadow-registers=yes` is given, the Valgrind gdbserver will let GDB examine and/or modify Valgrind's shadow registers. GDB version 7.1 or later is needed for this to work. For x86 and amd64, GDB version 7.2 or later is needed.

For each CPU register, the Valgrind core maintains two shadow register sets. These shadow registers can be accessed from GDB by giving a postfix `s1` or `s2` for respectively the first and second shadow register. For example, the x86 register `eax` and its two shadows can be examined using the following commands:

```
(gdb) p $eax
$1 = 0
(gdb) p $eaxs1
$2 = 0
(gdb) p $eaxs2
$3 = 0
(gdb)
```

Float shadow registers are shown by GDB as unsigned integer values instead of float values, as it is expected that these shadow values are mostly used for memcheck validity bits.

Intel/amd64 AVX registers ymm0 to ymm15 have also their shadow registers. However, GDB presents the shadow values using two "half" registers. For example, the half shadow registers for ymm9 are xmm9s1 (lower half for set 1), ymm9hs1 (upper half for set 1), xmm9s2 (lower half for set 2), ymm9hs2 (upper half for set 2). Note the inconsistent notation for the names of the half registers: the lower part starts with an x, the upper part starts with an y and has an h before the shadow postfix.

The special presentation of the AVX shadow registers is due to the fact that GDB independently retrieves the lower and upper half of the ymm registers. GDB does not however know that the shadow half registers have to be shown combined.

3.2.8. Limitations of the Valgrind gdbserver

Debugging with the Valgrind gdbserver is very similar to native debugging. Valgrind's gdbserver implementation is quite complete, and so provides most of the GDB debugging functionality. There are however some limitations and peculiarities:

- Precision of "stop-at" commands.

  GDB commands such as "step", "next", "stepi", breakpoints and watchpoints, will stop the execution of the process. With the option --vgdb=yes, the process might not stop at the exact requested instruction. Instead, it might continue execution of the current basic block and stop at one of the following basic blocks. This is linked to the fact that Valgrind gdbserver has to instrument a block to allow stopping at the exact instruction requested. Currently, re-instrumentation of the block currently being executed is not supported. So, if the action requested by GDB (e.g. single stepping or inserting a breakpoint) implies re-instrumentation of the current block, the GDB action may not be executed precisely.

  This limitation applies when the basic block currently being executed has not yet been instrumented for debugging. This typically happens when the gdbserver is activated due to the tool reporting an error or to a watchpoint. If the gdbserver block has been activated following a breakpoint, or if a breakpoint has been inserted in the block before its execution, then the block has already been instrumented for debugging.

  If you use the option --vgdb=full, then GDB "stop-at" commands will be obeyed precisely. The downside is that this requires each instruction to be instrumented with an additional call to a gdbserver helper function, which gives considerable overhead (+500% for memcheck) compared to --vgdb=no. Option --vgdb=yes has neglectible overhead compared to --vgdb=no.

- Processor registers and flags values.

  When Valgrind gdbserver stops on an error, on a breakpoint or when single stepping, registers and flags values might not be always up to date due to the optimisations done by the Valgrind core. The default value --vex-iropt-register-updates=unwindregs-at-mem-access ensures that the registers needed to make a stack trace (typically PC/SP/FP) are up to date at each memory access (i.e. memory exception points). Disabling some optimisations using the following values will increase the precision of registers and flags values (a typical performance impact for memcheck is given for each option).

  - --vex-iropt-register-updates=allregs-at-mem-access (+10%) ensures that all registers and flags are up to date at each memory access.

  - --vex-iropt-register-updates=allregs-at-each-insn (+25%) ensures that all registers and flags are up to date at each instruction.

Note that `--vgdb=full` (+500%, see above Precision of "stop-at" commands) automatically activates `--vex-iropt-register-updates=allregs-at-each-insn`.

• Hardware watchpoint support by the Valgrind gdbserver.

The Valgrind gdbserver can simulate hardware watchpoints if the selected tool provides support for it. Currently, only Memcheck provides hardware watchpoint simulation. The hardware watchpoint simulation provided by Memcheck is much faster that GDB software watchpoints, which are implemented by GDB checking the value of the watched zone(s) after each instruction. Hardware watchpoint simulation also provides read watchpoints. The hardware watchpoint simulation by Memcheck has some limitations compared to real hardware watchpoints. However, the number and length of simulated watchpoints are not limited.

Typically, the number of (real) hardware watchpoints is limited. For example, the x86 architecture supports a maximum of 4 hardware watchpoints, each watchpoint watching 1, 2, 4 or 8 bytes. The Valgrind gdbserver does not have any limitation on the number of simulated hardware watchpoints. It also has no limitation on the length of the memory zone being watched. Using GDB version 7.4 or later allow full use of the flexibility of the Valgrind gdbserver's simulated hardware watchpoints. Previous GDB versions do not understand that Valgrind gdbserver watchpoints have no length limit.

Memcheck implements hardware watchpoint simulation by marking the watched address ranges as being unaddressable. When a hardware watchpoint is removed, the range is marked as addressable and defined. Hardware watchpoint simulation of addressable but undefined memory zones works properly, but has the undesirable side effect of marking the zone as defined when the watchpoint is removed.

Write watchpoints might not be reported at the exact instruction that writes the monitored area, unless option `--vgdb=full` is given. Read watchpoints will always be reported at the exact instruction reading the watched memory.

It is better to avoid using hardware watchpoint of not addressable (yet) memory: in such a case, GDB will fall back to extremely slow software watchpoints. Also, if you do not quit GDB between two debugging sessions, the hardware watchpoints of the previous sessions will be re-inserted as software watchpoints if the watched memory zone is not addressable at program startup.

• Stepping inside shared libraries on ARM.

For unknown reasons, stepping inside shared libraries on ARM may fail. A workaround is to use the `ldd` command to find the list of shared libraries and their loading address and inform GDB of the loading address using the GDB command "add-symbol-file". Example:

```
(gdb) shell ldd ./prog
 libc.so.6 => /lib/libc.so.6 (0x4002c000)
 /lib/ld-linux.so.3 (0x40000000)
(gdb) add-symbol-file /lib/libc.so.6 0x4002c000
add symbol table from file "/lib/libc.so.6" at
 .text_addr = 0x4002c000
(y or n) y
Reading symbols from /lib/libc.so.6...(no debugging symbols found)...done.
(gdb)
```

- GDB version needed for ARM and PPC32/64.

  You must use a GDB version which is able to read XML target description sent by a gdbserver. This is the standard setup if GDB was configured and built with the "expat" library. If your GDB was not configured with XML support, it will report an error message when using the "target" command. Debugging will not work because GDB will then not be able to fetch the registers from the Valgrind gdbserver. For ARM programs using the Thumb instruction set, you must use a GDB version of 7.1 or later, as earlier versions have problems with next/step/breakpoints in Thumb code.

- Stack unwinding on PPC32/PPC64.

  On PPC32/PPC64, stack unwinding for leaf functions (functions that do not call any other functions) works properly only when you give the option `--vex-iropt-register-updates=allregs-at-mem-access` or `--vex-iropt-register-updates=allregs-at-each-insn`. You must also pass this option in order to get a precise stack when a signal is trapped by GDB.

- Breakpoints encountered multiple times.

  Some instructions (e.g. x86 "rep movsb") are translated by Valgrind using a loop. If a breakpoint is placed on such an instruction, the breakpoint will be encountered multiple times -- once for each step of the "implicit" loop implementing the instruction.

- Execution of Inferior function calls by the Valgrind gdbserver.

  GDB allows the user to "call" functions inside the process being debugged. Such calls are named "inferior calls" in the GDB terminology. A typical use of an inferior call is to execute a function that prints a human-readable version of a complex data structure. To make an inferior call, use the GDB "print" command followed by the function to call and its arguments. As an example, the following GDB command causes an inferior call to the libc "printf" function to be executed by the process being debugged:

```
(gdb) p printf("process being debugged has pid %d\n", getpid())
$5 = 36
(gdb)
```

The Valgrind gdbserver supports inferior function calls. Whilst an inferior call is running, the Valgrind tool will report errors as usual. If you do not want to have such errors stop the execution of the inferior call, you can use `v.set vgdb-error` to set a big value before the call, then manually reset it to its original value when the call is complete.

To execute inferior calls, GDB changes registers such as the program counter, and then continues the execution of the program. In a multithreaded program, all threads are continued, not just the thread instructed to make the inferior call. If another thread reports an error or encounters a breakpoint, the evaluation of the inferior call is abandoned.

Note that inferior function calls are a powerful GDB feature, but should be used with caution. For example, if the program being debugged is stopped inside the function "printf", forcing a recursive call to printf via an inferior call will very probably create problems. The Valgrind tool might also add another level of complexity to inferior calls, e.g. by reporting tool errors during the Inferior call or due to the instrumentation done.

- Connecting to or interrupting a Valgrind process blocked in a system call.

Connecting to or interrupting a Valgrind process blocked in a system call requires the "ptrace" system call to be usable. This may be disabled in your kernel for security reasons.

When running your program, Valgrind's scheduler periodically checks whether there is any work to be handled by the gdbserver. Unfortunately this check is only done if at least one thread of the process is runnable. If all the threads of the process are blocked in a system call, then the checks do not happen, and the Valgrind scheduler will not invoke the gdbserver. In such a case, the vgdb relay application will "force" the gdbserver to be invoked, without the intervention of the Valgrind scheduler.

Such forced invocation of the Valgrind gdbserver is implemented by vgdb using ptrace system calls. On a properly implemented kernel, the ptrace calls done by vgdb will not influence the behaviour of the program running under Valgrind. If however they do, giving the option `--max-invoke-ms=0` to the vgdb relay application will disable the usage of ptrace calls. The consequence of disabling ptrace usage in vgdb is that a Valgrind process blocked in a system call cannot be woken up or interrupted from GDB until it executes enough basic blocks to let the Valgrind scheduler's normal checking take effect.

When ptrace is disabled in vgdb, you can increase the responsiveness of the Valgrind gdbserver to commands or interrupts by giving a lower value to the option `--vgdb-poll`. If your application is blocked in system calls most of the time, using a very low value for `--vgdb-poll` will cause a the gdbserver to be invoked sooner. The gdbserver polling done by Valgrind's scheduler is very efficient, so the increased polling frequency should not cause significant performance degradation.

When ptrace is disabled in vgdb, a query packet sent by GDB may take significant time to be handled by the Valgrind gdbserver. In such cases, GDB might encounter a protocol timeout. To avoid this, you can increase the value of the timeout by using the GDB command "set remotetimeout".

Ubuntu versions 10.10 and later may restrict the scope of ptrace to the children of the process calling ptrace. As the Valgrind process is not a child of vgdb, such restricted scoping causes the ptrace calls to fail. To avoid that, Valgrind will automatically allow all processes belonging to the same userid to "ptrace" a Valgrind process, by using PR_SET_PTRACER.

Unblocking processes blocked in system calls is not currently implemented on Mac OS X and Android. So you cannot connect to or interrupt a process blocked in a system call on Mac OS X or Android.

- Changing register values.

The Valgrind gdbserver will only modify the values of the thread's registers when the thread is in status Runnable or Yielding. In other states (typically, WaitSys), attempts to change register values will fail. Amongst other things, this means that inferior calls are not executed for a thread which is in a system call, since the Valgrind gdbserver does not implement system call restart.

- Unsupported GDB functionality.

GDB provides a lot of debugging functionality and not all of it is supported. Specifically, the following are not supported: reversible debugging and tracepoints.

- Unknown limitations or problems.

The combination of GDB, Valgrind and the Valgrind gdbserver probably has unknown other limitations and problems. If you encounter strange or unexpected behaviour, feel free to report a bug. But first please verify that the limitation or problem is not inherent to GDB or the GDB remote protocol. You may be able to do so by checking the behaviour when using standard gdbserver part of the GDB package.

3.2.9. vgdb command line options

Usage: `vgdb [OPTION]...  [[-c] COMMAND]...`

vgdb ("Valgrind to GDB") is a small program that is used as an intermediary between Valgrind and GDB or a shell. Therefore, it has two usage modes:

1. As a standalone utility, it is used from a shell command line to send monitor commands to a process running under Valgrind. For this usage, the vgdb OPTION(s) must be followed by the monitor command to send. To send more than one command, separate them with the `-c` option.

2. In combination with GDB "target remote |" command, it is used as the relay application between GDB and the Valgrind gdbserver. For this usage, only OPTION(s) can be given, but no COMMAND can be given.

`vgdb` accepts the following options:

`--pid=<number>`
Specifies the PID of the process to which vgdb must connect to. This option is useful in case more than one Valgrind gdbserver can be connected to. If the `--pid` argument is not given and multiple Valgrind gdbserver processes are running, vgdb will report the list of such processes and then exit.

`--vgdb-prefix`
Must be given to both Valgrind and vgdb if you want to change the default prefix for the FIFOs (named pipes) used for communication between the Valgrind gdbserver and vgdb.

`--wait=<number>`
Instructs vgdb to search for available Valgrind gdbservers for the specified number of seconds. This makes it possible start a vgdb process before starting the Valgrind gdbserver with which you intend the vgdb to communicate. This option is useful when used in conjunction with a `--vgdb-prefix` that is unique to the process you want to wait for. Also, if you use the `--wait` argument in the GDB "target remote" command, you must set the GDB remotetimeout to a value bigger than the --wait argument value. See option `--max-invoke-ms` (just below) for an example of setting the remotetimeout value.

`--max-invoke-ms=<number>`
Gives the number of milliseconds after which vgdb will force the invocation of gdbserver embedded in Valgrind. The default value is 100 milliseconds. A value of 0 disables forced invocation. The forced invocation is used when vgdb is connected to a Valgrind gdbserver, and the Valgrind process has all its threads blocked in a system call.

If you specify a large value, you might need to increase the GDB "remotetimeout" value from its default value of 2 seconds. You should ensure that the timeout (in seconds) is bigger than the `--max-invoke-ms` value. For example, for `--max-invoke-ms=5000`, the following GDB command is suitable:

```
(gdb) set remotetimeout 6
```

`--cmd-time-out=<number>`
Instructs a standalone vgdb to exit if the Valgrind gdbserver it is connected to does not process a command in the specified number of seconds. The default value is to never time out.

```
--port=<portnr>
```
Instructs vgdb to use tcp/ip and listen for GDB on the specified port nr rather than to use a pipe to communicate with GDB. Using tcp/ip allows to have GDB running on one computer and debugging a Valgrind process running on another target computer. Example:

```
# On the target computer, start your program under valgrind using
valgrind --vgdb-error=0 prog
# and then in another shell, run:
vgdb --port=1234
```

On the computer which hosts GDB, execute the command:

```
gdb prog
(gdb) target remote targetip:1234
```

where targetip is the ip address or hostname of the target computer.

```
c
```
To give more than one command to a standalone vgdb, separate the commands by an option -c. Example:

```
vgdb v.set log_output -c leak_check any
```

```
-l
```
Instructs a standalone vgdb to report the list of the Valgrind gdbserver processes running and then exit.

```
-D
```
Instructs a standalone vgdb to show the state of the shared memory used by the Valgrind gdbserver. vgdb will exit after having shown the Valgrind gdbserver shared memory state.

```
-d
```
Instructs vgdb to produce debugging output. Give multiple -d args to increase the verbosity. When giving -d to a relay vgdb, you better redirect the standard error (stderr) of vgdb to a file to avoid interaction between GDB and vgdb debugging output.

3.2.10. Valgrind monitor commands

This section describes the Valgrind monitor commands, available regardless of the Valgrind tool selected. For the tool specific commands, refer to Memcheck Monitor Commands, Helgrind Monitor Commands, Callgrind Monitor Commands and Massif Monitor Commands.

The monitor commands can be sent either from a shell command line, by using a standalone vgdb, or from GDB, by using GDB's "monitor" command (see Monitor command handling by the Valgrind gdbserver). They can also be launched by the client program, using the VALGRIND_MONITOR_COMMAND client request.

- `help [debug]` instructs Valgrind's gdbserver to give the list of all monitor commands of the Valgrind core and of the tool. The optional "debug" argument tells to also give help for the monitor commands aimed at Valgrind internals debugging.

- `v.info all_errors` shows all errors found so far.

- `v.info last_error` shows the last error found.

- `v.info location <addr>` outputs information about the location <addr>. Possibly, the following are described: global variables, local (stack) variables, allocated or freed blocks, ... The information produced depends on the tool and on the options given to valgrind. Some tools (e.g. memcheck and helgrind) produce more detailed information for client heap blocks. For example, these tools show the stacktrace where the heap block was allocated. If a tool does not replace the malloc/free/... functions, then client heap blocks will not be described. Use the option `--read-var-info=yes` to obtain more detailed information about global or local (stack) variables.

```
(gdb) monitor v.info location 0x8050b20
 Location 0x8050b20 is 0 bytes inside global var "mx"
 declared at tc19_shadowmem.c:19

(gdb) mo v.in loc 0x582f33c
 Location 0x582f33c is 0 bytes inside local var "info"
 declared at tc19_shadowmem.c:282, in frame #1 of thread 3
(gdb)
```

- `v.info n_errs_found [msg]` shows the number of errors found so far, the nr of errors shown so far and the current value of the `--vgdb-error` argument. The optional `msg` (one or more words) is appended. Typically, this can be used to insert markers in a process output file between several tests executed in sequence by a process started only once. This allows to associate the errors reported by Valgrind with the specific test that produced these errors.

- `v.info open_fds` shows the list of open file descriptors and details related to the file descriptor. This only works if `--track-fds=yes` was given at Valgrind startup.

- `v.set {gdb_output | log_output | mixed_output}` allows redirection of the Valgrind output (e.g. the errors detected by the tool). The default setting is `mixed_output`.

With `mixed_output`, the Valgrind output goes to the Valgrind log (typically stderr) while the output of the interactive GDB monitor commands (e.g. `v.info last_error`) is displayed by GDB.

With `gdb_output`, both the Valgrind output and the interactive GDB monitor commands output are displayed by GDB.

With `log_output`, both the Valgrind output and the interactive GDB monitor commands output go to the Valgrind log.

- `v.wait [ms (default 0)]` instructs Valgrind gdbserver to sleep "ms" milli-seconds and then continue. When sent from a standalone vgdb, if this is the last command, the Valgrind process will continue the execution of the guest process. The typical usage of this is to use vgdb to send a "no-op" command to a Valgrind gdbserver so as to continue the execution of the guest process.

- `v.kill` requests the gdbserver to kill the process. This can be used from a standalone vgdb to properly kill a Valgrind process which is currently expecting a vgdb connection.

- `v.set vgdb-error <errornr>` dynamically changes the value of the `--vgdb-error` argument. A typical usage of this is to start with `--vgdb-error=0` on the command line, then set a few breakpoints, set the vgdb-error value to a huge value and continue execution.

The following Valgrind monitor commands are useful for investigating the behaviour of Valgrind or its gdbserver in case of problems or bugs.

- `v.do expensive_sanity_check_general` executes various sanity checks. In particular, the sanity of the Valgrind heap is verified. This can be useful if you suspect that your program and/or Valgrind has a bug corrupting Valgrind data structure. It can also be used when a Valgrind tool reports a client error to the connected GDB, in order to verify the sanity of Valgrind before continuing the execution.

- `v.info gdbserver_status` shows the gdbserver status. In case of problems (e.g. of communications), this shows the values of some relevant Valgrind gdbserver internal variables. Note that the variables related to breakpoints and watchpoints (e.g. the number of breakpoint addresses and the number of watchpoints) will be zero, as GDB by default removes all watchpoints and breakpoints when execution stops, and re-inserts them when resuming the execution of the debugged process. You can change this GDB behaviour by using the GDB command `set breakpoint always-inserted on`.

- `v.info memory [aspacemgr]` shows the statistics of Valgrind's internal heap management. If option `--profile-heap=yes` was given, detailed statistics will be output. With the optional argument `aspacemgr`, the segment list maintained by valgrind address space manager will be output. Note that this list of segments is always output on the Valgrind log.

- `v.info exectxt` shows informations about the "executable contexts" (i.e. the stack traces) recorded by Valgrind. For some programs, Valgrind can record a very high number of such stack traces, causing a high memory usage. This monitor command shows all the recorded stack traces, followed by some statistics. This can be used to analyse the reason for having a big number of stack traces. Typically, you will use this command if `v.info memory` has shown significant memory usage by the "exectxt" arena.

- `v.info scheduler` shows various information about threads. First, it outputs the host stack trace, i.e. the Valgrind code being executed. Then, for each thread, it outputs the thread state. For non terminated threads, the state is followed by the guest (client) stack trace. Finally, for each active thread or for each terminated thread slot not yet re-used, it shows the max usage of the valgrind stack.

  Showing the client stack traces allows to compare the stack traces produced by the Valgrind unwinder with the stack traces produced by GDB+Valgrind gdbserver. Pay attention that GDB and Valgrind scheduler status have their own thread numbering scheme. To make the link between the GDB thread number and the corresponding Valgrind scheduler thread number, use the GDB command `info threads`. The output of this command shows the GDB thread number and the valgrind 'tid'. The 'tid' is the thread number output by `v.info scheduler`. When using the callgrind tool, the callgrind monitor command `status` outputs internal callgrind information about the stack/call graph it maintains.

- `v.info stats` shows various valgrind core and tool statistics. With this, Valgrind and tool statistics can be examined while running, even without option `--stats=yes`.

- `v.info unwind <addr> [<len>]` shows the CFI unwind debug info for the address range [addr, addr+len-1]. The default value of <len> is 1, giving the unwind information for the instruction at <addr>.

- `v.set debuglog <intvalue>` sets the Valgrind debug log level to <intvalue>. This allows to dynamically change the log level of Valgrind e.g. when a problem is detected.

- `v.set hostvisibility [yes*|no]` The value "yes" indicates to gdbserver that GDB can look at the Valgrind 'host' (internal) status/memory. "no" disables this access. When hostvisibility is activated, GDB can e.g. look at Valgrind global variables. As an example, to examine a Valgrind global variable of the memcheck tool on an x86, do the following setup:

```
(gdb) monitor v.set hostvisibility yes
(gdb) add-symbol-file /path/to/tool/executable/file/memcheck-x86-linux 0x38000000

add symbol table from file "/path/to/tool/executable/file/memcheck-x86-linux" at

 .text_addr = 0x38000000
(y or n) y
Reading symbols from /path/to/tool/executable/file/memcheck-x86-linux...done.
(gdb)
```

After that, variables defined in memcheck-x86-linux can be accessed, e.g.

```
(gdb) p /x vgPlain_threads[1].os_state
$3 = {lwpid = 0x4688, threadgroup = 0x4688, parent = 0x0,
  valgrind_stack_base = 0x62e78000, valgrind_stack_init_SP = 0x62f79fe0,
  exitcode = 0x0, fatalsig = 0x0}
(gdb) p vex_control
$5 = {iropt_verbosity = 0, iropt_level = 2,
  iropt_register_updates = VexRegUpdUnwindregsAtMemAccess,
  iropt_unroll_thresh = 120, guest_max_insns = 60, guest_chase_thresh = 10,
  guest_chase_cond = 0 '\000'}
(gdb)
```

- `v.translate <address> [<traceflags>]` shows the translation of the block containing `address` with the given trace flags. The `traceflags` value bit patterns have similar meaning to Valgrind's `--trace-flags` option. It can be given in hexadecimal (e.g. 0x20) or decimal (e.g. 32) or in binary 1s and 0s bit (e.g. 0b00100000). The default value of the traceflags is 0b00100000, corresponding to "show after instrumentation". The output of this command always goes to the Valgrind log.

The additional bit flag 0b100000000 (bit 8) has no equivalent in the `--trace-flags` option. It enables tracing of the gdbserver specific instrumentation. Note that this bit 8 can only enable the addition of gdbserver instrumentation in the trace. Setting it to 0 will not disable the tracing of the gdbserver instrumentation if it is active for some other reason, for example because there is a breakpoint at this address or because gdbserver is in single stepping mode.

3.3. Function wrapping

Valgrind allows calls to some specified functions to be intercepted and rerouted to a different, user-supplied function. This can do whatever it likes, typically examining the arguments, calling onwards to the original, and possibly examining the result. Any number of functions may be wrapped.

Function wrapping is useful for instrumenting an API in some way. For example, Helgrind wraps functions in the POSIX pthreads API so it can know about thread status changes, and the core is able to wrap functions in the MPI (message-passing) API so it can know of memory status changes associated with message arrival/departure. Such information is usually passed to Valgrind by using client requests in the wrapper functions, although the exact mechanism may vary.

3.3.1. A Simple Example

Supposing we want to wrap some function

```
int foo ( int x, int y ) { return x + y; }
```

A wrapper is a function of identical type, but with a special name which identifies it as the wrapper for `foo`. Wrappers need to include supporting macros from `valgrind.h`. Here is a simple wrapper which prints the arguments and return value:

```
#include <stdio.h>
#include "valgrind.h"
int I_WRAP_SONAME_FNNAME_ZU(NONE,foo)( int x, int y )
{
   int    result;
   OrigFn fn;
   VALGRIND_GET_ORIG_FN(fn);
   printf("foo's wrapper: args %d %d\n", x, y);
   CALL_FN_W_WW(result, fn, x,y);
   printf("foo's wrapper: result %d\n", result);
   return result;
}
```

To become active, the wrapper merely needs to be present in a text section somewhere in the same process' address space as the function it wraps, and for its ELF symbol name to be visible to Valgrind. In practice, this means either compiling to a `.o` and linking it in, or compiling to a `.so` and `LD_PRELOAD`ing it in. The latter is more convenient in that it doesn't require relinking.

All wrappers have approximately the above form. There are three crucial macros:

`I_WRAP_SONAME_FNNAME_ZU`: this generates the real name of the wrapper. This is an encoded name which Valgrind notices when reading symbol table information. What it says is: I am the wrapper for any function named `foo` which is found in an ELF shared object with an empty (`"NONE"`) soname field. The specification mechanism is powerful in that wildcards are allowed for both sonames and function names. The details are discussed below.

`VALGRIND_GET_ORIG_FN`: once in the wrapper, the first priority is to get hold of the address of the original (and any other supporting information needed). This is stored in a value of opaque type `OrigFn`. The information is acquired using `VALGRIND_GET_ORIG_FN`. It is crucial to make this macro call before calling any other wrapped function in the same thread.

`CALL_FN_W_WW`: eventually we will want to call the function being wrapped. Calling it directly does not work, since that just gets us back to the wrapper and leads to an infinite loop. Instead, the result lvalue, `OrigFn` and arguments are handed to one of a family of macros of the form `CALL_FN_*`. These cause Valgrind to call the original and avoid recursion back to the wrapper.

3.3.2. Wrapping Specifications

This scheme has the advantage of being self-contained. A library of wrappers can be compiled to object code in the normal way, and does not rely on an external script telling Valgrind which wrappers pertain to which originals.

Each wrapper has a name which, in the most general case says: I am the wrapper for any function whose name matches FNPATT and whose ELF "soname" matches SOPATT. Both FNPATT and SOPATT may contain wildcards (asterisks) and other characters (spaces, dots, @, etc) which are not generally regarded as valid C identifier names.

This flexibility is needed to write robust wrappers for POSIX pthread functions, where typically we are not completely sure of either the function name or the soname, or alternatively we want to wrap a whole set of functions at once.

For example, `pthread_create` in GNU libpthread is usually a versioned symbol - one whose name ends in, eg, `@GLIBC_2.3`. Hence we are not sure what its real name is. We also want to cover any soname of the form `libpthread.so*`. So the header of the wrapper will be

```
int I_WRAP_SONAME_FNNAME_ZZ(libpthreadZdsoZd0,pthreadZucreateZAZa)
  ( ... formals ... )
  { ... body ... }
```

In order to write unusual characters as valid C function names, a Z-encoding scheme is used. Names are written literally, except that a capital Z acts as an escape character, with the following encoding:

```
Za    encodes    *
Zp               +
Zc               :
Zd               .
Zu               _
Zh               -
Zs               (space)
ZA               @
ZZ               Z
ZL               (       # only in valgrind 3.3.0 and later
ZR               )       # only in valgrind 3.3.0 and later
```

Hence `libpthreadZdsoZd0` is an encoding of the soname `libpthread.so.0` and `pthreadZucreateZAZa` is an encoding of the function name `pthread_create@*`.

The macro `I_WRAP_SONAME_FNNAME_ZZ` constructs a wrapper name in which both the soname (first component) and function name (second component) are Z-encoded. Encoding the function name can be tiresome and is often unnecessary, so a second macro, `I_WRAP_SONAME_FNNAME_ZU`, can be used instead. The `_ZU` variant is also useful for writing wrappers for C++ functions, in which the function name is usually already mangled using some other convention in which Z plays an important role. Having to encode a second time quickly becomes confusing.

Since the function name field may contain wildcards, it can be anything, including just `*`. The same is true for the soname. However, some ELF objects - specifically, main executables - do not have sonames. Any object lacking a soname is treated as if its soname was NONE, which is why the original example above had a name `I_WRAP_SONAME_FNNAME_ZU(NONE,foo)`.

Note that the soname of an ELF object is not the same as its file name, although it is often similar. You can find the soname of an object `libfoo.so` using the command `readelf -a libfoo.so | grep soname`.

3.3.3. Wrapping Semantics

The ability for a wrapper to replace an infinite family of functions is powerful but brings complications in situations where ELF objects appear and disappear (are dlopen'd and dlclose'd) on the fly. Valgrind tries to maintain sensible behaviour in such situations.

For example, suppose a process has dlopened (an ELF object with soname) object1.so, which contains function1. It starts to use function1 immediately.

After a while it dlopens wrappers.so, which contains a wrapper for function1 in (soname) object1.so. All subsequent calls to function1 are rerouted to the wrapper.

If wrappers.so is later dlclose'd, calls to function1 are naturally routed back to the original.

Alternatively, if object1.so is dlclose'd but wrappers.so remains, then the wrapper exported by wrappers.so becomes inactive, since there is no way to get to it - there is no original to call any more. However, Valgrind remembers that the wrapper is still present. If object1.so is eventually dlopen'd again, the wrapper will become active again.

In short, valgrind inspects all code loading/unloading events to ensure that the set of currently active wrappers remains consistent.

A second possible problem is that of conflicting wrappers. It is easily possible to load two or more wrappers, both of which claim to be wrappers for some third function. In such cases Valgrind will complain about conflicting wrappers when the second one appears, and will honour only the first one.

3.3.4. Debugging

Figuring out what's going on given the dynamic nature of wrapping can be difficult. The --trace-redir=yes option makes this possible by showing the complete state of the redirection subsystem after every mmap/munmap event affecting code (text).

There are two central concepts:

- A "redirection specification" is a binding of a (soname pattern, fnname pattern) pair to a code address. These bindings are created by writing functions with names made with the I_WRAP_SONAME_FNNAME_{ZZ,_ZU} macros.

- An "active redirection" is a code-address to code-address binding currently in effect.

The state of the wrapping-and-redirection subsystem comprises a set of specifications and a set of active bindings. The specifications are acquired/discarded by watching all mmap/munmap events on code (text) sections. The active binding set is (conceptually) recomputed from the specifications, and all known symbol names, following any change to the specification set.

--trace-redir=yes shows the contents of both sets following any such event.

-v prints a line of text each time an active specification is used for the first time.

Hence for maximum debugging effectiveness you will need to use both options.

One final comment. The function-wrapping facility is closely tied to Valgrind's ability to replace (redirect) specified functions, for example to redirect calls to malloc to its own implementation. Indeed, a replacement function can be regarded as a wrapper function which does not call the original. However, to make the implementation more robust, the two kinds of interception (wrapping vs replacement) are treated differently.

--trace-redir=yes shows specifications and bindings for both replacement and wrapper functions. To differentiate the two, replacement bindings are printed using R-> whereas wraps are printed using W->.

3.3.5. Limitations - control flow

For the most part, the function wrapping implementation is robust. The only important caveat is: in a wrapper, get hold of the OrigFn information using VALGRIND_GET_ORIG_FN before calling any other wrapped function. Once you have the OrigFn, arbitrary calls between, recursion between, and longjumps out of wrappers should work correctly. There is never any interaction between wrapped functions and merely replaced functions (eg malloc), so you can call malloc etc safely from within wrappers.

The above comments are true for {x86,amd64,ppc32,arm,mips32,s390}-linux. On ppc64-linux function wrapping is more fragile due to the (arguably poorly designed) ppc64-linux ABI. This mandates the use of a shadow stack which tracks entries/exits of both wrapper and replacement functions. This gives two limitations: firstly, longjumping out of wrappers will rapidly lead to disaster, since the shadow stack will not get correctly cleared. Secondly, since the shadow stack has finite size, recursion between wrapper/replacement functions is only possible to a limited depth, beyond which Valgrind has to abort the run. This depth is currently 16 calls.

For all platforms ({x86,amd64,ppc32,ppc64,arm,mips32,s390}-linux) all the above comments apply on a per-thread basis. In other words, wrapping is thread-safe: each thread must individually observe the above restrictions, but there is no need for any kind of inter-thread cooperation.

3.3.6. Limitations - original function signatures

As shown in the above example, to call the original you must use a macro of the form CALL_FN_*. For technical reasons it is impossible to create a single macro to deal with all argument types and numbers, so a family of macros covering the most common cases is supplied. In what follows, 'W' denotes a machine-word-typed value (a pointer or a C long), and 'v' denotes C's void type. The currently available macros are:

```
CALL_FN_v_v     -- call an original of type  void fn ( void )
CALL_FN_W_v     -- call an original of type  long fn ( void )

CALL_FN_v_W     -- call an original of type  void fn ( long )
CALL_FN_W_W     -- call an original of type  long fn ( long )

CALL_FN_v_WW    -- call an original of type  void fn ( long, long )
CALL_FN_W_WW    -- call an original of type  long fn ( long, long )

CALL_FN_v_WWW   -- call an original of type  void fn ( long, long, long )
CALL_FN_W_WWW   -- call an original of type  long fn ( long, long, long )

CALL_FN_W_WWWW  -- call an original of type  long fn ( long, long, long, long )
CALL_FN_W_5W    -- call an original of type  long fn ( long, long, long, long, long )

CALL_FN_W_6W    -- call an original of type  long fn ( long, long, long, long, long, long )

and so on, up to
CALL_FN_W_12W
```

The set of supported types can be expanded as needed. It is regrettable that this limitation exists. Function wrapping has proven difficult to implement, with a certain apparently unavoidable level of ickiness. After several implementation attempts, the present arrangement appears to be the least-worst tradeoff. At least it works reliably in the presence of dynamic linking and dynamic code loading/unloading.

You should not attempt to wrap a function of one type signature with a wrapper of a different type signature. Such trickery will surely lead to crashes or strange behaviour. This is not a limitation of the function wrapping implementation, merely a reflection of the fact that it gives you sweeping powers to shoot yourself in the foot if you are not careful. Imagine the instant havoc you could wreak by writing a wrapper which matched any function name in any soname - in effect, one which claimed to be a wrapper for all functions in the process.

3.3.7. Examples

In the source tree, `memcheck/tests/wrap[1-8].c` provide a series of examples, ranging from very simple to quite advanced.

`mpi/libmpiwrap.c` is an example of wrapping a big, complex API (the MPI-2 interface). This file defines almost 300 different wrappers.

4. Memcheck: a memory error detector

To use this tool, you may specify `--tool=memcheck` on the Valgrind command line. You don't have to, though, since Memcheck is the default tool.

4.1. Overview

Memcheck is a memory error detector. It can detect the following problems that are common in C and C++ programs.

- Accessing memory you shouldn't, e.g. overrunning and underrunning heap blocks, overrunning the top of the stack, and accessing memory after it has been freed.

- Using undefined values, i.e. values that have not been initialised, or that have been derived from other undefined values.

- Incorrect freeing of heap memory, such as double-freeing heap blocks, or mismatched use of `malloc`/`new`/`new[]` versus `free`/`delete`/`delete[]`

- Overlapping `src` and `dst` pointers in `memcpy` and related functions.

- Passing a fishy (presumably negative) value to the `size` parameter of a memory allocation function.

- Memory leaks.

Problems like these can be difficult to find by other means, often remaining undetected for long periods, then causing occasional, difficult-to-diagnose crashes.

4.2. Explanation of error messages from Memcheck

Memcheck issues a range of error messages. This section presents a quick summary of what error messages mean. The precise behaviour of the error-checking machinery is described in Details of Memcheck's checking machinery.

4.2.1. Illegal read / Illegal write errors

For example:

```
Invalid read of size 4
   at 0x40F6BBCC: (within /usr/lib/libpng.so.2.1.0.9)
   by 0x40F6B804: (within /usr/lib/libpng.so.2.1.0.9)
   by 0x40B07FF4: read_png_image(QImageIO *) (kernel/qpngio.cpp:326)
   by 0x40AC751B: QImageIO::read() (kernel/qimage.cpp:3621)
 Address 0xBFFFF0E0 is not stack'd, malloc'd or free'd
```

This happens when your program reads or writes memory at a place which Memcheck reckons it shouldn't. In this example, the program did a 4-byte read at address 0xBFFFF0E0, somewhere within the system-supplied library libpng.so.2.1.0.9, which was called from somewhere else in the same library, called from line 326 of qpngio.cpp, and so on.

Memcheck tries to establish what the illegal address might relate to, since that's often useful. So, if it points into a block of memory which has already been freed, you'll be informed of this, and also where the block was freed. Likewise, if it should turn out to be just off the end of a heap block, a common result of off-by-one-errors in array subscripting, you'll be informed of this fact, and also where the block was allocated. If you use the `--read-var-info` option Memcheck will run more slowly but may give a more detailed description of any illegal address.

In this example, Memcheck can't identify the address. Actually the address is on the stack, but, for some reason, this is not a valid stack address -- it is below the stack pointer and that isn't allowed. In this particular case it's probably caused by GCC generating invalid code, a known bug in some ancient versions of GCC. ·

Note that Memcheck only tells you that your program is about to access memory at an illegal address. It can't stop the access from happening. So, if your program makes an access which normally would result in a segmentation fault, you program will still suffer the same fate -- but you will get a message from Memcheck immediately prior to this. In this particular example, reading junk on the stack is non-fatal, and the program stays alive.

4.2.2. Use of uninitialised values

For example:

```
Conditional jump or move depends on uninitialised value(s)
   at 0x402DFA94: _IO_vfprintf (_itoa.h:49)
   by 0x402E8476: _IO_printf (printf.c:36)
   by 0x8048472: main (tests/manuel1.c:8)
```

An uninitialised-value use error is reported when your program uses a value which hasn't been initialised -- in other words, is undefined. Here, the undefined value is used somewhere inside the `printf` machinery of the C library. This error was reported when running the following small program:

```
int main()
{
  int x;
  printf ("x = %d\n", x);
}
```

It is important to understand that your program can copy around junk (uninitialised) data as much as it likes. Memcheck observes this and keeps track of the data, but does not complain. A complaint is issued only when your program attempts to make use of uninitialised data in a way that might affect your program's externally-visible behaviour. In this example, x is uninitialised. Memcheck observes the value being passed to `_IO_printf` and thence to `_IO_vfprintf`, but makes no comment. However, `_IO_vfprintf` has to examine the value of x so it can turn it into the corresponding ASCII string, and it is at this point that Memcheck complains.

Sources of uninitialised data tend to be:

• Local variables in procedures which have not been initialised, as in the example above.

• The contents of heap blocks (allocated with `malloc`, `new`, or a similar function) before you (or a constructor) write something there.

To see information on the sources of uninitialised data in your program, use the `--track-origins=yes` option. This makes Memcheck run more slowly, but can make it much easier to track down the root causes of uninitialised value errors.

4.2.3. Use of uninitialised or unaddressable values in system calls

Memcheck checks all parameters to system calls:

- It checks all the direct parameters themselves, whether they are initialised.

- Also, if a system call needs to read from a buffer provided by your program, Memcheck checks that the entire buffer is addressable and its contents are initialised.

- Also, if the system call needs to write to a user-supplied buffer, Memcheck checks that the buffer is addressable.

After the system call, Memcheck updates its tracked information to precisely reflect any changes in memory state caused by the system call.

Here's an example of two system calls with invalid parameters:

```
#include <stdlib.h>
#include <unistd.h>
int main( void )
{
  char* arr  = malloc(10);
  int*  arr2 = malloc(sizeof(int));
  write( 1 /* stdout */, arr, 10 );
  exit(arr2[0]);
}
```

You get these complaints ...

```
Syscall param write(buf) points to uninitialised byte(s)
   at 0x25A48723: __write_nocancel (in /lib/tls/libc-2.3.3.so)
   by 0x259AFAD3: __libc_start_main (in /lib/tls/libc-2.3.3.so)
   by 0x8048348: (within /auto/homes/njn25/grind/head4/a.out)
 Address 0x25AB8028 is 0 bytes inside a block of size 10 alloc'd
   at 0x259852B0: malloc (vg_replace_malloc.c:130)
   by 0x80483F1: main (a.c:5)

Syscall param exit(error_code) contains uninitialised byte(s)
   at 0x25A21B44: __GI__exit (in /lib/tls/libc-2.3.3.so)
   by 0x8048426: main (a.c:8)
```

... because the program has (a) written uninitialised junk from the heap block to the standard output, and (b) passed an uninitialised value to `exit`. Note that the first error refers to the memory pointed to by `buf` (not `buf` itself), but the second error refers directly to `exit`'s argument `arr2[0]`.

4.2.4. Illegal frees

For example:

```
Invalid free()
   at 0x4004FFDF: free (vg_clientmalloc.c:577)
   by 0x80484C7: main (tests/doublefree.c:10)
 Address 0x3807F7B4 is 0 bytes inside a block of size 177 free'd
   at 0x4004FFDF: free (vg_clientmalloc.c:577)
   by 0x80484C7: main (tests/doublefree.c:10)
```

Memcheck keeps track of the blocks allocated by your program with malloc/new, so it can know exactly whether or not the argument to free/delete is legitimate or not. Here, this test program has freed the same block twice. As with the illegal read/write errors, Memcheck attempts to make sense of the address freed. If, as here, the address is one which has previously been freed, you wil be told that -- making duplicate frees of the same block easy to spot. You will also get this message if you try to free a pointer that doesn't point to the start of a heap block.

4.2.5. When a heap block is freed with an inappropriate deallocation function

In the following example, a block allocated with new[] has wrongly been deallocated with free:

```
Mismatched free() / delete / delete []
   at 0x40043249: free (vg_clientfuncs.c:171)
   by 0x4102BB4E: QGArray::~QGArray(void) (tools/qgarray.cpp:149)
   by 0x4C261C41: PptDoc::~PptDoc(void) (include/qmemarray.h:60)
   by 0x4C261F0E: PptXml::~PptXml(void) (pptxml.cc:44)
 Address 0x4BB292A8 is 0 bytes inside a block of size 64 alloc'd
   at 0x4004318C: operator new[](unsigned int) (vg_clientfuncs.c:152)
   by 0x4C21BC15: KLaola::readSBStream(int) const (klaola.cc:314)
   by 0x4C21C155: KLaola::stream(KLaola::OLENode const *) (klaola.cc:416)
   by 0x4C21788F: OLEFilter::convert(QCString const &) (olefilter.cc:272)
```

In C++ it's important to deallocate memory in a way compatible with how it was allocated. The deal is:

- If allocated with malloc, calloc, realloc, valloc or memalign, you must deallocate with free.

- If allocated with new, you must deallocate with delete.

- If allocated with new[], you must deallocate with delete[].

The worst thing is that on Linux apparently it doesn't matter if you do mix these up, but the same program may then crash on a different platform, Solaris for example. So it's best to fix it properly. According to the KDE folks "it's amazing how many C++ programmers don't know this".

The reason behind the requirement is as follows. In some C++ implementations, delete[] must be used for objects allocated by new[] because the compiler stores the size of the array and the pointer-to-member to the destructor of the array's content just before the pointer actually returned. delete doesn't account for this and will get confused, possibly corrupting the heap.

4.2.6. Overlapping source and destination blocks

The following C library functions copy some data from one memory block to another (or something similar): memcpy, strcpy, strncpy, strcat, strncat. The blocks pointed to by their src and dst pointers aren't allowed to overlap. The POSIX standards have wording along the lines "If copying takes place between objects that overlap, the behavior is undefined." Therefore, Memcheck checks for this.

For example:

```
==27492== Source and destination overlap in memcpy(0xbffff294, 0xbffff280, 21)
==27492==    at 0x40026CDC: memcpy (mc_replace_strmem.c:71)
==27492==    by 0x804865A: main (overlap.c:40)
```

You don't want the two blocks to overlap because one of them could get partially overwritten by the copying.

You might think that Memcheck is being overly pedantic reporting this in the case where dst is less than src. For example, the obvious way to implement memcpy is by copying from the first byte to the last. However, the optimisation guides of some architectures recommend copying from the last byte down to the first. Also, some implementations of memcpy zero dst before copying, because zeroing the destination's cache line(s) can improve performance.

The moral of the story is: if you want to write truly portable code, don't make any assumptions about the language implementation.

4.2.7. Fishy argument values

All memory allocation functions take an argument specifying the size of the memory block that should be allocated. Clearly, the requested size should be a non-negative value and is typically not excessively large. For instance, it is extremely unlikly that the size of an allocation request exceeds 2**63 bytes on a 64-bit machine. It is much more likely that such a value is the result of an erroneous size calculation and is in effect a negative value (that just happens to appear excessively large because the bit pattern is interpreted as an unsigned integer). Such a value is called a "fishy value". The size argument of the following allocation functions is checked for being fishy: malloc, calloc, realloc, memalign, new, new []. __builtin_new, __builtin_vec_new, For calloc both arguments are being checked.

For example:

```
==32233== Argument 'size' of function malloc has a fishy (possibly negative) value: -3

==32233==    at 0x4C2CFA7: malloc (vg_replace_malloc.c:298)
==32233==    by 0x400555: foo (fishy.c:15)
==32233==    by 0x400583: main (fishy.c:23)
```

In earlier Valgrind versions those values were being referred to as "silly arguments" and no back-trace was included.

4.2.8. Memory leak detection

Memcheck keeps track of all heap blocks issued in response to calls to `malloc`/`new` et al. So when the program exits, it knows which blocks have not been freed.

If `--leak-check` is set appropriately, for each remaining block, Memcheck determines if the block is reachable from pointers within the root-set. The root-set consists of (a) general purpose registers of all threads, and (b) initialised, aligned, pointer-sized data words in accessible client memory, including stacks.

There are two ways a block can be reached. The first is with a "start-pointer", i.e. a pointer to the start of the block. The second is with an "interior-pointer", i.e. a pointer to the middle of the block. There are several ways we know of that an interior-pointer can occur:

- The pointer might have originally been a start-pointer and have been moved along deliberately (or not deliberately) by the program. In particular, this can happen if your program uses tagged pointers, i.e. if it uses the bottom one, two or three bits of a pointer, which are normally always zero due to alignment, in order to store extra information.

- It might be a random junk value in memory, entirely unrelated, just a coincidence.

- It might be a pointer to the inner char array of a C++ `std::string`. For example, some compilers add 3 words at the beginning of the std::string to store the length, the capacity and a reference count before the memory containing the array of characters. They return a pointer just after these 3 words, pointing at the char array.

- Some code might allocate a block of memory, and use the first 8 bytes to store (block size - 8) as a 64bit number. `sqlite3MemMalloc` does this.

- It might be a pointer to an array of C++ objects (which possess destructors) allocated with `new[]`. In this case, some compilers store a "magic cookie" containing the array length at the start of the allocated block, and return a pointer to just past that magic cookie, i.e. an interior-pointer. See this page for more information.

- It might be a pointer to an inner part of a C++ object using multiple inheritance.

You can optionally activate heuristics to use during the leak search to detect the interior pointers corresponding to the stdstring, length64, newarray and multipleinheritance cases. If the heuristic detects that an interior pointer corresponds to such a case, the block will be considered as reachable by the interior pointer. In other words, the interior pointer will be treated as if it were a start pointer.

With that in mind, consider the nine possible cases described by the following figure.

```
    Pointer chain          AAA Leak Case  BBB Leak Case
    -------------          -------------  -------------
(1) RRR ------------> BBB                 DR
(2) RRR ---> AAA ---> BBB    DR           IR
(3) RRR          BBB              DL
(4) RRR      AAA ---> BBB    DL           IL
(5) RRR ------?-----> BBB              (y)DR, (n)DL
(6) RRR ---> AAA -?-> BBB    DR        (y)IR, (n)DL
(7) RRR -?-> AAA ---> BBB  (y)DR, (n)DL  (y)IR, (n)IL
(8) RRR -?-> AAA -?-> BBB  (y)DR, (n)DL  (y,y)IR, (n,y)IL, (_,n)DL
(9) RRR      AAA -?-> BBB    DL        (y)IL, (n)DL
```

```
Pointer chain legend:
- RRR: a root set node or DR block
- AAA, BBB: heap blocks
- --->: a start-pointer
- -?->: an interior-pointer
```

```
Leak Case legend:
- DR: Directly reachable
- IR: Indirectly reachable
- DL: Directly lost
- IL: Indirectly lost
- (y)XY: it's XY if the interior-pointer is a real pointer
- (n)XY: it's XY if the interior-pointer is not a real pointer
- (_)XY: it's XY in either case
```

Every possible case can be reduced to one of the above nine. Memcheck merges some of these cases in its output, resulting in the following four leak kinds.

- "Still reachable". This covers cases 1 and 2 (for the BBB blocks) above. A start-pointer or chain of start-pointers to the block is found. Since the block is still pointed at, the programmer could, at least in principle, have freed it before program exit. "Still reachable" blocks are very common and arguably not a problem. So, by default, Memcheck won't report such blocks individually.

- "Definitely lost". This covers case 3 (for the BBB blocks) above. This means that no pointer to the block can be found. The block is classified as "lost", because the programmer could not possibly have freed it at program exit, since no pointer to it exists. This is likely a symptom of having lost the pointer at some earlier point in the program. Such cases should be fixed by the programmer.

- "Indirectly lost". This covers cases 4 and 9 (for the BBB blocks) above. This means that the block is lost, not because there are no pointers to it, but rather because all the blocks that point to it are themselves lost. For example, if you have a binary tree and the root node is lost, all its children nodes will be indirectly lost. Because the problem will disappear if the definitely lost block that caused the indirect leak is fixed, Memcheck won't report such blocks individually by default.

- "Possibly lost". This covers cases 5--8 (for the BBB blocks) above. This means that a chain of one or more pointers to the block has been found, but at least one of the pointers is an interior-pointer. This could just be a random value in memory that happens to point into a block, and so you shouldn't consider this ok unless you know you have interior-pointers.

(Note: This mapping of the nine possible cases onto four leak kinds is not necessarily the best way that leaks could be reported; in particular, interior-pointers are treated inconsistently. It is possible the categorisation may be improved in the future.)

Furthermore, if suppressions exists for a block, it will be reported as "suppressed" no matter what which of the above four kinds it belongs to.

The following is an example leak summary.

```
LEAK SUMMARY:
   definitely lost: 48 bytes in 3 blocks.
   indirectly lost: 32 bytes in 2 blocks.
     possibly lost: 96 bytes in 6 blocks.
   still reachable: 64 bytes in 4 blocks.
        suppressed: 0 bytes in 0 blocks.
```

If heuristics have been used to consider some blocks as reachable, the leak summary details the heuristically reachable subset of 'still reachable:' per heuristic. In the below example, of the 95 bytes still reachable, 87 bytes (56+7+8+16) have been considered heuristically reachable.

```
LEAK SUMMARY:
   definitely lost: 4 bytes in 1 blocks
   indirectly lost: 0 bytes in 0 blocks
     possibly lost: 0 bytes in 0 blocks
   still reachable: 95 bytes in 6 blocks
                of which reachable via heuristic:
                   stdstring          : 56 bytes in 2 blocks
                   length64           : 16 bytes in 1 blocks
                   newarray           : 7 bytes in 1 blocks
                   multipleinheritance: 8 bytes in 1 blocks
        suppressed: 0 bytes in 0 blocks
```

If --leak-check=full is specified, Memcheck will give details for each definitely lost or possibly lost block, including where it was allocated. (Actually, it merges results for all blocks that have the same leak kind and sufficiently similar stack traces into a single "loss record". The --leak-resolution lets you control the meaning of "sufficiently similar".) It cannot tell you when or how or why the pointer to a leaked block was lost; you have to work that out for yourself. In general, you should attempt to ensure your programs do not have any definitely lost or possibly lost blocks at exit.

For example:

```
8 bytes in 1 blocks are definitely lost in loss record 1 of 14
  at 0x........: malloc (vg_replace_malloc.c:...)
  by 0x........: mk (leak-tree.c:11)
  by 0x........: main (leak-tree.c:39)

88 (8 direct, 80 indirect) bytes in 1 blocks are definitely lost in loss record 13 of 14

  at 0x........: malloc (vg_replace_malloc.c:...)
  by 0x........: mk (leak-tree.c:11)
  by 0x........: main (leak-tree.c:25)
```

The first message describes a simple case of a single 8 byte block that has been definitely lost. The second case mentions another 8 byte block that has been definitely lost; the difference is that a further 80 bytes in other blocks are indirectly lost because of this lost block. The loss records are not presented in any notable order, so the loss record numbers aren't particularly meaningful. The loss record numbers can be used in the Valgrind gdbserver to list the addresses of the leaked blocks and/or give more details about how a block is still reachable.

The option `--show-leak-kinds=<set>` controls the set of leak kinds to show when `--leak-check=full` is specified.

The `<set>` of leak kinds is specified in one of the following ways:

- a comma separated list of one or more of `definite indirect possible reachable`.

- `all` to specify the complete set (all leak kinds).

- `none` for the empty set.

The default value for the leak kinds to show is `--show-leak-kinds=definite,possible`.

To also show the reachable and indirectly lost blocks in addition to the definitely and possibly lost blocks, you can use `--show-leak-kinds=all`. To only show the reachable and indirectly lost blocks, use `--show-leak-kinds=indirect,reachable`. The reachable and indirectly lost blocks will then be presented as shown in the following two examples.

```
64 bytes in 4 blocks are still reachable in loss record 2 of 4
  at 0x........: malloc (vg_replace_malloc.c:177)
  by 0x........: mk (leak-cases.c:52)
  by 0x........: main (leak-cases.c:74)

32 bytes in 2 blocks are indirectly lost in loss record 1 of 4
  at 0x........: malloc (vg_replace_malloc.c:177)
  by 0x........: mk (leak-cases.c:52)
  by 0x........: main (leak-cases.c:80)
```

Because there are different kinds of leaks with different severities, an interesting question is: which leaks should be counted as true "errors" and which should not?

The answer to this question affects the numbers printed in the ERROR SUMMARY line, and also the effect of the --error-exitcode option. First, a leak is only counted as a true "error" if --leak-check=full is specified. Then, the option --errors-for-leak-kinds=<set> controls the set of leak kinds to consider as errors. The default value is --errors-for-leak-kinds=definite,possible

4.3. Memcheck Command-Line Options

--leak-check=<no|summary|yes|full> [default: summary]
When enabled, search for memory leaks when the client program finishes. If set to summary, it says how many leaks occurred. If set to full or yes, each individual leak will be shown in detail and/or counted as an error, as specified by the options --show-leak-kinds and --errors-for-leak-kinds.

--leak-resolution=<low|med|high> [default: high]
When doing leak checking, determines how willing Memcheck is to consider different backtraces to be the same for the purposes of merging multiple leaks into a single leak report. When set to low, only the first two entries need match. When med, four entries have to match. When high, all entries need to match.

For hardcore leak debugging, you probably want to use --leak-resolution=high together with --num-callers=40 or some such large number.

Note that the --leak-resolution setting does not affect Memcheck's ability to find leaks. It only changes how the results are presented.

--show-leak-kinds=<set> [default: definite,possible]
Specifies the leak kinds to show in a full leak search, in one of the following ways:

- a comma separated list of one or more of definite indirect possible reachable.

- all to specify the complete set (all leak kinds). It is equivalent to --show-leak-kinds=definite,indirect,pos

- none for the empty set.

--errors-for-leak-kinds=<set> [default: definite,possible]
Specifies the leak kinds to count as errors in a full leak search. The <set> is specified similarly to --show-leak-kinds

--leak-check-heuristics=<set> [default: all]
Specifies the set of leak check heuristics to be used during leak searches. The heuristics control which interior pointers to a block cause it to be considered as reachable. The heuristic set is specified in one of the following ways:

- a comma separated list of one or more of stdstring length64 newarray multipleinheritance.

- all to activate the complete set of heuristics. It is equivalent to --leak-check-heuristics=stdstring,length6

- none for the empty set.

--show-reachable=<yes|no> , --show-possibly-lost=<yes|no>
These options provide an alternative way to specify the leak kinds to show:

- --show-reachable=no --show-possibly-lost=yes is equivalent to --show-leak-kinds=definite,p

- --show-reachable=no --show-possibly-lost=no is equivalent to --show-leak-kinds=definite.

- --show-reachable=yes is equivalent to --show-leak-kinds=all.

`--undef-value-errors=<yes|no> [default: yes]`
Controls whether Memcheck reports uses of undefined value errors. Set this to `no` if you don't want to see undefined value errors. It also has the side effect of speeding up Memcheck somewhat.

`--track-origins=<yes|no> [default: no]`
Controls whether Memcheck tracks the origin of uninitialised values. By default, it does not, which means that although it can tell you that an uninitialised value is being used in a dangerous way, it cannot tell you where the uninitialised value came from. This often makes it difficult to track down the root problem.

When set to `yes`, Memcheck keeps track of the origins of all uninitialised values. Then, when an uninitialised value error is reported, Memcheck will try to show the origin of the value. An origin can be one of the following four places: a heap block, a stack allocation, a client request, or miscellaneous other sources (eg, a call to `brk`).

For uninitialised values originating from a heap block, Memcheck shows where the block was allocated. For uninitialised values originating from a stack allocation, Memcheck can tell you which function allocated the value, but no more than that -- typically it shows you the source location of the opening brace of the function. So you should carefully check that all of the function's local variables are initialised properly.

Performance overhead: origin tracking is expensive. It halves Memcheck's speed and increases memory use by a minimum of 100MB, and possibly more. Nevertheless it can drastically reduce the effort required to identify the root cause of uninitialised value errors, and so is often a programmer productivity win, despite running more slowly.

Accuracy: Memcheck tracks origins quite accurately. To avoid very large space and time overheads, some approximations are made. It is possible, although unlikely, that Memcheck will report an incorrect origin, or not be able to identify any origin.

Note that the combination `--track-origins=yes` and `--undef-value-errors=no` is nonsensical. Memcheck checks for and rejects this combination at startup.

`--partial-loads-ok=<yes|no> [default: yes]`
Controls how Memcheck handles 32-, 64-, 128- and 256-bit naturally aligned loads from addresses for which some bytes are addressable and others are not. When `yes`, such loads do not produce an address error. Instead, loaded bytes originating from illegal addresses are marked as uninitialised, and those corresponding to legal addresses are handled in the normal way.

When `no`, loads from partially invalid addresses are treated the same as loads from completely invalid addresses: an illegal-address error is issued, and the resulting bytes are marked as initialised.

Note that code that behaves in this way is in violation of the ISO C/C++ standards, and should be considered broken. If at all possible, such code should be fixed.

`--expensive-definedness-checks=<yes|no> [default: no]`
Controls whether Memcheck should employ more precise but also more expensive (time consuming) algorithms when checking the definedness of a value. The default setting is not to do that and it is usually sufficient. However, for highly optimised code valgrind may sometimes incorrectly complain. Invoking valgrind with `--expensive-definedness-checks=yes` helps but comes at a performance cost. Runtime degradation of 25% have been observed but the extra cost depends a lot on the application at hand.

`--keep-stacktraces=alloc|free|alloc-and-free|alloc-then-free|none [default: alloc-and-free]`
Controls which stack trace(s) to keep for malloc'd and/or free'd blocks.

With `alloc-then-free`, a stack trace is recorded at allocation time, and is associated with the block. When the block is freed, a second stack trace is recorded, and this replaces the allocation stack trace. As a result, any "use after free" errors relating to this block can only show a stack trace for where the block was freed.

With `alloc-and-free`, both allocation and the deallocation stack traces for the block are stored. Hence a "use after free" error will show both, which may make the error easier to diagnose. Compared to `alloc-then-free`, this setting slightly increases Valgrind's memory use as the block contains two references instead of one.

With `alloc`, only the allocation stack trace is recorded (and reported). With `free`, only the deallocation stack trace is recorded (and reported). These values somewhat decrease Valgrind's memory and cpu usage. They can be useful depending on the error types you are searching for and the level of detail you need to analyse them. For example, if you are only interested in memory leak errors, it is sufficient to record the allocation stack traces.

With `none`, no stack traces are recorded for malloc and free operations. If your program allocates a lot of blocks and/or allocates/frees from many different stack traces, this can significantly decrease cpu and/or memory required. Of course, few details will be reported for errors related to heap blocks.

Note that once a stack trace is recorded, Valgrind keeps the stack trace in memory even if it is not referenced by any block. Some programs (for example, recursive algorithms) can generate a huge number of stack traces. If Valgrind uses too much memory in such circumstances, you can reduce the memory required with the options `--keep-stacktraces` and/or by using a smaller value for the option `--num-callers`.

`--freelist-vol=<number> [default: 20000000]`
When the client program releases memory using `free` (in C) or `delete` (C++), that memory is not immediately made available for re-allocation. Instead, it is marked inaccessible and placed in a queue of freed blocks. The purpose is to defer as long as possible the point at which freed-up memory comes back into circulation. This increases the chance that Memcheck will be able to detect invalid accesses to blocks for some significant period of time after they have been freed.

This option specifies the maximum total size, in bytes, of the blocks in the queue. The default value is twenty million bytes. Increasing this increases the total amount of memory used by Memcheck but may detect invalid uses of freed blocks which would otherwise go undetected.

`--freelist-big-blocks=<number> [default: 1000000]`
When making blocks from the queue of freed blocks available for re-allocation, Memcheck will in priority re-circulate the blocks with a size greater or equal to `--freelist-big-blocks`. This ensures that freeing big blocks (in particular freeing blocks bigger than `--freelist-vol`) does not immediately lead to a re-circulation of all (or a lot of) the small blocks in the free list. In other words, this option increases the likelihood to discover dangling pointers for the "small" blocks, even when big blocks are freed.

Setting a value of 0 means that all the blocks are re-circulated in a FIFO order.

`--workaround-gcc296-bugs=<yes|no> [default: no]`
When enabled, assume that reads and writes some small distance below the stack pointer are due to bugs in GCC 2.96, and does not report them. The "small distance" is 256 bytes by default. Note that GCC 2.96 is the default compiler on some ancient Linux distributions (RedHat 7.X) and so you may need to use this option. Do not use it if you do not have to, as it can cause real errors to be overlooked. A better alternative is to use a more recent GCC in which this bug is fixed.

You may also need to use this option when working with GCC 3.X or 4.X on 32-bit PowerPC Linux. This is because GCC generates code which occasionally accesses below the stack pointer, particularly for floating-point to/from integer conversions. This is in violation of the 32-bit PowerPC ELF specification, which makes no provision for locations below the stack pointer to be accessible.

`--show-mismatched-frees=<yes|no> [default: yes]`
When enabled, Memcheck checks that heap blocks are deallocated using a function that matches the allocating function. That is, it expects `free` to be used to deallocate blocks allocated by `malloc`, `delete` for blocks allocated by `new`, and `delete[]` for blocks allocated by `new[]`. If a mismatch is detected, an error is reported. This is in general important because in some environments, freeing with a non-matching function can cause crashes.

There is however a scenario where such mismatches cannot be avoided. That is when the user provides implementations of `new/new[]` that call `malloc` and of `delete/delete[]` that call `free`, and these functions are asymmetrically inlined. For example, imagine that `delete[]` is inlined but `new[]` is not. The result is that Memcheck "sees" all `delete[]` calls as direct calls to `free`, even when the program source contains no mismatched calls.

This causes a lot of confusing and irrelevant error reports. `--show-mismatched-frees=no` disables these checks. It is not generally advisable to disable them, though, because you may miss real errors as a result.

`--ignore-ranges=0xPP-0xQQ[,0xRR-0xSS]`
Any ranges listed in this option (and multiple ranges can be specified, separated by commas) will be ignored by Memcheck's addressability checking.

`--malloc-fill=<hexnumber>`
Fills blocks allocated by `malloc`, `new`, etc, but not by `calloc`, with the specified byte. This can be useful when trying to shake out obscure memory corruption problems. The allocated area is still regarded by Memcheck as undefined -- this option only affects its contents. Note that `--malloc-fill` does not affect a block of memory when it is used as argument to client requests VALGRIND_MEMPOOL_ALLOC or VALGRIND_MALLOCLIKE_BLOCK.

`--free-fill=<hexnumber>`
Fills blocks freed by `free`, `delete`, etc, with the specified byte value. This can be useful when trying to shake out obscure memory corruption problems. The freed area is still regarded by Memcheck as not valid for access -- this option only affects its contents. Note that `--free-fill` does not affect a block of memory when it is used as argument to client requests VALGRIND_MEMPOOL_FREE or VALGRIND_FREELIKE_BLOCK.

4.4. Writing suppression files

The basic suppression format is described in Suppressing errors.

The suppression-type (second) line should have the form:

`Memcheck:suppression_type`

The Memcheck suppression types are as follows:

- `Value1`, `Value2`, `Value4`, `Value8`, `Value16`, meaning an uninitialised-value error when using a value of 1, 2, 4, 8 or 16 bytes.

- `Cond` (or its old name, `Value0`), meaning use of an uninitialised CPU condition code.

- `Addr1`, `Addr2`, `Addr4`, `Addr8`, `Addr16`, meaning an invalid address during a memory access of 1, 2, 4, 8 or 16 bytes respectively.

- `Jump`, meaning an jump to an unaddressable location error.

- `Param`, meaning an invalid system call parameter error.

- `Free`, meaning an invalid or mismatching free.

- `Overlap`, meaning a `src` / `dst` overlap in `memcpy` or a similar function.

- `Leak`, meaning a memory leak.

`Param` errors have a mandatory extra information line at this point, which is the name of the offending system call parameter.

`Leak` errors have an optional extra information line, with the following format:

```
match-leak-kinds:<set>
```

where `<set>` specifies which leak kinds are matched by this suppression entry. `<set>` is specified in the same way as with the option `--show-leak-kinds`, that is, one of the following:

- a comma separated list of one or more of `definite indirect possible reachable`.

- `all` to specify the complete set (all leak kinds).

- `none` for the empty set.

If this optional extra line is not present, the suppression entry will match all leak kinds.

Be aware that leak suppressions that are created using `--gen-suppressions` will contain this optional extra line, and therefore may match fewer leaks than you expect. You may want to remove the line before using the generated suppressions.

The other Memcheck error kinds do not have extra lines.

If you give the `-v` option, Valgrind will print the list of used suppressions at the end of execution. For a leak suppression, this output gives the number of different loss records that match the suppression, and the number of bytes and blocks suppressed by the suppression. If the run contains multiple leak checks, the number of bytes and blocks are reset to zero before each new leak check. Note that the number of different loss records is not reset to zero.

In the example below, in the last leak search, 7 blocks and 96 bytes have been suppressed by a suppression with the name `some_leak_suppression`:

```
--21041-- used_suppression:    10 some_other_leak_suppression s.supp:14 suppressed: 12

--21041-- used_suppression:    39 some_leak_suppression s.supp:2 suppressed: 96 bytes i
```

For `ValueN` and `AddrN` errors, the first line of the calling context is either the name of the function in which the error occurred, or, failing that, the full path of the `.so` file or executable containing the error location. For `Free` errors, the first line is the name of the function doing the freeing (eg, `free`, `__builtin_vec_delete`, etc). For `Overlap` errors, the first line is the name of the function with the overlapping arguments (eg. `memcpy`, `strcpy`, etc).

The last part of any suppression specifies the rest of the calling context that needs to be matched.

4.5. Details of Memcheck's checking machinery

Read this section if you want to know, in detail, exactly what and how Memcheck is checking.

4.5.1. Valid-value (V) bits

It is simplest to think of Memcheck implementing a synthetic CPU which is identical to a real CPU, except for one crucial detail. Every bit (literally) of data processed, stored and handled by the real CPU has, in the synthetic CPU, an associated "valid-value" bit, which says whether or not the accompanying bit has a legitimate value. In the discussions which follow, this bit is referred to as the V (valid-value) bit.

Each byte in the system therefore has a 8 V bits which follow it wherever it goes. For example, when the CPU loads a word-size item (4 bytes) from memory, it also loads the corresponding 32 V bits from a bitmap which stores the V bits for the process' entire address space. If the CPU should later write the whole or some part of that value to memory at a different address, the relevant V bits will be stored back in the V-bit bitmap.

In short, each bit in the system has (conceptually) an associated V bit, which follows it around everywhere, even inside the CPU. Yes, all the CPU's registers (integer, floating point, vector and condition registers) have their own V bit vectors. For this to work, Memcheck uses a great deal of compression to represent the V bits compactly.

Copying values around does not cause Memcheck to check for, or report on, errors. However, when a value is used in a way which might conceivably affect your program's externally-visible behaviour, the associated V bits are immediately checked. If any of these indicate that the value is undefined (even partially), an error is reported.

Here's an (admittedly nonsensical) example:

```
int i, j;
int a[10], b[10];
for ( i = 0; i < 10; i++ ) {
  j = a[i];
  b[i] = j;
}
```

Memcheck emits no complaints about this, since it merely copies uninitialised values from a[] into b[], and doesn't use them in a way which could affect the behaviour of the program. However, if the loop is changed to:

```
for ( i = 0; i < 10; i++ ) {
  j += a[i];
}
if ( j == 77 )
  printf("hello there\n");
```

then Memcheck will complain, at the if, that the condition depends on uninitialised values. Note that it **doesn't** complain at the j += a[i];, since at that point the undefinedness is not "observable". It's only when a decision has to be made as to whether or not to do the printf -- an observable action of your program -- that Memcheck complains.

Most low level operations, such as adds, cause Memcheck to use the V bits for the operands to calculate the V bits for the result. Even if the result is partially or wholly undefined, it does not complain.

Checks on definedness only occur in three places: when a value is used to generate a memory address, when control flow decision needs to be made, and when a system call is detected, Memcheck checks definedness of parameters as required.

If a check should detect undefinedness, an error message is issued. The resulting value is subsequently regarded as well-defined. To do otherwise would give long chains of error messages. In other words, once Memcheck reports an undefined value error, it tries to avoid reporting further errors derived from that same undefined value.

This sounds overcomplicated. Why not just check all reads from memory, and complain if an undefined value is loaded into a CPU register? Well, that doesn't work well, because perfectly legitimate C programs routinely copy uninitialised values around in memory, and we don't want endless complaints about that. Here's the canonical example. Consider a struct like this:

```
struct S { int x; char c; };
struct S s1, s2;
s1.x = 42;
s1.c = 'z';
s2 = s1;
```

The question to ask is: how large is `struct S`, in bytes? An `int` is 4 bytes and a `char` one byte, so perhaps a `struct S` occupies 5 bytes? Wrong. All non-toy compilers we know of will round the size of `struct S` up to a whole number of words, in this case 8 bytes. Not doing this forces compilers to generate truly appalling code for accessing arrays of `struct S`'s on some architectures.

So `s1` occupies 8 bytes, yet only 5 of them will be initialised. For the assignment `s2 = s1`, GCC generates code to copy all 8 bytes wholesale into `s2` without regard for their meaning. If Memcheck simply checked values as they came out of memory, it would yelp every time a structure assignment like this happened. So the more complicated behaviour described above is necessary. This allows GCC to copy `s1` into `s2` any way it likes, and a warning will only be emitted if the uninitialised values are later used.

4.5.2. Valid-address (A) bits

Notice that the previous subsection describes how the validity of values is established and maintained without having to say whether the program does or does not have the right to access any particular memory location. We now consider the latter question.

As described above, every bit in memory or in the CPU has an associated valid-value (V) bit. In addition, all bytes in memory, but not in the CPU, have an associated valid-address (A) bit. This indicates whether or not the program can legitimately read or write that location. It does not give any indication of the validity of the data at that location -- that's the job of the V bits -- only whether or not the location may be accessed.

Every time your program reads or writes memory, Memcheck checks the A bits associated with the address. If any of them indicate an invalid address, an error is emitted. Note that the reads and writes themselves do not change the A bits, only consult them.

So how do the A bits get set/cleared? Like this:

- When the program starts, all the global data areas are marked as accessible.

- When the program does `malloc/new`, the A bits for exactly the area allocated, and not a byte more, are marked as accessible. Upon freeing the area the A bits are changed to indicate inaccessibility.

- When the stack pointer register (SP) moves up or down, A bits are set. The rule is that the area from SP up to the base of the stack is marked as accessible, and below SP is inaccessible. (If that sounds illogical, bear in mind that the stack grows down, not up, on almost all Unix systems, including GNU/Linux.) Tracking SP like this has the useful side-effect that the section of stack used by a function for local variables etc is automatically marked accessible on function entry and inaccessible on exit.

- When doing system calls, A bits are changed appropriately. For example, mmap magically makes files appear in the process' address space, so the A bits must be updated if mmap succeeds.

- Optionally, your program can tell Memcheck about such changes explicitly, using the client request mechanism described above.

4.5.3. Putting it all together

Memcheck's checking machinery can be summarised as follows:

- Each byte in memory has 8 associated V (valid-value) bits, saying whether or not the byte has a defined value, and a single A (valid-address) bit, saying whether or not the program currently has the right to read/write that address. As mentioned above, heavy use of compression means the overhead is typically around 25%.

- When memory is read or written, the relevant A bits are consulted. If they indicate an invalid address, Memcheck emits an Invalid read or Invalid write error.

- When memory is read into the CPU's registers, the relevant V bits are fetched from memory and stored in the simulated CPU. They are not consulted.

- When a register is written out to memory, the V bits for that register are written back to memory too.

- When values in CPU registers are used to generate a memory address, or to determine the outcome of a conditional branch, the V bits for those values are checked, and an error emitted if any of them are undefined.

- When values in CPU registers are used for any other purpose, Memcheck computes the V bits for the result, but does not check them.

- Once the V bits for a value in the CPU have been checked, they are then set to indicate validity. This avoids long chains of errors.

- When values are loaded from memory, Memcheck checks the A bits for that location and issues an illegal-address warning if needed. In that case, the V bits loaded are forced to indicate Valid, despite the location being invalid.

  This apparently strange choice reduces the amount of confusing information presented to the user. It avoids the unpleasant phenomenon in which memory is read from a place which is both unaddressable and contains invalid values, and, as a result, you get not only an invalid-address (read/write) error, but also a potentially large set of uninitialised-value errors, one for every time the value is used.

  There is a hazy boundary case to do with multi-byte loads from addresses which are partially valid and partially invalid. See details of the option --partial-loads-ok for details.

Memcheck intercepts calls to malloc, calloc, realloc, valloc, memalign, free, new, new[], delete and delete[]. The behaviour you get is:

- malloc/new/new[]: the returned memory is marked as addressable but not having valid values. This means you have to write to it before you can read it.

- `calloc`: returned memory is marked both addressable and valid, since `calloc` clears the area to zero.

- `realloc`: if the new size is larger than the old, the new section is addressable but invalid, as with `malloc`. If the new size is smaller, the dropped-off section is marked as unaddressable. You may only pass to `realloc` a pointer previously issued to you by `malloc`/`calloc`/`realloc`.

- `free/delete/delete[]`: you may only pass to these functions a pointer previously issued to you by the corresponding allocation function. Otherwise, Memcheck complains. If the pointer is indeed valid, Memcheck marks the entire area it points at as unaddressable, and places the block in the freed-blocks-queue. The aim is to defer as long as possible reallocation of this block. Until that happens, all attempts to access it will elicit an invalid-address error, as you would hope.

4.6. Memcheck Monitor Commands

The Memcheck tool provides monitor commands handled by Valgrind's built-in gdbserver (see Monitor command handling by the Valgrind gdbserver).

- `xb <addr> [<len>]` shows the definedness (V) bits and values for <len> (default 1) bytes starting at <addr>. For each 8 bytes, two lines are output.

The first line shows the validity bits for 8 bytes. The definedness of each byte in the range is given using two hexadecimal digits. These hexadecimal digits encode the validity of each bit of the corresponding byte, using 0 if the bit is defined and 1 if the bit is undefined. If a byte is not addressable, its validity bits are replaced by __ (a double underscore).

The second line shows the values of the bytes below the corresponding validity bits. The format used to show the bytes data is similar to the GDB command 'x /<len>xb <addr>'. The value for a non addressable bytes is shown as ?? (two question marks).

In the following example, `string10` is an array of 10 characters, in which the even numbered bytes are undefined. In the below example, the byte corresponding to `string10[5]` is not addressable.

```
(gdb) p &string10
$4 = (char (*)[10]) 0x804a2f0
(gdb) mo xb 0x804a2f0 10
             ff      00      ff      00      ff      __      ff      00
0x804A2F0:    0x3f    0x6e    0x3f    0x65    0x3f    0x??    0x3f    0x65
             ff      00
0x804A2F8:    0x3f    0x00
Address 0x804A2F0 len 10 has 1 bytes unaddressable
(gdb)
```

The command xb cannot be used with registers. To get the validity bits of a register, you must start Valgrind with the option `--vgdb-shadow-registers=yes`. The validity bits of a register can then be obtained by printing the 'shadow 1' corresponding register. In the below x86 example, the register eax has all its bits undefined, while the register ebx is fully defined.

```
(gdb) p /x $eaxs1
$9 = 0xffffffff
(gdb) p /x $ebxs1
```

```
$10 = 0x0
(gdb)
```

- get_vbits <addr> [<len>] shows the definedness (V) bits for <len> (default 1) bytes starting at <addr> using the same convention as the xb command. get_vbits only shows the V bits (grouped by 4 bytes). It does not show the values. If you want to associate V bits with the corresponding byte values, the xb command will be easier to use, in particular on little endian computers when associating undefined parts of an integer with their V bits values.

The following example shows the result of get_vibts on the string10 used in the xb command explanation.

```
(gdb) monitor get_vbits 0x804a2f0 10
ff00ff00 ff__ff00 ff00
Address 0x804A2F0 len 10 has 1 bytes unaddressable
(gdb)
```

- make_memory [noaccess|undefined|defined|Definedifaddressable] <addr> [<len>] marks the range of <len> (default 1) bytes at <addr> as having the given status. Parameter noaccess marks the range as non-accessible, so Memcheck will report an error on any access to it. undefined or defined mark the area as accessible, but Memcheck regards the bytes in it respectively as having undefined or defined values. Definedifaddressable marks as defined, bytes in the range which are already addressible, but makes no change to the status of bytes in the range which are not addressible. Note that the first letter of Definedifaddressable is an uppercase D to avoid confusion with defined.

In the following example, the first byte of the string10 is marked as defined:

```
(gdb) monitor make_memory defined 0x8049e28  1
(gdb) monitor get_vbits 0x8049e28 10
0000ff00 ff00ff00 ff00
(gdb)
```

- check_memory [addressable|defined] <addr> [<len>] checks that the range of <len> (default 1) bytes at <addr> has the specified accessibility. It then outputs a description of <addr>. In the following example, a detailed description is available because the option --read-var-info=yes was given at Valgrind startup:

```
(gdb) monitor check_memory defined 0x8049e28  1
Address 0x8049E28 len 1 defined
==14698==  Location 0x8049e28 is 0 bytes inside string10[0],
==14698==  declared at prog.c:10, in frame #0 of thread 1
(gdb)
```

- `leak_check [full*|summary] [kinds <set>|reachable|possibleleak*|definiteleak]`
  `[heuristics heur1,heur2,...] [increased*|changed|any] [unlimited*|limited`
  `<max_loss_records_output>]` performs a leak check. The * in the arguments indicates the default
  values.

If the `[full*|summary]` argument is `summary`, only a summary of the leak search is given; otherwise a full
leak report is produced. A full leak report gives detailed information for each leak: the stack trace where the leaked
blocks were allocated, the number of blocks leaked and their total size. When a full report is requested, the next
two arguments further specify what kind of leaks to report. A leak's details are shown if they match both the second
and third argument. A full leak report might output detailed information for many leaks. The nr of leaks for which
information is output can be controlled using the `limited` argument followed by the maximum nr of leak records
to output. If this maximum is reached, the leak search outputs the records with the biggest number of bytes.

The `kinds` argument controls what kind of blocks are shown for a `full` leak search. The set of leak kinds to show
can be specified using a `<set>` similarly to the command line option `--show-leak-kinds`. Alternatively, the
value `definiteleak` is equivalent to `kinds definite`, the value `possibleleak` is equivalent to `kinds`
`definite,possible` : it will also show possibly leaked blocks, .i.e those for which only an interior pointer was
found. The value `reachable` will show all block categories (i.e. is equivalent to `kinds all`).

The `heuristics` argument controls the heuristics used during the leak search. The set of heuristics to use can
be specified using a `<set>` similarly to the command line option `--leak-check-heuristics`. The default
value for the `heuristics` argument is `heuristics none`.

The `[increased*|changed|any]` argument controls what kinds of changes are shown for a `full` leak
search. The value `increased` specifies that only block allocation stacks with an increased number of leaked
bytes or blocks since the previous leak check should be shown. The value `changed` specifies that allocation
stacks with any change since the previous leak check should be shown. The value `any` specifies that all leak entries
should be shown, regardless of any increase or decrease. When If `increased` or `changed` are specified, the
leak report entries will show the delta relative to the previous leak report.

The following example shows usage of the `leak_check` monitor command on the `memcheck/tests/leak-cases.c`
regression test. The first command outputs one entry having an increase in the leaked bytes. The second command
is the same as the first command, but uses the abbreviated forms accepted by GDB and the Valgrind gdbserver. It
only outputs the summary information, as there was no increase since the previous leak search.

```
(gdb) monitor leak_check full possibleleak increased
==19520== 16 (+16) bytes in 1 (+1) blocks are possibly lost in loss record 9 of 12

==19520==    at 0x40070B4: malloc (vg_replace_malloc.c:263)
==19520==    by 0x80484D5: mk (leak-cases.c:52)
==19520==    by 0x804855F: f (leak-cases.c:81)
==19520==    by 0x80488E0: main (leak-cases.c:107)
==19520==
==19520== LEAK SUMMARY:
==19520==    definitely lost: 32 (+0) bytes in 2 (+0) blocks
==19520==    indirectly lost: 16 (+0) bytes in 1 (+0) blocks
==19520==      possibly lost: 32 (+16) bytes in 2 (+1) blocks
==19520==    still reachable: 96 (+16) bytes in 6 (+1) blocks
==19520==         suppressed: 0 (+0) bytes in 0 (+0) blocks
==19520== Reachable blocks (those to which a pointer was found) are not shown.
==19520== To see them, add 'reachable any' args to leak_check
==19520==
(gdb) mo l
==19520== LEAK SUMMARY:
```

```
==19520==    definitely lost: 32 (+0) bytes in 2 (+0) blocks
==19520==    indirectly lost: 16 (+0) bytes in 1 (+0) blocks
==19520==     possibly lost: 32 (+0) bytes in 2 (+0) blocks
==19520==    still reachable: 96 (+0) bytes in 6 (+0) blocks
==19520==          suppressed: 0 (+0) bytes in 0 (+0) blocks
==19520== Reachable blocks (those to which a pointer was found) are not shown.
==19520== To see them, add 'reachable any' args to leak_check
==19520==
(gdb)
```

Note that when using Valgrind's gdbserver, it is not necessary to rerun with `--leak-check=full --show-reachable=yes` to see the reachable blocks. You can obtain the same information without rerunning by using the GDB command `monitor leak_check full reachable any` (or, using abbreviation: `mo l f r a`).

- `block_list <loss_record_nr>|<loss_record_nr_from>..<loss_record_nr_to>`
  `[unlimited*|limited <max_blocks>] [heuristics heur1,heur2,...]`   shows the list of blocks belonging to `<loss_record_nr>` (or to the loss records range `<loss_record_nr_from>..<loss_recorc`
  The nr of blocks to print can be controlled using the `limited` argument followed by the maximum nr of blocks to output. If one or more heuristics are given, only prints the loss records and blocks found via one of the given `heur1,heur2,...` heuristics.

A leak search merges the allocated blocks in loss records : a loss record re-groups all blocks having the same state (for example, Definitely Lost) and the same allocation backtrace. Each loss record is identified in the leak search result by a loss record number. The `block_list` command shows the loss record information followed by the addresses and sizes of the blocks which have been merged in the loss record. If a block was found using an heuristic, the block size is followed by the heuristic.

If a directly lost block causes some other blocks to be indirectly lost, the block_list command will also show these indirectly lost blocks. The indirectly lost blocks will be indented according to the level of indirection between the directly lost block and the indirectly lost block(s). Each indirectly lost block is followed by the reference of its loss record.

The block_list command can be used on the results of a leak search as long as no block has been freed after this leak search: as soon as the program frees a block, a new leak search is needed before block_list can be used again.

In the below example, the program leaks a tree structure by losing the pointer to the block A (top of the tree). So, the block A is directly lost, causing an indirect loss of blocks B to G. The first block_list command shows the loss record of A (a definitely lost block with address 0x4028028, size 16). The addresses and sizes of the indirectly lost blocks due to block A are shown below the block A. The second command shows the details of one of the indirect loss records output by the first command.

```
          A
         / \
        B   C
       / \ / \
      D  E F  G
```

```
(gdb) bt
#0  main () at leak-tree.c:69
(gdb) monitor leak_check full any
```

```
==19552== 112 (16 direct, 96 indirect) bytes in 1 blocks are definitely lost in loss re

==19552==    at 0x40070B4: malloc (vg_replace_malloc.c:263)
==19552==    by 0x80484D5: mk (leak-tree.c:28)
==19552==    by 0x80484FC: f (leak-tree.c:41)
==19552==    by 0x8048856: main (leak-tree.c:63)
==19552==
==19552== LEAK SUMMARY:
==19552==    definitely lost: 16 bytes in 1 blocks
==19552==    indirectly lost: 96 bytes in 6 blocks
==19552==      possibly lost: 0 bytes in 0 blocks
==19552==    still reachable: 0 bytes in 0 blocks
==19552==         suppressed: 0 bytes in 0 blocks
==19552==
(gdb) monitor block_list 7
==19552== 112 (16 direct, 96 indirect) bytes in 1 blocks are definitely lost in loss re

==19552==    at 0x40070B4: malloc (vg_replace_malloc.c:263)
==19552==    by 0x80484D5: mk (leak-tree.c:28)
==19552==    by 0x80484FC: f (leak-tree.c:41)
==19552==    by 0x8048856: main (leak-tree.c:63)
==19552== 0x4028028[16]
==19552==   0x4028068[16] indirect loss record 1
==19552==      0x40280E8[16] indirect loss record 3
==19552==      0x4028128[16] indirect loss record 4
==19552==   0x40280A8[16] indirect loss record 2
==19552==      0x4028168[16] indirect loss record 5
==19552==      0x40281A8[16] indirect loss record 6
(gdb) mo b 2
==19552== 16 bytes in 1 blocks are indirectly lost in loss record 2 of 7
==19552==    at 0x40070B4: malloc (vg_replace_malloc.c:263)
==19552==    by 0x80484D5: mk (leak-tree.c:28)
==19552==    by 0x8048519: f (leak-tree.c:43)
==19552==    by 0x8048856: main (leak-tree.c:63)
==19552== 0x40280A8[16]
==19552==   0x4028168[16] indirect loss record 5
==19552==   0x40281A8[16] indirect loss record 6
(gdb)
```

- who_points_at <addr> [<len>] shows all the locations where a pointer to addr is found. If len is equal to 1, the command only shows the locations pointing exactly at addr (i.e. the "start pointers" to addr). If len is > 1, "interior pointers" pointing at the len first bytes will also be shown.

The locations searched for are the same as the locations used in the leak search. So, who_points_at can a.o. be used to show why the leak search still can reach a block, or can search for dangling pointers to a freed block. Each location pointing at addr (or pointing inside addr if interior pointers are being searched for) will be described.

In the below example, the pointers to the 'tree block A' (see example in command block_list) is shown before the tree was leaked. The descriptions are detailed as the option --read-var-info=yes was given at Valgrind startup. The second call shows the pointers (start and interior pointers) to block G. The block G (0x40281A8) is reachable via block C (0x40280a8) and register ECX of tid 1 (tid is the Valgrind thread id). It is "interior reachable" via the register EBX.

```
(gdb) monitor who_points_at 0x4028028
==20852== Searching for pointers to 0x4028028
==20852== *0x8049e20 points at 0x4028028
==20852==  Location 0x8049e20 is 0 bytes inside global var "t"
==20852==  declared at leak-tree.c:35
(gdb) monitor who_points_at 0x40281A8 16
==20852== Searching for pointers pointing in 16 bytes from 0x40281a8
==20852== *0x40280ac points at 0x40281a8
==20852==  Address 0x40280ac is 4 bytes inside a block of size 16 alloc'd
==20852==    at 0x40070B4: malloc (vg_replace_malloc.c:263)
==20852==    by 0x80484D5: mk (leak-tree.c:28)
==20852==    by 0x8048519: f (leak-tree.c:43)
==20852==    by 0x8048856: main (leak-tree.c:63)
==20852== tid 1 register ECX points at 0x40281a8
==20852== tid 1 register EBX interior points at 2 bytes inside 0x40281a8
(gdb)
```

When who_points_at finds an interior pointer, it will report the heuristic(s) with which this interior pointer will be considered as reachable. Note that this is done independently of the value of the option --leak-check-heuristics. In the below example, the loss record 6 indicates a possibly lost block. who_points_at reports that there is an interior pointer pointing in this block, and that the block can be considered reachable using the heuristic multipleinheritance.

```
(gdb) monitor block_list 6
==3748== 8 bytes in 1 blocks are possibly lost in loss record 6 of 7
==3748==    at 0x4007D77: operator new(unsigned int) (vg_replace_malloc.c:313)
==3748==    by 0x8048954: main (leak_cpp_interior.cpp:43)
==3748== 0x402A0E0[8]
(gdb) monitor who_points_at 0x402A0E0 8
==3748== Searching for pointers pointing in 8 bytes from 0x402a0e0
==3748== *0xbe8ee078 interior points at 4 bytes inside 0x402a0e0
==3748==  Address 0xbe8ee078 is on thread 1's stack
==3748== block at 0x402a0e0 considered reachable by ptr 0x402a0e4 using multipleinher:

(gdb)
```

4.7. Client Requests

The following client requests are defined in memcheck.h. See memcheck.h for exact details of their arguments.

- VALGRIND_MAKE_MEM_NOACCESS, VALGRIND_MAKE_MEM_UNDEFINED and VALGRIND_MAKE_MEM_DEFINED. These mark address ranges as completely inaccessible, accessible but containing undefined data, and accessible and containing defined data, respectively. They return -1, when run on Valgrind and 0 otherwise.

- VALGRIND_MAKE_MEM_DEFINED_IF_ADDRESSABLE. This is just like VALGRIND_MAKE_MEM_DEFINED but only affects those bytes that are already addressable.

- `VALGRIND_CHECK_MEM_IS_ADDRESSABLE` and `VALGRIND_CHECK_MEM_IS_DEFINED`: check immediately whether or not the given address range has the relevant property, and if not, print an error message. Also, for the convenience of the client, returns zero if the relevant property holds; otherwise, the returned value is the address of the first byte for which the property is not true. Always returns 0 when not run on Valgrind.

- `VALGRIND_CHECK_VALUE_IS_DEFINED`: a quick and easy way to find out whether Valgrind thinks a particular value (lvalue, to be precise) is addressable and defined. Prints an error message if not. It has no return value.

- `VALGRIND_DO_LEAK_CHECK`: does a full memory leak check (like `--leak-check=full`) right now. This is useful for incrementally checking for leaks between arbitrary places in the program's execution. It has no return value.

- `VALGRIND_DO_ADDED_LEAK_CHECK`: same as `VALGRIND_DO_LEAK_CHECK` but only shows the entries for which there was an increase in leaked bytes or leaked number of blocks since the previous leak search. It has no return value.

- `VALGRIND_DO_CHANGED_LEAK_CHECK`: same as `VALGRIND_DO_LEAK_CHECK` but only shows the entries for which there was an increase or decrease in leaked bytes or leaked number of blocks since the previous leak search. It has no return value.

- `VALGRIND_DO_QUICK_LEAK_CHECK`: like `VALGRIND_DO_LEAK_CHECK`, except it produces only a leak summary (like `--leak-check=summary`). It has no return value.

- `VALGRIND_COUNT_LEAKS`: fills in the four arguments with the number of bytes of memory found by the previous leak check to be leaked (i.e. the sum of direct leaks and indirect leaks), dubious, reachable and suppressed. This is useful in test harness code, after calling `VALGRIND_DO_LEAK_CHECK` or `VALGRIND_DO_QUICK_LEAK_CHECK`.

- `VALGRIND_COUNT_LEAK_BLOCKS`: identical to `VALGRIND_COUNT_LEAKS` except that it returns the number of blocks rather than the number of bytes in each category.

- `VALGRIND_GET_VBITS` and `VALGRIND_SET_VBITS`: allow you to get and set the V (validity) bits for an address range. You should probably only set V bits that you have got with `VALGRIND_GET_VBITS`. Only for those who really know what they are doing.

- `VALGRIND_CREATE_BLOCK` and `VALGRIND_DISCARD`. `VALGRIND_CREATE_BLOCK` takes an address, a number of bytes and a character string. The specified address range is then associated with that string. When Memcheck reports an invalid access to an address in the range, it will describe it in terms of this block rather than in terms of any other block it knows about. Note that the use of this macro does not actually change the state of memory in any way -- it merely gives a name for the range.

At some point you may want Memcheck to stop reporting errors in terms of the block named by `VALGRIND_CREATE_BLOCK`. To make this possible, `VALGRIND_CREATE_BLOCK` returns a "block handle", which is a C `int` value. You can pass this block handle to `VALGRIND_DISCARD`. After doing so, Valgrind will no longer relate addressing errors in the specified range to the block. Passing invalid handles to `VALGRIND_DISCARD` is harmless.

4.8. Memory Pools: describing and working with custom allocators

Some programs use custom memory allocators, often for performance reasons. Left to itself, Memcheck is unable to understand the behaviour of custom allocation schemes as well as it understands the standard allocators, and so may miss errors and leaks in your program. What this section describes is a way to give Memcheck enough of a description of your custom allocator that it can make at least some sense of what is happening.

There are many different sorts of custom allocator, so Memcheck attempts to reason about them using a loose, abstract model. We use the following terminology when describing custom allocation systems:

• Custom allocation involves a set of independent "memory pools".

• Memcheck's notion of a a memory pool consists of a single "anchor address" and a set of non-overlapping "chunks" associated with the anchor address.

• Typically a pool's anchor address is the address of a book-keeping "header" structure.

• Typically the pool's chunks are drawn from a contiguous "superblock" acquired through the system `malloc` or `mmap`.

Keep in mind that the last two points above say "typically": the Valgrind mempool client request API is intentionally vague about the exact structure of a mempool. There is no specific mention made of headers or superblocks. Nevertheless, the following picture may help elucidate the intention of the terms in the API:

```
"pool"
(anchor address)
|
v
+--------+---+
| header | o |
+--------+-|-+
         |
         v            superblock
       +------+---+-------------+---+-----------------+
       |      |rzB|  allocation |rzB|                 |
       +------+---+-------------+---+-----------------+
              ^                 ^
              |                 |
           "addr"      "addr"+"size"
```

Note that the header and the superblock may be contiguous or discontiguous, and there may be multiple superblocks associated with a single header; such variations are opaque to Memcheck. The API only requires that your allocation scheme can present sensible values of "pool", "addr" and "size".

Typically, before making client requests related to mempools, a client program will have allocated such a header and superblock for their mempool, and marked the superblock NOACCESS using the `VALGRIND_MAKE_MEM_NOACCESS` client request.

When dealing with mempools, the goal is to maintain a particular invariant condition: that Memcheck believes the unallocated portions of the pool's superblock (including redzones) are NOACCESS. To maintain this invariant, the client program must ensure that the superblock starts out in that state; Memcheck cannot make it so, since Memcheck never explicitly learns about the superblock of a pool, only the allocated chunks within the pool.

Once the header and superblock for a pool are established and properly marked, there are a number of client requests programs can use to inform Memcheck about changes to the state of a mempool:

- `VALGRIND_CREATE_MEMPOOL(pool, rzB, is_zeroed)`: This request registers the address `pool` as the anchor address for a memory pool. It also provides a size `rzB`, specifying how large the redzones placed around chunks allocated from the pool should be. Finally, it provides an `is_zeroed` argument that specifies whether the pool's chunks are zeroed (more precisely: defined) when allocated.

    Upon completion of this request, no chunks are associated with the pool. The request simply tells Memcheck that the pool exists, so that subsequent calls can refer to it as a pool.

- `VALGRIND_DESTROY_MEMPOOL(pool)`: This request tells Memcheck that a pool is being torn down. Memcheck then removes all records of chunks associated with the pool, as well as its record of the pool's existence. While destroying its records of a mempool, Memcheck resets the redzones of any live chunks in the pool to NOACCESS.

- `VALGRIND_MEMPOOL_ALLOC(pool, addr, size)`: This request informs Memcheck that a `size`-byte chunk has been allocated at `addr`, and associates the chunk with the specified `pool`. If the pool was created with nonzero `rzB` redzones, Memcheck will mark the `rzB` bytes before and after the chunk as NOACCESS. If the pool was created with the `is_zeroed` argument set, Memcheck will mark the chunk as DEFINED, otherwise Memcheck will mark the chunk as UNDEFINED.

- `VALGRIND_MEMPOOL_FREE(pool, addr)`: This request informs Memcheck that the chunk at `addr` should no longer be considered allocated. Memcheck will mark the chunk associated with `addr` as NOACCESS, and delete its record of the chunk's existence.

- `VALGRIND_MEMPOOL_TRIM(pool, addr, size)`: This request trims the chunks associated with `pool`. The request only operates on chunks associated with `pool`. Trimming is formally defined as:

    - All chunks entirely inside the range `addr..(addr+size-1)` are preserved.

    - All chunks entirely outside the range `addr..(addr+size-1)` are discarded, as though `VALGRIND_MEMPOOL_FREE` was called on them.

    - All other chunks must intersect with the range `addr..(addr+size-1)`; areas outside the intersection are marked as NOACCESS, as though they had been independently freed with `VALGRIND_MEMPOOL_FREE`.

    This is a somewhat rare request, but can be useful in implementing the type of mass-free operations common in custom LIFO allocators.

- `VALGRIND_MOVE_MEMPOOL(poolA, poolB)`: This request informs Memcheck that the pool previously anchored at address `poolA` has moved to anchor address `poolB`. This is a rare request, typically only needed if you `realloc` the header of a mempool.

    No memory-status bits are altered by this request.

- `VALGRIND_MEMPOOL_CHANGE(pool, addrA, addrB, size)`: This request informs Memcheck that the chunk previously allocated at address `addrA` within `pool` has been moved and/or resized, and should be changed to cover the region `addrB..(addrB+size-1)`. This is a rare request, typically only needed if you `realloc` a superblock or wish to extend a chunk without changing its memory-status bits.

    No memory-status bits are altered by this request.

• VALGRIND_MEMPOOL_EXISTS(pool): This request informs the caller whether or not Memcheck is currently tracking a mempool at anchor address pool. It evaluates to 1 when there is a mempool associated with that address, 0 otherwise. This is a rare request, only useful in circumstances when client code might have lost track of the set of active mempools.

4.9. Debugging MPI Parallel Programs with Valgrind

Memcheck supports debugging of distributed-memory applications which use the MPI message passing standard. This support consists of a library of wrapper functions for the PMPI_* interface. When incorporated into the application's address space, either by direct linking or by LD_PRELOAD, the wrappers intercept calls to PMPI_Send, PMPI_Recv, etc. They then use client requests to inform Memcheck of memory state changes caused by the function being wrapped. This reduces the number of false positives that Memcheck otherwise typically reports for MPI applications.

The wrappers also take the opportunity to carefully check size and definedness of buffers passed as arguments to MPI functions, hence detecting errors such as passing undefined data to PMPI_Send, or receiving data into a buffer which is too small.

Unlike most of the rest of Valgrind, the wrapper library is subject to a BSD-style license, so you can link it into any code base you like. See the top of mpi/libmpiwrap.c for license details.

4.9.1. Building and installing the wrappers

The wrapper library will be built automatically if possible. Valgrind's configure script will look for a suitable mpicc to build it with. This must be the same mpicc you use to build the MPI application you want to debug. By default, Valgrind tries mpicc, but you can specify a different one by using the configure-time option --with-mpicc. Currently the wrappers are only buildable with mpiccs which are based on GNU GCC or Intel's C++ Compiler.

Check that the configure script prints a line like this:

```
checking for usable MPI2-compliant mpicc and mpi.h... yes, mpicc
```

If it says . . . no, your mpicc has failed to compile and link a test MPI2 program.

If the configure test succeeds, continue in the usual way with make and make install. The final install tree should then contain libmpiwrap-<platform>.so.

Compile up a test MPI program (eg, MPI hello-world) and try this:

```
LD_PRELOAD=$prefix/lib/valgrind/libmpiwrap-<platform>.so  \
      mpirun [args] $prefix/bin/valgrind ./hello
```

You should see something similar to the following

```
valgrind MPI wrappers 31901: Active for pid 31901
valgrind MPI wrappers 31901: Try MPIWRAP_DEBUG=help for possible options
```

repeated for every process in the group. If you do not see these, there is an build/installation problem of some kind.

The MPI functions to be wrapped are assumed to be in an ELF shared object with soname matching libmpi.so*. This is known to be correct at least for Open MPI and Quadrics MPI, and can easily be changed if required.

4.9.2. Getting started

Compile your MPI application as usual, taking care to link it using the same mpicc that your Valgrind build was configured with.

Use the following basic scheme to run your application on Valgrind with the wrappers engaged:

```
MPIWRAP_DEBUG=[wrapper-args]                              \
  LD_PRELOAD=$prefix/lib/valgrind/libmpiwrap-<platform>.so  \
  mpirun [mpirun-args]                                   \
  $prefix/bin/valgrind [valgrind-args]                     \
  [application] [app-args]
```

As an alternative to LD_PRELOADing libmpiwrap-<platform>.so, you can simply link it to your application if desired. This should not disturb native behaviour of your application in any way.

4.9.3. Controlling the wrapper library

Environment variable MPIWRAP_DEBUG is consulted at startup. The default behaviour is to print a starting banner

```
valgrind MPI wrappers 16386: Active for pid 16386
valgrind MPI wrappers 16386: Try MPIWRAP_DEBUG=help for possible options
```

and then be relatively quiet.

You can give a list of comma-separated options in MPIWRAP_DEBUG. These are

- verbose: show entries/exits of all wrappers. Also show extra debugging info, such as the status of outstanding MPI_Requests resulting from uncompleted MPI_Irecvs.

- quiet: opposite of verbose, only print anything when the wrappers want to report a detected programming error, or in case of catastrophic failure of the wrappers.

- warn: by default, functions which lack proper wrappers are not commented on, just silently ignored. This causes a warning to be printed for each unwrapped function used, up to a maximum of three warnings per function.

- strict: print an error message and abort the program if a function lacking a wrapper is used.

If you want to use Valgrind's XML output facility (`--xml=yes`), you should pass `quiet` in `MPIWRAP_DEBUG` so as to get rid of any extraneous printing from the wrappers.

4.9.4. Functions

All MPI2 functions except `MPI_Wtick`, `MPI_Wtime` and `MPI_Pcontrol` have wrappers. The first two are not wrapped because they return a `double`, which Valgrind's function-wrap mechanism cannot handle (but it could easily be extended to do so). `MPI_Pcontrol` cannot be wrapped as it has variable arity: `int MPI_Pcontrol(const int level, ...)`

Most functions are wrapped with a default wrapper which does nothing except complain or abort if it is called, depending on settings in `MPIWRAP_DEBUG` listed above. The following functions have "real", do-something-useful wrappers:

```
PMPI_Send PMPI_Bsend PMPI_Ssend PMPI_Rsend

PMPI_Recv PMPI_Get_count

PMPI_Isend PMPI_Ibsend PMPI_Issend PMPI_Irsend

PMPI_Irecv
PMPI_Wait PMPI_Waitall
PMPI_Test PMPI_Testall

PMPI_Iprobe PMPI_Probe

PMPI_Cancel

PMPI_Sendrecv

PMPI_Type_commit PMPI_Type_free

PMPI_Pack PMPI_Unpack

PMPI_Bcast PMPI_Gather PMPI_Scatter PMPI_Alltoall
PMPI_Reduce PMPI_Allreduce PMPI_Op_create

PMPI_Comm_create PMPI_Comm_dup PMPI_Comm_free PMPI_Comm_rank PMPI_Comm_size

PMPI_Error_string
PMPI_Init PMPI_Initialized PMPI_Finalize
```

A few functions such as `PMPI_Address` are listed as `HAS_NO_WRAPPER`. They have no wrapper at all as there is nothing worth checking, and giving a no-op wrapper would reduce performance for no reason.

Note that the wrapper library itself can itself generate large numbers of calls to the MPI implementation, especially when walking complex types. The most common functions called are `PMPI_Extent`, `PMPI_Type_get_envelope`, `PMPI_Type_get_contents`, and `PMPI_Type_free`.

4.9.5. Types

MPI-1.1 structured types are supported, and walked exactly. The currently supported combiners are `MPI_COMBINER_NAMED`, `MPI_COMBINER_CONTIGUOUS`, `MPI_COMBINER_VECTOR`, `MPI_COMBINER_HVECTOR` `MPI_COMBINER_INDEXED`, `MPI_COMBINER_HINDEXED` and `MPI_COMBINER_STRUCT` This should cover all MPI-1.1 types. The mechanism (function `walk_type`) should extend easily to cover MPI2 combiners.

MPI defines some named structured types (`MPI_FLOAT_INT`, `MPI_DOUBLE_INT`, `MPI_LONG_INT`, `MPI_2INT`, `MPI_SHORT_INT`, `MPI_LONG_DOUBLE_INT`) which are pairs of some basic type and a C `int`. Unfortunately the MPI specification makes it impossible to look inside these types and see where the fields are. Therefore these wrappers assume the types are laid out as `struct { float val; int loc; }` (for `MPI_FLOAT_INT`), etc, and act accordingly. This appears to be correct at least for Open MPI 1.0.2 and for Quadrics MPI.

If `strict` is an option specified in `MPIWRAP_DEBUG`, the application will abort if an unhandled type is encountered. Otherwise, the application will print a warning message and continue.

Some effort is made to mark/check memory ranges corresponding to arrays of values in a single pass. This is important for performance since asking Valgrind to mark/check any range, no matter how small, carries quite a large constant cost. This optimisation is applied to arrays of primitive types (`double`, `float`, `int`, `long`, `long long`, `short`, `char`, and `long double` on platforms where `sizeof(long double) == 8`). For arrays of all other types, the wrappers handle each element individually and so there can be a very large performance cost.

4.9.6. Writing new wrappers

For the most part the wrappers are straightforward. The only significant complexity arises with nonblocking receives.

The issue is that `MPI_Irecv` states the recv buffer and returns immediately, giving a handle (`MPI_Request`) for the transaction. Later the user will have to poll for completion with `MPI_Wait` etc, and when the transaction completes successfully, the wrappers have to paint the recv buffer. But the recv buffer details are not presented to `MPI_Wait` -- only the handle is. The library therefore maintains a shadow table which associates uncompleted `MPI_Requests` with the corresponding buffer address/count/type. When an operation completes, the table is searched for the associated address/count/type info, and memory is marked accordingly.

Access to the table is guarded by a (POSIX pthreads) lock, so as to make the library thread-safe.

The table is allocated with `malloc` and never `freed`, so it will show up in leak checks.

Writing new wrappers should be fairly easy. The source file is `mpi/libmpiwrap.c`. If possible, find an existing wrapper for a function of similar behaviour to the one you want to wrap, and use it as a starting point. The wrappers are organised in sections in the same order as the MPI 1.1 spec, to aid navigation. When adding a wrapper, remember to comment out the definition of the default wrapper in the long list of defaults at the bottom of the file (do not remove it, just comment it out).

4.9.7. What to expect when using the wrappers

The wrappers should reduce Memcheck's false-error rate on MPI applications. Because the wrapping is done at the MPI interface, there will still potentially be a large number of errors reported in the MPI implementation below the interface. The best you can do is try to suppress them.

You may also find that the input-side (buffer length/definedness) checks find errors in your MPI use, for example passing too short a buffer to `MPI_Recv`.

Functions which are not wrapped may increase the false error rate. A possible approach is to run with `MPI_DEBUG` containing `warn`. This will show you functions which lack proper wrappers but which are nevertheless used. You can then write wrappers for them.

A known source of potential false errors are the `PMPI_Reduce` family of functions, when using a custom (user-defined) reduction function. In a reduction operation, each node notionally sends data to a "central point" which uses the specified reduction function to merge the data items into a single item. Hence, in general, data is passed between nodes and fed to the reduction function, but the wrapper library cannot mark the transferred data as initialised before it is handed to the reduction function, because all that happens "inside" the `PMPI_Reduce` call. As a result you may see false positives reported in your reduction function.

5. Cachegrind: a cache and branch-prediction profiler

To use this tool, you must specify `--tool=cachegrind` on the Valgrind command line.

5.1. Overview

Cachegrind simulates how your program interacts with a machine's cache hierarchy and (optionally) branch predictor. It simulates a machine with independent first-level instruction and data caches (I1 and D1), backed by a unified second-level cache (L2). This exactly matches the configuration of many modern machines.

However, some modern machines have three or four levels of cache. For these machines (in the cases where Cachegrind can auto-detect the cache configuration) Cachegrind simulates the first-level and last-level caches. The reason for this choice is that the last-level cache has the most influence on runtime, as it masks accesses to main memory. Furthermore, the L1 caches often have low associativity, so simulating them can detect cases where the code interacts badly with this cache (eg. traversing a matrix column-wise with the row length being a power of 2).

Therefore, Cachegrind always refers to the I1, D1 and LL (last-level) caches.

Cachegrind gathers the following statistics (abbreviations used for each statistic is given in parentheses):

- I cache reads (`Ir`, which equals the number of instructions executed), I1 cache read misses (`I1mr`) and LL cache instruction read misses (`ILmr`).

- D cache reads (`Dr`, which equals the number of memory reads), D1 cache read misses (`D1mr`), and LL cache data read misses (`DLmr`).

- D cache writes (`Dw`, which equals the number of memory writes), D1 cache write misses (`D1mw`), and LL cache data write misses (`DLmw`).

- Conditional branches executed (`Bc`) and conditional branches mispredicted (`Bcm`).

- Indirect branches executed (`Bi`) and indirect branches mispredicted (`Bim`).

Note that D1 total accesses is given by `D1mr + D1mw`, and that LL total accesses is given by `ILmr + DLmr + DLmw`.

These statistics are presented for the entire program and for each function in the program. You can also annotate each line of source code in the program with the counts that were caused directly by it.

On a modern machine, an L1 miss will typically cost around 10 cycles, an LL miss can cost as much as 200 cycles, and a mispredicted branch costs in the region of 10 to 30 cycles. Detailed cache and branch profiling can be very useful for understanding how your program interacts with the machine and thus how to make it faster.

Also, since one instruction cache read is performed per instruction executed, you can find out how many instructions are executed per line, which can be useful for traditional profiling.

5.2. Using Cachegrind, cg_annotate and cg_merge

First off, as for normal Valgrind use, you probably want to compile with debugging info (the -g option). But by contrast with normal Valgrind use, you probably do want to turn optimisation on, since you should profile your program as it will be normally run.

Then, you need to run Cachegrind itself to gather the profiling information, and then run cg_annotate to get a detailed presentation of that information. As an optional intermediate step, you can use cg_merge to sum together the outputs of multiple Cachegrind runs into a single file which you then use as the input for cg_annotate. Alternatively, you can use cg_diff to difference the outputs of two Cachegrind runs into a single file which you then use as the input for cg_annotate.

5.2.1. Running Cachegrind

To run Cachegrind on a program prog, run:

```
valgrind --tool=cachegrind prog
```

The program will execute (slowly). Upon completion, summary statistics that look like this will be printed:

```
==31751== I   refs:      27,742,716
==31751== I1  misses:           276
==31751== LLi misses:           275
==31751== I1  miss rate:        0.0%
==31751== LLi miss rate:        0.0%
==31751==
==31751== D   refs:      15,430,290  (10,955,517 rd + 4,474,773 wr)
==31751== D1  misses:        41,185  (    21,905 rd +    19,280 wr)
==31751== LLd misses:        23,085  (     3,987 rd +    19,098 wr)
==31751== D1  miss rate:        0.2% (       0.1% +       0.4%)
==31751== LLd miss rate:        0.1% (       0.0% +       0.4%)
==31751==
==31751== LL misses:         23,360  (     4,262 rd +    19,098 wr)
==31751== LL miss rate:         0.0% (       0.0% +       0.4%)
```

Cache accesses for instruction fetches are summarised first, giving the number of fetches made (this is the number of instructions executed, which can be useful to know in its own right), the number of I1 misses, and the number of LL instruction (LLi) misses.

Cache accesses for data follow. The information is similar to that of the instruction fetches, except that the values are also shown split between reads and writes (note each row's rd and wr values add up to the row's total).

Combined instruction and data figures for the LL cache follow that. Note that the LL miss rate is computed relative to the total number of memory accesses, not the number of L1 misses. I.e. it is (ILmr + DLmr + DLmw) / (Ir + Dr + Dw) not (ILmr + DLmr + DLmw) / (I1mr + D1mr + D1mw).

Branch prediction statistics are not collected by default. To do so, add the option --branch-sim=yes.

5.2.2. Output File

As well as printing summary information, Cachegrind also writes more detailed profiling information to a file. By default this file is named cachegrind.out.<pid> (where <pid> is the program's process ID), but its name can be changed with the `--cachegrind-out-file` option. This file is human-readable, but is intended to be interpreted by the accompanying program cg_annotate, described in the next section.

The default `.<pid>` suffix on the output file name serves two purposes. Firstly, it means you don't have to rename old log files that you don't want to overwrite. Secondly, and more importantly, it allows correct profiling with the `--trace-children=yes` option of programs that spawn child processes.

The output file can be big, many megabytes for large applications built with full debugging information.

5.2.3. Running cg_annotate

Before using cg_annotate, it is worth widening your window to be at least 120-characters wide if possible, as the output lines can be quite long.

To get a function-by-function summary, run:
```
cg_annotate <filename>
```

on a Cachegrind output file.

5.2.4. The Output Preamble

The first part of the output looks like this:

```
---------------------------------------------------------------------

I1 cache:          65536 B, 64 B, 2-way associative
D1 cache:          65536 B, 64 B, 2-way associative
LL cache:          262144 B, 64 B, 8-way associative
Command:           concord vg_to_ucode.c
Events recorded:    Ir I1mr ILmr Dr D1mr DLmr Dw D1mw DLmw
Events shown:       Ir I1mr ILmr Dr D1mr DLmr Dw D1mw DLmw
Event sort order:   Ir I1mr ILmr Dr D1mr DLmr Dw D1mw DLmw
Threshold:         99%
Chosen for annotation:
Auto-annotation:    off
```

This is a summary of the annotation options:

• I1 cache, D1 cache, LL cache: cache configuration. So you know the configuration with which these results were obtained.

• Command: the command line invocation of the program under examination.

• Events recorded: which events were recorded.

• Events shown: the events shown, which is a subset of the events gathered. This can be adjusted with the `--show` option.

- Event sort order: the sort order in which functions are shown. For example, in this case the functions are sorted from highest Ir counts to lowest. If two functions have identical Ir counts, they will then be sorted by I1mr counts, and so on. This order can be adjusted with the --sort option.

  Note that this dictates the order the functions appear. It is *not* the order in which the columns appear; that is dictated by the "events shown" line (and can be changed with the --show option).

- Threshold: cg_annotate by default omits functions that cause very low counts to avoid drowning you in information. In this case, cg_annotate shows summaries the functions that account for 99% of the Ir counts; Ir is chosen as the threshold event since it is the primary sort event. The threshold can be adjusted with the --threshold option.

- Chosen for annotation: names of files specified manually for annotation; in this case none.

- Auto-annotation: whether auto-annotation was requested via the --auto=yes option. In this case no.

5.2.5. The Global and Function-level Counts

Then follows summary statistics for the whole program:

```
--------------------------------------------------------------------------

Ir         I1mr ILmr Dr         D1mr   DLmr  Dw         D1mw   DLmw
--------------------------------------------------------------------------

27,742,716  276  275 10,955,517 21,905 3,987 4,474,773 19,280 19,098  PROGRAM TOTALS
```

These are similar to the summary provided when Cachegrind finishes running.

Then comes function-by-function statistics:

```
----------------------------------------------------------------------------

Ir          I1mr ILmr Dr         D1mr  DLmr  Dw         D1mw   DLmw   file:function
----------------------------------------------------------------------------

8,821,482    5    5 2,242,702 1,621    73 1,794,230     0      0 getc.c:_IO_getc
5,222,023    4    4 2,276,334   16     12   875,959     1      1 concord.c:get_word
2,649,248    2    2 1,344,810 7,326 1,385        .      .      . vg_main.c:strcmp
2,521,927    2    2   591,215    0      0   179,398     0      0 concord.c:hash
2,242,740    2    2 1,046,612  568     22   448,548     0      0 ctype.c:tolower
1,496,937    4    4   630,874 9,000 1,400   279,388     0      0 concord.c:insert
  897,991   51   51   897,831   95     30        62     1      1 ???:???
  598,068    1    1   299,034    0      0   149,517     0      0 ../sysdeps/generic/lockfile.c

  598,068    0    0   299,034    0      0   149,517     0      0 ../sysdeps/generic/lockfile.c

  598,024    4    4   213,580   35     16   149,506     0      0 vg_clientmalloc.c:malloc

  446,587    1    1   215,973 2,167   430   129,948 14,057 13,957 concord.c:add_existing

  341,760    2    2   128,160    0      0   128,160     0      0 vg_clientmalloc.c:vg_trap_her

  320,782    4    4   150,711  276      0    56,027    53     53 concord.c:init_hash_table

  298,998    1    1   106,785    0      0    64,071     1      1 concord.c:create
  149,518    0    0   149,516    0      0         1     0      0 ???:tolower@@GLIBC_2.0
  149,518    0    0   149,516    0      0         1     0      0 ???:fgetc@@GLIBC_2.0
   95,983    4    4    38,031    0      0    34,409 3,152  3,150 concord.c:new_word_node

   85,440    0    0    42,720    0      0    21,360     0      0 vg_clientmalloc.c:vg_bogus_epi
```

Each function is identified by a file_name:function_name pair. If a column contains only a dot it means the function never performs that event (e.g. the third row shows that strcmp() contains no instructions that write to memory). The name ??? is used if the file name and/or function name could not be determined from debugging information. If most of the entries have the form ???:??? the program probably wasn't compiled with -g.

It is worth noting that functions will come both from the profiled program (e.g. concord.c) and from libraries (e.g. getc.c)

5.2.6. Line-by-line Counts

There are two ways to annotate source files -- by specifying them manually as arguments to cg_annotate, or with the --auto=yes option. For example, the output from running cg_annotate <filename> concord.c for our example produces the same output as above followed by an annotated version of concord.c, a section of which looks like:

```
---------------------------------------------------------------------------
-- User-annotated source: concord.c
---------------------------------------------------------------------------

Ir        I1mr ILmr Dr       D1mr DLmr Dw       D1mw  DLmw

    .        .    .    .        .    .    .        .     .  void init_hash_table(char *file_name,
    3        1    1    .        .    .    1        0     0  {
    .        .    .    .        .    .    .        .     .      FILE *file_ptr;
    .        .    .    .        .    .    .        .     .      Word_Info *data;
    1        0    0    .        .    .    1        1     1      int line = 1, i;
    .        .    .    .        .    .    .        .     .
    5        0    0    .        .    .    3        0     0      data = (Word_Info *) create(sizeof(
    .        .    .    .        .    .    .        .     .
4,991        0    0 1,995       0    0  998        0     0      for (i = 0; i < TABLE_SIZE; i++)

3,988        1    1 1,994       0    0  997       53    52          table[i] = NULL;
    .        .    .    .        .    .    .        .     .
    .        .    .    .        .    .    .        .     .      /* Open file, check it. */
    6        0    0    1        0    0    4        0     0      file_ptr = fopen(file_name, "r");

    2        0    0    1        0    0    .        .     .      if (!(file_ptr)) {
    .        .    .    .        .    .    .        .     .          fprintf(stderr, "Couldn't open '
    1        1    1    .        .    .    .        .     .          exit(EXIT_FAILURE);
    .        .    .    .        .    .    .        .     .      }
    .        .    .    .        .    .    .        .     .
165,062      1    1 73,360      0    0 91,700      0     0      while ((line = get_word(data, :

146,712      0    0 73,356      0    0 73,356      0     0          insert(data->;word, data->l

    .        .    .    .        .    .    .        .     .
    4        0    0    1        0    0    2        0     0      free(data);
    4        0    0    1        0    0    2        0     0      fclose(file_ptr);
    3        0    0    2        0    0    .        .     .  }
```

(Although column widths are automatically minimised, a wide terminal is clearly useful.)

Each source file is clearly marked (User-annotated source) as having been chosen manually for annotation. If the file was found in one of the directories specified with the -I/--include option, the directory and file are both given.

Each line is annotated with its event counts. Events not applicable for a line are represented by a dot. This is useful for distinguishing between an event which cannot happen, and one which can but did not.

Sometimes only a small section of a source file is executed. To minimise uninteresting output, Cachegrind only shows annotated lines and lines within a small distance of annotated lines. Gaps are marked with the line numbers so you know which part of a file the shown code comes from, eg:

```
(figures and code for line 704)
-- line 704 --------------------------------------
-- line 878 --------------------------------------
(figures and code for line 878)
```

The amount of context to show around annotated lines is controlled by the `--context` option.

To get automatic annotation, use the `--auto=yes` option. cg_annotate will automatically annotate every source file it can find that is mentioned in the function-by-function summary. Therefore, the files chosen for auto-annotation are affected by the `--sort` and `--threshold` options. Each source file is clearly marked (`Auto-annotated source`) as being chosen automatically. Any files that could not be found are mentioned at the end of the output, eg:

```
--------------------------------------------------------------
The following files chosen for auto-annotation could not be found:
--------------------------------------------------------------
  getc.c
  ctype.c
  ../sysdeps/generic/lockfile.c
```

This is quite common for library files, since libraries are usually compiled with debugging information, but the source files are often not present on a system. If a file is chosen for annotation both manually and automatically, it is marked as `User-annotated source`. Use the `-I/--include` option to tell Valgrind where to look for source files if the filenames found from the debugging information aren't specific enough.

Beware that cg_annotate can take some time to digest large `cachegrind.out.<pid>` files, e.g. 30 seconds or more. Also beware that auto-annotation can produce a lot of output if your program is large!

5.2.7. Annotating Assembly Code Programs

Valgrind can annotate assembly code programs too, or annotate the assembly code generated for your C program. Sometimes this is useful for understanding what is really happening when an interesting line of C code is translated into multiple instructions.

To do this, you just need to assemble your `.s` files with assembly-level debug information. You can use compile with the `-S` to compile C/C++ programs to assembly code, and then assemble the assembly code files with `-g` to achieve this. You can then profile and annotate the assembly code source files in the same way as C/C++ source files.

5.2.8. Forking Programs

If your program forks, the child will inherit all the profiling data that has been gathered for the parent.

If the output file format string (controlled by `--cachegrind-out-file`) does not contain `%p`, then the outputs from the parent and child will be intermingled in a single output file, which will almost certainly make it unreadable by cg_annotate.

5.2.9. cg_annotate Warnings

There are a couple of situations in which cg_annotate issues warnings.

• If a source file is more recent than the cachegrind.out.<pid> file. This is because the information in cachegrind.out.<pid> is only recorded with line numbers, so if the line numbers change at all in the source (e.g. lines added, deleted, swapped), any annotations will be incorrect.

• If information is recorded about line numbers past the end of a file. This can be caused by the above problem, i.e. shortening the source file while using an old cachegrind.out.<pid> file. If this happens, the figures for the bogus lines are printed anyway (clearly marked as bogus) in case they are important.

5.2.10. Unusual Annotation Cases

Some odd things that can occur during annotation:

• If annotating at the assembler level, you might see something like this:

```
1   0   0   .   .   .   .   .   .       leal -12(%ebp),%eax
1   0   0   .   .   . 1   0   0       movl %eax,84(%ebx)
2   0   0   0   0   0 1   0   0       movl $1,-20(%ebp)
.   .   .   .   .   .   .   .   .       .align 4,0x90
1   0   0   .   .   .   .   .   .       movl $.LnrB,%eax
1   0   0   .   .   . 1   0   0       movl %eax,-16(%ebp)
```

How can the third instruction be executed twice when the others are executed only once? As it turns out, it isn't. Here's a dump of the executable, using objdump -d:

```
8048f25:    8d 45 f4            lea    0xfffffff4(%ebp),%eax
8048f28:    89 43 54            mov    %eax,0x54(%ebx)
8048f2b:    c7 45 ec 01 00 00 00   movl   $0x1,0xffffffec(%ebp)
8048f32:    89 f6               mov    %esi,%esi
8048f34:    b8 08 8b 07 08      mov    $0x8078b08,%eax
8048f39:    89 45 f0            mov    %eax,0xfffffff0(%ebp)
```

Notice the extra mov %esi,%esi instruction. Where did this come from? The GNU assembler inserted it to serve as the two bytes of padding needed to align the movl $.LnrB,%eax instruction on a four-byte boundary, but pretended it didn't exist when adding debug information. Thus when Valgrind reads the debug info it thinks that the movl $0x1,0xffffffec(%ebp) instruction covers the address range 0x8048f2b--0x804833 by itself, and attributes the counts for the mov %esi,%esi to it.

• Sometimes, the same filename might be represented with a relative name and with an absolute name in different parts of the debug info, eg: /home/user/proj/proj.h and ../proj.h. In this case, if you use auto-annotation, the file will be annotated twice with the counts split between the two.

• If you compile some files with -g and some without, some events that take place in a file without debug info could be attributed to the last line of a file with debug info (whichever one gets placed before the non-debug-info file in the executable).

This list looks long, but these cases should be fairly rare.

5.2.11. Merging Profiles with cg_merge

cg_merge is a simple program which reads multiple profile files, as created by Cachegrind, merges them together, and writes the results into another file in the same format. You can then examine the merged results using `cg_annotate <filename>`, as described above. The merging functionality might be useful if you want to aggregate costs over multiple runs of the same program, or from a single parallel run with multiple instances of the same program.

cg_merge is invoked as follows:

```
cg_merge -o outputfile file1 file2 file3 ...
```

It reads and checks `file1`, then read and checks `file2` and merges it into the running totals, then the same with `file3`, etc. The final results are written to `outputfile`, or to standard out if no output file is specified.

Costs are summed on a per-function, per-line and per-instruction basis. Because of this, the order in which the input files does not matter, although you should take care to only mention each file once, since any file mentioned twice will be added in twice.

cg_merge does not attempt to check that the input files come from runs of the same executable. It will happily merge together profile files from completely unrelated programs. It does however check that the `Events:` lines of all the inputs are identical, so as to ensure that the addition of costs makes sense. For example, it would be nonsensical for it to add a number indicating D1 read references to a number from a different file indicating LL write misses.

A number of other syntax and sanity checks are done whilst reading the inputs. cg_merge will stop and attempt to print a helpful error message if any of the input files fail these checks.

5.2.12. Differencing Profiles with cg_diff

cg_diff is a simple program which reads two profile files, as created by Cachegrind, finds the difference between them, and writes the results into another file in the same format. You can then examine the merged results using `cg_annotate <filename>`, as described above. This is very useful if you want to measure how a change to a program affected its performance.

cg_diff is invoked as follows:

```
cg_diff file1 file2
```

It reads and checks `file1`, then read and checks `file2`, then computes the difference (effectively `file1 - file2`). The final results are written to standard output.

Costs are summed on a per-function basis. Per-line costs are not summed, because doing so is too difficult. For example, consider differencing two profiles, one from a single-file program A, and one from the same program A where a single blank line was inserted at the top of the file. Every single per-line count has changed. In comparison, the per-function counts have not changed. The per-function count differences are still very useful for determining differences between programs. Note that because the result is the difference of two profiles, many of the counts will be negative; this indicates that the counts for the relevant function are fewer in the second version than those in the first version.

cg_diff does not attempt to check that the input files come from runs of the same executable. It will happily merge together profile files from completely unrelated programs. It does however check that the `Events:` lines of all the inputs are identical, so as to ensure that the addition of costs makes sense. For example, it would be nonsensical for it to add a number indicating D1 read references to a number from a different file indicating LL write misses.

A number of other syntax and sanity checks are done whilst reading the inputs. cg_diff will stop and attempt to print a helpful error message if any of the input files fail these checks.

Sometimes you will want to compare Cachegrind profiles of two versions of a program that you have sitting side-by-side. For example, you might have `version1/prog.c` and `version2/prog.c`, where the second is slightly different to the first. A straight comparison of the two will not be useful -- because functions are qualified with filenames, a function `f` will be listed as `version1/prog.c:f` for the first version but `version2/prog.c:f` for the second version.

When this happens, you can use the `--mod-filename` option. Its argument is a Perl search-and-replace expression that will be applied to all the filenames in both Cachegrind output files. It can be used to remove minor differences in filenames. For example, the option `--mod-filename='s/version[0-9]/versionN/'` will suffice for this case.

Similarly, sometimes compilers auto-generate certain functions and give them randomized names. For example, GCC sometimes auto-generates functions with names like `T.1234`, and the suffixes vary from build to build. You can use the `--mod-funcname` option to remove small differences like these; it works in the same way as `--mod-filename`.

5.3. Cachegrind Command-line Options

Cachegrind-specific options are:

`--I1=<size>,<associativity>,<line size>`
Specify the size, associativity and line size of the level 1 instruction cache.

`--D1=<size>,<associativity>,<line size>`
Specify the size, associativity and line size of the level 1 data cache.

`--LL=<size>,<associativity>,<line size>`
Specify the size, associativity and line size of the last-level cache.

`--cache-sim=no|yes [yes]`
Enables or disables collection of cache access and miss counts.

`--branch-sim=no|yes [no]`
Enables or disables collection of branch instruction and misprediction counts. By default this is disabled as it slows Cachegrind down by approximately 25%. Note that you cannot specify `--cache-sim=no` and `--branch-sim=no` together, as that would leave Cachegrind with no information to collect.

`--cachegrind-out-file=<file>`
Write the profile data to `file` rather than to the default output file, `cachegrind.out.<pid>`. The `%p` and `%q` format specifiers can be used to embed the process ID and/or the contents of an environment variable in the name, as is the case for the core option `--log-file`.

5.4. cg_annotate Command-line Options

`-h --help`
Show the help message.

`--version`
Show the version number.

`--show=A,B,C [default: all, using order in cachegrind.out.<pid>]`
Specifies which events to show (and the column order). Default is to use all present in the `cachegrind.out.<pid>` file (and use the order in the file). Useful if you want to concentrate on, for example, I cache misses (`--show=I1mr,ILmr`), or data read misses (`--show=D1mr,DLmr`), or LL data misses (`--show=DLmr,DLmw`). Best used in conjunction with `--sort`.

`--sort=A,B,C [default: order in cachegrind.out.<pid>]`
Specifies the events upon which the sorting of the function-by-function entries will be based.

`--threshold=X [default: 0.1%]`
Sets the threshold for the function-by-function summary. A function is shown if it accounts for more than X% of the counts for the primary sort event. If auto-annotating, also affects which files are annotated.

Note: thresholds can be set for more than one of the events by appending any events for the `--sort` option with a colon and a number (no spaces, though). E.g. if you want to see each function that covers more than 1% of LL read misses or 1% of LL write misses, use this option:

`--sort=DLmr:1,DLmw:1`

`--auto=<no|yes> [default: no]`
When enabled, automatically annotates every file that is mentioned in the function-by-function summary that can be found. Also gives a list of those that couldn't be found.

`--context=N [default: 8]`
Print N lines of context before and after each annotated line. Avoids printing large sections of source files that were not executed. Use a large number (e.g. 100000) to show all source lines.

`-I<dir> --include=<dir> [default: none]`
Adds a directory to the list in which to search for files. Multiple `-I`/`--include` options can be given to add multiple directories.

5.5. cg_merge Command-line Options

`-o outfile`
Write the profile data to `outfile` rather than to standard output.

5.6. cg_diff Command-line Options

`-h --help`
Show the help message.

`--version`
Show the version number.

`--mod-filename=<expr> [default: none]`
Specifies a Perl search-and-replace expression that is applied to all filenames. Useful for removing minor differences in paths between two different versions of a program that are sitting in different directories.

```
--mod-funcname=<expr> [default:  none]
```
Like `--mod-filename`, but for filenames. Useful for removing minor differences in randomized names of auto-generated functions generated by some compilers.

5.7. Acting on Cachegrind's Information

Cachegrind gives you lots of information, but acting on that information isn't always easy. Here are some rules of thumb that we have found to be useful.

First of all, the global hit/miss counts and miss rates are not that useful. If you have multiple programs or multiple runs of a program, comparing the numbers might identify if any are outliers and worthy of closer investigation. Otherwise, they're not enough to act on.

The function-by-function counts are more useful to look at, as they pinpoint which functions are causing large numbers of counts. However, beware that inlining can make these counts misleading. If a function `f` is always inlined, counts will be attributed to the functions it is inlined into, rather than itself. However, if you look at the line-by-line annotations for `f` you'll see the counts that belong to `f`. (This is hard to avoid, it's how the debug info is structured.) So it's worth looking for large numbers in the line-by-line annotations.

The line-by-line source code annotations are much more useful. In our experience, the best place to start is by looking at the `Ir` numbers. They simply measure how many instructions were executed for each line, and don't include any cache information, but they can still be very useful for identifying bottlenecks.

After that, we have found that LL misses are typically a much bigger source of slow-downs than L1 misses. So it's worth looking for any snippets of code with high `DLmr` or `DLmw` counts. (You can use `--show=DLmr` `--sort=DLmr` with cg_annotate to focus just on `DLmr` counts, for example.) If you find any, it's still not always easy to work out how to improve things. You need to have a reasonable understanding of how caches work, the principles of locality, and your program's data access patterns. Improving things may require redesigning a data structure, for example.

Looking at the `Bcm` and `Bim` misses can also be helpful. In particular, `Bim` misses are often caused by `switch` statements, and in some cases these `switch` statements can be replaced with table-driven code. For example, you might replace code like this:

```
enum E { A, B, C };
enum E e;
int i;
...
switch (e)
{
   case A: i += 1; break;
   case B: i += 2; break;
   case C: i += 3; break;
}
```

with code like this:

```
enum E { A, B, C };
enum E e;
enum E table[] = { 1, 2, 3 };
int i;
...
i += table[e];
```

This is obviously a contrived example, but the basic principle applies in a wide variety of situations.

In short, Cachegrind can tell you where some of the bottlenecks in your code are, but it can't tell you how to fix them. You have to work that out for yourself. But at least you have the information!

5.8. Simulation Details

This section talks about details you don't need to know about in order to use Cachegrind, but may be of interest to some people.

5.8.1. Cache Simulation Specifics

Specific characteristics of the cache simulation are as follows:

- Write-allocate: when a write miss occurs, the block written to is brought into the D1 cache. Most modern caches have this property.

- Bit-selection hash function: the set of line(s) in the cache to which a memory block maps is chosen by the middle bits M--(M+N-1) of the byte address, where:

  - line size = 2^M bytes

  - (cache size / line size / associativity) = 2^N bytes

- Inclusive LL cache: the LL cache typically replicates all the entries of the L1 caches, because fetching into L1 involves fetching into LL first (this does not guarantee strict inclusiveness, as lines evicted from LL still could reside in L1). This is standard on Pentium chips, but AMD Opterons, Athlons and Durons use an exclusive LL cache that only holds blocks evicted from L1. Ditto most modern VIA CPUs.

The cache configuration simulated (cache size, associativity and line size) is determined automatically using the x86 CPUID instruction. If you have a machine that (a) doesn't support the CPUID instruction, or (b) supports it in an early incarnation that doesn't give any cache information, then Cachegrind will fall back to using a default configuration (that of a model 3/4 Athlon). Cachegrind will tell you if this happens. You can manually specify one, two or all three levels (I1/D1/LL) of the cache from the command line using the --I1, --D1 and --LL options. For cache parameters to be valid for simulation, the number of sets (with associativity being the number of cache lines in each set) has to be a power of two.

On PowerPC platforms Cachegrind cannot automatically determine the cache configuration, so you will need to specify it with the --I1, --D1 and --LL options.

Other noteworthy behaviour:

- References that straddle two cache lines are treated as follows:

  - If both blocks hit --> counted as one hit

  - If one block hits, the other misses --> counted as one miss.

  - If both blocks miss --> counted as one miss (not two)

- Instructions that modify a memory location (e.g. `inc` and `dec`) are counted as doing just a read, i.e. a single data reference. This may seem strange, but since the write can never cause a miss (the read guarantees the block is in the cache) it's not very interesting.

  Thus it measures not the number of times the data cache is accessed, but the number of times a data cache miss could occur.

If you are interested in simulating a cache with different properties, it is not particularly hard to write your own cache simulator, or to modify the existing ones in `cg_sim.c`. We'd be interested to hear from anyone who does.

5.8.2. Branch Simulation Specifics

Cachegrind simulates branch predictors intended to be typical of mainstream desktop/server processors of around 2004.

Conditional branches are predicted using an array of 16384 2-bit saturating counters. The array index used for a branch instruction is computed partly from the low-order bits of the branch instruction's address and partly using the taken/not-taken behaviour of the last few conditional branches. As a result the predictions for any specific branch depend both on its own history and the behaviour of previous branches. This is a standard technique for improving prediction accuracy.

For indirect branches (that is, jumps to unknown destinations) Cachegrind uses a simple branch target address predictor. Targets are predicted using an array of 512 entries indexed by the low order 9 bits of the branch instruction's address. Each branch is predicted to jump to the same address it did last time. Any other behaviour causes a mispredict.

More recent processors have better branch predictors, in particular better indirect branch predictors. Cachegrind's predictor design is deliberately conservative so as to be representative of the large installed base of processors which pre-date widespread deployment of more sophisticated indirect branch predictors. In particular, late model Pentium 4s (Prescott), Pentium M, Core and Core 2 have more sophisticated indirect branch predictors than modelled by Cachegrind.

Cachegrind does not simulate a return stack predictor. It assumes that processors perfectly predict function return addresses, an assumption which is probably close to being true.

See Hennessy and Patterson's classic text "Computer Architecture: A Quantitative Approach", 4th edition (2007), Section 2.3 (pages 80-89) for background on modern branch predictors.

5.8.3. Accuracy

Valgrind's cache profiling has a number of shortcomings:

- It doesn't account for kernel activity -- the effect of system calls on the cache and branch predictor contents is ignored.

- It doesn't account for other process activity. This is probably desirable when considering a single program.

- It doesn't account for virtual-to-physical address mappings. Hence the simulation is not a true representation of what's happening in the cache. Most caches and branch predictors are physically indexed, but Cachegrind simulates caches using virtual addresses.

- It doesn't account for cache misses not visible at the instruction level, e.g. those arising from TLB misses, or speculative execution.

- Valgrind will schedule threads differently from how they would be when running natively. This could warp the results for threaded programs.

- The x86/amd64 instructions `bts`, `btr` and `btc` will incorrectly be counted as doing a data read if both the arguments are registers, eg:

```
btsl %eax, %edx
```

This should only happen rarely.

- x86/amd64 FPU instructions with data sizes of 28 and 108 bytes (e.g. `fsave`) are treated as though they only access 16 bytes. These instructions seem to be rare so hopefully this won't affect accuracy much.

Another thing worth noting is that results are very sensitive. Changing the size of the executable being profiled, or the sizes of any of the shared libraries it uses, or even the length of their file names, can perturb the results. Variations will be small, but don't expect perfectly repeatable results if your program changes at all.

More recent GNU/Linux distributions do address space randomisation, in which identical runs of the same program have their shared libraries loaded at different locations, as a security measure. This also perturbs the results.

While these factors mean you shouldn't trust the results to be super-accurate, they should be close enough to be useful.

5.9. Implementation Details

This section talks about details you don't need to know about in order to use Cachegrind, but may be of interest to some people.

5.9.1. How Cachegrind Works

The best reference for understanding how Cachegrind works is chapter 3 of "Dynamic Binary Analysis and Instrumentation", by Nicholas Nethercote. It is available on the Valgrind publications page.

5.9.2. Cachegrind Output File Format

The file format is fairly straightforward, basically giving the cost centre for every line, grouped by files and functions. It's also totally generic and self-describing, in the sense that it can be used for any events that can be counted on a line-by-line basis, not just cache and branch predictor events. For example, earlier versions of Cachegrind didn't have a branch predictor simulation. When this was added, the file format didn't need to change at all. So the format (and consequently, cg_annotate) could be used by other tools.

The file format:

```
file         ::= desc_line* cmd_line events_line data_line+ summary_line
desc_line    ::= "desc:" ws? non_nl_string
cmd_line     ::= "cmd:" ws? cmd
events_line  ::= "events:" ws? (event ws)+
data_line    ::= file_line | fn_line | count_line
file_line    ::= "fl=" filename
fn_line      ::= "fn=" fn_name
count_line   ::= line_num ws? (count ws)+
summary_line ::= "summary:" ws? (count ws)+
count        ::= num | "."
```

Where:

- non_nl_string is any string not containing a newline.

- cmd is a string holding the command line of the profiled program.

- event is a string containing no whitespace.

- filename and fn_name are strings.

- num and line_num are decimal numbers.

- ws is whitespace.

The contents of the "desc:" lines are printed out at the top of the summary. This is a generic way of providing simulation specific information, e.g. for giving the cache configuration for cache simulation.

More than one line of info can be presented for each file/fn/line number. In such cases, the counts for the named events will be accumulated.

Counts can be "." to represent zero. This makes the files easier for humans to read.

The number of counts in each line and the summary_line should not exceed the number of events in the event_line. If the number in each line is less, cg_annotate treats those missing as though they were a "." entry. This saves space.

A file_line changes the current file name. A fn_line changes the current function name. A count_line contains counts that pertain to the current filename/fn_name. A "fn=" file_line and a fn_line must appear before any count_lines to give the context of the first count_lines.

Each file_line will normally be immediately followed by a fn_line. But it doesn't have to be.

The summary line is redundant, because it just holds the total counts for each event. But this serves as a useful sanity check of the data; if the totals for each event don't match the summary line, something has gone wrong.

6. Callgrind: a call-graph generating cache and branch prediction profiler

To use this tool, you must specify `--tool=callgrind` on the Valgrind command line.

6.1. Overview

Callgrind is a profiling tool that records the call history among functions in a program's run as a call-graph. By default, the collected data consists of the number of instructions executed, their relationship to source lines, the caller/callee relationship between functions, and the numbers of such calls. Optionally, cache simulation and/or branch prediction (similar to Cachegrind) can produce further information about the runtime behavior of an application.

The profile data is written out to a file at program termination. For presentation of the data, and interactive control of the profiling, two command line tools are provided:

callgrind_annotate

This command reads in the profile data, and prints a sorted lists of functions, optionally with source annotation.

For graphical visualization of the data, try KCachegrind, which is a KDE/Qt based GUI that makes it easy to navigate the large amount of data that Callgrind produces.

callgrind_control

This command enables you to interactively observe and control the status of a program currently running under Callgrind's control, without stopping the program. You can get statistics information as well as the current stack trace, and you can request zeroing of counters or dumping of profile data.

6.1.1. Functionality

Cachegrind collects flat profile data: event counts (data reads, cache misses, etc.) are attributed directly to the function they occurred in. This cost attribution mechanism is called *self* or *exclusive* attribution.

Callgrind extends this functionality by propagating costs across function call boundaries. If function `foo` calls `bar`, the costs from `bar` are added into `foo`'s costs. When applied to the program as a whole, this builds up a picture of so called *inclusive* costs, that is, where the cost of each function includes the costs of all functions it called, directly or indirectly.

As an example, the inclusive cost of `main` should be almost 100 percent of the total program cost. Because of costs arising before `main` is run, such as initialization of the run time linker and construction of global C++ objects, the inclusive cost of `main` is not exactly 100 percent of the total program cost.

Together with the call graph, this allows you to find the specific call chains starting from `main` in which the majority of the program's costs occur. Caller/callee cost attribution is also useful for profiling functions called from multiple call sites, and where optimization opportunities depend on changing code in the callers, in particular by reducing the call count.

Callgrind's cache simulation is based on that of Cachegrind. Read the documentation for Cachegrind: a cache and branch-prediction profiler first. The material below describes the features supported in addition to Cachegrind's features.

Callgrind's ability to detect function calls and returns depends on the instruction set of the platform it is run on. It works best on x86 and amd64, and unfortunately currently does not work so well on PowerPC, ARM, Thumb or MIPS code. This is because there are no explicit call or return instructions in these instruction sets, so Callgrind has to rely on heuristics to detect calls and returns.

6.1.2. Basic Usage

As with Cachegrind, you probably want to compile with debugging info (the -g option) and with optimization turned on.

To start a profile run for a program, execute:
```
valgrind --tool=callgrind [callgrind options] your-program [program options]
```

While the simulation is running, you can observe execution with:
```
callgrind_control -b
```

This will print out the current backtrace. To annotate the backtrace with event counts, run
```
callgrind_control -e -b
```

After program termination, a profile data file named `callgrind.out.<pid>` is generated, where *pid* is the process ID of the program being profiled. The data file contains information about the calls made in the program among the functions executed, together with **Instruction Read** (Ir) event counts.

To generate a function-by-function summary from the profile data file, use
```
callgrind_annotate [options] callgrind.out.<pid>
```

This summary is similar to the output you get from a Cachegrind run with cg_annotate: the list of functions is ordered by exclusive cost of functions, which also are the ones that are shown. Important for the additional features of Callgrind are the following two options:

- `--inclusive=yes`: Instead of using exclusive cost of functions as sorting order, use and show inclusive cost.

- `--tree=both`: Interleave into the top level list of functions, information on the callers and the callees of each function. In these lines, which represents executed calls, the cost gives the number of events spent in the call. Indented, above each function, there is the list of callers, and below, the list of callees. The sum of events in calls to a given function (caller lines), as well as the sum of events in calls from the function (callee lines) together with the self cost, gives the total inclusive cost of the function.

Use `--auto=yes` to get annotated source code for all relevant functions for which the source can be found. In addition to source annotation as produced by `cg_annotate`, you will see the annotated call sites with call counts. For all other options, consult the (Cachegrind) documentation for `cg_annotate`.

For better call graph browsing experience, it is highly recommended to use KCachegrind. If your code has a significant fraction of its cost in *cycles* (sets of functions calling each other in a recursive manner), you have to use KCachegrind, as `callgrind_annotate` currently does not do any cycle detection, which is important to get correct results in this case.

If you are additionally interested in measuring the cache behavior of your program, use Callgrind with the option `--cache-sim=yes`. For branch prediction simulation, use `--branch-sim=yes`. Expect a further slow down approximately by a factor of 2.

If the program section you want to profile is somewhere in the middle of the run, it is beneficial to *fast forward* to this section without any profiling, and then enable profiling. This is achieved by using the command line option `--instr-atstart=no` and running, in a shell: `callgrind_control -i on` just before the interesting code section is executed. To exactly specify the code position where profiling should start, use the client request `CALLGRIND_START_INSTRUMENTATION`.

If you want to be able to see assembly code level annotation, specify `--dump-instr=yes`. This will produce profile data at instruction granularity. Note that the resulting profile data can only be viewed with KCachegrind. For assembly annotation, it also is interesting to see more details of the control flow inside of functions, i.e. (conditional) jumps. This will be collected by further specifying `--collect-jumps=yes`.

6.2. Advanced Usage

6.2.1. Multiple profiling dumps from one program run

Sometimes you are not interested in characteristics of a full program run, but only of a small part of it, for example execution of one algorithm. If there are multiple algorithms, or one algorithm running with different input data, it may even be useful to get different profile information for different parts of a single program run.

Profile data files have names of the form

```
callgrind.out.pid.part-threadID
```

where *pid* is the PID of the running program, *part* is a number incremented on each dump (".part" is skipped for the dump at program termination), and *threadID* is a thread identification ("-threadID" is only used if you request dumps of individual threads with `--separate-threads=yes`).

There are different ways to generate multiple profile dumps while a program is running under Callgrind's supervision. Nevertheless, all methods trigger the same action, which is "dump all profile information since the last dump or program start, and zero cost counters afterwards". To allow for zeroing cost counters without dumping, there is a second action "zero all cost counters now". The different methods are:

- **Dump on program termination.** This method is the standard way and doesn't need any special action on your part.

- **Spontaneous, interactive dumping.** Use

```
callgrind_control -d [hint [PID/Name]]
```
to request the dumping of profile information of the supervised application with PID or Name. *hint* is an arbitrary string you can optionally specify to later be able to distinguish profile dumps. The control program will not terminate before the dump is completely written. Note that the application must be actively running for detection of the dump command. So, for a GUI application, resize the window, or for a server, send a request.

If you are using KCachegrind for browsing of profile information, you can use the toolbar button **Force dump**. This will request a dump and trigger a reload after the dump is written.

- **Periodic dumping after execution of a specified number of basic blocks**. For this, use the command line option `--dump-every-bb=count`.

- **Dumping at enter/leave of specified functions.** Use the option `--dump-before=function` and `--dump-after=function`. To zero cost counters before entering a function, use `--zero-before=function`.

You can specify these options multiple times for different functions. Function specifications support wildcards: e.g. use `--dump-before='foo*'` to generate dumps before entering any function starting with *foo*.

- **Program controlled dumping.** Insert `CALLGRIND_DUMP_STATS;` at the position in your code where you want a profile dump to happen. Use `CALLGRIND_ZERO_STATS;` to only zero profile counters. See Client request reference for more information on Callgrind specific client requests.

If you are running a multi-threaded application and specify the command line option `--separate-threads=yes`, every thread will be profiled on its own and will create its own profile dump. Thus, the last two methods will only generate one dump of the currently running thread. With the other methods, you will get multiple dumps (one for each thread) on a dump request.

6.2.2. Limiting the range of collected events

By default, whenever events are happening (such as an instruction execution or cache hit/miss), Callgrind is aggregating them into event counters. However, you may be interested only in what is happening within a given function or starting from a given program phase. To this end, you can disable event aggregation for uninteresting program parts. While attribution of events to functions as well as producing seperate output per program phase can be done by other means (see previous section), there are two benefits by disabling aggregation. First, this is very fine-granular (e.g. just for a loop within a function). Second, disabling event aggregation for complete program phases allows to switch off time-consuming cache simulation and allows Callgrind to progress at much higher speed with an slowdown of around factor 2 (identical to `valgrind --tool=none`).

There are two aspects which influence whether Callgrind is aggregating events at some point in time of program execution. First, there is the *collection state*. If this is off, no aggregation will be done. By changing the collection state, you can control event aggregation at a very fine granularity. However, there is not much difference in regard to execution speed of Callgrind. By default, collection is switched on, but can be disabled by different means (see below). Second, there is the *instrumentation mode* in which Callgrind is running. This mode either can be on or off. If instrumentation is off, no observation of actions in the program will be done and thus, no actions will be forwarded to the simulator which could trigger events. In the end, no events will be aggregated. The huge benefit is the much higher speed with instrumentation switched off. However, this only should be used with care and in a coarse fashion: every mode change resets the simulator state (ie. whether a memory block is cached or not) and flushes Valgrinds internal cache of instrumented code blocks, resulting in latency penalty at switching time. Also, cache simulator results directly after switching on instrumentation will be skewed due to identified cache misses which would not happen in reality (if you care about this warm-up effect, you should make sure to temporarily have collection state switched off directly after turning instrumentation mode on). However, switching instrumentation state is very useful to skip larger program phases such as an initialization phase. By default, instrumentation is switched on, but as with the collection state, can be changed by various means.

Callgrind can start with instrumentation mode switched off by specifying option `--instr-atstart=no`. Afterwards, instrumentation can be controlled in two ways: first, interactively with:
`callgrind_control -i on`

(and switching off again by specifying "off" instead of "on"). Second, instrumentation state can be programatically changed with the macros `CALLGRIND_START_INSTRUMENTATION;` and `CALLGRIND_STOP_INSTRUMENTATION;`.

Similarly, the collection state at program start can be switched off by `--instr-atstart=no`. During execution, it can be controlled programatically with the macro `CALLGRIND_TOGGLE_COLLECT;`. Further, you can limit event collection to a specific function by using `--toggle-collect=function`. This will toggle the collection state on entering and leaving the specified function. When this option is in effect, the default collection state at program start is "off". Only events happening while running inside of the given function will be collected. Recursive calls of the given function do not trigger any action. This option can be given multiple times to specify different functions of interest.

6.2.3. Counting global bus events

For access to shared data among threads in a multithreaded code, synchronization is required to avoid raced conditions. Synchronization primitives are usually implemented via atomic instructions. However, excessive use of such instructions can lead to performance issues.

To enable analysis of this problem, Callgrind optionally can count the number of atomic instructions executed. More precisely, for x86/x86_64, these are instructions using a lock prefix. For architectures supporting LL/SC, these are the number of SC instructions executed. For both, the term "global bus events" is used.

The short name of the event type used for global bus events is "Ge". To count global bus events, use `--collect-bus=yes`.

6.2.4. Avoiding cycles

Informally speaking, a cycle is a group of functions which call each other in a recursive way.

Formally speaking, a cycle is a nonempty set S of functions, such that for every pair of functions F and G in S, it is possible to call from F to G (possibly via intermediate functions) and also from G to F. Furthermore, S must be maximal -- that is, be the largest set of functions satisfying this property. For example, if a third function H is called from inside S and calls back into S, then H is also part of the cycle and should be included in S.

Recursion is quite usual in programs, and therefore, cycles sometimes appear in the call graph output of Callgrind. However, the title of this chapter should raise two questions: What is bad about cycles which makes you want to avoid them? And: How can cycles be avoided without changing program code?

Cycles are not bad in itself, but tend to make performance analysis of your code harder. This is because inclusive costs for calls inside of a cycle are meaningless. The definition of inclusive cost, i.e. self cost of a function plus inclusive cost of its callees, needs a topological order among functions. For cycles, this does not hold true: callees of a function in a cycle include the function itself. Therefore, KCachegrind does cycle detection and skips visualization of any inclusive cost for calls inside of cycles. Further, all functions in a cycle are collapsed into artifical functions called like `Cycle 1`.

Now, when a program exposes really big cycles (as is true for some GUI code, or in general code using event or callback based programming style), you lose the nice property to let you pinpoint the bottlenecks by following call chains from `main`, guided via inclusive cost. In addition, KCachegrind loses its ability to show interesting parts of the call graph, as it uses inclusive costs to cut off uninteresting areas.

Despite the meaningless of inclusive costs in cycles, the big drawback for visualization motivates the possibility to temporarily switch off cycle detection in KCachegrind, which can lead to misguiding visualization. However, often cycles appear because of unlucky superposition of independent call chains in a way that the profile result will see a cycle. Neglecting uninteresting calls with very small measured inclusive cost would break these cycles. In such cases, incorrect handling of cycles by not detecting them still gives meaningful profiling visualization.

It has to be noted that currently, **callgrind_annotate** does not do any cycle detection at all. For program executions with function recursion, it e.g. can print nonsense inclusive costs way above 100%.

After describing why cycles are bad for profiling, it is worth talking about cycle avoidance. The key insight here is that symbols in the profile data do not have to exactly match the symbols found in the program. Instead, the symbol name could encode additional information from the current execution context such as recursion level of the current function, or even some part of the call chain leading to the function. While encoding of additional information into symbols is quite capable of avoiding cycles, it has to be used carefully to not cause symbol explosion. The latter imposes large memory requirement for Callgrind with possible out-of-memory conditions, and big profile data files.

A further possibility to avoid cycles in Callgrind's profile data output is to simply leave out given functions in the call graph. Of course, this also skips any call information from and to an ignored function, and thus can break a cycle. Candidates for this typically are dispatcher functions in event driven code. The option to ignore calls to a function is `--fn-skip=function`. Aside from possibly breaking cycles, this is used in Callgrind to skip trampoline functions in the PLT sections for calls to functions in shared libraries. You can see the difference if you profile with `--skip-plt=no`. If a call is ignored, its cost events will be propagated to the enclosing function.

If you have a recursive function, you can distinguish the first 10 recursion levels by specifying `--separate-recs10=function`. Or for all functions with `--separate-recs=10`, but this will give you much bigger profile data files. In the profile data, you will see the recursion levels of "func" as the different functions with names "func", "func'2", "func'3" and so on.

If you have call chains "A > B > C" and "A > C > B" in your program, you usually get a "false" cycle "B <> C". Use `--separate-callers2=B --separate-callers2=C`, and functions "B" and "C" will be treated as different functions depending on the direct caller. Using the apostrophe for appending this "context" to the function name, you get "A > B'A > C'B" and "A > C'A > B'C", and there will be no cycle. Use `--separate-callers=2` to get a 2-caller dependency for all functions. Note that doing this will increase the size of profile data files.

6.2.5. Forking Programs

If your program forks, the child will inherit all the profiling data that has been gathered for the parent. To start with empty profile counter values in the child, the client request `CALLGRIND_ZERO_STATS;` can be inserted into code to be executed by the child, directly after `fork`.

However, you will have to make sure that the output file format string (controlled by `--callgrind-out-file`) does contain `%p` (which is true by default). Otherwise, the outputs from the parent and child will overwrite each other or will be intermingled, which almost certainly is not what you want.

You will be able to control the new child independently from the parent via callgrind_control.

6.3. Callgrind Command-line Options

In the following, options are grouped into classes.

Some options allow the specification of a function/symbol name, such as `--dump-before=function`, or `--fn-skip=function`. All these options can be specified multiple times for different functions. In addition, the function specifications actually are patterns by supporting the use of wildcards '*' (zero or more arbitrary characters) and '?' (exactly one arbitrary character), similar to file name globbing in the shell. This feature is important especially for C++, as without wildcard usage, the function would have to be specified in full extent, including parameter signature.

6.3.1. Dump creation options

These options influence the name and format of the profile data files.

`--callgrind-out-file=<file>`
Write the profile data to `file` rather than to the default output file, `callgrind.out.<pid>`. The `%p` and `%q` format specifiers can be used to embed the process ID and/or the contents of an environment variable in the name, as is the case for the core option `--log-file`. When multiple dumps are made, the file name is modified further; see below.

`--dump-line=<no|yes> [default: yes]`
This specifies that event counting should be performed at source line granularity. This allows source annotation for sources which are compiled with debug information (`-g`).

`--dump-instr=<no|yes> [default: no]`
This specifies that event counting should be performed at per-instruction granularity. This allows for assembly code annotation. Currently the results can only be displayed by KCachegrind.

`--compress-strings=<no|yes> [default: yes]`
This option influences the output format of the profile data. It specifies whether strings (file and function names) should be identified by numbers. This shrinks the file, but makes it more difficult for humans to read (which is not recommended in any case).

`--compress-pos=<no|yes> [default: yes]`
This option influences the output format of the profile data. It specifies whether numerical positions are always specified as absolute values or are allowed to be relative to previous numbers. This shrinks the file size.

`--combine-dumps=<no|yes> [default: no]`
When enabled, when multiple profile data parts are to be generated these parts are appended to the same output file. Not recommended.

6.3.2. Activity options

These options specify when actions relating to event counts are to be executed. For interactive control use callgrind_control.

`--dump-every-bb=<count> [default: 0, never]`
Dump profile data every `count` basic blocks. Whether a dump is needed is only checked when Valgrind's internal scheduler is run. Therefore, the minimum setting useful is about 100000. The count is a 64-bit value to make long dump periods possible.

`--dump-before=<function>`
Dump when entering `function`.

`--zero-before=<function>`
Zero all costs when entering `function`.

`--dump-after=<function>`
Dump when leaving `function`.

6.3.3. Data collection options

These options specify when events are to be aggregated into event counts. Also see Limiting range of event collection.

`--instr-atstart=<yes|no> [default:  yes]`
Specify if you want Callgrind to start simulation and profiling from the beginning of the program. When set to `no`, Callgrind will not be able to collect any information, including calls, but it will have at most a slowdown of around 4, which is the minimum Valgrind overhead. Instrumentation can be interactively enabled via `callgrind_control -i on`.

Note that the resulting call graph will most probably not contain `main`, but will contain all the functions executed after instrumentation was enabled. Instrumentation can also programatically enabled/disabled. See the Callgrind include file `callgrind.h` for the macro you have to use in your source code.

For cache simulation, results will be less accurate when switching on instrumentation later in the program run, as the simulator starts with an empty cache at that moment. Switch on event collection later to cope with this error.

`--collect-atstart=<yes|no> [default:  yes]`
Specify whether event collection is enabled at beginning of the profile run.

To only look at parts of your program, you have two possibilities:

1. Zero event counters before entering the program part you want to profile, and dump the event counters to a file after leaving that program part.

2. Switch on/off collection state as needed to only see event counters happening while inside of the program part you want to profile.

The second option can be used if the program part you want to profile is called many times. Option 1, i.e. creating a lot of dumps is not practical here.

Collection state can be toggled at entry and exit of a given function with the option `--toggle-collect`. If you use this option, collection state should be disabled at the beginning. Note that the specification of `--toggle-collect` implicitly sets `--collect-state=no`.

Collection state can be toggled also by inserting the client request `CALLGRIND_TOGGLE_COLLECT ;` at the needed code positions.

`--toggle-collect=<function>`
Toggle collection on entry/exit of `function`.

`--collect-jumps=<no|yes> [default:  no]`
This specifies whether information for (conditional) jumps should be collected. As above, callgrind_annotate currently is not able to show you the data. You have to use KCachegrind to get jump arrows in the annotated code.

`--collect-systime=<no|yes> [default:  no]`
This specifies whether information for system call times should be collected.

```
--collect-bus=<no|yes> [default:  no]
```
This specifies whether the number of global bus events executed should be collected. The event type "Ge" is used for these events.

6.3.4. Cost entity separation options

These options specify how event counts should be attributed to execution contexts. For example, they specify whether the recursion level or the call chain leading to a function should be taken into account, and whether the thread ID should be considered. Also see Avoiding cycles.

```
--separate-threads=<no|yes> [default:  no]
```
This option specifies whether profile data should be generated separately for every thread. If yes, the file names get "-threadID" appended.

```
--separate-callers=<callers> [default:  0]
```
Separate contexts by at most <callers> functions in the call chain. See Avoiding cycles.

```
--separate-callers<number>=<function>
```
Separate number callers for function. See Avoiding cycles.

```
--separate-recs=<level> [default:  2]
```
Separate function recursions by at most level levels. See Avoiding cycles.

```
--separate-recs<number>=<function>
```
Separate number recursions for function. See Avoiding cycles.

```
--skip-plt=<no|yes> [default:  yes]
```
Ignore calls to/from PLT sections.

```
--skip-direct-rec=<no|yes> [default:  yes]
```
Ignore direct recursions.

```
--fn-skip=<function>
```
Ignore calls to/from a given function. E.g. if you have a call chain A > B > C, and you specify function B to be ignored, you will only see A > C.

This is very convenient to skip functions handling callback behaviour. For example, with the signal/slot mechanism in the Qt graphics library, you only want to see the function emitting a signal to call the slots connected to that signal. First, determine the real call chain to see the functions needed to be skipped, then use this option.

6.3.5. Simulation options

```
--cache-sim=<yes|no> [default:  no]
```
Specify if you want to do full cache simulation. By default, only instruction read accesses will be counted ("Ir"). With cache simulation, further event counters are enabled: Cache misses on instruction reads ("I1mr"/"ILmr"), data read accesses ("Dr") and related cache misses ("D1mr"/"DLmr"), data write accesses ("Dw") and related cache misses ("D1mw"/"DLmw"). For more information, see Cachegrind: a cache and branch-prediction profiler.

`--branch-sim=<yes|no> [default:  no]`
Specify if you want to do branch prediction simulation. Further event counters are enabled: Number of executed conditional branches and related predictor misses ("Bc"/"Bcm"), executed indirect jumps and related misses of the jump address predictor ("Bi"/"Bim").

6.3.6. Cache simulation options

`--simulate-wb=<yes|no> [default:  no]`
Specify whether write-back behavior should be simulated, allowing to distinguish LL caches misses with and without write backs. The cache model of Cachegrind/Callgrind does not specify write-through vs. write-back behavior, and this also is not relevant for the number of generated miss counts. However, with explicit write-back simulation it can be decided whether a miss triggers not only the loading of a new cache line, but also if a write back of a dirty cache line had to take place before. The new dirty miss events are ILdmr, DLdmr, and DLdmw, for misses because of instruction read, data read, and data write, respectively. As they produce two memory transactions, they should account for a doubled time estimation in relation to a normal miss.

`--simulate-hwpref=<yes|no> [default:  no]`
Specify whether simulation of a hardware prefetcher should be added which is able to detect stream access in the second level cache by comparing accesses to separate to each page. As the simulation can not decide about any timing issues of prefetching, it is assumed that any hardware prefetch triggered succeeds before a real access is done. Thus, this gives a best-case scenario by covering all possible stream accesses.

`--cacheuse=<yes|no> [default:  no]`
Specify whether cache line use should be collected. For every cache line, from loading to it being evicted, the number of accesses as well as the number of actually used bytes is determined. This behavior is related to the code which triggered loading of the cache line. In contrast to miss counters, which shows the position where the symptoms of bad cache behavior (i.e. latencies) happens, the use counters try to pinpoint at the reason (i.e. the code with the bad access behavior). The new counters are defined in a way such that worse behavior results in higher cost. AcCost1 and AcCost2 are counters showing bad temporal locality for L1 and LL caches, respectively. This is done by summing up reciprocal values of the numbers of accesses of each cache line, multiplied by 1000 (as only integer costs are allowed). E.g. for a given source line with 5 read accesses, a value of 5000 AcCost means that for every access, a new cache line was loaded and directly evicted afterwards without further accesses. Similarly, SpLoss1/2 shows bad spatial locality for L1 and LL caches, respectively. It gives the *spatial loss* count of bytes which were loaded into cache but never accessed. It pinpoints at code accessing data in a way such that cache space is wasted. This hints at bad layout of data structures in memory. Assuming a cache line size of 64 bytes and 100 L1 misses for a given source line, the loading of 6400 bytes into L1 was triggered. If SpLoss1 shows a value of 3200 for this line, this means that half of the loaded data was never used, or using a better data layout, only half of the cache space would have been needed. Please note that for cache line use counters, it currently is not possible to provide meaningful inclusive costs. Therefore, inclusive cost of these counters should be ignored.

`--I1=<size>,<associativity>,<line size>`
Specify the size, associativity and line size of the level 1 instruction cache.

`--D1=<size>,<associativity>,<line size>`
Specify the size, associativity and line size of the level 1 data cache.

`--LL=<size>,<associativity>,<line size>`
Specify the size, associativity and line size of the last-level cache.

6.4. Callgrind Monitor Commands

The Callgrind tool provides monitor commands handled by the Valgrind gdbserver (see Monitor command handling by the Valgrind gdbserver).

- `dump [<dump_hint>]` requests to dump the profile data.

- `zero` requests to zero the profile data counters.

- `instrumentation [on|off]` requests to set (if parameter on/off is given) or get the current instrumentation state.

- `status` requests to print out some status information.

6.5. Callgrind specific client requests

Callgrind provides the following specific client requests in `callgrind.h`. See that file for the exact details of their arguments.

`CALLGRIND_DUMP_STATS`
Force generation of a profile dump at specified position in code, for the current thread only. Written counters will be reset to zero.

`CALLGRIND_DUMP_STATS_AT(string)`
Same as `CALLGRIND_DUMP_STATS`, but allows to specify a string to be able to distinguish profile dumps.

`CALLGRIND_ZERO_STATS`
Reset the profile counters for the current thread to zero.

`CALLGRIND_TOGGLE_COLLECT`
Toggle the collection state. This allows to ignore events with regard to profile counters. See also options `--collect-atstart` and `--toggle-collect`.

`CALLGRIND_START_INSTRUMENTATION`
Start full Callgrind instrumentation if not already enabled. When cache simulation is done, this will flush the simulated cache and lead to an artifical cache warmup phase afterwards with cache misses which would not have happened in reality. See also option `--instr-atstart`.

`CALLGRIND_STOP_INSTRUMENTATION`
Stop full Callgrind instrumentation if not already disabled. This flushes Valgrinds translation cache, and does no additional instrumentation afterwards: it effectivly will run at the same speed as Nulgrind, i.e. at minimal slowdown. Use this to speed up the Callgrind run for uninteresting code parts. Use `CALLGRIND_START_INSTRUMENTATION` to enable instrumentation again. See also option `--instr-atstart`.

6.6. callgrind_annotate Command-line Options

```
-h --help
```
Show summary of options.

```
--version
```
Show version of callgrind_annotate.

```
--show=A,B,C [default:  all]
```
Only show figures for events A,B,C.

```
--sort=A,B,C
```
Sort columns by events A,B,C [event column order].

```
--threshold=<0--100> [default:  99%]
```
Percentage of counts (of primary sort event) we are interested in.

```
--auto=<yes|no> [default:  no]
```
Annotate all source files containing functions that helped reach the event count threshold.

```
--context=N [default:  8]
```
Print N lines of context before and after annotated lines.

```
--inclusive=<yes|no> [default:  no]
```
Add subroutine costs to functions calls.

```
--tree=<none|caller|calling|both> [default:  none]
```
Print for each function their callers, the called functions or both.

```
-I, --include=<dir>
```
Add `dir` to the list of directories to search for source files.

6.7. callgrind_control Command-line Options

By default, callgrind_control acts on all programs run by the current user under Callgrind. It is possible to limit the actions to specified Callgrind runs by providing a list of pids or program names as argument. The default action is to give some brief information about the applications being run under Callgrind.

```
-h --help
```
Show a short description, usage, and summary of options.

```
--version
```
Show version of callgrind_control.

```
-l --long
```
Show also the working directory, in addition to the brief information given by default.

```
-s --stat
```
Show statistics information about active Callgrind runs.

```
-b --back
```
Show stack/back traces of each thread in active Callgrind runs. For each active function in the stack trace, also the number of invocations since program start (or last dump) is shown. This option can be combined with -e to show inclusive cost of active functions.

-e [A,B,...]   (default: all)
Show the current per-thread, exclusive cost values of event counters. If no explicit event names are given, figures for all event types which are collected in the given Callgrind run are shown. Otherwise, only figures for event types A, B, ... are shown. If this option is combined with -b, inclusive cost for the functions of each active stack frame is provided, too.

--dump[=<desc>]   (default: no description)
Request the dumping of profile information. Optionally, a description can be specified which is written into the dump as part of the information giving the reason which triggered the dump action. This can be used to distinguish multiple dumps.

-z --zero
Zero all event counters.

-k --kill
Force a Callgrind run to be terminated.

--instr=<on|off>
Switch instrumentation mode on or off. If a Callgrind run has instrumentation disabled, no simulation is done and no events are counted. This is useful to skip uninteresting program parts, as there is much less slowdown (same as with the Valgrind tool "none"). See also the Callgrind option --instr-atstart.

--vgdb-prefix=<prefix>
Specify the vgdb prefix to use by callgrind_control. callgrind_control internally uses vgdb to find and control the active Callgrind runs. If the --vgdb-prefix option was used for launching valgrind, then the same option must be given to callgrind_control.

7. Helgrind: a thread error detector

To use this tool, you must specify `--tool=helgrind` on the Valgrind command line.

7.1. Overview

Helgrind is a Valgrind tool for detecting synchronisation errors in C, C++ and Fortran programs that use the POSIX pthreads threading primitives.

The main abstractions in POSIX pthreads are: a set of threads sharing a common address space, thread creation, thread joining, thread exit, mutexes (locks), condition variables (inter-thread event notifications), reader-writer locks, spinlocks, semaphores and barriers.

Helgrind can detect three classes of errors, which are discussed in detail in the next three sections:

1. Misuses of the POSIX pthreads API.

2. Potential deadlocks arising from lock ordering problems.

3. Data races -- accessing memory without adequate locking or synchronisation.

Problems like these often result in unreproducible, timing-dependent crashes, deadlocks and other misbehaviour, and can be difficult to find by other means.

Helgrind is aware of all the pthread abstractions and tracks their effects as accurately as it can. On x86 and amd64 platforms, it understands and partially handles implicit locking arising from the use of the LOCK instruction prefix. On PowerPC/POWER and ARM platforms, it partially handles implicit locking arising from load-linked and store-conditional instruction pairs.

Helgrind works best when your application uses only the POSIX pthreads API. However, if you want to use custom threading primitives, you can describe their behaviour to Helgrind using the ANNOTATE_* macros defined in `helgrind.h`.

Following those is a section containing hints and tips on how to get the best out of Helgrind.

Then there is a summary of command-line options.

Finally, there is a brief summary of areas in which Helgrind could be improved.

7.2. Detected errors: Misuses of the POSIX pthreads API

Helgrind intercepts calls to many POSIX pthreads functions, and is therefore able to report on various common problems. Although these are unglamourous errors, their presence can lead to undefined program behaviour and hard-to-find bugs later on. The detected errors are:

- unlocking an invalid mutex

- unlocking a not-locked mutex

- unlocking a mutex held by a different thread

- destroying an invalid or a locked mutex

- recursively locking a non-recursive mutex

- deallocation of memory that contains a locked mutex

- passing mutex arguments to functions expecting reader-writer lock arguments, and vice versa

- when a POSIX pthread function fails with an error code that must be handled

- when a thread exits whilst still holding locked locks

- calling `pthread_cond_wait` with a not-locked mutex, an invalid mutex, or one locked by a different thread

- inconsistent bindings between condition variables and their associated mutexes

- invalid or duplicate initialisation of a pthread barrier

- initialisation of a pthread barrier on which threads are still waiting

- destruction of a pthread barrier object which was never initialised, or on which threads are still waiting

- waiting on an uninitialised pthread barrier

- for all of the pthreads functions that Helgrind intercepts, an error is reported, along with a stack trace, if the system threading library routine returns an error code, even if Helgrind itself detected no error

Checks pertaining to the validity of mutexes are generally also performed for reader-writer locks.

Various kinds of this-can't-possibly-happen events are also reported. These usually indicate bugs in the system threading library.

Reported errors always contain a primary stack trace indicating where the error was detected. They may also contain auxiliary stack traces giving additional information. In particular, most errors relating to mutexes will also tell you where that mutex first came to Helgrind's attention (the "was first observed at" part), so you have a chance of figuring out which mutex it is referring to. For example:

```
Thread #1 unlocked a not-locked lock at 0x7FEFFFA90
   at 0x4C2408D: pthread_mutex_unlock (hg_intercepts.c:492)
   by 0x40073A: nearly_main (tc09_bad_unlock.c:27)
   by 0x40079B: main (tc09_bad_unlock.c:50)
 Lock at 0x7FEFFFA90 was first observed
   at 0x4C25D01: pthread_mutex_init (hg_intercepts.c:326)
   by 0x40071F: nearly_main (tc09_bad_unlock.c:23)
   by 0x40079B: main (tc09_bad_unlock.c:50)
```

Helgrind has a way of summarising thread identities, as you see here with the text "Thread #1". This is so that it can speak about threads and sets of threads without overwhelming you with details. See below for more information on interpreting error messages.

7.3. Detected errors: Inconsistent Lock Orderings

In this section, and in general, to "acquire" a lock simply means to lock that lock, and to "release" a lock means to unlock it.

Helgrind monitors the order in which threads acquire locks. This allows it to detect potential deadlocks which could arise from the formation of cycles of locks. Detecting such inconsistencies is useful because, whilst actual deadlocks are fairly obvious, potential deadlocks may never be discovered during testing and could later lead to hard-to-diagnose in-service failures.

The simplest example of such a problem is as follows.

- Imagine some shared resource R, which, for whatever reason, is guarded by two locks, L1 and L2, which must both be held when R is accessed.

- Suppose a thread acquires L1, then L2, and proceeds to access R. The implication of this is that all threads in the program must acquire the two locks in the order first L1 then L2. Not doing so risks deadlock.

- The deadlock could happen if two threads -- call them T1 and T2 -- both want to access R. Suppose T1 acquires L1 first, and T2 acquires L2 first. Then T1 tries to acquire L2, and T2 tries to acquire L1, but those locks are both already held. So T1 and T2 become deadlocked.

Helgrind builds a directed graph indicating the order in which locks have been acquired in the past. When a thread acquires a new lock, the graph is updated, and then checked to see if it now contains a cycle. The presence of a cycle indicates a potential deadlock involving the locks in the cycle.

In general, Helgrind will choose two locks involved in the cycle and show you how their acquisition ordering has become inconsistent. It does this by showing the program points that first defined the ordering, and the program points which later violated it. Here is a simple example involving just two locks:

```
Thread #1: lock order "0x7FF0006D0 before 0x7FF0006A0" violated

Observed (incorrect) order is: acquisition of lock at 0x7FF0006A0
   at 0x4C2BC62: pthread_mutex_lock (hg_intercepts.c:494)
   by 0x400825: main (tc13_laog1.c:23)

 followed by a later acquisition of lock at 0x7FF0006D0
   at 0x4C2BC62: pthread_mutex_lock (hg_intercepts.c:494)
   by 0x400853: main (tc13_laog1.c:24)

Required order was established by acquisition of lock at 0x7FF0006D0
   at 0x4C2BC62: pthread_mutex_lock (hg_intercepts.c:494)
   by 0x40076D: main (tc13_laog1.c:17)

 followed by a later acquisition of lock at 0x7FF0006A0
   at 0x4C2BC62: pthread_mutex_lock (hg_intercepts.c:494)
   by 0x40079B: main (tc13_laog1.c:18)
```

When there are more than two locks in the cycle, the error is equally serious. However, at present Helgrind does not show the locks involved, sometimes because that information is not available, but also so as to avoid flooding you with information. For example, a naive implementation of the famous Dining Philosophers problem involves a cycle of five locks (see `helgrind/tests/tc14_laog_dinphils.c`). In this case Helgrind has detected that all 5 philosophers could simultaneously pick up their left fork and then deadlock whilst waiting to pick up their right forks.

```
Thread #6: lock order "0x80499A0 before 0x8049A00" violated

Observed (incorrect) order is: acquisition of lock at 0x8049A00
   at 0x40085BC: pthread_mutex_lock (hg_intercepts.c:495)
   by 0x80485B4: dine (tc14_laog_dinphils.c:18)
   by 0x400BDA4: mythread_wrapper (hg_intercepts.c:219)
   by 0x39B924: start_thread (pthread_create.c:297)
   by 0x2F107D: clone (clone.S:130)

 followed by a later acquisition of lock at 0x80499A0
   at 0x40085BC: pthread_mutex_lock (hg_intercepts.c:495)
   by 0x80485CD: dine (tc14_laog_dinphils.c:19)
   by 0x400BDA4: mythread_wrapper (hg_intercepts.c:219)
   by 0x39B924: start_thread (pthread_create.c:297)
   by 0x2F107D: clone (clone.S:130)
```

7.4. Detected errors: Data Races

A data race happens, or could happen, when two threads access a shared memory location without using suitable locks or other synchronisation to ensure single-threaded access. Such missing locking can cause obscure timing dependent bugs. Ensuring programs are race-free is one of the central difficulties of threaded programming.

Reliably detecting races is a difficult problem, and most of Helgrind's internals are devoted to dealing with it. We begin with a simple example.

7.4.1. A Simple Data Race

About the simplest possible example of a race is as follows. In this program, it is impossible to know what the value of var is at the end of the program. Is it 2 ? Or 1 ?

```
#include <pthread.h>

int var = 0;

void* child_fn ( void* arg ) {
  var++; /* Unprotected relative to parent */ /* this is line 6 */
  return NULL;
}

int main ( void ) {
  pthread_t child;
  pthread_create(&child, NULL, child_fn, NULL);
  var++; /* Unprotected relative to child */ /* this is line 13 */
  pthread_join(child, NULL);
  return 0;
}
```

The problem is there is nothing to stop var being updated simultaneously by both threads. A correct program would protect var with a lock of type pthread_mutex_t, which is acquired before each access and released afterwards. Helgrind's output for this program is:

```
Thread #1 is the program's root thread

Thread #2 was created
   at 0x511C08E: clone (in /lib64/libc-2.8.so)
   by 0x4E333A4: do_clone (in /lib64/libpthread-2.8.so)
   by 0x4E33A30: pthread_create@@GLIBC_2.2.5 (in /lib64/libpthread-2.8.so)
   by 0x4C299D4: pthread_create@* (hg_intercepts.c:214)
   by 0x400605: main (simple_race.c:12)

Possible data race during read of size 4 at 0x601038 by thread #1
Locks held: none
   at 0x400606: main (simple_race.c:13)

This conflicts with a previous write of size 4 by thread #2
Locks held: none
   at 0x4005DC: child_fn (simple_race.c:6)
   by 0x4C29AFF: mythread_wrapper (hg_intercepts.c:194)
   by 0x4E3403F: start_thread (in /lib64/libpthread-2.8.so)
   by 0x511C0CC: clone (in /lib64/libc-2.8.so)

Location 0x601038 is 0 bytes inside global var "var"
declared at simple_race.c:3
```

This is quite a lot of detail for an apparently simple error. The last clause is the main error message. It says there is a race as a result of a read of size 4 (bytes), at 0x601038, which is the address of var, happening in function main at line 13 in the program.

Two important parts of the message are:

- Helgrind shows two stack traces for the error, not one. By definition, a race involves two different threads accessing the same location in such a way that the result depends on the relative speeds of the two threads.

  The first stack trace follows the text "Possible data race during read of size 4 ..." and the second trace follows the text "This conflicts with a previous write of size 4 ...". Helgrind is usually able to show both accesses involved in a race. At least one of these will be a write (since two concurrent, unsynchronised reads are harmless), and they will of course be from different threads.

  By examining your program at the two locations, you should be able to get at least some idea of what the root cause of the problem is. For each location, Helgrind shows the set of locks held at the time of the access. This often makes it clear which thread, if any, failed to take a required lock. In this example neither thread holds a lock during the access.

- For races which occur on global or stack variables, Helgrind tries to identify the name and defining point of the variable. Hence the text `"Location 0x601038 is 0 bytes inside global var "var" declared at simple_race.c:3"`.

Showing names of stack and global variables carries no run-time overhead once Helgrind has your program up and running. However, it does require Helgrind to spend considerable extra time and memory at program startup to read the relevant debug info. Hence this facility is disabled by default. To enable it, you need to give the `--read-var-info=yes` option to Helgrind.

The following section explains Helgrind's race detection algorithm in more detail.

7.4.2. Helgrind's Race Detection Algorithm

Most programmers think about threaded programming in terms of the basic functionality provided by the threading library (POSIX Pthreads): thread creation, thread joining, locks, condition variables, semaphores and barriers.

The effect of using these functions is to impose constraints upon the order in which memory accesses can happen. This implied ordering is generally known as the "happens-before relation". Once you understand the happens-before relation, it is easy to see how Helgrind finds races in your code. Fortunately, the happens-before relation is itself easy to understand, and is by itself a useful tool for reasoning about the behaviour of parallel programs. We now introduce it using a simple example.

Consider first the following buggy program:

```
Parent thread:                  Child thread:

int var;

// create child thread
pthread_create(...)
var = 20;                           var = 10;
                                    exit

// wait for child
pthread_join(...)
printf("%d\n", var);
```

The parent thread creates a child. Both then write different values to some variable `var`, and the parent then waits for the child to exit.

What is the value of `var` at the end of the program, 10 or 20? We don't know. The program is considered buggy (it has a race) because the final value of `var` depends on the relative rates of progress of the parent and child threads. If the parent is fast and the child is slow, then the child's assignment may happen later, so the final value will be 10; and vice versa if the child is faster than the parent.

The relative rates of progress of parent vs child is not something the programmer can control, and will often change from run to run. It depends on factors such as the load on the machine, what else is running, the kernel's scheduling strategy, and many other factors.

The obvious fix is to use a lock to protect `var`. It is however instructive to consider a somewhat more abstract solution, which is to send a message from one thread to the other:

```
Parent thread:                    Child thread:

int var;

// create child thread
pthread_create(...)
var = 20;
// send message to child
                                  // wait for message to arrive
                                  var = 10;
                                  exit


// wait for child
pthread_join(...)
printf("%d\n", var);
```

Now the program reliably prints "10", regardless of the speed of the threads. Why? Because the child's assignment cannot happen until after it receives the message. And the message is not sent until after the parent's assignment is done.

The message transmission creates a "happens-before" dependency between the two assignments: `var = 20;` must now happen-before `var = 10;`. And so there is no longer a race on `var`.

Note that it's not significant that the parent sends a message to the child. Sending a message from the child (after its assignment) to the parent (before its assignment) would also fix the problem, causing the program to reliably print "20".

Helgrind's algorithm is (conceptually) very simple. It monitors all accesses to memory locations. If a location -- in this example, `var`, is accessed by two different threads, Helgrind checks to see if the two accesses are ordered by the happens-before relation. If so, that's fine; if not, it reports a race.

It is important to understand that the happens-before relation creates only a partial ordering, not a total ordering. An example of a total ordering is comparison of numbers: for any two numbers x and y, either x is less than, equal to, or greater than y. A partial ordering is like a total ordering, but it can also express the concept that two elements are neither equal, less or greater, but merely unordered with respect to each other.

In the fixed example above, we say that `var = 20;` "happens-before" `var = 10;`. But in the original version, they are unordered: we cannot say that either happens-before the other.

What does it mean to say that two accesses from different threads are ordered by the happens-before relation? It means that there is some chain of inter-thread synchronisation operations which cause those accesses to happen in a particular order, irrespective of the actual rates of progress of the individual threads. This is a required property for a reliable threaded program, which is why Helgrind checks for it.

The happens-before relations created by standard threading primitives are as follows:

- When a mutex is unlocked by thread T1 and later (or immediately) locked by thread T2, then the memory accesses in T1 prior to the unlock must happen-before those in T2 after it acquires the lock.

- The same idea applies to reader-writer locks, although with some complication so as to allow correct handling of reads vs writes.

• When a condition variable (CV) is signalled on by thread T1 and some other thread T2 is thereby released from a wait on the same CV, then the memory accesses in T1 prior to the signalling must happen-before those in T2 after it returns from the wait. If no thread was waiting on the CV then there is no effect.

• If instead T1 broadcasts on a CV, then all of the waiting threads, rather than just one of them, acquire a happens-before dependency on the broadcasting thread at the point it did the broadcast.

• A thread T2 that continues after completing sem_wait on a semaphore that thread T1 posts on, acquires a happens-before dependence on the posting thread, a bit like dependencies caused mutex unlock-lock pairs. However, since a semaphore can be posted on many times, it is unspecified from which of the post calls the wait call gets its happens-before dependency.

• For a group of threads T1 .. Tn which arrive at a barrier and then move on, each thread after the call has a happens-after dependency from all threads before the barrier.

• A newly-created child thread acquires an initial happens-after dependency on the point where its parent created it. That is, all memory accesses performed by the parent prior to creating the child are regarded as happening-before all the accesses of the child.

• Similarly, when an exiting thread is reaped via a call to pthread_join, once the call returns, the reaping thread acquires a happens-after dependency relative to all memory accesses made by the exiting thread.

In summary: Helgrind intercepts the above listed events, and builds a directed acyclic graph represented the collective happens-before dependencies. It also monitors all memory accesses.

If a location is accessed by two different threads, but Helgrind cannot find any path through the happens-before graph from one access to the other, then it reports a race.

There are a couple of caveats:

• Helgrind doesn't check for a race in the case where both accesses are reads. That would be silly, since concurrent reads are harmless.

• Two accesses are considered to be ordered by the happens-before dependency even through arbitrarily long chains of synchronisation events. For example, if T1 accesses some location L, and then pthread_cond_signals T2, which later pthread_cond_signals T3, which then accesses L, then a suitable happens-before dependency exists between the first and second accesses, even though it involves two different inter-thread synchronisation events.

7.4.3. Interpreting Race Error Messages

Helgrind's race detection algorithm collects a lot of information, and tries to present it in a helpful way when a race is detected. Here's an example:

```
Thread #2 was created
   at 0x511C08E: clone (in /lib64/libc-2.8.so)
   by 0x4E333A4: do_clone (in /lib64/libpthread-2.8.so)
   by 0x4E33A30: pthread_create@@GLIBC_2.2.5 (in /lib64/libpthread-2.8.so)
   by 0x4C299D4: pthread_create@* (hg_intercepts.c:214)
   by 0x4008F2: main (tc21_pthonce.c:86)

Thread #3 was created
   at 0x511C08E: clone (in /lib64/libc-2.8.so)
   by 0x4E333A4: do_clone (in /lib64/libpthread-2.8.so)
   by 0x4E33A30: pthread_create@@GLIBC_2.2.5 (in /lib64/libpthread-2.8.so)
   by 0x4C299D4: pthread_create@* (hg_intercepts.c:214)
   by 0x4008F2: main (tc21_pthonce.c:86)

Possible data race during read of size 4 at 0x601070 by thread #3
Locks held: none
   at 0x40087A: child (tc21_pthonce.c:74)
   by 0x4C29AFF: mythread_wrapper (hg_intercepts.c:194)
   by 0x4E3403F: start_thread (in /lib64/libpthread-2.8.so)
   by 0x511C0CC: clone (in /lib64/libc-2.8.so)

This conflicts with a previous write of size 4 by thread #2
Locks held: none
   at 0x400883: child (tc21_pthonce.c:74)
   by 0x4C29AFF: mythread_wrapper (hg_intercepts.c:194)
   by 0x4E3403F: start_thread (in /lib64/libpthread-2.8.so)
   by 0x511C0CC: clone (in /lib64/libc-2.8.so)

Location 0x601070 is 0 bytes inside local var "unprotected2"
declared at tc21_pthonce.c:51, in frame #0 of thread 3
```

Helgrind first announces the creation points of any threads referenced in the error message. This is so it can speak concisely about threads without repeatedly printing their creation point call stacks. Each thread is only ever announced once, the first time it appears in any Helgrind error message.

The main error message begins at the text "Possible data race during read". At the start is information you would expect to see -- address and size of the racing access, whether a read or a write, and the call stack at the point it was detected.

A second call stack is presented starting at the text "This conflicts with a previous write". This shows a previous access which also accessed the stated address, and which is believed to be racing against the access in the first call stack. Note that this second call stack is limited to a maximum of 8 entries to limit the memory usage.

Finally, Helgrind may attempt to give a description of the raced-on address in source level terms. In this example, it identifies it as a local variable, shows its name, declaration point, and in which frame (of the first call stack) it lives. Note that this information is only shown when --read-var-info=yes is specified on the command line. That's because reading the DWARF3 debug information in enough detail to capture variable type and location information makes Helgrind much slower at startup, and also requires considerable amounts of memory, for large programs.

Once you have your two call stacks, how do you find the root cause of the race?

The first thing to do is examine the source locations referred to by each call stack. They should both show an access to the same location, or variable.

Now figure out how how that location should have been made thread-safe:

- Perhaps the location was intended to be protected by a mutex? If so, you need to lock and unlock the mutex at both access points, even if one of the accesses is reported to be a read. Did you perhaps forget the locking at one or other of the accesses? To help you do this, Helgrind shows the set of locks held by each threads at the time they accessed the raced-on location.

- Alternatively, perhaps you intended to use a some other scheme to make it safe, such as signalling on a condition variable. In all such cases, try to find a synchronisation event (or a chain thereof) which separates the earlier-observed access (as shown in the second call stack) from the later-observed access (as shown in the first call stack). In other words, try to find evidence that the earlier access "happens-before" the later access. See the previous subsection for an explanation of the happens-before relation.

  The fact that Helgrind is reporting a race means it did not observe any happens-before relation between the two accesses. If Helgrind is working correctly, it should also be the case that you also cannot find any such relation, even on detailed inspection of the source code. Hopefully, though, your inspection of the code will show where the missing synchronisation operation(s) should have been.

7.5. Hints and Tips for Effective Use of Helgrind

Helgrind can be very helpful in finding and resolving threading-related problems. Like all sophisticated tools, it is most effective when you understand how to play to its strengths.

Helgrind will be less effective when you merely throw an existing threaded program at it and try to make sense of any reported errors. It will be more effective if you design threaded programs from the start in a way that helps Helgrind verify correctness. The same is true for finding memory errors with Memcheck, but applies more here, because thread checking is a harder problem. Consequently it is much easier to write a correct program for which Helgrind falsely reports (threading) errors than it is to write a correct program for which Memcheck falsely reports (memory) errors.

With that in mind, here are some tips, listed most important first, for getting reliable results and avoiding false errors. The first two are critical. Any violations of them will swamp you with huge numbers of false data-race errors.

1. Make sure your application, and all the libraries it uses, use the POSIX threading primitives. Helgrind needs to be able to see all events pertaining to thread creation, exit, locking and other synchronisation events. To do so it intercepts many POSIX pthreads functions.

   Do not roll your own threading primitives (mutexes, etc) from combinations of the Linux futex syscall, atomic counters, etc. These throw Helgrind's internal what's-going-on models way off course and will give bogus results.

   Also, do not reimplement existing POSIX abstractions using other POSIX abstractions. For example, don't build your own semaphore routines or reader-writer locks from POSIX mutexes and condition variables. Instead use POSIX reader-writer locks and semaphores directly, since Helgrind supports them directly.

   Helgrind directly supports the following POSIX threading abstractions: mutexes, reader-writer locks, condition variables (but see below), semaphores and barriers. Currently spinlocks are not supported, although they could be in future.

   At the time of writing, the following popular Linux packages are known to implement their own threading primitives:

- Qt version 4.X. Qt 3.X is harmless in that it only uses POSIX pthreads primitives. Unfortunately Qt 4.X has its
- Runtime support library for GNU OpenMP (part of GCC), at least for GCC versions 4.2 and 4.3. The GNU own implementation of mutexes (QMutex) and thread reaping. Helgrind 3.4.x contains direct support for Qt 4.X OpenMP runtime library (libgomp.so) constructs its own synchronisation primitives using combinations of threading, which is experimental but is believed to work fairly well. A side effect of supporting Qt 4 directly is atomic memory instructions and the futex syscall, which causes total chaos since in Helgrind since it cannot that Helgrind can be used to debug KDE4 applications. As this is an experimental feature, we would particularly "see" those. appreciate feedback from folks who have used Helgrind to successfully debug Qt 4 and/or KDE4 applications.

Fortunately, this can be solved using a configuration-time option (for GCC). Rebuild GCC from source, and configure using --disable-linux-futex. This makes libgomp.so use the standard POSIX threading primitives instead. Note that this was tested using GCC 4.2.3 and has not been re-tested using more recent GCC versions. We would appreciate hearing about any successes or failures with more recent versions.

If you must implement your own threading primitives, there are a set of client request macros in helgrind.h to help you describe your primitives to Helgrind. You should be able to mark up mutexes, condition variables, etc, without difficulty.

It is also possible to mark up the effects of thread-safe reference counting using the ANNOTATE_HAPPENS_BEFORE, ANNOTATE_HAPPENS_AFTER and ANNOTATE_HAPPENS_BEFORE_FORGET_ALL, macros. Thread-safe reference counting using an atomically incremented/decremented refcount variable causes Helgrind problems because a one-to-zero transition of the reference count means the accessing thread has exclusive ownership of the associated resource (normally, a C++ object) and can therefore access it (normally, to run its destructor) without locking. Helgrind doesn't understand this, and markup is essential to avoid false positives.

Here are recommended guidelines for marking up thread safe reference counting in C++. You only need to mark up your release methods -- the ones which decrement the reference count. Given a class like this:

```
class MyClass {
  unsigned int mRefCount;

  void Release ( void ) {
    unsigned int newCount = atomic_decrement(&mRefCount);
    if (newCount == 0) {
      delete this;
    }
  }
}
```

the release method should be marked up as follows:

```
  void Release ( void ) {
    unsigned int newCount = atomic_decrement(&mRefCount);
    if (newCount == 0) {
      ANNOTATE_HAPPENS_AFTER(&mRefCount);
      ANNOTATE_HAPPENS_BEFORE_FORGET_ALL(&mRefCount);
      delete this;
    } else {
      ANNOTATE_HAPPENS_BEFORE(&mRefCount);
    }
  }
```

There are a number of complex, mostly-theoretical objections to this scheme. From a theoretical standpoint it appears to be impossible to devise a markup scheme which is completely correct in the sense of guaranteeing to remove all false races. The proposed scheme however works well in practice.

2. Avoid memory recycling.   If you can't avoid it, you must use tell Helgrind what is going on via the
   VALGRIND_HG_CLEAN_MEMORY client request (in helgrind.h).

   Helgrind is aware of standard heap memory allocation and deallocation that occurs via malloc/free/new/delete
   and from entry and exit of stack frames.   In particular, when memory is deallocated via free, delete, or
   function exit, Helgrind considers that memory clean, so when it is eventually reallocated, its history is irrelevant.

   However, it is common practice to implement memory recycling schemes.   In these, memory to be freed is not
   handed to free/delete, but instead put into a pool of free buffers to be handed out again as required.   The
   problem is that Helgrind has no way to know that such memory is logically no longer in use, and its history is
   irrelevant.   Hence you must make that explicit, using the VALGRIND_HG_CLEAN_MEMORY client request to
   specify the relevant address ranges.   It's easiest to put these requests into the pool manager code, and use them
   either when memory is returned to the pool, or is allocated from it.

3. Avoid POSIX condition variables.   If you can, use POSIX semaphores (sem_t, sem_post, sem_wait) to do
   inter-thread event signalling. Semaphores with an initial value of zero are particularly useful for this.

   Helgrind only partially correctly handles POSIX condition variables.   This is because Helgrind can see inter-thread
   dependencies between a pthread_cond_wait call and a pthread_cond_signal/pthread_cond_broadcast
   call only if the waiting thread actually gets to the rendezvous first (so that it actually calls pthread_cond_wait).
   It can't see dependencies between the threads if the signaller arrives first.   In the latter case, POSIX guidelines
   imply that the associated boolean condition still provides an inter-thread synchronisation event, but one which is
   invisible to Helgrind.

   The result of Helgrind missing some inter-thread synchronisation events is to cause it to report false positives.

   The root cause of this synchronisation lossage is particularly hard to understand, so an example is helpful.   It was
   discussed at length by Arndt Muehlenfeld ("Runtime Race Detection in Multi-Threaded Programs", Dissertation,
   TU Graz, Austria).   The canonical POSIX-recommended usage scheme for condition variables is as follows:

```
b   is a Boolean condition, which is False most of the time
cv  is a condition variable
mx  is its associated mutex

Signaller:                      Waiter:

lock(mx)                        lock(mx)
b = True                        while (b == False)
signal(cv)                         wait(cv,mx)
unlock(mx)                      unlock(mx)
```

   Assume b is False most of the time.   If the waiter arrives at the rendezvous first, it enters its while-loop, waits for
   the signaller to signal, and eventually proceeds.   Helgrind sees the signal, notes the dependency, and all is well.

   If the signaller arrives first, b is set to true, and the signal disappears into nowhere.   When the waiter later arrives, it
   does not enter its while-loop and simply carries on.   But even in this case, the waiter code following the while-loop
   cannot execute until the signaller sets b to True.   Hence there is still the same inter-thread dependency, but this
   time it is through an arbitrary in-memory condition, and Helgrind cannot see it.

   By comparison, Helgrind's detection of inter-thread dependencies caused by semaphore operations is believed to
   be exactly correct.

   As far as I know, a solution to this problem that does not require source-level annotation of condition-variable wait
   loops is beyond the current state of the art.

4. Make sure you are using a supported Linux distribution. At present, Helgrind only properly supports glibc-2.3 or later. This in turn means we only support glibc's NPTL threading implementation. The old LinuxThreads implementation is not supported.

5. If your application is using thread local variables, helgrind might report false positive race conditions on these variables, despite being very probably race free. On Linux, you can use `--sim-hints=deactivate-pthread-stack-cache-via-hack` to avoid such false positive error messages (see --sim-hints).

6. Round up all finished threads using `pthread_join`. Avoid detaching threads: don't create threads in the detached state, and don't call `pthread_detach` on existing threads.

Using `pthread_join` to round up finished threads provides a clear synchronisation point that both Helgrind and programmers can see. If you don't call `pthread_join` on a thread, Helgrind has no way to know when it finishes, relative to any significant synchronisation points for other threads in the program. So it assumes that the thread lingers indefinitely and can potentially interfere indefinitely with the memory state of the program. It has every right to assume that -- after all, it might really be the case that, for scheduling reasons, the exiting thread did run very slowly in the last stages of its life.

7. Perform thread debugging (with Helgrind) and memory debugging (with Memcheck) together.

Helgrind tracks the state of memory in detail, and memory management bugs in the application are liable to cause confusion. In extreme cases, applications which do many invalid reads and writes (particularly to freed memory) have been known to crash Helgrind. So, ideally, you should make your application Memcheck-clean before using Helgrind.

It may be impossible to make your application Memcheck-clean unless you first remove threading bugs. In particular, it may be difficult to remove all reads and writes to freed memory in multithreaded C++ destructor sequences at program termination. So, ideally, you should make your application Helgrind-clean before using Memcheck.

Since this circularity is obviously unresolvable, at least bear in mind that Memcheck and Helgrind are to some extent complementary, and you may need to use them together.

8. POSIX requires that implementations of standard I/O (`printf`, `fprintf`, `fwrite`, `fread`, etc) are thread safe. Unfortunately GNU libc implements this by using internal locking primitives that Helgrind is unable to intercept. Consequently Helgrind generates many false race reports when you use these functions.

Helgrind attempts to hide these errors using the standard Valgrind error-suppression mechanism. So, at least for simple test cases, you don't see any. Nevertheless, some may slip through. Just something to be aware of.

9. Helgrind's error checks do not work properly inside the system threading library itself (`libpthread.so`), and it usually observes large numbers of (false) errors in there. Valgrind's suppression system then filters these out, so you should not see them.

If you see any race errors reported where `libpthread.so` or `ld.so` is the object associated with the innermost stack frame, please file a bug report at http://www.valgrind.org/.

7.6. Helgrind Command-line Options

The following end-user options are available:

`--free-is-write=no|yes [default: no]`
When enabled (not the default), Helgrind treats freeing of heap memory as if the memory was written immediately before the free. This exposes races where memory is referenced by one thread, and freed by another, but there is no observable synchronisation event to ensure that the reference happens before the free.

This functionality is new in Valgrind 3.7.0, and is regarded as experimental. It is not enabled by default because its interaction with custom memory allocators is not well understood at present. User feedback is welcomed.

`--track-lockorders=no|yes [default: yes]`
When enabled (the default), Helgrind performs lock order consistency checking. For some buggy programs, the large number of lock order errors reported can become annoying, particularly if you're only interested in race errors. You may therefore find it helpful to disable lock order checking.

`--history-level=none|approx|full [default: full]`
`--history-level=full` (the default) causes Helgrind collects enough information about "old" accesses that it can produce two stack traces in a race report -- both the stack trace for the current access, and the trace for the older, conflicting access. To limit memory usage, "old" accesses stack traces are limited to a maximum of 8 entries, even if `--num-callers` value is bigger.

Collecting such information is expensive in both speed and memory, particularly for programs that do many inter-thread synchronisation events (locks, unlocks, etc). Without such information, it is more difficult to track down the root causes of races. Nonetheless, you may not need it in situations where you just want to check for the presence or absence of races, for example, when doing regression testing of a previously race-free program.

`--history-level=none` is the opposite extreme. It causes Helgrind not to collect any information about previous accesses. This can be dramatically faster than `--history-level=full`.

`--history-level=approx` provides a compromise between these two extremes. It causes Helgrind to show a full trace for the later access, and approximate information regarding the earlier access. This approximate information consists of two stacks, and the earlier access is guaranteed to have occurred somewhere between program points denoted by the two stacks. This is not as useful as showing the exact stack for the previous access (as `--history-level=full` does), but it is better than nothing, and it is almost as fast as `--history-level=none`.

`--conflict-cache-size=N [default: 1000000]`
This flag only has any effect at `--history-level=full`.

Information about "old" conflicting accesses is stored in a cache of limited size, with LRU-style management. This is necessary because it isn't practical to store a stack trace for every single memory access made by the program. Historical information on not recently accessed locations is periodically discarded, to free up space in the cache.

This option controls the size of the cache, in terms of the number of different memory addresses for which conflicting access information is stored. If you find that Helgrind is showing race errors with only one stack instead of the expected two stacks, try increasing this value.

The minimum value is 10,000 and the maximum is 30,000,000 (thirty times the default value). Increasing the value by 1 increases Helgrind's memory requirement by very roughly 100 bytes, so the maximum value will easily eat up three extra gigabytes or so of memory.

`--check-stack-refs=no|yes [default: yes]`
By default Helgrind checks all data memory accesses made by your program. This flag enables you to skip checking for accesses to thread stacks (local variables). This can improve performance, but comes at the cost of missing races on stack-allocated data.

`--ignore-thread-creation=<yes|no> [default: no]`
Controls whether all activities during thread creation should be ignored. By default enabled only on Solaris. Solaris provides higher throughput, parallelism and scalability than other operating systems, at the cost of more fine-grained locking activity. This means for example that when a thread is created under glibc, just one big lock is used for all thread setup. Solaris libc uses several fine-grained locks and the creator thread resumes its activities as soon as possible, leaving for example stack and TLS setup sequence to the created thread. This situation confuses Helgrind as it assumes there is some false ordering in place between creator and created thread; and therefore many types of race conditions in the application would not be reported. To prevent such false ordering, this command line option is set to `yes` by default on Solaris. All activity (loads, stores, client requests) is therefore ignored during:

- pthread_create() call in the creator thread

- thread creation phase (stack and TLS setup) in the created thread

Also new memory allocated during thread creation is untracked, that is race reporting is suppressed there. DRD does the same thing implicitly. This is necessary because Solaris libc caches many objects and reuses them for different threads and that confuses Helgrind.

7.7. Helgrind Monitor Commands

The Helgrind tool provides monitor commands handled by Valgrind's built-in gdbserver (see Monitor command handling by the Valgrind gdbserver).

- `info locks [lock_addr]` shows the list of locks and their status. If `lock_addr` is given, only shows the lock located at this address.

  In the following example, helgrind knows about one lock. This lock is located at the guest address `ga 0x8049a20`. The lock kind is `rdwr` indicating a reader-writer lock. Other possible lock kinds are `nonRec` (simple mutex, non recursive) and `mbRec` (simple mutex, possibly recursive). The lock kind is then followed by the list of threads helding the lock. In the below example, `R1:thread #6 tid 3` indicates that the helgrind thread #6 has acquired (once, as the counter following the letter R is one) the lock in read mode. The helgrind thread nr is incremented for each started thread. The presence of 'tid 3' indicates that the thread #6 is has not exited yet and is the valgrind tid 3. If a thread has terminated, then this is indicated with 'tid (exited)'.

```
(gdb) monitor info locks
Lock ga 0x8049a20 {
  kind  rdwr
 { R1:thread #6 tid 3 }
}
(gdb)
```

  If you give the option `--read-var-info=yes`, then more information will be provided about the lock location, such as the global variable or the heap block that contains the lock:

```
Lock ga 0x8049a20 {
 Location 0x8049a20 is 0 bytes inside global var "s_rwlock"
 declared at rwlock_race.c:17
  kind  rdwr
 { R1:thread #3 tid 3 }
}
```

- `accesshistory` `<addr>` `[<len>]` shows the access history recorded for <len> (default 1) bytes starting at <addr>. For each recorded access that overlaps with the given range, `accesshistory` shows the operation type (read or write), the address and size read or written, the helgrind thread nr/valgrind tid number that did the operation and the locks held by the thread at the time of the operation. The oldest access is shown first, the most recent access is shown last.

In the following example, we see first a recorded write of 4 bytes by thread #7 that has modified the given 2 bytes range. The second recorded write is the most recent recorded write : thread #9 modified the same 2 bytes as part of a 4 bytes write operation. The list of locks held by each thread at the time of the write operation are also shown.

```
(gdb) monitor accesshistory 0x8049D8A 2
write of size 4 at 0x8049D88 by thread #7 tid 3
==6319== Locks held: 2, at address 0x8049D8C (and 1 that can't be shown)
==6319==    at 0x804865F: child_fn1 (locked_vs_unlocked2.c:29)
==6319==    by 0x400AE61: mythread_wrapper (hg_intercepts.c:234)
==6319==    by 0x39B924: start_thread (pthread_create.c:297)
==6319==    by 0x2F107D: clone (clone.S:130)

write of size 4 at 0x8049D88 by thread #9 tid 2
==6319== Locks held: 2, at addresses 0x8049DA4 0x8049DD4
==6319==    at 0x804877B: child_fn2 (locked_vs_unlocked2.c:45)
==6319==    by 0x400AE61: mythread_wrapper (hg_intercepts.c:234)
==6319==    by 0x39B924: start_thread (pthread_create.c:297)
==6319==    by 0x2F107D: clone (clone.S:130)
```

7.8. Helgrind Client Requests

The following client requests are defined in `helgrind.h`. See that file for exact details of their arguments.

- `VALGRIND_HG_CLEAN_MEMORY`

This makes Helgrind forget everything it knows about a specified memory range. This is particularly useful for memory allocators that wish to recycle memory.

- `ANNOTATE_HAPPENS_BEFORE`

- `ANNOTATE_HAPPENS_AFTER`

- `ANNOTATE_NEW_MEMORY`

- `ANNOTATE_RWLOCK_CREATE`

- `ANNOTATE_RWLOCK_DESTROY`

- `ANNOTATE_RWLOCK_ACQUIRED`

- `ANNOTATE_RWLOCK_RELEASED`

These are used to describe to Helgrind, the behaviour of custom (non-POSIX) synchronisation primitives, which it otherwise has no way to understand. See comments in `helgrind.h` for further documentation.

7.9. A To-Do List for Helgrind

The following is a list of loose ends which should be tidied up some time.

- For lock order errors, print the complete lock cycle, rather than only doing for size-2 cycles as at present.

- The conflicting access mechanism sometimes mysteriously fails to show the conflicting access' stack, even when provided with unbounded storage for conflicting access info. This should be investigated.

- Document races caused by GCC's thread-unsafe code generation for speculative stores. In the interim see `http://gcc.gnu.org/ml/gcc/2007-10/msg00266.html` and `http://lkml.org/lkml/2007/10/24`,

- Don't update the lock-order graph, and don't check for errors, when a "try"-style lock operation happens (e.g. `pthread_mutex_trylock`). Such calls do not add any real restrictions to the locking order, since they can always fail to acquire the lock, resulting in the caller going off and doing Plan B (presumably it will have a Plan B). Doing such checks could generate false lock-order errors and confuse users.

- Performance can be very poor. Slowdowns on the order of 100:1 are not unusual. There is limited scope for performance improvements.

8. DRD: a thread error detector

To use this tool, you must specify `--tool=drd` on the Valgrind command line.

8.1. Overview

DRD is a Valgrind tool for detecting errors in multithreaded C and C++ programs. The tool works for any program that uses the POSIX threading primitives or that uses threading concepts built on top of the POSIX threading primitives.

8.1.1. Multithreaded Programming Paradigms

There are two possible reasons for using multithreading in a program:

- To model concurrent activities. Assigning one thread to each activity can be a great simplification compared to multiplexing the states of multiple activities in a single thread. This is why most server software and embedded software is multithreaded.

- To use multiple CPU cores simultaneously for speeding up computations. This is why many High Performance Computing (HPC) applications are multithreaded.

Multithreaded programs can use one or more of the following programming paradigms. Which paradigm is appropriate depends e.g. on the application type. Some examples of multithreaded programming paradigms are:

- Locking. Data that is shared over threads is protected from concurrent accesses via locking. E.g. the POSIX threads library, the Qt library and the Boost.Thread library support this paradigm directly.

- Message passing. No data is shared between threads, but threads exchange data by passing messages to each other. Examples of implementations of the message passing paradigm are MPI and CORBA.

- Automatic parallelization. A compiler converts a sequential program into a multithreaded program. The original program may or may not contain parallelization hints. One example of such parallelization hints is the OpenMP standard. In this standard a set of directives are defined which tell a compiler how to parallelize a C, C++ or Fortran program. OpenMP is well suited for computational intensive applications. As an example, an open source image processing software package is using OpenMP to maximize performance on systems with multiple CPU cores. GCC supports the OpenMP standard from version 4.2.0 on.

- Software Transactional Memory (STM). Any data that is shared between threads is updated via transactions. After each transaction it is verified whether there were any conflicting transactions. If there were conflicts, the transaction is aborted, otherwise it is committed. This is a so-called optimistic approach. There is a prototype of the Intel C++ Compiler available that supports STM. Research about the addition of STM support to GCC is ongoing.

DRD supports any combination of multithreaded programming paradigms as long as the implementation of these paradigms is based on the POSIX threads primitives. DRD however does not support programs that use e.g. Linux' futexes directly. Attempts to analyze such programs with DRD will cause DRD to report many false positives.

8.1.2. POSIX Threads Programming Model

POSIX threads, also known as Pthreads, is the most widely available threading library on Unix systems.

The POSIX threads programming model is based on the following abstractions:

- A shared address space. All threads running within the same process share the same address space. All data, whether shared or not, is identified by its address.

- Regular load and store operations, which allow to read values from or to write values to the memory shared by all threads running in the same process.

- Atomic store and load-modify-store operations. While these are not mentioned in the POSIX threads standard, most microprocessors support atomic memory operations.

- Threads. Each thread represents a concurrent activity.

- Synchronization objects and operations on these synchronization objects. The following types of synchronization objects have been defined in the POSIX threads standard: mutexes, condition variables, semaphores, reader-writer synchronization objects, barriers and spinlocks.

Which source code statements generate which memory accesses depends on the *memory model* of the programming language being used. There is not yet a definitive memory model for the C and C++ languages. For a draft memory model, see also the document WG21/N2338: Concurrency memory model compiler consequences.

For more information about POSIX threads, see also the Single UNIX Specification version 3, also known as IEEE Std 1003.1.

8.1.3. Multithreaded Programming Problems

Depending on which multithreading paradigm is being used in a program, one or more of the following problems can occur:

- Data races. One or more threads access the same memory location without sufficient locking. Most but not all data races are programming errors and are the cause of subtle and hard-to-find bugs.

- Lock contention. One thread blocks the progress of one or more other threads by holding a lock too long.

- Improper use of the POSIX threads API. Most implementations of the POSIX threads API have been optimized for runtime speed. Such implementations will not complain on certain errors, e.g. when a mutex is being unlocked by another thread than the thread that obtained a lock on the mutex.

- Deadlock. A deadlock occurs when two or more threads wait for each other indefinitely.

- False sharing. If threads that run on different processor cores access different variables located in the same cache line frequently, this will slow down the involved threads a lot due to frequent exchange of cache lines.

Although the likelihood of the occurrence of data races can be reduced through a disciplined programming style, a tool for automatic detection of data races is a necessity when developing multithreaded software. DRD can detect these, as well as lock contention and improper use of the POSIX threads API.

8.1.4. Data Race Detection

The result of load and store operations performed by a multithreaded program depends on the order in which memory operations are performed. This order is determined by:

1. All memory operations performed by the same thread are performed in *program order*, that is, the order determined by the program source code and the results of previous load operations.

2. Synchronization operations determine certain ordering constraints on memory operations performed by different threads. These ordering constraints are called the *synchronization order*.

The combination of program order and synchronization order is called the *happens-before relationship*. This concept was first defined by S. Adve et al in the paper *Detecting data races on weak memory systems*, ACM SIGARCH Computer Architecture News, v.19 n.3, p.234-243, May 1991.

Two memory operations *conflict* if both operations are performed by different threads, refer to the same memory location and at least one of them is a store operation.

A multithreaded program is *data-race free* if all conflicting memory accesses are ordered by synchronization operations.

A well known way to ensure that a multithreaded program is data-race free is to ensure that a locking discipline is followed. It is e.g. possible to associate a mutex with each shared data item, and to hold a lock on the associated mutex while the shared data is accessed.

All programs that follow a locking discipline are data-race free, but not all data-race free programs follow a locking discipline. There exist multithreaded programs where access to shared data is arbitrated via condition variables, semaphores or barriers. As an example, a certain class of HPC applications consists of a sequence of computation steps separated in time by barriers, and where these barriers are the only means of synchronization. Although there are many conflicting memory accesses in such applications and although such applications do not make use mutexes, most of these applications do not contain data races.

There exist two different approaches for verifying the correctness of multithreaded programs at runtime. The approach of the so-called Eraser algorithm is to verify whether all shared memory accesses follow a consistent locking strategy. And the happens-before data race detectors verify directly whether all interthread memory accesses are ordered by synchronization operations. While the last approach is more complex to implement, and while it is more sensitive to OS scheduling, it is a general approach that works for all classes of multithreaded programs. An important advantage of happens-before data race detectors is that these do not report any false positives.

DRD is based on the happens-before algorithm.

8.2. Using DRD

8.2.1. DRD Command-line Options

The following command-line options are available for controlling the behavior of the DRD tool itself:

```
--check-stack-var=<yes|no> [default:  no]
```
Controls whether DRD detects data races on stack variables. Verifying stack variables is disabled by default because most programs do not share stack variables over threads.

```
--exclusive-threshold=<n> [default:  off]
```
Print an error message if any mutex or writer lock has been held longer than the time specified in milliseconds. This option enables the detection of lock contention.

```
--join-list-vol=<n> [default:  10]
```
Data races that occur between a statement at the end of one thread and another thread can be missed if memory access information is discarded immediately after a thread has been joined. This option allows to specify for how many joined threads memory access information should be retained.

`--first-race-only=<yes|no> [default:  no]`
Whether to report only the first data race that has been detected on a memory location or all data races that have been detected on a memory location.

`--free-is-write=<yes|no> [default:  no]`
Whether to report races between accessing memory and freeing memory. Enabling this option may cause DRD to run slightly slower. Notes:

• Don't enable this option when using custom memory allocators that use the `VG_USERREQ__MALLOCLIKE_BLOCK` and `VG_USERREQ__FREELIKE_BLOCK` because that would result in false positives.

• Don't enable this option when using reference-counted objects because that will result in false positives, even when that code has been annotated properly with `ANNOTATE_HAPPENS_BEFORE` and `ANNOTATE_HAPPENS_AFTER`. See e.g. the output of the following command for an example: `valgrind --tool=drd --free-is-write=yes drd/tests/annotate_smart_pointer`.

`--report-signal-unlocked=<yes|no> [default:  yes]`
Whether to report calls to `pthread_cond_signal` and `pthread_cond_broadcast` where the mutex associated with the signal through `pthread_cond_wait` or `pthread_cond_timed_wait` is not locked at the time the signal is sent. Sending a signal without holding a lock on the associated mutex is a common programming error which can cause subtle race conditions and unpredictable behavior. There exist some uncommon synchronization patterns however where it is safe to send a signal without holding a lock on the associated mutex.

`--segment-merging=<yes|no> [default:  yes]`
Controls segment merging. Segment merging is an algorithm to limit memory usage of the data race detection algorithm. Disabling segment merging may improve the accuracy of the so-called 'other segments' displayed in race reports but can also trigger an out of memory error.

`--segment-merging-interval=<n> [default:  10]`
Perform segment merging only after the specified number of new segments have been created. This is an advanced configuration option that allows to choose whether to minimize DRD's memory usage by choosing a low value or to let DRD run faster by choosing a slightly higher value. The optimal value for this parameter depends on the program being analyzed. The default value works well for most programs.

`--shared-threshold=<n> [default:  off]`
Print an error message if a reader lock has been held longer than the specified time (in milliseconds). This option enables the detection of lock contention.

`--show-confl-seg=<yes|no> [default:  yes]`
Show conflicting segments in race reports. Since this information can help to find the cause of a data race, this option is enabled by default. Disabling this option makes the output of DRD more compact.

`--show-stack-usage=<yes|no> [default:  no]`
Print stack usage at thread exit time. When a program creates a large number of threads it becomes important to limit the amount of virtual memory allocated for thread stacks. This option makes it possible to observe how much stack memory has been used by each thread of the client program. Note: the DRD tool itself allocates some temporary data on the client thread stack. The space necessary for this temporary data must be allocated by the client program when it allocates stack memory, but is not included in stack usage reported by DRD.

`--ignore-thread-creation=<yes|no> [default: no]`
Controls whether all activities during thread creation should be ignored. By default enabled only on Solaris. Solaris provides higher throughput, parallelism and scalability than other operating systems, at the cost of more fine-grained locking activity. This means for example that when a thread is created under glibc, just one big lock is used for all thread setup. Solaris libc uses several fine-grained locks and the creator thread resumes its activities as soon as possible, leaving for example stack and TLS setup sequence to the created thread. This situation confuses DRD as it assumes there is some false ordering in place between creator and created thread; and therefore many types of race conditions in the application would not be reported. To prevent such false ordering, this command line option is set to `yes` by default on Solaris. All activity (loads, stores, client requests) is therefore ignored during:

- pthread_create() call in the creator thread

- thread creation phase (stack and TLS setup) in the created thread

The following options are available for monitoring the behavior of the client program:

`--trace-addr=<address> [default: none]`
Trace all load and store activity for the specified address. This option may be specified more than once.

`--ptrace-addr=<address> [default: none]`
Trace all load and store activity for the specified address and keep doing that even after the memory at that address has been freed and reallocated.

`--trace-alloc=<yes|no> [default: no]`
Trace all memory allocations and deallocations. May produce a huge amount of output.

`--trace-barrier=<yes|no> [default: no]`
Trace all barrier activity.

`--trace-cond=<yes|no> [default: no]`
Trace all condition variable activity.

`--trace-fork-join=<yes|no> [default: no]`
Trace all thread creation and all thread termination events.

`--trace-hb=<yes|no> [default: no]`
Trace execution of the `ANNOTATE_HAPPENS_BEFORE()`, `ANNOTATE_HAPPENS_AFTER()` and `ANNOTATE_HAPPENS_DONE()` client requests.

`--trace-mutex=<yes|no> [default: no]`
Trace all mutex activity.

`--trace-rwlock=<yes|no> [default: no]`
Trace all reader-writer lock activity.

```
--trace-semaphore=<yes|no> [default:  no]
```
Trace all semaphore activity.

8.2.2. Detected Errors: Data Races

DRD prints a message every time it detects a data race. Please keep the following in mind when interpreting DRD's output:

- Every thread is assigned a *thread ID* by the DRD tool. A thread ID is a number. Thread ID's start at one and are never recycled.

- The term *segment* refers to a consecutive sequence of load, store and synchronization operations, all issued by the same thread. A segment always starts and ends at a synchronization operation. Data race analysis is performed between segments instead of between individual load and store operations because of performance reasons.

- There are always at least two memory accesses involved in a data race. Memory accesses involved in a data race are called *conflicting memory accesses*. DRD prints a report for each memory access that conflicts with a past memory access.

Below you can find an example of a message printed by DRD when it detects a data race:

```
$ valgrind --tool=drd --read-var-info=yes drd/tests/rwlock_race
...
==9466== Thread 3:
==9466== Conflicting load by thread 3 at 0x006020b8 size 4
==9466==    at 0x400B6C: thread_func (rwlock_race.c:29)
==9466==    by 0x4C291DF: vg_thread_wrapper (drd_pthread_intercepts.c:186)
==9466==    by 0x4E3403F: start_thread (in /lib64/libpthread-2.8.so)
==9466==    by 0x53250CC: clone (in /lib64/libc-2.8.so)
==9466== Location 0x6020b8 is 0 bytes inside local var "s_racy"
==9466== declared at rwlock_race.c:18, in frame #0 of thread 3
==9466== Other segment start (thread 2)
==9466==    at 0x4C2847D: pthread_rwlock_rdlock* (drd_pthread_intercepts.c:813)
==9466==    by 0x400B6B: thread_func (rwlock_race.c:28)
==9466==    by 0x4C291DF: vg_thread_wrapper (drd_pthread_intercepts.c:186)
==9466==    by 0x4E3403F: start_thread (in /lib64/libpthread-2.8.so)
==9466==    by 0x53250CC: clone (in /lib64/libc-2.8.so)
==9466== Other segment end (thread 2)
==9466==    at 0x4C28B54: pthread_rwlock_unlock* (drd_pthread_intercepts.c:912)
==9466==    by 0x400B84: thread_func (rwlock_race.c:30)
==9466==    by 0x4C291DF: vg_thread_wrapper (drd_pthread_intercepts.c:186)
==9466==    by 0x4E3403F: start_thread (in /lib64/libpthread-2.8.so)
==9466==    by 0x53250CC: clone (in /lib64/libc-2.8.so)
...
```

The above report has the following meaning:

- The number in the column on the left is the process ID of the process being analyzed by DRD.

- The first line ("Thread 3") tells you the thread ID for the thread in which context the data race has been detected.

- The next line tells which kind of operation was performed (load or store) and by which thread. On the same line the start address and the number of bytes involved in the conflicting access are also displayed.

- Next, the call stack of the conflicting access is displayed. If your program has been compiled with debug information (-g), this call stack will include file names and line numbers. The two bottommost frames in this call stack (clone and start_thread) show how the NPTL starts a thread. The third frame (vg_thread_wrapper) is added by DRD. The fourth frame (thread_func) is the first interesting line because it shows the thread entry point, that is the function that has been passed as the third argument to pthread_create.

- Next, the allocation context for the conflicting address is displayed. For dynamically allocated data the allocation call stack is shown. For static variables and stack variables the allocation context is only shown when the option --read-var-info=yes has been specified. Otherwise DRD will print Allocation context: unknown.

- A conflicting access involves at least two memory accesses. For one of these accesses an exact call stack is displayed, and for the other accesses an approximate call stack is displayed, namely the start and the end of the segments of the other accesses. This information can be interpreted as follows:

  1. Start at the bottom of both call stacks, and count the number stack frames with identical function name, file name and line number. In the above example the three bottommost frames are identical (clone, start_thread and vg_thread_wrapper).

  2. The next higher stack frame in both call stacks now tells you between in which source code region the other memory access happened. The above output tells that the other memory access involved in the data race happened between source code lines 28 and 30 in file rwlock_race.c.

8.2.3. Detected Errors: Lock Contention

Threads must be able to make progress without being blocked for too long by other threads. Sometimes a thread has to wait until a mutex or reader-writer synchronization object is unlocked by another thread. This is called *lock contention*.

Lock contention causes delays. Such delays should be as short as possible. The two command line options --exclusive-threshold=<n> and --shared-threshold=<n> make it possible to detect excessive lock contention by making DRD report any lock that has been held longer than the specified threshold. An example:

```
$ valgrind --tool=drd --exclusive-threshold=10 drd/tests/hold_lock -i 500
...
==10668== Acquired at:
==10668==    at 0x4C267C8: pthread_mutex_lock (drd_pthread_intercepts.c:395)
==10668==    by 0x400D92: main (hold_lock.c:51)
==10668== Lock on mutex 0x7fefffd50 was held during 503 ms (threshold: 10 ms).
==10668==    at 0x4C26ADA: pthread_mutex_unlock (drd_pthread_intercepts.c:441)
==10668==    by 0x400DB5: main (hold_lock.c:55)
...
```

The hold_lock test program holds a lock as long as specified by the -i (interval) argument. The DRD output reports that the lock acquired at line 51 in source file hold_lock.c and released at line 55 was held during 503 ms, while a threshold of 10 ms was specified to DRD.

8.2.4. Detected Errors: Misuse of the POSIX threads API

DRD is able to detect and report the following misuses of the POSIX threads API:

- Passing the address of one type of synchronization object (e.g. a mutex) to a POSIX API call that expects a pointer to another type of synchronization object (e.g. a condition variable).

- Attempts to unlock a mutex that has not been locked.

- Attempts to unlock a mutex that was locked by another thread.

- Attempts to lock a mutex of type `PTHREAD_MUTEX_NORMAL` or a spinlock recursively.

- Destruction or deallocation of a locked mutex.

- Sending a signal to a condition variable while no lock is held on the mutex associated with the condition variable.

- Calling `pthread_cond_wait` on a mutex that is not locked, that is locked by another thread or that has been locked recursively.

- Associating two different mutexes with a condition variable through `pthread_cond_wait`.

- Destruction or deallocation of a condition variable that is being waited upon.

- Destruction or deallocation of a locked reader-writer synchronization object.

- Attempts to unlock a reader-writer synchronization object that was not locked by the calling thread.

- Attempts to recursively lock a reader-writer synchronization object exclusively.

- Attempts to pass the address of a user-defined reader-writer synchronization object to a POSIX threads function.

- Attempts to pass the address of a POSIX reader-writer synchronization object to one of the annotations for user-defined reader-writer synchronization objects.

- Reinitialization of a mutex, condition variable, reader-writer lock, semaphore or barrier.

- Destruction or deallocation of a semaphore or barrier that is being waited upon.

- Missing synchronization between barrier wait and barrier destruction.

- Exiting a thread without first unlocking the spinlocks, mutexes or reader-writer synchronization objects that were locked by that thread.

- Passing an invalid thread ID to `pthread_join` or `pthread_cancel`.

8.2.5. Client Requests

Just as for other Valgrind tools it is possible to let a client program interact with the DRD tool through client requests. In addition to the client requests several macros have been defined that allow to use the client requests in a convenient way.

The interface between client programs and the DRD tool is defined in the header file `<valgrind/drd.h>`. The available macros and client requests are:

- The macro `DRD_GET_VALGRIND_THREADID` and the corresponding client request `VG_USERREQ__DRD_GET_VALGRI` Query the thread ID that has been assigned by the Valgrind core to the thread executing this client request. Valgrind's thread ID's start at one and are recycled in case a thread stops.

- The macro `DRD_GET_DRD_THREADID` and the corresponding client request `VG_USERREQ__DRD_GET_DRD_THREAD_` Query the thread ID that has been assigned by DRD to the thread executing this client request. These are the thread ID's reported by DRD in data race reports and in trace messages. DRD's thread ID's start at one and are never recycled.

- The macros `DRD_IGNORE_VAR(x)`, `ANNOTATE_TRACE_MEMORY(&x)` and the corresponding client request `VG_USERREQ__DRD_START_SUPPRESSION`. Some applications contain intentional races. There exist e.g. applications where the same value is assigned to a shared variable from two different threads. It may be more convenient to suppress such races than to solve these. This client request allows to suppress such races.

- The macro `DRD_STOP_IGNORING_VAR(x)` and the corresponding client request `VG_USERREQ__DRD_FINISH_SUPP` Tell DRD to no longer ignore data races for the address range that was suppressed either via the macro `DRD_IGNORE_VAR(x)` or via the client request `VG_USERREQ__DRD_START_SUPPRESSION`.

- The macro `DRD_TRACE_VAR(x)`. Trace all load and store activity for the address range starting at `&x` and occupying `sizeof(x)` bytes. When DRD reports a data race on a specified variable, and it's not immediately clear which source code statements triggered the conflicting accesses, it can be very helpful to trace all activity on the offending memory location.

- The macro `DRD_STOP_TRACING_VAR(x)`. Stop tracing load and store activity for the address range starting at `&x` and occupying `sizeof(x)` bytes.

- The macro `ANNOTATE_TRACE_MEMORY(&x)`. Trace all load and store activity that touches at least the single byte at the address `&x`.

- The client request `VG_USERREQ__DRD_START_TRACE_ADDR`, which allows to trace all load and store activity for the specified address range.

- The client request `VG_USERREQ__DRD_STOP_TRACE_ADDR`. Do no longer trace load and store activity for the specified address range.

- The macro `ANNOTATE_HAPPENS_BEFORE(addr)` tells DRD to insert a mark. Insert this macro just after an access to the variable at the specified address has been performed.

- The macro `ANNOTATE_HAPPENS_AFTER(addr)` tells DRD that the next access to the variable at the specified address should be considered to have happened after the access just before the latest `ANNOTATE_HAPPENS_BEFORE(addr)` annotation that references the same variable. The purpose of these two macros is to tell DRD about the order of inter-thread memory accesses implemented via atomic memory operations. See also `drd/tests/annotate_smart_pointer.cpp` for an example.

- The macro `ANNOTATE_RWLOCK_CREATE(rwlock)` tells DRD that the object at address `rwlock` is a reader-writer synchronization object that is not a `pthread_rwlock_t` synchronization object. See also `drd/tests/annotate_rwlock.c` for an example.

- The macro `ANNOTATE_RWLOCK_DESTROY(rwlock)` tells DRD that the reader-writer synchronization object at address `rwlock` has been destroyed.

- The macro `ANNOTATE_WRITERLOCK_ACQUIRED(rwlock)` tells DRD that a writer lock has been acquired on the reader-writer synchronization object at address `rwlock`.

- The macro `ANNOTATE_READERLOCK_ACQUIRED(rwlock)` tells DRD that a reader lock has been acquired on the reader-writer synchronization object at address `rwlock`.

- The macro ANNOTATE_RWLOCK_ACQUIRED(rwlock, is_w) tells DRD that a writer lock (when is_w != 0) or that a reader lock (when is_w == 0) has been acquired on the reader-writer synchronization object at address rwlock.

- The macro ANNOTATE_WRITERLOCK_RELEASED(rwlock) tells DRD that a writer lock has been released on the reader-writer synchronization object at address rwlock.

- The macro ANNOTATE_READERLOCK_RELEASED(rwlock) tells DRD that a reader lock has been released on the reader-writer synchronization object at address rwlock.

- The macro ANNOTATE_RWLOCK_RELEASED(rwlock, is_w) tells DRD that a writer lock (when is_w != 0) or that a reader lock (when is_w == 0) has been released on the reader-writer synchronization object at address rwlock.

- The macro ANNOTATE_BARRIER_INIT(barrier, count, reinitialization_allowed) tells DRD that a new barrier object at the address barrier has been initialized, that count threads participate in each barrier and also whether or not barrier reinitialization without intervening destruction should be reported as an error. See also drd/tests/annotate_barrier.c for an example.

- The macro ANNOTATE_BARRIER_DESTROY(barrier) tells DRD that a barrier object is about to be destroyed.

- The macro ANNOTATE_BARRIER_WAIT_BEFORE(barrier) tells DRD that waiting for a barrier will start.

- The macro ANNOTATE_BARRIER_WAIT_AFTER(barrier) tells DRD that waiting for a barrier has finished.

- The macro ANNOTATE_BENIGN_RACE_SIZED(addr, size, descr) tells DRD that any races detected on the specified address are benign and hence should not be reported. The descr argument is ignored but can be used to document why data races on addr are benign.

- The macro ANNOTATE_BENIGN_RACE_STATIC(var, descr) tells DRD that any races detected on the specified static variable are benign and hence should not be reported. The descr argument is ignored but can be used to document why data races on var are benign. Note: this macro can only be used in C++ programs and not in C programs.

- The macro ANNOTATE_IGNORE_READS_BEGIN tells DRD to ignore all memory loads performed by the current thread.

- The macro ANNOTATE_IGNORE_READS_END tells DRD to stop ignoring the memory loads performed by the current thread.

- The macro ANNOTATE_IGNORE_WRITES_BEGIN tells DRD to ignore all memory stores performed by the current thread.

- The macro ANNOTATE_IGNORE_WRITES_END tells DRD to stop ignoring the memory stores performed by the current thread.

- The macro ANNOTATE_IGNORE_READS_AND_WRITES_BEGIN tells DRD to ignore all memory accesses performed by the current thread.

- The macro ANNOTATE_IGNORE_READS_AND_WRITES_END tells DRD to stop ignoring the memory accesses performed by the current thread.

- The macro ANNOTATE_NEW_MEMORY(addr, size) tells DRD that the specified memory range has been allocated by a custom memory allocator in the client program and that the client program will start using this memory range.

- The macro ANNOTATE_THREAD_NAME(name) tells DRD to associate the specified name with the current thread and to include this name in the error messages printed by DRD.

- The macros VALGRIND_MALLOCLIKE_BLOCK and VALGRIND_FREELIKE_BLOCK from the Valgrind core are implemented; they are described in The Client Request mechanism.

Note: if you compiled Valgrind yourself, the header file <valgrind/drd.h> will have been installed in the directory /usr/include by the command make install. If you obtained Valgrind by installing it as a package however, you will probably have to install another package with a name like valgrind-devel before Valgrind's header files are available.

8.2.6. Debugging C++11 Programs

If you want to use the C++11 class std::thread you will need to do the following to annotate the std::shared_ptr<> objects used in the implementation of that class:

- Add the following code at the start of a common header or at the start of each source file, before any C++ header files are included:

```
#include <valgrind/drd.h>
#define _GLIBCXX_SYNCHRONIZATION_HAPPENS_BEFORE(addr) ANNOTATE_HAPPENS_BEFORE(addr)

#define _GLIBCXX_SYNCHRONIZATION_HAPPENS_AFTER(addr)  ANNOTATE_HAPPENS_AFTER(addr)
```

- Download the gcc source code and from source file libstdc++-v3/src/c++11/thread.cc copy the implementation of the execute_native_thread_routine() and std::thread::_M_start_thread() functions into a source file that is linked with your application. Make sure that also in this source file the _GLIBCXX_SYNCHRONIZATION_HAPPENS_*() macros are defined properly.

For more information, see also *The GNU C++ Library Manual, Debugging Support* (http://gcc.gnu.org/onlinedocs/libstdc++/ma

8.2.7. Debugging GNOME Programs

GNOME applications use the threading primitives provided by the glib and gthread libraries. These libraries are built on top of POSIX threads, and hence are directly supported by DRD. Please keep in mind that you have to call g_thread_init before creating any threads, or DRD will report several data races on glib functions. See also the GLib Reference Manual for more information about g_thread_init.

One of the many facilities provided by the glib library is a block allocator, called g_slice. You have to disable this block allocator when using DRD by adding the following to the shell environment variables: G_SLICE=always-malloc. See also the GLib Reference Manual for more information.

8.2.8. Debugging Boost.Thread Programs

The Boost.Thread library is the threading library included with the cross-platform Boost Libraries. This threading library is an early implementation of the upcoming C++0x threading library.

Applications that use the Boost.Thread library should run fine under DRD.

More information about Boost.Thread can be found here:

- Anthony Williams, Boost.Thread Library Documentation, Boost website, 2007.

- Anthony Williams, What's New in Boost Threads?, Recent changes to the Boost Thread library, Dr. Dobbs Magazine, October 2008.

8.2.9. Debugging OpenMP Programs

OpenMP stands for *Open Multi-Processing*. The OpenMP standard consists of a set of compiler directives for C, C++ and Fortran programs that allows a compiler to transform a sequential program into a parallel program. OpenMP is well suited for HPC applications and allows to work at a higher level compared to direct use of the POSIX threads API. While OpenMP ensures that the POSIX API is used correctly, OpenMP programs can still contain data races. So it definitely makes sense to verify OpenMP programs with a thread checking tool.

DRD supports OpenMP shared-memory programs generated by GCC. GCC supports OpenMP since version 4.2.0. GCC's runtime support for OpenMP programs is provided by a library called `libgomp`. The synchronization primitives implemented in this library use Linux' futex system call directly, unless the library has been configured with the `--disable-linux-futex` option. DRD only supports libgomp libraries that have been configured with this option and in which symbol information is present. For most Linux distributions this means that you will have to recompile GCC. See also the script `drd/scripts/download-and-build-gcc` in the Valgrind source tree for an example of how to compile GCC. You will also have to make sure that the newly compiled `libgomp.so` library is loaded when OpenMP programs are started. This is possible by adding a line similar to the following to your shell startup script:

```
export LD_LIBRARY_PATH=~/gcc-4.4.0/lib64:~/gcc-4.4.0/lib:
```

As an example, the test OpenMP test program `drd/tests/omp_matinv` triggers a data race when the option -r has been specified on the command line. The data race is triggered by the following code:

```
#pragma omp parallel for private(j)
for (j = 0; j < rows; j++)
{
  if (i != j)
  {
    const elem_t factor = a[j * cols + i];
    for (k = 0; k < cols; k++)
    {
      a[j * cols + k] -= a[i * cols + k] * factor;
    }
  }
}
```

The above code is racy because the variable k has not been declared private. DRD will print the following error message for the above code:

```
$ valgrind --tool=drd --check-stack-var=yes --read-var-info=yes drd/tests/omp_matinv 3
...
Conflicting store by thread 1/1 at 0x7fefffbc4 size 4
   at 0x4014A0: gj.omp_fn.0 (omp_matinv.c:203)
   by 0x401211: gj (omp_matinv.c:159)
   by 0x40166A: invert_matrix (omp_matinv.c:238)
   by 0x4019B4: main (omp_matinv.c:316)
Location 0x7fefffbc4 is 0 bytes inside local var "k"
declared at omp_matinv.c:160, in frame #0 of thread 1
...
```

In the above output the function name `gj.omp_fn.0` has been generated by GCC from the function name `gj`. The allocation context information shows that the data race has been caused by modifying the variable `k`.

Note: for GCC versions before 4.4.0, no allocation context information is shown. With these GCC versions the most usable information in the above output is the source file name and the line number where the data race has been detected (`omp_matinv.c:203`).

For more information about OpenMP, see also openmp.org.

8.2.10. DRD and Custom Memory Allocators

DRD tracks all memory allocation events that happen via the standard memory allocation and deallocation functions (`malloc`, `free`, `new` and `delete`), via entry and exit of stack frames or that have been annotated with Valgrind's memory pool client requests. DRD uses memory allocation and deallocation information for two purposes:

- To know where the scope ends of POSIX objects that have not been destroyed explicitly. It is e.g. not required by the POSIX threads standard to call `pthread_mutex_destroy` before freeing the memory in which a mutex object resides.

- To know where the scope of variables ends. If e.g. heap memory has been used by one thread, that thread frees that memory, and another thread allocates and starts using that memory, no data races must be reported for that memory.

It is essential for correct operation of DRD that the tool knows about memory allocation and deallocation events. When analyzing a client program with DRD that uses a custom memory allocator, either instrument the custom memory allocator with the `VALGRIND_MALLOCLIKE_BLOCK` and `VALGRIND_FREELIKE_BLOCK` macros or disable the custom memory allocator.

As an example, the GNU libstdc++ library can be configured to use standard memory allocation functions instead of memory pools by setting the environment variable `GLIBCXX_FORCE_NEW`. For more information, see also the libstdc++ manual.

8.2.11. DRD Versus Memcheck

It is essential for correct operation of DRD that there are no memory errors such as dangling pointers in the client program. Which means that it is a good idea to make sure that your program is Memcheck-clean before you analyze it with DRD. It is possible however that some of the Memcheck reports are caused by data races. In this case it makes sense to run DRD before Memcheck.

So which tool should be run first? In case both DRD and Memcheck complain about a program, a possible approach is to run both tools alternatingly and to fix as many errors as possible after each run of each tool until none of the two tools prints any more error messages.

8.2.12. Resource Requirements

The requirements of DRD with regard to heap and stack memory and the effect on the execution time of client programs are as follows:

- When running a program under DRD with default DRD options, between 1.1 and 3.6 times more memory will be needed compared to a native run of the client program. More memory will be needed if loading debug information has been enabled (`--read-var-info=yes`).

- DRD allocates some of its temporary data structures on the stack of the client program threads. This amount of data is limited to 1 - 2 KB. Make sure that thread stacks are sufficiently large.

- Most applications will run between 20 and 50 times slower under DRD than a native single-threaded run. The slowdown will be most noticeable for applications which perform frequent mutex lock / unlock operations.

8.2.13. Hints and Tips for Effective Use of DRD

The following information may be helpful when using DRD:

- Make sure that debug information is present in the executable being analyzed, such that DRD can print function name and line number information in stack traces. Most compilers can be told to include debug information via compiler option `-g`.

- Compile with option `-O1` instead of `-O0`. This will reduce the amount of generated code, may reduce the amount of debug info and will speed up DRD's processing of the client program. For more information, see also Getting started.

- If DRD reports any errors on libraries that are part of your Linux distribution like e.g. `libc.so` or `libstdc++.so`, installing the debug packages for these libraries will make the output of DRD a lot more detailed.

- When using C++, do not send output from more than one thread to `std::cout`. Doing so would not only generate multiple data race reports, it could also result in output from several threads getting mixed up. Either use `printf` or do the following:

  1. Derive a class from `std::ostreambuf` and let that class send output line by line to `stdout`. This will avoid that individual lines of text produced by different threads get mixed up.

  2. Create one instance of `std::ostream` for each thread. This makes stream formatting settings thread-local. Pass a per-thread instance of the class derived from `std::ostreambuf` to the constructor of each instance.

  3. Let each thread send its output to its own instance of `std::ostream` instead of `std::cout`.

8.3. Using the POSIX Threads API Effectively

8.3.1. Mutex types

The Single UNIX Specification version two defines the following four mutex types (see also the documentation of `pthread_mutexattr_settype`):

normal, which means that no error checking is performed, and that the mutex is non-recursive.

- *error checking*, which means that the mutex is non-recursive and that error checking is performed.

- *recursive*, which means that a mutex may be locked recursively.

- *default*, which means that error checking behavior is undefined, and that the behavior for recursive locking is also undefined. Or: portable code must neither trigger error conditions through the Pthreads API nor attempt to lock a mutex of default type recursively.

In complex applications it is not always clear from beforehand which mutex will be locked recursively and which mutex will not be locked recursively. Attempts lock a non-recursive mutex recursively will result in race conditions that are very hard to find without a thread checking tool. So either use the error checking mutex type and consistently check the return value of Pthread API mutex calls, or use the recursive mutex type.

8.3.2. Condition variables

A condition variable allows one thread to wake up one or more other threads. Condition variables are often used to notify one or more threads about state changes of shared data. Unfortunately it is very easy to introduce race conditions by using condition variables as the only means of state information propagation. A better approach is to let threads poll for changes of a state variable that is protected by a mutex, and to use condition variables only as a thread wakeup mechanism. See also the source file `drd/tests/monitor_example.cpp` for an example of how to implement this concept in C++. The monitor concept used in this example is a well known and very useful concept -- see also Wikipedia for more information about the monitor concept.

8.3.3. pthread_cond_timedwait and timeouts

Historically the function `pthread_cond_timedwait` only allowed the specification of an absolute timeout, that is a timeout independent of the time when this function was called. However, almost every call to this function expresses a relative timeout. This typically happens by passing the sum of `clock_gettime(CLOCK_REALTIME)` and a relative timeout as the third argument. This approach is incorrect since forward or backward clock adjustments by e.g. ntpd will affect the timeout. A more reliable approach is as follows:

- When initializing a condition variable through `pthread_cond_init`, specify that the timeout of `pthread_cond_timedwait` will use the clock `CLOCK_MONOTONIC` instead of `CLOCK_REALTIME`. You can do this via `pthread_condattr_setclock(..., CLOCK_MONOTONIC)`.

- When calling `pthread_cond_timedwait`, pass the sum of `clock_gettime(CLOCK_MONOTONIC)` and a relative timeout as the third argument.

See also `drd/tests/monitor_example.cpp` for an example.

8.4. Limitations

DRD currently has the following limitations:

- DRD, just like Memcheck, will refuse to start on Linux distributions where all symbol information has been removed from `ld.so`. This is e.g. the case for the PPC editions of openSUSE and Gentoo. You will have to install the glibc debuginfo package on these platforms before you can use DRD. See also openSUSE bug 396197 and Gentoo bug 214065.

- With gcc 4.4.3 and before, DRD may report data races on the C++ class `std::string` in a multithreaded program. This is a know `libstdc++` issue -- see also GCC bug 40518 for more information.

- If you compile the DRD source code yourself, you need GCC 3.0 or later. GCC 2.95 is not supported.

- Of the two POSIX threads implementations for Linux, only the NPTL (Native POSIX Thread Library) is supported. The older LinuxThreads library is not supported.

8.5. Feedback

If you have any comments, suggestions, feedback or bug reports about DRD, feel free to either post a message on the Valgrind users mailing list or to file a bug report. See also http://www.valgrind.org/ for more information.

9. Massif: a heap profiler

To use this tool, you must specify `--tool=massif` on the Valgrind command line.

9.1. Overview

Massif is a heap profiler. It measures how much heap memory your program uses. This includes both the useful space, and the extra bytes allocated for book-keeping and alignment purposes. It can also measure the size of your program's stack(s), although it does not do so by default.

Heap profiling can help you reduce the amount of memory your program uses. On modern machines with virtual memory, this provides the following benefits:

- It can speed up your program -- a smaller program will interact better with your machine's caches and avoid paging.

- If your program uses lots of memory, it will reduce the chance that it exhausts your machine's swap space.

Also, there are certain space leaks that aren't detected by traditional leak-checkers, such as Memcheck's. That's because the memory isn't ever actually lost -- a pointer remains to it -- but it's not in use. Programs that have leaks like this can unnecessarily increase the amount of memory they are using over time. Massif can help identify these leaks.

Importantly, Massif tells you not only how much heap memory your program is using, it also gives very detailed information that indicates which parts of your program are responsible for allocating the heap memory.

9.2. Using Massif and ms_print

First off, as for the other Valgrind tools, you should compile with debugging info (the `-g` option). It shouldn't matter much what optimisation level you compile your program with, as this is unlikely to affect the heap memory usage.

Then, you need to run Massif itself to gather the profiling information, and then run ms_print to present it in a readable way.

9.2.1. An Example Program

An example will make things clear. Consider the following C program (annotated with line numbers) which allocates a number of different blocks on the heap.

```
1      #include <stdlib.h>
2
3      void g(void)
4      {
5         malloc(4000);
6      }
7
8      void f(void)
9      {
10        malloc(2000);
11        g();
12     }
13
14     int main(void)
15     {
16        int i;
17        int* a[10];
18
19        for (i = 0; i < 10; i++) {
20           a[i] = malloc(1000);
21        }
22
23        f();
24
25        g();
26
27        for (i = 0; i < 10; i++) {
28           free(a[i]);
29        }
30
31        return 0;
32     }
```

9.2.2. Running Massif

To gather heap profiling information about the program prog, type:

```
valgrind --tool=massif prog
```

The program will execute (slowly). Upon completion, no summary statistics are printed to Valgrind's commentary; all of Massif's profiling data is written to a file. By default, this file is called massif.out.<pid>, where <pid> is the process ID, although this filename can be changed with the --massif-out-file option.

9.2.3. Running ms_print

To see the information gathered by Massif in an easy-to-read form, use ms_print.   If the output file's name is massif.out.12345, type:

```
ms_print massif.out.12345
```

ms_print will produce (a) a graph showing the memory consumption over the program's execution, and (b) detailed information about the responsible allocation sites at various points in the program, including the point of peak memory allocation. The use of a separate script for presenting the results is deliberate: it separates the data gathering from its presentation, and means that new methods of presenting the data can be added in the future.

9.2.4. The Output Preamble

After running this program under Massif, the first part of ms_print's output contains a preamble which just states how the program, Massif and ms_print were each invoked:

```
--------------------------------------------------------------------------------

Command:            example
Massif arguments:   (none)
ms_print arguments: massif.out.12797
--------------------------------------------------------------------------------
```

9.2.5. The Output Graph

The next part is the graph that shows how memory consumption occurred as the program executed:

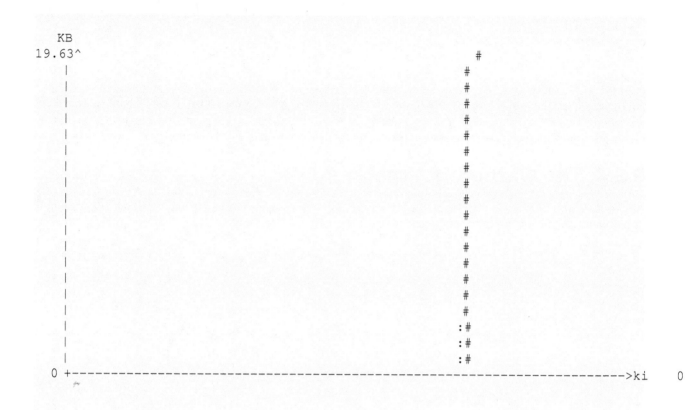

```
    KB
19.63^                                                          #
     |                                                          #
     |                                                          #
     |                                                          #
     |                                                          #
     |                                                          #
     |                                                          #
     |                                                          #
     |                                                          #
     |                                                          #
     |                                                          #
     |                                                          #
     |                                                          #
     |                                                          #
     |                                                          #
     |                                                          #
     |                                                          #
     |                                                        : #
     |                                                        : #
     |                                                        : #
   0 +----------------------------------------------------------------->ki     0
```

Number of snapshots: 25
Detailed snapshots: [9, 14 (peak), 24]

Why is most of the graph empty, with only a couple of bars at the very end? By default, Massif uses "instructions executed" as the unit of time. For very short-run programs such as the example, most of the executed instructions involve the loading and dynamic linking of the program. The execution of main (and thus the heap allocations) only occur at the very end. For a short-running program like this, we can use the --time-unit=B option to specify that we want the time unit to instead be the number of bytes allocated/deallocated on the heap and stack(s).

If we re-run the program under Massif with this option, and then re-run ms_print, we get this more useful graph:

```
19.63^                                        ###
     |                                        #
     |                                        #   ::
     |                                        #   : :::
     |                             :::::::::::#   : :  ::
     |                             :           #   : :  : ::
     |                             :           #   : :  : : :::
     |                             :           #   : :  : : :  ::
     |                   :::::::::::::          #   : :  : : :  : :::
     |                   :           :          #   : :  : : :  : : ::
     |                 :::::          :          #   : :  : : :  : : :  : ::
     |              @@@:    :          :          #   : :  : : :  : :  : : @
     |            ::@   :   :          :          #   : :  : : :  : :  : : @
     |          ::::: @   :   :             :          #   : :  : : :  : :  : : @
     |          ::: : @   :   :             :          #   : :  : : :  : :  : : @
     |          ::: :   @  :   :             :          #   : :  : : :  : :  : : @
     |        :::::: :  : @   :   :             :          #   : :  : : :  : :  : : @
     |        ::: : :  : : @   :   :             :          #   : :  : : :  : :  : : @
     |       ::::: :  : : :  : @   :   :             :          #   : :  : : :  : :  : : @
     |       :::  : :  : : :  : @   :   :             :          #   : :  : : :  : :  : : @
   0 +-------------------------------------------------------------------------->KB     0
```

Number of snapshots: 25
Detailed snapshots: [9, 14 (peak), 24]

The size of the graph can be changed with ms_print's --x and --y options. Each vertical bar represents a snapshot, i.e. a measurement of the memory usage at a certain point in time. If the next snapshot is more than one column away, a horizontal line of characters is drawn from the top of the snapshot to just before the next snapshot column. The text at the bottom show that 25 snapshots were taken for this program, which is one per heap allocation/deallocation, plus a couple of extras. Massif starts by taking snapshots for every heap allocation/deallocation, but as a program runs for longer, it takes snapshots less frequently. It also discards older snapshots as the program goes on; when it reaches the maximum number of snapshots (100 by default, although changeable with the --max-snapshots option) half of them are deleted. This means that a reasonable number of snapshots are always maintained.

Most snapshots are *normal*, and only basic information is recorded for them. Normal snapshots are represented in the graph by bars consisting of ':' characters.

Some snapshots are *detailed*. Information about where allocations happened are recorded for these snapshots, as we will see shortly. Detailed snapshots are represented in the graph by bars consisting of '@' characters. The text at the bottom show that 3 detailed snapshots were taken for this program (snapshots 9, 14 and 24). By default, every 10th snapshot is detailed, although this can be changed via the --detailed-freq option.

Finally, there is at most one *peak* snapshot. The peak snapshot is a detailed snapshot, and records the point where memory consumption was greatest. The peak snapshot is represented in the graph by a bar consisting of '#' characters. The text at the bottom shows that snapshot 14 was the peak.

Massif's determination of when the peak occurred can be wrong, for two reasons.

- Peak snapshots are only ever taken after a deallocation happens. This avoids lots of unnecessary peak snapshot recordings (imagine what happens if your program allocates a lot of heap blocks in succession, hitting a new peak every time). But it means that if your program never deallocates any blocks, no peak will be recorded. It also means that if your program does deallocate blocks but later allocates to a higher peak without subsequently deallocating, the reported peak will be too low.

- Even with this behaviour, recording the peak accurately is slow. So by default Massif records a peak whose size is within 1% of the size of the true peak. This inaccuracy in the peak measurement can be changed with the `--peak-inaccuracy` option.

The following graph is from an execution of Konqueror, the KDE web browser. It shows what graphs for larger programs look like.

```
    MB
3.952^                                                              #
    |                                                             @#:
    |                                                            :@@#:
    |                                                          @@::::@@#:
    |                                                          @ :: :@@#::
    |                                                        @@@ :: :@@#::
    |                                                      @@:@@@ :: :@@#::
    |                                                    :::@ :@@@ :: :@@#::
    |                                                    : :@ :@@@ :: :@@#::
    |                                                  :@: :@ :@@@ :: :@@#::
    |                                                @@:@: :@ :@@@ :: :@@#:::
    |               :          ::                  ::@@:@: :@ :@@@ :: :@@#:::
    |            :@@:       :::::  ::::@@@:::@@:@: :@ :@@@ :: :@@#:::
    |          ::::@@:      ::: :::::::: @  :::@@:@: :@ :@@@ :: :@@#:::
    |          @: ::@@:     ::: :::::::: @  :::@@:@: :@ :@@@ :: :@@#:::
    |          @: ::@@:     ::: :::::::: @  :::@@:@: :@ :@@@ :: :@@#:::
    |          @: ::@@:::::::: :::::::: @  :::@@:@: :@ :@@@ :: :@@#:::
    |          ::@@@: ::@@:: ::: ::::::: @  :::@@:@: :@ :@@@ :: :@@#:::
    |          :::::@ @: ::@@:: ::: ::::::: @  :::@@:@: :@ :@@@ :: :@@#:::
    |          @@:::::@ @: ::@@:: ::: ::::::: @  :::@@:@: :@ :@@@ :: :@@#:::
  0 +-------------------------------------------------------------------------->Mi


    0                                                             626.4
```

```
Number of snapshots: 63
 Detailed snapshots: [3, 4, 10, 11, 15, 16, 29, 33, 34, 36, 39, 41,
              42, 43, 44, 49, 50, 51, 53, 55, 56, 57 (peak)]
```

Note that the larger size units are KB, MB, GB, etc. As is typical for memory measurements, these are based on a multiplier of 1024, rather than the standard SI multiplier of 1000. Strictly speaking, they should be written KiB, MiB, GiB, etc.

9.2.6. The Snapshot Details

Returning to our example, the graph is followed by the detailed information for each snapshot. The first nine snapshots are normal, so only a small amount of information is recorded for each one:

```
-------------------------------------------------------------------------
 n        time(B)       total(B)   useful-heap(B) extra-heap(B)    stacks(B)
-------------------------------------------------------------------------

 0          0             0            0            0            0
 1        1,008         1,008        1,000          8            0
 2        2,016         2,016        2,000         16            0
 3        3,024         3,024        3,000         24            0
 4        4,032         4,032        4,000         32            0
 5        5,040         5,040        5,000         40            0
 6        6,048         6,048        6,000         48            0
 7        7,056         7,056        7,000         56            0
 8        8,064         8,064        8,000         64            0
```

Each normal snapshot records several things.

• Its number.

• The time it was taken. In this case, the time unit is bytes, due to the use of --time-unit=B.

• The total memory consumption at that point.

• The number of useful heap bytes allocated at that point. This reflects the number of bytes asked for by the program.

• The number of extra heap bytes allocated at that point. This reflects the number of bytes allocated in excess of what the program asked for. There are two sources of extra heap bytes.

First, every heap block has administrative bytes associated with it. The exact number of administrative bytes depends on the details of the allocator. By default Massif assumes 8 bytes per block, as can be seen from the example, but this number can be changed via the --heap-admin option.

Second, allocators often round up the number of bytes asked for to a larger number, usually 8 or 16. This is required to ensure that elements within the block are suitably aligned. If N bytes are asked for, Massif rounds N up to the nearest multiple of the value specified by the --alignment option.

• The size of the stack(s). By default, stack profiling is off as it slows Massif down greatly. Therefore, the stack column is zero in the example. Stack profiling can be turned on with the --stacks=yes option.

The next snapshot is detailed. As well as the basic counts, it gives an allocation tree which indicates exactly which pieces of code were responsible for allocating heap memory:

```
9         9,072           9,072           9,000           72              0
99.21% (9,000B) (heap allocation functions) malloc/new/new[], --alloc-fns, etc.
->99.21% (9,000B) 0x804841A: main (example.c:20)
```

The allocation tree can be read from the top down. The first line indicates all heap allocation functions such as malloc and C++ new. All heap allocations go through these functions, and so all 9,000 useful bytes (which is 99.21% of all allocated bytes) go through them. But how were malloc and new called? At this point, every allocation so far has been due to line 20 inside main, hence the second line in the tree. The -> indicates that main (line 20) called malloc.

Let's see what the subsequent output shows happened next:

```
-----------------------------------------------------------------------------

    n       time(B)         total(B)    useful-heap(B) extra-heap(B)     stacks(B)
-----------------------------------------------------------------------------

   10       10,080          10,080          10,000          80              0
   11       12,088          12,088          12,000          88              0
   12       16,096          16,096          16,000          96              0
   13       20,104          20,104          20,000         104              0
   14       20,104          20,104          20,000         104              0
99.48% (20,000B) (heap allocation functions) malloc/new/new[], --alloc-fns, etc.
->49.74% (10,000B) 0x804841A: main (example.c:20)
|
->39.79% (8,000B) 0x80483C2: g (example.c:5)
| ->19.90% (4,000B) 0x80483E2: f (example.c:11)
| | ->19.90% (4,000B) 0x8048431: main (example.c:23)
| |
| ->19.90% (4,000B) 0x8048436: main (example.c:25)
|
->09.95% (2,000B) 0x80483DA: f (example.c:10)
  ->09.95% (2,000B) 0x8048431: main (example.c:23)
```

The first four snapshots are similar to the previous ones. But then the global allocation peak is reached, and a detailed snapshot (number 14) is taken. Its allocation tree shows that 20,000B of useful heap memory has been allocated, and the lines and arrows indicate that this is from three different code locations: line 20, which is responsible for 10,000B (49.74%); line 5, which is responsible for 8,000B (39.79%); and line 10, which is responsible for 2,000B (9.95%).

We can then drill down further in the allocation tree. For example, of the 8,000B asked for by line 5, half of it was due to a call from line 11, and half was due to a call from line 25.

In short, Massif collates the stack trace of every single allocation point in the program into a single tree, which gives a complete picture at a particular point in time of how and why all heap memory was allocated.

Note that the tree entries correspond not to functions, but to individual code locations. For example, if function A calls malloc, and function B calls A twice, once on line 10 and once on line 11, then the two calls will result in two distinct stack traces in the tree. In contrast, if B calls A repeatedly from line 15 (e.g. due to a loop), then each of those calls will be represented by the same stack trace in the tree.

Note also that each tree entry with children in the example satisfies an invariant: the entry's size is equal to the sum of its children's sizes. For example, the first entry has size 20,000B, and its children have sizes 10,000B, 8,000B, and 2,000B. In general, this invariant almost always holds. However, in rare circumstances stack traces can be malformed, in which case a stack trace can be a sub-trace of another stack trace. This means that some entries in the tree may not satisfy the invariant -- the entry's size will be greater than the sum of its children's sizes. This is not a big problem, but could make the results confusing. Massif can sometimes detect when this happens; if it does, it issues a warning:

```
Warning: Malformed stack trace detected.  In Massif's output,
        the size of an entry's child entries may not sum up
        to the entry's size as they normally do.
```

However, Massif does not detect and warn about every such occurrence. Fortunately, malformed stack traces are rare in practice.

Returning now to ms_print's output, the final part is similar:

```
--------------------------------------------------------------------------------
 n       time(B)       total(B)    useful-heap(B) extra-heap(B)     stacks(B)
--------------------------------------------------------------------------------

 15      21,112        19,096        19,000          96              0
 16      22,120        18,088        18,000          88              0
 17      23,128        17,080        17,000          80              0
 18      24,136        16,072        16,000          72              0
 19      25,144        15,064        15,000          64              0
 20      26,152        14,056        14,000          56              0
 21      27,160        13,048        13,000          48              0
 22      28,168        12,040        12,000          40              0
 23      29,176        11,032        11,000          32              0
 24      30,184        10,024        10,000          24              0
99.76% (10,000B) (heap allocation functions) malloc/new/new[], --alloc-fns, etc.
->79.81% (8,000B) 0x80483C2: g (example.c:5)
| ->39.90% (4,000B) 0x80483E2: f (example.c:11)
| | ->39.90% (4,000B) 0x8048431: main (example.c:23)
| |
| ->39.90% (4,000B) 0x8048436: main (example.c:25)
|
->19.95% (2,000B) 0x80483DA: f (example.c:10)
| ->19.95% (2,000B) 0x8048431: main (example.c:23)
|
->00.00% (0B) in 1+ places, all below ms_print's threshold (01.00%)
```

The final detailed snapshot shows how the heap looked at termination. The 00.00% entry represents the code locations for which memory was allocated and then freed (line 20 in this case, the memory for which was freed on line 28). However, no code location details are given for this entry; by default, Massif only records the details for code locations responsible for more than 1% of useful memory bytes, and ms_print likewise only prints the details for code locations responsible for more than 1%. The entries that do not meet this threshold are aggregated. This avoids filling up the output with large numbers of unimportant entries. The thresholds can be changed with the `--threshold` option that both Massif and ms_print support.

9.2.7. Forking Programs

If your program forks, the child will inherit all the profiling data that has been gathered for the parent.

If the output file format string (controlled by `--massif-out-file`) does not contain `%p`, then the outputs from the parent and child will be intermingled in a single output file, which will almost certainly make it unreadable by ms_print.

9.2.8. Measuring All Memory in a Process

It is worth emphasising that by default Massif measures only heap memory, i.e. memory allocated with `malloc`, `calloc`, `realloc`, `memalign`, `new`, `new[]`, and a few other, similar functions. (And it can optionally measure stack memory, of course.) This means it does *not* directly measure memory allocated with lower-level system calls such as `mmap`, `mremap`, and `brk`.

Heap allocation functions such as `malloc` are built on top of these system calls. For example, when needed, an allocator will typically call `mmap` to allocate a large chunk of memory, and then hand over pieces of that memory chunk to the client program in response to calls to `malloc` et al. Massif directly measures only these higher-level `malloc` et al calls, not the lower-level system calls.

Furthermore, a client program may use these lower-level system calls directly to allocate memory. By default, Massif does not measure these. Nor does it measure the size of code, data and BSS segments. Therefore, the numbers reported by Massif may be significantly smaller than those reported by tools such as `top` that measure a program's total size in memory.

However, if you wish to measure *all* the memory used by your program, you can use the `--pages-as-heap=yes`. When this option is enabled, Massif's normal heap block profiling is replaced by lower-level page profiling. Every page allocated via `mmap` and similar system calls is treated as a distinct block. This means that code, data and BSS segments are all measured, as they are just memory pages. Even the stack is measured, since it is ultimately allocated (and extended when necessary) via `mmap`; for this reason `--stacks=yes` is not allowed in conjunction with `--pages-as-heap=yes`.

After `--pages-as-heap=yes` is used, ms_print's output is mostly unchanged. One difference is that the start of each detailed snapshot says:

```
(page allocation syscalls) mmap/mremap/brk, --alloc-fns, etc.
```

instead of the usual
:

```
(heap allocation functions) malloc/new/new[], --alloc-fns, etc.
```

The stack traces in the output may be more difficult to read, and interpreting them may require some detailed understanding of the lower levels of a program like the memory allocators. But for some programs having the full information about memory usage can be very useful.

9.2.9. Acting on Massif's Information

Massif's information is generally fairly easy to act upon. The obvious place to start looking is the peak snapshot.

It can also be useful to look at the overall shape of the graph, to see if memory usage climbs and falls as you expect; spikes in the graph might be worth investigating.

The detailed snapshots can get quite large. It is worth viewing them in a very wide window. It's also a good idea to view them with a text editor. That makes it easy to scroll up and down while keeping the cursor in a particular column, which makes following the allocation chains easier.

9.3. Massif Command-line Options

Massif-specific command-line options are:

`--heap=<yes|no> [default: yes]`
Specifies whether heap profiling should be done.

`--heap-admin=<size> [default: 8]`
If heap profiling is enabled, gives the number of administrative bytes per block to use. This should be an estimate of the average, since it may vary. For example, the allocator used by glibc on Linux requires somewhere between 4 to 15 bytes per block, depending on various factors. That allocator also requires admin space for freed blocks, but Massif cannot account for this.

`--stacks=<yes|no> [default: no]`
Specifies whether stack profiling should be done. This option slows Massif down greatly, and so is off by default. Note that Massif assumes that the main stack has size zero at start-up. This is not true, but doing otherwise accurately is difficult. Furthermore, starting at zero better indicates the size of the part of the main stack that a user program actually has control over.

`--pages-as-heap=<yes|no> [default: no]`
Tells Massif to profile memory at the page level rather than at the malloc'd block level. See above for details.

`--depth=<number> [default: 30]`
Maximum depth of the allocation trees recorded for detailed snapshots. Increasing it will make Massif run somewhat more slowly, use more memory, and produce bigger output files.

`--alloc-fn=<name>`
Functions specified with this option will be treated as though they were a heap allocation function such as `malloc`. This is useful for functions that are wrappers to `malloc` or `new`, which can fill up the allocation trees with uninteresting information. This option can be specified multiple times on the command line, to name multiple functions.

Note that the named function will only be treated this way if it is the top entry in a stack trace, or just below another function treated this way. For example, if you have a function `malloc1` that wraps `malloc`, and `malloc2` that wraps `malloc1`, just specifying `--alloc-fn=malloc2` will have no effect. You need to specify `--alloc-fn=malloc1` as well. This is a little inconvenient, but the reason is that checking for allocation functions is slow, and it saves a lot of time if Massif can stop looking through the stack trace entries as soon as it finds one that doesn't match rather than having to continue through all the entries.

Note that C++ names are demangled. Note also that overloaded C++ names must be written in full. Single quotes may be necessary to prevent the shell from breaking them up. For example:

`--alloc-fn='operator new(unsigned, std::nothrow_t const&)'`

`--ignore-fn=<name>`
Any direct heap allocation (i.e. a call to `malloc`, `new`, etc, or a call to a function named by an `--alloc-fn` option) that occurs in a function specified by this option will be ignored. This is mostly useful for testing purposes. This option can be specified multiple times on the command line, to name multiple functions.

Any `realloc` of an ignored block will also be ignored, even if the `realloc` call does not occur in an ignored function. This avoids the possibility of negative heap sizes if ignored blocks are shrunk with `realloc`.

The rules for writing C++ function names are the same as for `--alloc-fn` above.

`--threshold=<m.n>` `[default: 1.0]`
The significance threshold for heap allocations, as a percentage of total memory size. Allocation tree entries that account for less than this will be aggregated. Note that this should be specified in tandem with ms_print's option of the same name.

`--peak-inaccuracy=<m.n>` `[default: 1.0]`
Massif does not necessarily record the actual global memory allocation peak; by default it records a peak only when the global memory allocation size exceeds the previous peak by at least 1.0%. This is because there can be many local allocation peaks along the way, and doing a detailed snapshot for every one would be expensive and wasteful, as all but one of them will be later discarded. This inaccuracy can be changed (even to 0.0%) via this option, but Massif will run drastically slower as the number approaches zero.

`--time-unit=<i|ms|B>` `[default: i]`
The time unit used for the profiling. There are three possibilities: instructions executed (i), which is good for most cases; real (wallclock) time (ms, i.e. milliseconds), which is sometimes useful; and bytes allocated/deallocated on the heap and/or stack (B), which is useful for very short-run programs, and for testing purposes, because it is the most reproducible across different machines.

`--detailed-freq=<n>` `[default: 10]`
Frequency of detailed snapshots. With `--detailed-freq=1`, every snapshot is detailed.

`--max-snapshots=<n>` `[default: 100]`
The maximum number of snapshots recorded. If set to N, for all programs except very short-running ones, the final number of snapshots will be between N/2 and N.

`--massif-out-file=<file>` [default: massif.out.%p]
Write the profile data to `file` rather than to the default output file, `massif.out.<pid>`. The %p and %q format specifiers can be used to embed the process ID and/or the contents of an environment variable in the name, as is the case for the core option `--log-file`.

9.4. Massif Monitor Commands

The Massif tool provides monitor commands handled by the Valgrind gdbserver (see Monitor command handling by the Valgrind gdbserver).

- `snapshot [<filename>]` requests to take a snapshot and save it in the given <filename> (default massif.vgdb.out).

- `detailed_snapshot [<filename>]` requests to take a detailed snapshot and save it in the given <filename> (default massif.vgdb.out).

- `all_snapshots [<filename>]` requests to take all captured snapshots so far and save them in the given <filename> (default massif.vgdb.out).

9.5. Massif Client Requests

Massif does not have a `massif.h` file, but it does implement two of the core client requests: `VALGRIND_MALLOCLIKE_BLOCK` and `VALGRIND_FREELIKE_BLOCK`; they are described in The Client Request mechanism.

9.6. ms_print Command-line Options

ms_print's options are:

`-h --help`
Show the help message.

`--version`
Show the version number.

`--threshold=<m.n>` [default: 1.0]
Same as Massif's `--threshold` option, but applied after profiling rather than during.

`--x=<4..1000>` [default: 72]
Width of the graph, in columns.

`--y=<4..1000>` [default: 20]
Height of the graph, in rows.

9.7. Massif's Output File Format

Massif's file format is plain text (i.e. not binary) and deliberately easy to read for both humans and machines. Nonetheless, the exact format is not described here. This is because the format is currently very Massif-specific. In the future we hope to make the format more general, and thus suitable for possible use with other tools. Once this has been done, the format will be documented here.

10. DHAT: a dynamic heap analysis tool

To use this tool, you must specify `--tool=exp-dhat` on the Valgrind command line.

10.1. Overview

DHAT is a tool for examining how programs use their heap allocations.

It tracks the allocated blocks, and inspects every memory access to find which block, if any, it is to. The following data is collected and presented per allocation point (allocation stack):

- Total allocation (number of bytes and blocks)

- maximum live volume (number of bytes and blocks)

- average block lifetime (number of instructions between allocation and freeing)

- average number of reads and writes to each byte in the block ("access ratios")

- for allocation points which always allocate blocks only of one size, and that size is 4096 bytes or less: counts showing how often each byte offset inside the block is accessed.

Using these statistics it is possible to identify allocation points with the following characteristics:

- potential process-lifetime leaks: blocks allocated by the point just accumulate, and are freed only at the end of the run.

- excessive turnover: points which chew through a lot of heap, even if it is not held onto for very long

- excessively transient: points which allocate very short lived blocks

- useless or underused allocations: blocks which are allocated but not completely filled in, or are filled in but not subsequently read.

- blocks with inefficient layout -- areas never accessed, or with hot fields scattered throughout the block.

As with the Massif heap profiler, DHAT measures program progress by counting instructions, and so presents all age/time related figures as instruction counts. This sounds a little odd at first, but it makes runs repeatable in a way which is not possible if CPU time is used.

10.2. Understanding DHAT's output

DHAT provides a lot of useful information on dynamic heap usage. Most of the art of using it is in interpretation of the resulting numbers. That is best illustrated via a set of examples.

10.2.1. Interpreting the max-live, tot-alloc and deaths fields

10.2.1.1. A simple example

```
======== SUMMARY STATISTICS ========

guest_insns:  1,045,339,534
[...]
max-live:     63,490 in 984 blocks
tot-alloc:    1,904,700 in 29,520 blocks (avg size 64.52)
deaths:       29,520, at avg age 22,227,424
acc-ratios:   6.37 rd, 1.14 wr  (12,141,526 b-read, 2,174,460 b-written)
   at 0x4C275B8: malloc (vg_replace_malloc.c:236)
   by 0x40350E: tcc_malloc (tinycc.c:6712)
   by 0x404580: tok_alloc_new (tinycc.c:7151)
   by 0x40870A: next_nomacro1 (tinycc.c:9305)
```

Over the entire run of the program, this stack (allocation point) allocated 29,520 blocks in total, containing 1,904,700 bytes in total. By looking at the max-live data, we see that not many blocks were simultaneously live, though: at the peak, there were 63,490 allocated bytes in 984 blocks. This tells us that the program is steadily freeing such blocks as it runs, rather than hanging on to all of them until the end and freeing them all.

The deaths entry tells us that 29,520 blocks allocated by this stack died (were freed) during the run of the program. Since 29,520 is also the number of blocks allocated in total, that tells us that all allocated blocks were freed by the end of the program.

It also tells us that the average age at death was 22,227,424 instructions. From the summary statistics we see that the program ran for 1,045,339,534 instructions, and so the average age at death is about 2% of the program's total run time.

10.2.1.2. Example of a potential process-lifetime leak

This next example (from a different program than the above) shows a potential process lifetime leak. A process lifetime leak occurs when a program keeps allocating data, but only frees the data just before it exits. Hence the program's heap grows constantly in size, yet Memcheck reports no leak, because the program has freed up everything at exit. This is particularly a hazard for long running programs.

```
======== SUMMARY STATISTICS ========

guest_insns:  418,901,537
[...]
max-live:    32,512 in 254 blocks
tot-alloc:   32,512 in 254 blocks (avg size 128.00)
deaths:      254, at avg age 300,467,389
acc-ratios:  0.26 rd, 0.20 wr  (8,756 b-read, 6,604 b-written)
   at 0x4C275B8: malloc (vg_replace_malloc.c:236)
   by 0x4C27632: realloc (vg_replace_malloc.c:525)
   by 0x56FF41D: QtFontStyle::pixelSize(unsigned short, bool) (qfontdatabase.cpp:269

   by 0x5700D69: loadFontConfig() (qfontdatabase_x11.cpp:1146)
```

There are two tell-tale signs that this might be a process-lifetime leak. Firstly, the max-live and tot-alloc numbers are identical. The only way that can happen is if these blocks are all allocated and then all deallocated.

Secondly, the average age at death (300 million insns) is 71% of the total program lifetime (419 million insns), hence this is not a transient allocation-free spike -- rather, it is spread out over a large part of the entire run. One interpretation is, roughly, that all 254 blocks were allocated in the first half of the run, held onto for the second half, and then freed just before exit.

10.2.2. Interpreting the acc-ratios fields

10.2.2.1. A fairly harmless allocation point record

```
max-live:    49,398 in 808 blocks
tot-alloc:   1,481,940 in 24,240 blocks (avg size 61.13)
deaths:      24,240, at avg age 34,611,026
acc-ratios:  2.13 rd, 0.91 wr  (3,166,650 b-read, 1,358,820 b-written)
   at 0x4C275B8: malloc (vg_replace_malloc.c:236)
   by 0x40350E: tcc_malloc (tinycc.c:6712)
   by 0x404580: tok_alloc_new (tinycc.c:7151)
   by 0x4046C4: tok_alloc (tinycc.c:7190)
```

The acc-ratios field tells us that each byte in the blocks allocated here is read an average of 2.13 times before the block is deallocated. Given that the blocks have an average age at death of 34,611,026, that's one read per block per approximately every 15 million instructions. So from that standpoint the blocks aren't "working" very hard.

More interesting is the write ratio: each byte is written an average of 0.91 times. This tells us that some parts of the allocated blocks are never written, at least 9% on average. To completely initialise the block would require writing each byte at least once, and that would give a write ratio of 1.0. The fact that some block areas are evidently unused might point to data alignment holes or other layout inefficiencies.

Well, at least all the blocks are freed (24,240 allocations, 24,240 deaths).

If all the blocks had been the same size, DHAT would also show the access counts by block offset, so we could see where exactly these unused areas are. However, that isn't the case: the blocks have varying sizes, so DHAT can't perform such an analysis. We can see that they must have varying sizes since the average block size, 61.13, isn't a whole number.

10.2.2.2. A more suspicious looking example

```
max-live:   180,224 in 22 blocks
tot-alloc:  180,224 in 22 blocks (avg size 8192.00)
deaths:     none (none of these blocks were freed)
acc-ratios: 0.00 rd, 0.00 wr  (0 b-read, 0 b-written)
  at 0x4C275B8: malloc (vg_replace_malloc.c:236)
  by 0x40350E: tcc_malloc (tinycc.c:6712)
  by 0x40369C: __sym_malloc (tinycc.c:6787)
  by 0x403711: sym_malloc (tinycc.c:6805)
```

Here, both the read and write access ratios are zero. Hence this point is allocating blocks which are never used, neither read nor written. Indeed, they are also not freed ("deaths: none") and are simply leaked. So, here is 180k of completely useless allocation that could be removed.

Re-running with Memcheck does indeed report the same leak. What DHAT can tell us, that Memcheck can't, is that not only are the blocks leaked, they are also never used.

10.2.2.3. Another suspicious example

Here's one where blocks are allocated, written to, but never read from. We see this immediately from the zero read access ratio. They do get freed, though:

```
max-live:   54 in 3 blocks
tot-alloc:  1,620 in 90 blocks (avg size 18.00)
deaths:     90, at avg age 34,558,236
acc-ratios: 0.00 rd, 1.11 wr  (0 b-read, 1,800 b-written)
  at 0x4C275B8: malloc (vg_replace_malloc.c:236)
  by 0x40350E: tcc_malloc (tinycc.c:6712)
  by 0x4035BD: tcc_strdup (tinycc.c:6750)
  by 0x41FEBB: tcc_add_sysinclude_path (tinycc.c:20931)
```

In the previous two examples, it is easy to see blocks that are never written to, or never read from, or some combination of both. Unfortunately, in C++ code, the situation is less clear. That's because an object's constructor will write to the underlying block, and its destructor will read from it. So the block's read and write ratios will be non-zero even if the object, once constructed, is never used, but only eventually destructed.

Really, what we want is to measure only memory accesses in between the end of an object's construction and the start of its destruction. Unfortunately I do not know of a reliable way to determine when those transitions are made.

10.2.3. Interpreting "Aggregated access counts by offset" data

For allocation points that always allocate blocks of the same size, and which are 4096 bytes or smaller, DHAT counts accesses per offset, for example:

```
max-live:   317,408 in 5,668 blocks
tot-alloc:  317,408 in 5,668 blocks (avg size 56.00)
deaths:     5,668, at avg age 622,890,597
acc-ratios: 1.03 rd, 1.28 wr  (327,642 b-read, 408,172 b-written)
   at 0x4C275B8: malloc (vg_replace_malloc.c:236)
   by 0x5440C16: QDesignerPropertySheetPrivate::ensureInfo (qhash.h:515)
   by 0x544350B: QDesignerPropertySheet::setVisible (qdesigner_propertysh...)
   by 0x5446232: QDesignerPropertySheet::QDesignerPropertySheet (qdesigne...)

Aggregated access counts by offset:

[   0]  28782 28782 28782 28782 28782 28782 28782 28782
[   8]  20638 20638 20638 20638 0 0 0 0
[  16]  22738 22738 22738 22738 22738 22738 22738 22738
[  24]  6013 6013 6013 6013 6013 6013 6013 6013
[  32]  18883 18883 18883 37422 0 0 0 0
[  36]  5668 11915 5668 5668 11336 11336 11336 11336
[  48]  6166 6166 6166 6166 0 0 0 0
```

This is fairly typical, for C++ code running on a 64-bit platform. Here, we have aggregated access statistics for 5668 blocks, all of size 56 bytes. Each byte has been accessed at least 5668 times, except for offsets 12--15, 36--39 and 52--55. These are likely to be alignment holes.

Careful interpretation of the numbers reveals useful information. Groups of N consecutive identical numbers that begin at an N-aligned offset, for N being 2, 4 or 8, are likely to indicate an N-byte object in the structure at that point. For example, the first 32 bytes of this object are likely to have the layout

```
[0 ]  64-bit type
[8 ]  32-bit type
[12]  32-bit alignment hole
[16]  64-bit type
[24]  64-bit type
```

As a counterexample, it's also clear that, whatever is at offset 32, it is not a 32-bit value. That's because the last number of the group (37422) is not the same as the first three (18883 18883 18883).

This example leads one to enquire (by reading the source code) whether the zeroes at 12--15 and 52--55 are alignment holes, and whether 48--51 is indeed a 32-bit type. If so, it might be possible to place what's at 48--51 at 12--15 instead, which would reduce the object size from 56 to 48 bytes.

Bear in mind that the above inferences are all only "maybes". That's because they are based on dynamic data, not static analysis of the object layout. For example, the zeroes might not be alignment holes, but rather just parts of the structure which were not used at all for this particular run. Experience shows that's unlikely to be the case, but it could happen.

10.3. DHAT Command-line Options

DHAT-specific command-line options are:

`--show-top-n=<number>` `[default: 10]`
At the end of the run, DHAT sorts the accumulated allocation points according to some metric, and shows the highest scoring entries. `--show-top-n` controls how many entries are shown. The default of 10 is quite small. For realistic applications you will probably need to set it much higher, at least several hundred.

`--sort-by=<string>` `[default: max-bytes-live]`
At the end of the run, DHAT sorts the accumulated allocation points according to some metric, and shows the highest scoring entries. `--sort-by` selects the metric used for sorting:

`max-bytes-live`   maximum live bytes [default]

`tot-bytes-allocd`   total allocation (turnover)

`max-blocks-live`   maximum live blocks

This controls the order in which allocation points are displayed. You can choose to look at allocation points with the highest maximum liveness, or the highest total turnover, or by the highest number of live blocks. These give usefully different pictures of program behaviour. For example, sorting by maximum live blocks tends to show up allocation points creating large numbers of small objects.

One important point to note is that each allocation stack counts as a seperate allocation point. Because stacks by default have 12 frames, this tends to spread data out over multiple allocation points. You may want to use the flag `--num-callers=4` or some such small number, to reduce the spreading.

11. SGCheck: an experimental stack and global array overrun detector

To use this tool, you must specify `--tool=exp-sgcheck` on the Valgrind command line.

11.1. Overview

SGCheck is a tool for finding overruns of stack and global arrays. It works by using a heuristic approach derived from an observation about the likely forms of stack and global array accesses.

11.2. SGCheck Command-line Options

There are no SGCheck-specific command-line options at present.

11.3. How SGCheck Works

When a source file is compiled with `-g`, the compiler attaches DWARF3 debugging information which describes the location of all stack and global arrays in the file.

Checking of accesses to such arrays would then be relatively simple, if the compiler could also tell us which array (if any) each memory referencing instruction was supposed to access. Unfortunately the DWARF3 debugging format does not provide a way to represent such information, so we have to resort to a heuristic technique to approximate it. The key observation is that *if a memory referencing instruction accesses inside a stack or global array once, then it is highly likely to always access that same array.*

To see how this might be useful, consider the following buggy fragment:

```
{ int i, a[10];  // both are auto vars
  for (i = 0; i <= 10; i++)
    a[i] = 42;
}
```

At run time we will know the precise address of `a[]` on the stack, and so we can observe that the first store resulting from `a[i] = 42` writes `a[]`, and we will (correctly) assume that that instruction is intended always to access `a[]`. Then, on the 11th iteration, it accesses somewhere else, possibly a different local, possibly an un-accounted for area of the stack (eg, spill slot), so SGCheck reports an error.

There is an important caveat.

Imagine a function such as `memcpy`, which is used to read and write many different areas of memory over the lifetime of the program. If we insist that the read and write instructions in its memory copying loop only ever access one particular stack or global variable, we will be flooded with errors resulting from calls to `memcpy`.

To avoid this problem, SGCheck instantiates fresh likely-target records for each entry to a function, and discards them on exit. This allows detection of cases where (e.g.) `memcpy` overflows its source or destination buffers for any specific call, but does not carry any restriction from one call to the next. Indeed, multiple threads may make multiple simultaneous calls to (e.g.) `memcpy` without mutual interference.

11.4. Comparison with Memcheck

SGCheck and Memcheck are complementary: their capabilities do not overlap. Memcheck performs bounds checks and use-after-free checks for heap arrays. It also finds uses of uninitialised values created by heap or stack allocations. But it does not perform bounds checking for stack or global arrays.

SGCheck, on the other hand, does do bounds checking for stack or global arrays, but it doesn't do anything else.

11.5. Limitations

This is an experimental tool, which relies rather too heavily on some not-as-robust-as-I-would-like assumptions on the behaviour of correct programs. There are a number of limitations which you should be aware of.

- False negatives (missed errors): it follows from the description above (How SGCheck Works) that the first access by a memory referencing instruction to a stack or global array creates an association between that instruction and the array, which is checked on subsequent accesses by that instruction, until the containing function exits. Hence, the first access by an instruction to an array (in any given function instantiation) is not checked for overrun, since SGCheck uses that as the "example" of how subsequent accesses should behave.

- False positives (false errors): similarly, and more serious, it is clearly possible to write legitimate pieces of code which break the basic assumption upon which the checking algorithm depends. For example:

```
{ int a[10], b[10], *p, i;
  for (i = 0; i < 10; i++) {
    p = /* arbitrary condition */ ? &a[i]  : &b[i];
    *p = 42;
  }
}
```

In this case the store sometimes accesses a[] and sometimes b[], but in no cases is the addressed array overrun. Nevertheless the change in target will cause an error to be reported.

It is hard to see how to get around this problem. The only mitigating factor is that such constructions appear very rare, at least judging from the results using the tool so far. Such a construction appears only once in the Valgrind sources (running Valgrind on Valgrind) and perhaps two or three times for a start and exit of Firefox. The best that can be done is to suppress the errors.

- Performance: SGCheck has to read all of the DWARF3 type and variable information on the executable and its shared objects. This is computationally expensive and makes startup quite slow. You can expect debuginfo reading time to be in the region of a minute for an OpenOffice sized application, on a 2.4 GHz Core 2 machine. Reading this information also requires a lot of memory. To make it viable, SGCheck goes to considerable trouble to compress the in-memory representation of the DWARF3 data, which is why the process of reading it appears slow.

- Performance: SGCheck runs slower than Memcheck. This is partly due to a lack of tuning, but partly due to algorithmic difficulties. The stack and global checks can sometimes require a number of range checks per memory access, and these are difficult to short-circuit, despite considerable efforts having been made. A redesign and reimplementation could potentially make it much faster.

- Coverage: Stack and global checking is fragile. If a shared object does not have debug information attached, then SGCheck will not be able to determine the bounds of any stack or global arrays defined within that shared object, and so will not be able to check accesses to them. This is true even when those arrays are accessed from some other shared object which was compiled with debug info.

  At the moment SGCheck accepts objects lacking debuginfo without comment. This is dangerous as it causes SGCheck to silently skip stack and global checking for such objects. It would be better to print a warning in such circumstances.

- Coverage: SGCheck does not check whether the areas read or written by system calls do overrun stack or global arrays. This would be easy to add.

- Platforms: the stack/global checks won't work properly on PowerPC, ARM or S390X platforms, only on X86 and AMD64 targets. That's because the stack and global checking requires tracking function calls and exits reliably, and there's no obvious way to do it on ABIs that use a link register for function returns.

- Robustness: related to the previous point. Function call/exit tracking for X86 and AMD64 is believed to work properly even in the presence of longjmps within the same stack (although this has not been tested). However, code which switches stacks is likely to cause breakage/chaos.

11.6. Still To Do: User-visible Functionality

- Extend system call checking to work on stack and global arrays.

- Print a warning if a shared object does not have debug info attached, or if, for whatever reason, debug info could not be found, or read.

- Add some heuristic filtering that removes obvious false positives. This would be easy to do. For example, an access transition from a heap to a stack object almost certainly isn't a bug and so should not be reported to the user.

11.7. Still To Do: Implementation Tidying

Items marked CRITICAL are considered important for correctness: non-fixage of them is liable to lead to crashes or assertion failures in real use.

- sg_main.c: Redesign and reimplement the basic checking algorithm. It could be done much faster than it is -- the current implementation isn't very good.

- sg_main.c: Improve the performance of the stack / global checks by doing some up-front filtering to ignore references in areas which "obviously" can't be stack or globals. This will require using information that m_aspacemgr knows about the address space layout.

- sg_main.c: fix compute_II_hash to make it a bit more sensible for ppc32/64 targets (except that sg_ doesn't work on ppc32/64 targets, so this is a bit academic at the moment).

12. BBV: an experimental basic block vector generation tool

To use this tool, you must specify `--tool=exp-bbv` on the Valgrind command line.

12.1. Overview

A basic block is a linear section of code with one entry point and one exit point. A *basic block vector* (BBV) is a list of all basic blocks entered during program execution, and a count of how many times each basic block was run.

BBV is a tool that generates basic block vectors for use with the SimPoint analysis tool. The SimPoint methodology enables speeding up architectural simulations by only running a small portion of a program and then extrapolating total behavior from this small portion. Most programs exhibit phase-based behavior, which means that at various times during execution a program will encounter intervals of time where the code behaves similarly to a previous interval. If you can detect these intervals and group them together, an approximation of the total program behavior can be obtained by only simulating a bare minimum number of intervals, and then scaling the results.

In computer architecture research, running a benchmark on a cycle-accurate simulator can cause slowdowns on the order of 1000 times, making it take days, weeks, or even longer to run full benchmarks. By utilizing SimPoint this can be reduced significantly, usually by 90 95%, while still retaining reasonable accuracy.

A more complete introduction to how SimPoint works can be found in the paper "Automatically Characterizing Large Scale Program Behavior" by T. Sherwood, E. Perelman, G. Hamerly, and B. Calder.

12.2. Using Basic Block Vectors to create SimPoints

To quickly create a basic block vector file, you will call Valgrind like this:
```
valgrind --tool=exp-bbv /bin/ls
```

In this case we are running on `/bin/ls`, but this can be any program. By default a file called `bb.out.PID` will be created, where PID is replaced by the process ID of the running process. This file contains the basic block vector. For long-running programs this file can be quite large, so it might be wise to compress it with gzip or some other compression program.

To create actual SimPoint results, you will need the SimPoint utility, available from the SimPoint webpage. Assuming you have downloaded SimPoint 3.2 and compiled it, create SimPoint results with a command like the following:

```
./SimPoint.3.2/bin/simpoint -inputVectorsGzipped \
  -loadFVFile bb.out.1234.gz \
  -k 5 -saveSimpoints results.simpts \
  -saveSimpointWeights results.weights
```

where bb.out.1234.gz is your compressed basic block vector file generated by BBV.

The SimPoint utility does random linear projection using 15-dimensions, then does k-mean clustering to calculate which intervals are of interest. In this example we specify 5 intervals with the -k 5 option.

The outputs from the SimPoint run are the `results.simpts` and `results.weights` files. The first holds the 5 most relevant intervals of the program. The seconds holds the weight to scale each interval by when extrapolating full-program behavior. The intervals and the weights can be used in conjunction with a simulator that supports fast-forwarding; you fast-forward to the interval of interest, collect stats for the desired interval length, then use statistics gathered in conjunction with the weights to calculate your results.

12.3. BBV Command-line Options

BBV-specific command-line options are:

`--bb-out-file=<name> [default: bb.out.%p]`
This option selects the name of the basic block vector file. The `%p` and `%q` format specifiers can be used to embed the process ID and/or the contents of an environment variable in the name, as is the case for the core option `--log-file`.

`--pc-out-file=<name> [default: pc.out.%p]`
This option selects the name of the PC file. This file holds program counter addresses and function name info for the various basic blocks. This can be used in conjunction with the basic block vector file to fast-forward via function names instead of just instruction counts. The `%p` and `%q` format specifiers can be used to embed the process ID and/or the contents of an environment variable in the name, as is the case for the core option `--log-file`.

`--interval-size=<number> [default: 100000000]`
This option selects the size of the interval to use. The default is 100 million instructions, which is a commonly used value. Other sizes can be used; smaller intervals can help programs with finer-grained phases. However smaller interval size can lead to accuracy issues due to warm-up effects (When fast-forwarding the various architectural features will be un-initialized, and it will take some number of instructions before they "warm up" to the state a full simulation would be at without the fast-forwarding. Large interval sizes tend to mitigate this.)

`--instr-count-only [default: no]`
This option tells the tool to only display instruction count totals, and to not generate the actual basic block vector file. This is useful for debugging, and for gathering instruction count info without generating the large basic block vector files.

12.4. Basic Block Vector File Format

The Basic Block Vector is dumped at fixed intervals. This is commonly done every 100 million instructions; the `--interval-size` option can be used to change this.

The output file looks like this:

```
T:45:1024 :189:99343
T:11:78573 :15:1353  :56:1
T:18:45 :12:135353 :56:78 314:4324263
```

Each new interval starts with a T. This is followed on the same line by a series of basic block and frequency pairs, one for each basic block that was entered during the interval. The format for each block/frequency pair is a colon, followed by a number that uniquely identifies the basic block, another colon, and then the frequency (which is the number of times the block was entered, multiplied by the number of instructions in the block). The pairs are separated from each other by a space.

The frequency count is multiplied by the number of instructions that are in the basic block, in order to weigh the count so that instructions in small basic blocks aren't counted as more important than instructions in large basic blocks.

The SimPoint program only processes lines that start with a "T". All other lines are ignored. Traditionally comments are indicated by starting a line with a "#" character. Some other BBV generation tools, such as PinPoints, generate lines beginning with letters other than "T" to indicate more information about the program being run. We do not generate these, as the SimPoint utility ignores them.

12.5. Implementation

Valgrind provides all of the information necessary to create BBV files. In the current implementation, all instructions are instrumented. This is slower (by approximately a factor of two) than a method that instruments at the basic block level, but there are some complications (especially with rep prefix detection) that make that method more difficult.

Valgrind actually provides instrumentation at a superblock level. A superblock has one entry point but unlike basic blocks can have multiple exit points. Once a branch occurs into the middle of a block, it is split into a new basic block. Because Valgrind cannot produce "true" basic blocks, the generated BBV vectors will be different than those generated by other tools. In practice this does not seem to affect the accuracy of the SimPoint results. We do internally force the `--vex-guest-chase-thresh=0` option to Valgrind which forces a more basic-block-like behavior.

When a superblock is run for the first time, it is instrumented with our BBV routine. A block info (bbInfo) structure is allocated which holds the various information and statistics for the block. A unique block ID is assigned to the block, and then the structure is placed into an ordered set. Then each native instruction in the block is instrumented to call an instruction counting routine with a pointer to the block info structure as an argument.

At run-time, our instruction counting routines are called once per native instruction. The relevant block info structure is accessed and the block count and total instruction count is updated. If the total instruction count overflows the interval size then we walk the ordered set, writing out the statistics for any block that was accessed in the interval, then resetting the block counters to zero.

On the x86 and amd64 architectures the counting code has extra code to handle rep-prefixed string instructions. This is because actual hardware counts a rep-prefixed instruction as one instruction, while a naive Valgrind implementation would count it as many (possibly hundreds, thousands or even millions) of instructions. We handle rep-prefixed instructions specially, in order to make the results match those obtained with hardware performance counters.

BBV also counts the fldcw instruction. This instruction is used on x86 machines in various ways; it is most commonly found when converting floating point values into integers. On Pentium 4 systems the retired instruction performance counter counts this instruction as two instructions (all other known processors only count it as one). This can affect results when using SimPoint on Pentium 4 systems. We provide the fldcw count so that users can evaluate whether it will impact their results enough to avoid using Pentium 4 machines for their experiments. It would be possible to add an option to this tool that mimics the double-counting so that the generated BBV files would be usable for experiments using hardware performance counters on Pentium 4 systems.

12.6. Threaded Executable Support

BBV supports threaded programs. When a program has multiple threads, an additional basic block vector file is created for each thread (each additional file is the specified filename with the thread number appended at the end).

There is no official method of using SimPoint with threaded workloads. The most common method is to run SimPoint on each thread's results independently, and use some method of deterministic execution to try to match the original workload. This should be possible with the current BBV.

12.7. Validation

BBV has been tested on x86, amd64, and ppc32 platforms. An earlier version of BBV was tested in detail using hardware performance counters, this work is described in a paper from the HiPEAC'08 conference, "Using Dynamic

Binary Instrumentation to Generate Multi-Platform SimPoints: Methodology and Accuracy" by V.M. Weaver and S.A. McKee.

12.8. Performance

Using this program slows down execution by roughly a factor of 40 over native execution. This varies depending on the machine used and the benchmark being run. On the SPEC CPU 2000 benchmarks running on a 3.4GHz Pentium D processor, the slowdown ranges from 24x (mcf) to 340x (vortex.2).

13. Lackey: an example tool

To use this tool, you must specify `--tool=lackey` on the Valgrind command line.

13.1. Overview

Lackey is a simple Valgrind tool that does various kinds of basic program measurement. It adds quite a lot of simple instrumentation to the program's code. It is primarily intended to be of use as an example tool, and consequently emphasises clarity of implementation over performance.

13.2. Lackey Command-line Options

Lackey-specific command-line options are:

`--basic-counts=<no|yes> [default: yes]`
When enabled, Lackey prints the following statistics and information about the execution of the client program:

1. The number of calls to the function specified by the `--fnname` option (the default is `main`). If the program has had its symbols stripped, the count will always be zero.

2. The number of conditional branches encountered and the number and proportion of those taken.

3. The number of superblocks entered and completed by the program. Note that due to optimisations done by the JIT, this is not at all an accurate value.

4. The number of guest (x86, amd64, ppc, etc.) instructions and IR statements executed. IR is Valgrind's RISC-like intermediate representation via which all instrumentation is done.

5. Ratios between some of these counts.

6. The exit code of the client program.

`--detailed-counts=<no|yes> [default: no]`
When enabled, Lackey prints a table containing counts of loads, stores and ALU operations, differentiated by their IR types. The IR types are identified by their IR name ("I1", "I8", ... "I128", "F32", "F64", and "V128").

`--trace-mem=<no|yes> [default: no]`
When enabled, Lackey prints the size and address of almost every memory access made by the program. See the comments at the top of the file `lackey/lk_main.c` for details about the output format, how it works, and inaccuracies in the address trace. Note that this option produces immense amounts of output.

`--trace-superblocks=<no|yes> [default: no]`
When enabled, Lackey prints out the address of every superblock (a single entry, multiple exit, linear chunk of code) executed by the program. This is primarily of interest to Valgrind developers. See the comments at the top of the file `lackey/lk_main.c` for details about the output format. Note that this option produces large amounts of output.

`--fnname=<name> [default: main]`
Changes the function for which calls are counted when `--basic-counts=yes` is specified.

14. Nulgrind: the minimal Valgrind tool

To use this tool, you must specify `--tool=none` on the Valgrind command line.

14.1. Overview

Nulgrind is the simplest possible Valgrind tool. It performs no instrumentation or analysis of a program, just runs it normally. It is mainly of use for Valgrind's developers for debugging and regression testing.

Nonetheless you can run programs with Nulgrind. They will run roughly 5 times more slowly than normal, for no useful effect. Note that you need to use the option `--tool=none` to run Nulgrind (ie. not `--tool=nulgrind`).

Valgrind FAQ

Release 3.11.0 22 September 2015
Copyright © 2000-2015 Valgrind Developers

Email: valgrind@valgrind.org

Table of Contents

Valgrind Frequently Asked Questions

1. Background

1.1. How do you pronounce "Valgrind"?

The "Val" as in the word "value". The "grind" is pronounced with a short 'i' -- ie. "grinned" (rhymes with "tinned") rather than "grined" (rhymes with "find").

Don't feel bad: almost everyone gets it wrong at first.

1.2. Where does the name "Valgrind" come from?

From Nordic mythology. Originally (before release) the project was named Heimdall, after the watchman of the Nordic gods. He could "see a hundred miles by day or night, hear the grass growing, see the wool growing on a sheep's back", etc. This would have been a great name, but it was already taken by a security package "Heimdal".

Keeping with the Nordic theme, Valgrind was chosen. Valgrind is the name of the main entrance to Valhalla (the Hall of the Chosen Slain in Asgard). Over this entrance there resides a wolf and over it there is the head of a boar and on it perches a huge eagle, whose eyes can see to the far regions of the nine worlds. Only those judged worthy by the guardians are allowed to pass through Valgrind. All others are refused entrance.

It's not short for "value grinder", although that's not a bad guess.

2. Compiling, installing and configuring

2.1. When building Valgrind, 'make' dies partway with an assertion failure, something like this:

```
% make: expand.c:489: allocated_variable_append:
        Assertion 'current_variable_set_list->next != 0' failed.
```

It's probably a bug in 'make'. Some, but not all, instances of version 3.79.1 have this bug, see this. Try upgrading to a more recent version of 'make'. Alternatively, we have heard that unsetting the CFLAGS environment variable avoids the problem.

2.2. When building Valgrind, 'make' fails with this:

```
/usr/bin/ld: cannot find -lc
collect2: ld returned 1 exit status
```

You need to install the glibc-static-devel package.

3. Valgrind aborts unexpectedly

3.1. Programs run OK on Valgrind, but at exit produce a bunch of errors involving __libc_freeres and then die with a segmentation fault.

When the program exits, Valgrind runs the procedure __libc_freeres in glibc. This is a hook for memory debuggers, so they can ask glibc to free up any memory it has used. Doing that is needed to ensure that Valgrind doesn't incorrectly report space leaks in glibc.

The problem is that running __libc_freeres in older glibc versions causes this crash.

Workaround for 1.1.X and later versions of Valgrind: use the --run-libc-freeres=no option. You may then get space leak reports for glibc allocations (please don't report these to the glibc people, since they are not real leaks), but at least the program runs.

3.2. My (buggy) program dies like this:

```
valgrind: m_mallocfree.c:248 (get_bszB_as_is): Assertion 'bszB_lo == bszB_hi' fai
```

or like this.

```
valgrind: m_mallocfree.c:442 (mk_inuse_bszB): Assertion 'bszB != 0' failed.
```

or otherwise aborts or crashes in m_mallocfree.c.

If Memcheck (the memory checker) shows any invalid reads, invalid writes or invalid frees in your program, the above may happen. Reason is that your program may trash Valgrind's low-level memory manager, which then dies with the above assertion, or something similar. The cure is to fix your program so that it doesn't do any illegal memory accesses. The above failure will hopefully go away after that.

3.3. My program dies, printing a message like this along the way:

```
vex x86->IR: unhandled instruction bytes: 0x66 0xF 0x2E 0x5
```

One possibility is that your program has a bug and erroneously jumps to a non-code address, in which case you'll get a SIGILL signal. Memcheck may issue a warning just before this happens, but it might not if the jump happens to land in addressable memory.

Another possibility is that Valgrind does not handle the instruction. If you are using an older Valgrind, a newer version might handle the instruction. However, all instruction sets have some obscure, rarely used instructions. Also, on amd64 there are an almost limitless number of combinations of redundant instruction prefixes, many of them undocumented but accepted by CPUs. So Valgrind will still have decoding failures from time to time. If this happens, please file a bug report.

3.4. I tried running a Java program (or another program that uses a just-in-time compiler) under Valgrind but something went wrong. Does Valgrind handle such programs?

Valgrind can handle dynamically generated code, so long as none of the generated code is later overwritten by other generated code. If this happens, though, things will go wrong as Valgrind will continue running its translations of the old code (this is true on x86 and amd64, on PowerPC there are explicit cache flush instructions which Valgrind detects and honours). You should try running with `--smc-check=all` in this case. Valgrind will run much more slowly, but should detect the use of the out-of-date code.

Alternatively, if you have the source code to the JIT compiler you can insert calls to the `VALGRIND_DISCARD_TRANSLATIONS` client request to mark out-of-date code, saving you from using `--smc-check=all`.

Apart from this, in theory Valgrind can run any Java program just fine, even those that use JNI and are partially implemented in other languages like C and C++. In practice, Java implementations tend to do nasty things that most programs do not, and Valgrind sometimes falls over these corner cases.

If your Java programs do not run under Valgrind, even with `--smc-check=all`, please file a bug report and hopefully we'll be able to fix the problem.

4. Valgrind behaves unexpectedly

4.1. My program uses the C++ STL and string classes. Valgrind reports 'still reachable' memory leaks involving these classes at the exit of the program, but there should be none.

First of all: relax, it's probably not a bug, but a feature. Many implementations of the C++ standard libraries use their own memory pool allocators. Memory for quite a number of destructed objects is not immediately freed and given back to the OS, but kept in the pool(s) for later re-use. The fact that the pools are not freed at the exit of the program cause Valgrind to report this memory as still reachable. The behaviour not to free pools at the exit could be called a bug of the library though.

Using GCC, you can force the STL to use malloc and to free memory as soon as possible by globally disabling memory caching. Beware! Doing so will probably slow down your program, sometimes drastically.

- With GCC 2.91, 2.95, 3.0 and 3.1, compile all source using the STL with `-D__USE_MALLOC`. Beware! This was removed from GCC starting with version 3.3.

- With GCC 3.2.2 and later, you should export the environment variable `GLIBCPP_FORCE_NEW` before running your program.

- With GCC 3.4 and later, that variable has changed name to `GLIBCXX_FORCE_NEW`.

There are other ways to disable memory pooling: using the `malloc_alloc` template with your objects (not portable, but should work for GCC) or even writing your own memory allocators. But all this goes beyond the scope of this FAQ. Start by reading http://gcc.gnu.org/onlinedocs/libstdc++/faq/index.html#4_4_leak if you absolutely want to do that. But beware: allocators belong to the more messy parts of the STL and people went to great lengths to make the STL portable across platforms. Chances are good that your solution will work on your platform, but not on others.

4.2. The stack traces given by Memcheck (or another tool) aren't helpful. How can I improve them?

If they're not long enough, use `--num-callers` to make them longer.

If they're not detailed enough, make sure you are compiling with `-g` to add debug information. And don't strip symbol tables (programs should be unstripped unless you run 'strip' on them; some libraries ship stripped).

Also, for leak reports involving shared objects, if the shared object is unloaded before the program terminates, Valgrind will discard the debug information and the error message will be full of `???` entries. The workaround here is to avoid calling `dlclose` on these shared objects.

Also, `-fomit-frame-pointer` and `-fstack-check` can make stack traces worse.

Some example sub-traces:

- With debug information and unstripped (best):

```
Invalid write of size 1
   at 0x80483BF: really (malloc1.c:20)
   by 0x8048370: main (malloc1.c:9)
```

- With no debug information, unstripped:

```
Invalid write of size 1
   at 0x80483BF: really (in /auto/homes/njn25/grind/head5/a.out)
   by 0x8048370: main (in /auto/homes/njn25/grind/head5/a.out)
```

- With no debug information, stripped:

```
Invalid write of size 1
   at 0x80483BF: (within /auto/homes/njn25/grind/head5/a.out)
   by 0x8048370: (within /auto/homes/njn25/grind/head5/a.out)
   by 0x42015703: __libc_start_main (in /lib/tls/libc-2.3.2.so)
   by 0x80482CC: (within /auto/homes/njn25/grind/head5/a.out)
```

- With debug information and -fomit-frame-pointer:

```
Invalid write of size 1
   at 0x80483C4: really (malloc1.c:20)
   by 0x42015703: __libc_start_main (in /lib/tls/libc-2.3.2.so)
   by 0x80482CC: ??? (start.S:81)
```

• A leak error message involving an unloaded shared object:

```
84 bytes in 1 blocks are possibly lost in loss record 488 of 713
   at 0x1B9036DA: operator new(unsigned) (vg_replace_malloc.c:132)
   by 0x1DB63EEB: ???
   by 0x1DB4B800: ???
   by 0x1D65E007: ???
   by 0x8049EE6: main (main.cpp:24)
```

4.3. The stack traces given by Memcheck (or another tool) seem to have the wrong function name in them. What's happening?

Occasionally Valgrind stack traces get the wrong function names. This is caused by glibc using aliases to effectively give one function two names. Most of the time Valgrind chooses a suitable name, but very occasionally it gets it wrong. Examples we know of are printing `bcmp` instead of `memcmp`, `index` instead of `strchr`, and `rindex` instead of `strrchr`.

4.4. My program crashes normally, but doesn't under Valgrind, or vice versa. What's happening?

When a program runs under Valgrind, its environment is slightly different to when it runs natively. For example, the memory layout is different, and the way that threads are scheduled is different.

Most of the time this doesn't make any difference, but it can, particularly if your program is buggy. For example, if your program crashes because it erroneously accesses memory that is unaddressable, it's possible that this memory will not be unaddressable when run under Valgrind. Alternatively, if your program has data races, these may not manifest under Valgrind.

There isn't anything you can do to change this, it's just the nature of the way Valgrind works that it cannot exactly replicate a native execution environment. In the case where your program crashes due to a memory error when run natively but not when run under Valgrind, in most cases Memcheck should identify the bad memory operation.

4.5. Memcheck doesn't report any errors and I know my program has errors.

There are two possible causes of this.

First, by default, Valgrind only traces the top-level process. So if your program spawns children, they won't be traced by Valgrind by default. Also, if your program is started by a shell script, Perl script, or something similar, Valgrind will trace the shell, or the Perl interpreter, or equivalent.

To trace child processes, use the `--trace-children=yes` option.

If you are tracing large trees of processes, it can be less disruptive to have the output sent over the network. Give Valgrind the option `--log-socket=127.0.0.1:12345` (if you want logging output sent to port `12345` on `localhost`). You can use the valgrind-listener program to listen on that port:

```
valgrind-listener 12345
```

Obviously you have to start the listener process first. See the manual for more details.

Second, if your program is statically linked, most Valgrind tools will only work well if they are able to replace certain functions, such as `malloc`, with their own versions. By default, statically linked `malloc functions` are not replaced. A key indicator of this is if Memcheck says:

```
All heap blocks were freed -- no leaks are possible
```

when you know your program calls `malloc`. The workaround is to use the option `--soname-synonyms=somalloc=NONE` or to avoid statically linking your program.

There will also be no replacement if you use an alternative `malloc library` such as tcmalloc, jemalloc, ... In such a case, the option `--soname-synonyms=somalloc=zzzz` (where *zzzz* is the soname of the alternative malloc library) will allow Valgrind to replace the functions.

4.6. Why doesn't Memcheck find the array overruns in this program?

```
int static[5];

int main(void)
{
  int stack[5];

  static[5] = 0;
  stack [5] = 0;

  return 0;
}
```

Unfortunately, Memcheck doesn't do bounds checking on global or stack arrays. We'd like to, but it's just not possible to do in a reasonable way that fits with how Memcheck works. Sorry.

However, the experimental tool SGcheck can detect errors like this. Run Valgrind with the `--tool=exp-sgcheck` option to try it, but be aware that it is not as robust as Memcheck.

5. Miscellaneous

5.1. I tried writing a suppression but it didn't work. Can you write my suppression for me?

Yes! Use the `--gen-suppressions=yes` feature to spit out suppressions automatically for you. You can then edit them if you like, eg. combining similar automatically generated suppressions using wildcards like `'*'`.

If you really want to write suppressions by hand, read the manual carefully. Note particularly that C++ function names must be mangled (that is, not demangled).

5.2. With Memcheck's memory leak detector, what's the difference between "definitely lost", "indirectly lost", "possibly lost", "still reachable", and "suppressed"?

The details are in the Memcheck section of the user manual.

In short:

- "definitely lost" means your program is leaking memory -- fix those leaks!

- "indirectly lost" means your program is leaking memory in a pointer-based structure. (E.g. if the root node of a binary tree is "definitely lost", all the children will be "indirectly lost".) If you fix the "definitely lost" leaks, the "indirectly lost" leaks should go away.

- "possibly lost" means your program is leaking memory, unless you're doing unusual things with pointers that could cause them to point into the middle of an allocated block; see the user manual for some possible causes. Use `--show-possibly-lost=no` if you don't want to see these reports.

- "still reachable" means your program is probably ok -- it didn't free some memory it could have. This is quite common and often reasonable. Don't use `--show-reachable=yes` if you don't want to see these reports.

- "suppressed" means that a leak error has been suppressed. There are some suppressions in the default suppression files. You can ignore suppressed errors.

5.3. Memcheck's uninitialised value errors are hard to track down, because they are often reported some time after they are caused. Could Memcheck record a trail of operations to better link the cause to the effect? Or maybe just eagerly report any copies of uninitialised memory values?

Prior to version 3.4.0, the answer was "we don't know how to do it without huge performance penalties". As of 3.4.0, try using the `--track-origins=yes` option. It will run slower than usual, but will give you extra information about the origin of uninitialised values.

Or if you want to do it the old fashioned way, you can use the client request `VALGRIND_CHECK_VALUE_IS_DEFINE` to help track these errors down -- work backwards from the point where the uninitialised error occurs, checking suspect values until you find the cause. This requires editing, compiling and re-running your program multiple times, which is a pain, but still easier than debugging the problem without Memcheck's help.

As for eager reporting of copies of uninitialised memory values, this has been suggested multiple times. Unfortunately, almost all programs legitimately copy uninitialised memory values around (because compilers pad structs to preserve alignment) and eager checking leads to hundreds of false positives. Therefore Memcheck does not support eager checking at this time.

5.4. Is it possible to attach Valgrind to a program that is already running?

No. The environment that Valgrind provides for running programs is significantly different to that for normal programs, e.g. due to different layout of memory. Therefore Valgrind has to have full control from the very start.

It is possible to achieve something like this by running your program without any instrumentation (which involves a slow-down of about 5x, less than that of most tools), and then adding instrumentation once you get to a point of interest. Support for this must be provided by the tool, however, and Callgrind is the only tool that currently has such support. See the instructions on the `callgrind_control` program for details.

6. How To Get Further Assistance

Read the appropriate section(s) of the Valgrind Documentation.

Search the valgrind-users mailing list archives, using the group name `gmane.comp.debugging.valgrind`.

If you think an answer in this FAQ is incomplete or inaccurate, please e-mail valgrind@valgrind.org.

If you have tried all of these things and are still stuck, you can try mailing the valgrind-users mailing list. Note that an email has a better change of being answered usefully if it is clearly written. Also remember that, despite the fact that most of the community are very helpful and responsive to emailed questions, you are probably requesting help from unpaid volunteers, so you have no guarantee of receiving an answer.

Valgrind Technical Documentation

Release 3.11.0 22 September 2015
Copyright © 2000-2015 Valgrind Developers

Email: valgrind@valgrind.org

Table of Contents

1. The Design and Implementation of Valgrind

A number of academic publications nicely describe many aspects of Valgrind's design and implementation. Online copies of all of them, and others, are available on the Valgrind publications page.

The following paper gives a good overview of Valgrind, and explains how it differs from other dynamic binary instrumentation frameworks such as Pin and DynamoRIO.

- **Valgrind: A Framework for Heavyweight Dynamic Binary Instrumentation.** Nicholas Nethercote and Julian Seward. Proceedings of ACM SIGPLAN 2007 Conference on Programming Language Design and Implementation (PLDI 2007), San Diego, California, USA, June 2007.

The following two papers together give a comprehensive description of how most of Memcheck works. The first paper describes in detail how Memcheck's undefined value error detection (a.k.a. V bits) works. The second paper describes in detail how Memcheck's shadow memory is implemented, and compares it to other alternative approaches.

- **Using Valgrind to detect undefined value errors with bit-precision.** Julian Seward and Nicholas Nethercote. Proceedings of the USENIX'05 Annual Technical Conference, Anaheim, California, USA, April 2005.

  How to Shadow Every Byte of Memory Used by a Program. Nicholas Nethercote and Julian Seward. Proceedings of the Third International ACM SIGPLAN/SIGOPS Conference on Virtual Execution Environments (VEE 2007), San Diego, California, USA, June 2007.

The following paper describes Callgrind.

- **A Tool Suite for Simulation Based Analysis of Memory Access Behavior.** Josef Weidendorfer, Markus Kowarschik and Carsten Trinitis. Proceedings of the 4th International Conference on Computational Science (ICCS 2004), Krakow, Poland, June 2004.

The following dissertation describes Valgrind in some detail (many of these details are now out-of-date) as well as Cachegrind, Annelid and Redux. It also covers some underlying theory about dynamic binary analysis in general and what all these tools have in common.

- **Dynamic Binary Analysis and Instrumentation.** Nicholas Nethercote. PhD Dissertation, University of Cambridge, November 2004.

2. Writing a New Valgrind Tool

So you want to write a Valgrind tool? Here are some instructions that may help.

2.1. Introduction

The key idea behind Valgrind's architecture is the division between its *core* and *tools*.

The core provides the common low-level infrastructure to support program instrumentation, including the JIT compiler, low-level memory manager, signal handling and a thread scheduler. It also provides certain services that are useful to some but not all tools, such as support for error recording, and support for replacing heap allocation functions such as `malloc`.

But the core leaves certain operations undefined, which must be filled by tools. Most notably, tools define how program code should be instrumented. They can also call certain functions to indicate to the core that they would like to use certain services, or be notified when certain interesting events occur. But the core takes care of all the hard work.

2.2. Basics

2.2.1. How tools work

Tools must define various functions for instrumenting programs that are called by Valgrind's core. They are then linked against Valgrind's core to define a complete Valgrind tool which will be used when the `--tool` option is used to select it.

2.2.2. Getting the code

To write your own tool, you'll need the Valgrind source code. You'll need a check-out of the Subversion repository for the automake/autoconf build instructions to work. See the information about how to do check-out from the repository at the Valgrind website.

2.2.3. Getting started

Valgrind uses GNU `automake` and `autoconf` for the creation of Makefiles and configuration. But don't worry, these instructions should be enough to get you started even if you know nothing about those tools.

In what follows, all filenames are relative to Valgrind's top-level directory `valgrind/`.

1. Choose a name for the tool, and a two-letter abbreviation that can be used as a short prefix. We'll use `foobar` and `fb` as an example.

2. Make three new directories `foobar/`, `foobar/docs/` and `foobar/tests/`.

3. Create an empty file `foobar/tests/Makefile.am`.

4. Copy `none/Makefile.am` into `foobar/`. Edit it by replacing all occurrences of the strings `"none"`, `"nl_"` and `"nl-"` with `"foobar"`, `"fb_"` and `"fb-"` respectively.

5. Copy `none/nl_main.c` into `foobar/`, renaming it as `fb_main.c`. Edit it by changing the `details` lines in `nl_pre_clo_init` to something appropriate for the tool. These fields are used in the startup message, except for `bug_reports_to` which is used if a tool assertion fails. Also, replace the string `"nl_"` throughout with `"fb_"` again.

6. Edit `Makefile.am`, adding the new directory `foobar` to the `TOOLS` or `EXP_TOOLS` variables.

7. Edit `configure.in`, adding `foobar/Makefile` and `foobar/tests/Makefile` to the `AC_OUTPUT` list.

8. Run:

```
autogen.sh
./configure --prefix=`pwd`/inst
make
make install
```

It should automake, configure and compile without errors, putting copies of the tool in `foobar/` and `inst/lib/valgrind/`.

9. You can test it with a command like:

```
inst/bin/valgrind --tool=foobar date
```

(almost any program should work; `date` is just an example). The output should be something like this:

```
==738== foobar-0.0.1, a foobarring tool.
==738== Copyright (C) 2002-2009, and GNU GPL'd, by J. Programmer.
==738== Using Valgrind-3.5.0.SVN and LibVEX; rerun with -h for copyright info
==738== Command: date
==738==
Tue Nov 27 12:40:49 EST 2007
==738==
```

The tool does nothing except run the program uninstrumented.

These steps don't have to be followed exactly -- you can choose different names for your source files, and use a different `--prefix` for `./configure`.

Now that we've setup, built and tested the simplest possible tool, onto the interesting stuff...

2.2.4. Writing the code

A tool must define at least these four functions:

```
pre_clo_init()
post_clo_init()
instrument()
fini()
```

The names can be different to the above, but these are the usual names. The first one is registered using the macro `VG_DETERMINE_INTERFACE_VERSION`. The last three are registered using the `VG_(basic_tool_funcs)` function.

In addition, if a tool wants to use some of the optional services provided by the core, it may have to define other functions and tell the core about them.

2.2.5. Initialisation

Most of the initialisation should be done in `pre_clo_init`. Only use `post_clo_init` if a tool provides command line options and must do some initialisation after option processing takes place (`"clo"` stands for "command line options").

First of all, various "details" need to be set for a tool, using the functions `VG_(details_*)`. Some are all compulsory, some aren't. Some are used when constructing the startup message, `detail_bug_reports_to` is used if `VG_(tool_panic)` is ever called, or a tool assertion fails. Others have other uses.

Second, various "needs" can be set for a tool, using the functions `VG_(needs_*)`. They are mostly booleans, and can be left untouched (they default to `False`). They determine whether a tool can do various things such as: record, report and suppress errors; process command line options; wrap system calls; record extra information about heap blocks; etc.

For example, if a tool wants the core's help in recording and reporting errors, it must call `VG_(needs_tool_errors)` and provide definitions of eight functions for comparing errors, printing out errors, reading suppressions from a suppressions file, etc. While writing these functions requires some work, it's much less than doing error handling from scratch because the core is doing most of the work.

Third, the tool can indicate which events in core it wants to be notified about, using the functions `VG_(track_*)`. These include things such as heap blocks being allocated, the stack pointer changing, a mutex being locked, etc. If a tool wants to know about this, it should provide a pointer to a function, which will be called when that event happens.

For example, if the tool want to be notified when a new heap block is allocated, it should call `VG_(track_new_mem_heap)` with an appropriate function pointer, and the assigned function will be called each time this happens.

More information about "details", "needs" and "trackable events" can be found in `include/pub_tool_tooliface.h`.

2.2.6. Instrumentation

`instrument` is the interesting one. It allows you to instrument *VEX IR*, which is Valgrind's RISC-like intermediate language. VEX IR is described in the comments of the header file `VEX/pub/libvex_ir.h`.

The easiest way to instrument VEX IR is to insert calls to C functions when interesting things happen. See the tool "Lackey" (`lackey/lk_main.c`) for a simple example of this, or Cachegrind (`cachegrind/cg_main.c`) for a more complex example.

2.2.7. Finalisation

This is where you can present the final results, such as a summary of the information collected. Any log files should be written out at this point.

2.2.8. Other Important Information

Please note that the core/tool split infrastructure is quite complex and not brilliantly documented. Here are some important points, but there are undoubtedly many others that I should note but haven't thought of.

The files `include/pub_tool_*.h` contain all the types, macros, functions, etc. that a tool should (hopefully) need, and are the only `.h` files a tool should need to `#include`. They have a reasonable amount of documentation in it that should hopefully be enough to get you going.

Note that you can't use anything from the C library (there are deep reasons for this, trust us). Valgrind provides an implementation of a reasonable subset of the C library, details of which are in `pub_tool_libc*.h`.

When writing a tool, in theory you shouldn't need to look at any of the code in Valgrind's core, but in practice it might be useful sometimes to help understand something.

The `include/pub_tool_basics.h` and `VEX/pub/libvex_basictypes.h` files have some basic types that are widely used.

Ultimately, the tools distributed (Memcheck, Cachegrind, Lackey, etc.) are probably the best documentation of all, for the moment.

The `VG_` macro is used heavily. This just prepends a longer string in front of names to avoid potential namespace clashes. It is defined in `include/pub_tool_basics.h`.

There are some assorted notes about various aspects of the implementation in `docs/internals/`. Much of it isn't that relevant to tool-writers, however.

2.3. Advanced Topics

Once a tool becomes more complicated, there are some extra things you may want/need to do.

2.3.1. Debugging Tips

Writing and debugging tools is not trivial. Here are some suggestions for solving common problems.

If you are getting segmentation faults in C functions used by your tool, the usual GDB command:

```
gdb <prog> core
```

usually gives the location of the segmentation fault.

If you want to debug C functions used by your tool, there are instructions on how to do so in the file `README_DEVELOPERS`.

If you are having problems with your VEX IR instrumentation, it's likely that GDB won't be able to help at all. In this case, Valgrind's `--trace-flags` option is invaluable for observing the results of instrumentation.

If you just want to know whether a program point has been reached, using the `OINK` macro (in `include/pub_tool_libcprint.h`) can be easier than using GDB.

The other debugging command line options can be useful too (run `valgrind --help-debug` for the list).

2.3.2. Suppressions

If your tool reports errors and you want to suppress some common ones, you can add suppressions to the suppression files. The relevant files are `*.supp`; the final suppression file is aggregated from these files by combining the relevant `.supp` files depending on the versions of linux, X and glibc on a system.

Suppression types have the form `tool_name:suppression_name`. The `tool_name` here is the name you specify for the tool during initialisation with `VG_(details_name)`.

2.3.3. Documentation

If you are feeling conscientious and want to write some documentation for your tool, please use XML as the rest of Valgrind does. The file `docs/README` has more details on getting the XML toolchain to work; this can be difficult, unfortunately.

To write the documentation, follow these steps (using `foobar` as the example tool name again):

1. The docs go in `foobar/docs/`, which you will have created when you started writing the tool.

2. Copy the XML documentation file for the tool Nulgrind from `none/docs/nl-manual.xml` to `foobar/docs/`, and rename it to `foobar/docs/fb-manual.xml`.

   Note: there is a tetex bug involving underscores in filenames, so don't use '_'.

3. Write the documentation. There are some helpful bits and pieces on using XML markup in `docs/xml/xml_help.txt`.

4. Include it in the User Manual by adding the relevant entry to `docs/xml/manual.xml`. Copy and edit an existing entry.

5. Include it in the man page by adding the relevant entry to `docs/xml/valgrind-manpage.xml`. Copy and edit an existing entry.

6. Validate `foobar/docs/fb-manual.xml` using the following command from within `docs/`:

   ```
   make valid
   ```

   You may get errors that look like this:

   ```
   ./xml/index.xml:5: element chapter: validity error : No declaration for
   attribute base of element chapter
   ```

   Ignore (only) these -- they're not important.

   Because the XML toolchain is fragile, it is important to ensure that `fb-manual.xml` won't break the documentation set build. Note that just because an XML file happily transforms to html does not necessarily mean the same holds true for pdf/ps.

7. You can (re-)generate the HTML docs while you are writing `fb-manual.xml` to help you see how it's looking. The generated files end up in `docs/html/`. Use the following command, within `docs/`:

   ```
   make html-docs
   ```

8. When you have finished, try to generate PDF and PostScript output to check all is well, from within `docs/`:

```
make print-docs
```

Check the output `.pdf` and `.ps` files in `docs/print/`.

Note that the toolchain is even more fragile for the print docs, so don't feel too bad if you can't get it working.

2.3.4. Regression Tests

Valgrind has some support for regression tests. If you want to write regression tests for your tool:

1. The tests go in `foobar/tests/`, which you will have created when you started writing the tool.

2. Write `foobar/tests/Makefile.am`. Use `memcheck/tests/Makefile.am` as an example.

3. Write the tests, `.vgtest` test description files, `.stdout.exp` and `.stderr.exp` expected output files. (Note that Valgrind's output goes to stderr.) Some details on writing and running tests are given in the comments at the top of the testing script `tests/vg_regtest`.

4. Write a filter for stderr results `foobar/tests/filter_stderr`. It can call the existing filters in `tests/`. See `memcheck/tests/filter_stderr` for an example; in particular note the `$dir` trick that ensures the filter works correctly from any directory.

2.3.5. Profiling

Lots of profiling tools have trouble running Valgrind. For example, trying to use gprof is hopeless.

Probably the best way to profile a tool is with OProfile on Linux.

You can also use Cachegrind on it. Read `README_DEVELOPERS` for details on running Valgrind under Valgrind; it's a bit fragile but can usually be made to work.

2.3.6. Other Makefile Hackery

If you add any directories under `foobar/`, you will need to add an appropriate `Makefile.am` to it, and add a corresponding entry to the `AC_OUTPUT` list in `configure.in`.

If you add any scripts to your tool (see Cachegrind for an example) you need to add them to the `bin_SCRIPTS` variable in `foobar/Makefile.am` and possible also to the `AC_OUTPUT` list in `configure.in`.

2.3.7. The Core/tool Interface

The core/tool interface evolves over time, but it's pretty stable. We deliberately do not provide backward compatibility with old interfaces, because it is too difficult and too restrictive. We view this as a good thing -- if we had to be backward compatible with earlier versions, many improvements now in the system could not have been added.

Because tools are statically linked with the core, if a tool compiles successfully then it should be compatible with the core. We would not deliberately violate this property by, for example, changing the behaviour of a core function without changing its prototype.

2.4. Final Words

Writing a new Valgrind tool is not easy, but the tools you can write with Valgrind are among the most powerful programming tools there are. Happy programming!

3. Callgrind Format Specification

This chapter describes the Callgrind Profile Format, Version 1.

A synonymous name is "Calltree Profile Format". These names actually mean the same since Callgrind was previously named Calltree.

The format description is meant for the user to be able to understand the file contents; but more important, it is given for authors of measurement or visualization tools to be able to write and read this format.

3.1. Overview

The profile data format is ASCII based. It is written by Callgrind, and it is upwards compatible to the format used by Cachegrind (ie. Cachegrind uses a subset). It can be read by callgrind_annotate and KCachegrind.

This chapter gives on overview of format features and examples. For detailed syntax, look at the format reference.

3.1.1. Basic Structure

Each file has a header part of an arbitrary number of lines of the format "key: value". After the header, lines specifying profile costs follow. Everywhere, comments on own lines starting with '#' are allowed. The header lines with keys "positions" and "events" define the meaning of cost lines in the second part of the file: the value of "positions" is a list of subpositions, and the value of "events" is a list of event type names. Cost lines consist of subpositions followed by 64-bit counters for the events, in the order specified by the "positions" and "events" header line.

The "events" header line is always required in contrast to the optional line for "positions", which defaults to "line", i.e. a line number of some source file. In addition, the second part of the file contains position specifications of the form "spec=name". "spec" can be e.g. "fn" for a function name or "fl" for a file name. Cost lines are always related to the function/file specifications given directly before.

3.1.2. Simple Example

The event names in the following example are quite arbitrary, and are not related to event names used by Callgrind. Especially, cycle counts matching real processors probably will never be generated by any Valgrind tools, as these are bound to simulations of simple machine models for acceptable slowdown. However, any profiling tool could use the format described in this chapter.

```
events: Cycles Instructions Flops
fl=file.f
fn=main
15 90 14 2
16 20 12
```

The above example gives profile information for event types "Cycles", "Instructions", and "Flops". Thus, cost lines give the number of CPU cycles passed by, number of executed instructions, and number of floating point operations executed while running code corresponding to some source position. As there is no line specifying the value of "positions", it defaults to "line", which means that the first number of a cost line is always a line number.

Thus, the first cost line specifies that in line 15 of source file file.f there is code belonging to function main. While running, 90 CPU cycles passed by, and 2 of the 14 instructions executed were floating point operations. Similarly, the next line specifies that there were 12 instructions executed in the context of function main which can be related to line 16 in file `file.f`, taking 20 CPU cycles. If a cost line specifies less event counts than given in the "events" line, the rest is assumed to be zero. I.e. there was no floating point instruction executed relating to line 16.

Note that regular cost lines always give self (also called exclusive) cost of code at a given position. If you specify multiple cost lines for the same position, these will be summed up. On the other hand, in the example above there is no specification of how many times function `main` actually was called: profile data only contains sums.

3.1.3. Associations

The most important extension to the original format of Cachegrind is the ability to specify call relationship among functions. More generally, you specify associations among positions. For this, the second part of the file also can contain association specifications. These look similar to position specifications, but consist of two lines. For calls, the format looks like

```
calls=(Call Count) (Target position)
(Source position) (Inclusive cost of call)
```

The destination only specifies subpositions like line number. Therefore, to be able to specify a call to another function in another source file, you have to precede the above lines with a "cfn=" specification for the name of the called function, and optionally a "cfi=" specification if the function is in another source file ("cfl=" is an alternative specification for "cfi=" because of historical reasons, and both should be supported by format readers). The second line looks like a regular cost line with the difference that inclusive cost spent inside of the function call has to be specified.

Other associations are for example (conditional) jumps. See the reference below for details.

3.1.4. Extended Example

The following example shows 3 functions, `main`, `func1`, and `func2`. Function `main` calls `func1` once and `func2` 3 times. `func1` calls `func2` 2 times.

```
events: Instructions

fl=file1.c
fn=main
16 20
cfn=func1
calls=1 50
16 400
cfi=file2.c
cfn=func2
calls=3 20
16 400

fn=func1
51 100
cfi=file2.c
cfn=func2
calls=2 20
51 300

fl=file2.c
fn=func2
20 700
```

One can see that in main only code from line 16 is executed where also the other functions are called. Inclusive cost of main is 820, which is the sum of self cost 20 and costs spent in the calls: 400 for the single call to func1 and 400 as sum for the three calls to func2.

Function func1 is located in file1.c, the same as main. Therefore, a "cfi=" specification for the call to func1 is not needed. The function func1 only consists of code at line 51 of file1.c, where func2 is called.

3.1.5. Name Compression

With the introduction of association specifications like calls it is needed to specify the same function or same file name multiple times. As absolute filenames or symbol names in C++ can be quite long, it is advantageous to be able to specify integer IDs for position specifications. Here, the term "position" corresponds to a file name (source or object file) or function name.

To support name compression, a position specification can be not only of the format "spec=name", but also "spec=(ID) name" to specify a mapping of an integer ID to a name, and "spec=(ID)" to reference a previously defined ID mapping. There is a separate ID mapping for each position specification, i.e. you can use ID 1 for both a file name and a symbol name.

With string compression, the example from 1.4 looks like this:

```
events: Instructions

fl=(1) file1.c
fn=(1) main
16 20
cfn=(2) func1
calls=1 50
16 400
cfi=(2) file2.c
cfn=(3) func2
calls=3 20
16 400

fn=(2)
51 100
cfi=(2)
cfn=(3)
calls=2 20
51 300

fl=(2)
fn=(3)
20 700
```

As position specifications carry no information themselves, but only change the meaning of subsequent cost lines or associations, they can appear everywhere in the file without any negative consequence. Especially, you can define name compression mappings directly after the header, and before any cost lines. Thus, the above example can also be written as

```
events: Instructions

# define file ID mapping
fl=(1) file1.c
fl=(2) file2.c
# define function ID mapping
fn=(1) main
fn=(2) func1
fn=(3) func2

fl=(1)
fn=(1)
16 20
...
```

3.1.6. Subposition Compression

If a Callgrind data file should hold costs for each assembler instruction of a program, you specify subposition "instr" in the "positions:" header line, and each cost line has to include the address of some instruction. Addresses are allowed to have a size of 64 bits to support 64-bit architectures. Thus, repeating similar, long addresses for almost every line in the data file can enlarge the file size quite significantly, and motivates for subposition compression: instead of every cost line starting with a 16 character long address, one is allowed to specify relative addresses. This relative specification is not only allowed for instruction addresses, but also for line numbers; both addresses and line numbers are called "subpositions".

A relative subposition always is based on the corresponding subposition of the last cost line, and starts with a "+" to specify a positive difference, a "-" to specify a negative difference, or consists of "*" to specify the same subposition. Because absolute subpositions always are positive (ie. never prefixed by "-"), any relative specification is non-ambiguous; additionally, absolute and relative subposition specifications can be mixed freely. Assume the following example (subpositions can always be specified as hexadecimal numbers, beginning with "0x"):

```
positions: instr line
events: ticks

fn=func
0x80001234 90 1
0x80001237 90 5
0x80001238 91 6
```

With subposition compression, this looks like

```
positions: instr line
events: ticks

fn=func
0x80001234 90 1
+3 * 5
+1 +1 6
```

Remark: For assembler annotation to work, instruction addresses have to be corrected to correspond to addresses found in the original binary. I.e. for relocatable shared objects, often a load offset has to be subtracted.

3.1.7. Miscellaneous

3.1.7.1. Cost Summary Information

For the visualization to be able to show cost percentage, a sum of the cost of the full run has to be known. Usually, it is assumed that this is the sum of all cost lines in a file. But sometimes, this is not correct. Thus, you can specify a "summary:" line in the header giving the full cost for the profile run. An import filter may use this to show a progress bar while loading a large data file.

3.1.7.2. Long Names for Event Types and inherited Types

Event types for cost lines are specified in the "events:" line with an abbreviated name. For visualization, it makes sense to be able to specify some longer, more descriptive name. For an event type "Ir" which means "Instruction Fetches", this can be specified the header line

```
event: Ir : Instruction Fetches
events: Ir Dr
```

In this example, "Dr" itself has no long name associated. The order of "event:" lines and the "events:" line is of no importance. Additionally, inherited event types can be introduced for which no raw data is available, but which are calculated from given types. Suppose the last example, you could add

```
event: Sum = Ir + Dr
```

to specify an additional event type "Sum", which is calculated by adding costs for "Ir and "Dr".

3.2. Reference

3.2.1. Grammar

```
ProfileDataFile := FormatVersion? Creator? PartData*


FormatVersion := "version: 1\n"


Creator := "creator:" NoNewLineChar* "\n"


PartData := (HeaderLine "\n")+ (BodyLine "\n")+


HeaderLine := (empty line)
  | ('#' NoNewLineChar*)
  | PartDetail
  | Description
  | EventSpecification
  | CostLineDef


PartDetail := TargetCommand | TargetID


TargetCommand := "cmd:" Space* NoNewLineChar*


TargetID := ("pid"|"thread"|"part") ":" Space* Number


Description := "desc:" Space* Name Space* ":" NoNewLineChar*


EventSpecification := "event:" Space* Name InheritedDef? LongNameDef?


InheritedDef := "=" InheritedExpr


InheritedExpr := Name
  | Number Space* ("*" Space*)? Name
  | InheritedExpr Space* "+" Space* InheritedExpr


LongNameDef := ":" NoNewLineChar*
```

```
CostLineDef := "events:" Space* Name (Space+ Name)*
  | "positions:" "instr"? (Space+ "line")?


BodyLine := (empty line)
  | ('#' NoNewLineChar*)
  | CostLine
  | PositionSpec
  | CallSpec
  | UncondJumpSpec
  | CondJumpSpec


CostLine := SubPositionList Costs?


SubPositionList := (SubPosition+ Space+)+


SubPosition := Number | "+" Number | "-" Number | "*"


Costs := (Number Space+)+


PositionSpec := Position "=" Space* PositionName


Position := CostPosition | CalledPosition


CostPosition := "ob" | "fl" | "fi" | "fe" | "fn"


CalledPosition := " "cob" | "cfi" | "cfl" | "cfn"


PositionName := ( "(" Number ")" )? (Space* NoNewLineChar* )?


CallSpec := CallLine "\n" CostLine


CallLine := "calls=" Space* Number Space+ SubPositionList


UncondJumpSpec := "jump=" Space* Number Space+ SubPositionList


CondJumpSpec := "jcnd=" Space* Number Space+ Number Space+ SubPositionList


Space := " " | "\t"
```

```
Number := HexNumber | (Digit)+


Digit := "0" | ... | "9"


HexNumber := "0x" (Digit | HexChar)+


HexChar := "a" | ... | "f" | "A" | ... | "F"


Name = Alpha (Digit | Alpha)*


Alpha = "a" | ... | "z" | "A" | ... | "Z"


NoNewLineChar := all characters without "\n"
```

A profile data file ("ProfileDataFile") starts with basic information such as the version and creator information, and then has a list of parts, where each part has its own header and body. Parts typically are different threads and/or time spans/phases within a profiled application run.

Note that callgrind_annotate currently only supports profile data files with one part. Callgrind may produce multiple parts for one profile run, but defaults to one output file for each part.

3.2.2. Description of Header Lines

Basic information in the first lines of a profile data file:

- `version:  number` [Callgrind]

  This is used to distinguish future profile data formats.   A major version of 0 or 1 is supposed to be upwards compatible with Cachegrind's format. It is optional; if not appearing, version 1 is assumed. Otherwise, this has to be the first header line.

- `creator:  string` [Callgrind]

  This is an arbitrary string to denote the creator of this file. Optional.

The header for each part has an arbitrary number of lines of the format "key: value". Possible *key* values for the header are:

- `pid:  process id` [Callgrind]

  Optional. This specifies the process ID of the supervised application for which this profile was generated.

- `cmd:  program name + args` [Cachegrind]

  Optional. This specifies the full command line of the supervised application for which this profile was generated.

- part: number [Callgrind]

Optional. This specifies a sequentially incremented number for each dump generated, starting at 1.

- desc: type: value [Cachegrind]

This specifies various information for this dump. For some types, the semantic is defined, but any description type is allowed. Unknown types should be ignored.

There are the types "I1 cache", "D1 cache", "LL cache", which specify parameters used for the cache simulator. These are the only types originally used by Cachegrind. Additionally, Callgrind uses the following types: "Timerange" gives a rough range of the basic block counter, for which the cost of this dump was collected. Type "Trigger" states the reason of why this trace was generated. E.g. program termination or forced interactive dump.

- positions: [instr] [line] [Callgrind]

For cost lines, this defines the semantic of the first numbers. Any combination of "instr", "bb" and "line" is allowed, but has to be in this order which corresponds to position numbers at the start of the cost lines later in the file.

If "instr" is specified, the position is the address of an instruction whose execution raised the events given later on the line. This address is relative to the offset of the binary/shared library file to not have to specify relocation info. For "line", the position is the line number of a source file, which is responsible for the events raised. Note that the mapping of "instr" and "line" positions are given by the debugging line information produced by the compiler.

This header line is optional, defaulting to "positions: line" if not specified.

- events: event type abbreviations [Cachegrind]

A list of short names of the event types logged in cost lines in this part of the profile data file. Arbitrary short names are allowed. The order given specifies the required order in cost lines. Thus, the first event type is the second or third number in a cost line, depending on the value of "positions". Required to appear for each header part exactly once.

- summary: costs [Callgrind]

Optional. This header line specifies a summary cost, which should be equal or larger than a total over all self costs. It may be larger as the cost lines may not represent all cost of the program run.

- totals: costs [Cachegrind]

Optional. Should appear at the end of the file (although looking like a header line). Must give the total of all cost lines, to allow for a consistency check.

3.2.3. Description of Body Lines

The regular body line is a cost line consisting of one or two position numbers (depending on "positions:" header line, see above) and an array of cost numbers. A position number either is a line numbers into a source file or an instruction address within binary code, with source/binary file names specified as position names (see below). The cost numbers get mapped to event types in the same order as specified in the "events:" header line. If less numbers than event types are given, the costs default to zero for the remaining event types.

Further, there exist lines `spec=position name`. A position name is an arbitrary string. If it starts with "(" and a digit, it's a string in compressed format. Otherwise it's the real position string. This allows for file and symbol names as position strings, as these never start with "(" + *digit*. The compressed format is either "(" *number* ")" *space position* or only "(" *number* ")". The first relates *position* to *number* in the context of the given format specification from this line to the end of the file; it makes the (*number*) an alias for *position*. Compressed format is always optional.

Position specifications allowed:

  `ob=` [Callgrind]

  The ELF object where the cost of next cost lines happens.

- `fl=` [Cachegrind]

- `fi=` [Cachegrind]

- `fe=` [Cachegrind]

  The source file including the code which is responsible for the cost of next cost lines. "fi="/"fe=" is used when the source file changes inside of a function, i.e. for inlined code.

- `fn=` [Cachegrind]

  The name of the function where the cost of next cost lines happens.

- `cob=` [Callgrind]

  The ELF object of the target of the next call cost lines.

- `cfi=` [Callgrind]

  The source file including the code of the target of the next call cost lines.

- `cfl=` [Callgrind]

  Alternative spelling for `cfi=` specification (because of historical reasons).

- `cfn=` [Callgrind]

  The name of the target function of the next call cost lines.

The last type of body line provides specific costs not just related to one position as regular cost lines. It starts with specific strings similar to position name specifications.

- `calls=count target-position` [Callgrind]

  Call executed "count" times to "target-position". After a "calls=" line there MUST be a cost line. This provides the source position of the call and the cost spent in the called function in total.

- `jump=count target-position` [Callgrind]

  Unconditional jump, executed "count" times, to "target-position".

- `jcnd=exe-count jump-count target-position` [Callgrind]

  Conditional jump, executed "exe-count" times with "jump-count" jumps happening (rest is fall-through) to "target-position".

- `calls=count target-position` [Callgrind]

Valgrind Distribution Documents

Release 3.11.0 22 September 2015
Copyright © 2000-2015 Valgrind Developers

Email: valgrind@valgrind.org

Table of Contents

1. AUTHORS

Julian Seward was the original founder, designer and author of
Valgrind, created the dynamic translation frameworks, wrote Memcheck,
the 3.X versions of Helgrind, SGCheck, DHAT, and did lots of other
things.

Nicholas Nethercote did the core/tool generalisation, wrote
Cachegrind and Massif, and tons of other stuff.

Tom Hughes did a vast number of bug fixes, helped out with support for
more recent Linux/glibc versions, set up the present build system, and has
helped out with test and build machines.

Jeremy Fitzhardinge wrote Helgrind (in the 2.X line) and totally
overhauled low-level syscall/signal and address space layout stuff,
among many other things.

Josef Weidendorfer wrote and maintains Callgrind and the associated
KCachegrind GUI.

Paul Mackerras did a lot of the initial per-architecture factoring
that forms the basis of the 3.0 line and was also seen in 2.4.0.
He also did UCode-based dynamic translation support for PowerPC, and
created a set of ppc-linux derivatives of the 2.X release line.

Greg Parker wrote the Mac OS X port.

Dirk Mueller contributed the malloc/free mismatch checking
and other bits and pieces, and acts as our KDE liaison.

Robert Walsh added file descriptor leakage checking, new library
interception machinery, support for client allocation pools, and minor
other tweakage.

Bart Van Assche wrote and maintains DRD.

Cerion Armour-Brown worked on PowerPC instruction set support in the
Vex dynamic-translation framework. Maynard Johnson improved the
Power6 support.

Kirill Batuzov and Dmitry Zhurikhin did the NEON instruction set
support for ARM. Donna Robinson did the v6 media instruction support.

Donna Robinson created and maintains the very excellent
http://www.valgrind.org.

Vince Weaver wrote and maintains BBV.

Frederic Gobry helped with autoconf and automake.

Daniel Berlin modified readelf's dwarf2 source line reader, written by Nick Clifton, for use in Valgrind.o

Michael Matz and Simon Hausmann modified the GNU binutils demangler(s) for use in Valgrind.

David Woodhouse has helped out with test and build machines over the course of many releases.

Florian Krohm and Christian Borntraeger wrote and maintain the S390X/Linux port. Florian improved and ruggedised the regression test system during 2011.

Philippe Waroquiers wrote and maintains the embedded GDB server. He also made a bunch of performance and memory-reduction fixes across diverse parts of the system.

Carl Love and Maynard Johnson contributed IBM Power6 and Power7 support, and generally deal with ppc{32,64}-linux issues.

Petar Jovanovic and Dejan Jevtic wrote and maintain the mips32-linux port.

Dragos Tatulea modified the arm-android port so it also works on x86-android.

Jakub Jelinek helped out extensively with the AVX and AVX2 support.

Mark Wielaard fixed a bunch of bugs and acts as our Fedora/RHEL liaison.

Maran Pakkirisamy implemented support for decimal floating point on s390.

Many, many people sent bug reports, patches, and helpful feedback.

Development of Valgrind was supported in part by the Tri-Lab Partners (Lawrence Livermore National Laboratory, Los Alamos National Laboratory, and Sandia National Laboratories) of the U.S. Department of Energy's Advanced Simulation & Computing (ASC) Program.

2. NEWS

Release 3.11.0 (22 September 2015)
~~~~~~~~~~~~~~~~~~~~~~~~~~~~~~~~~~

3.11.0 is a feature release with many improvements and the usual collection of bug fixes.

This release supports X86/Linux, AMD64/Linux, ARM32/Linux, ARM64/Linux, PPC32/Linux, PPC64BE/Linux, PPC64LE/Linux, S390X/Linux, MIPS32/Linux, MIPS64/Linux, ARM/Android, ARM64/Android, MIPS32/Android, X86/Android, X86/Solaris, AMD64/Solaris, X86/MacOSX 10.10 and AMD64/MacOSX 10.10. There is also preliminary support for X86/MacOSX 10.11, AMD64/MacOSX 10.11 and TILEGX/Linux.

* ================== PLATFORM CHANGES ==================

* Support for Solaris/x86 and Solaris/amd64 has been added.

* Preliminary support for Mac OS X 10.11 (El Capitan) has been added.

* Preliminary support for the Tilera TileGX architecture has been added.

* s390x: It is now required for the host to have the "long displacement" facility. The oldest supported machine model is z990.

* x86: on an SSE2 only host, Valgrind in 32 bit mode now claims to be a Pentium 4. 3.10.1 wrongly claimed to be a Core 2, which is SSSE3.

* The JIT's register allocator is significantly faster, making the JIT as a whole somewhat faster, so JIT-intensive activities, for example program startup, are modestly faster, around 5%.

* There have been changes to the default settings of several command line flags, as detailed below.

* Intel AVX2 support is more complete (64 bit targets only). On AVX2 capable hosts, the simulated CPUID will now indicate AVX2 support.

* ===================== TOOL CHANGES =====================

* Memcheck:

  - The default value for --leak-check-heuristics has been changed from "none" to "all". This helps to reduce the number of possibly lost blocks, in particular for C++ applications.

  - The default value for --keep-stacktraces has been changed from "malloc-then-free" to "malloc-and-free". This has a small cost in memory (one word per malloc-ed block) but allows Memcheck to show the 3 stacktraces of a dangling reference: where the block was allocated, where it was freed, and where it is acccessed after being freed.

- The default value for --partial-loads-ok has been changed from "no" to
  "yes", so as to avoid false positive errors resulting from some kinds
  of vectorised loops.

- A new monitor command 'xb <addr> <len>' shows the validity bits of
  <len> bytes at <addr>. The monitor command 'xb' is easier to use
  than get_vbits when you need to associate byte data value with
  their corresponding validity bits.

- The 'block_list' monitor command has been enhanced:
    o it can print a range of loss records
    o it now accepts an optional argument 'limited <max_blocks>'
      to control the number of blocks printed.
    o if a block has been found using a heuristic, then
      'block_list' now shows the heuristic after the block size.
    o the loss records/blocks to print can be limited to the blocks
      found via specified heuristics.

- The C helper functions used to instrument loads on
  x86-{linux,solaris} and arm-linux (both 32-bit only) have been
  replaced by handwritten assembly sequences. This gives speedups
  in the region of 0% to 7% for those targets only.

- A new command line option, --expensive-definedness-checks=yes|no,
  has been added. This is useful for avoiding occasional invalid
  uninitialised-value errors in optimised code. Watch out for
  runtime degradation, as this can be up to 25%. As always, though,
  the slowdown is highly application specific. The default setting
  is "no".

* Massif:

  - A new monitor command 'all_snapshots <filename>' dumps all
    snapshots taken so far.

* Helgrind:

  - Significant memory reduction and moderate speedups for
    --history-level=full for applications accessing a lot of memory
    with many different stacktraces.

  - The default value for --conflict-cache-size=N has been doubled to
    2000000. Users that were not using the default value should
    preferably also double the value they give.

    The default was changed due to the changes in the "full history"
    implementation. Doubling the value gives on average a slightly more
    complete history and uses similar memory (or significantly less memory
    in the worst case) than the previous implementation.

  - The Helgrind monitor command 'info locks' now accepts an optional
    argument 'lock_addr', which shows information about the lock at the

given address only.

- When using --history-level=full, the new Helgrind monitor command
  'accesshistory <addr> [<len>]' will show the recorded accesses for
  <len> (or 1) bytes at <addr>.

* ==================== OTHER CHANGES ====================

* The default value for the --smc-check option has been changed from
  "stack" to "all-non-file" on targets that provide automatic D-I
  cache coherence (x86, amd64 and s390x). The result is to provide,
  by default, transparent support for JIT generated and self-modifying
  code on all targets.

* Mac OS X only: the default value for the --dsymutil option has been
  changed from "no" to "yes", since any serious usage on Mac OS X
  always required it to be "yes".

* The command line options --db-attach and --db-command have been removed.
  They were deprecated in 3.10.0.

* When a process dies due to a signal, Valgrind now shows the signal
  and the stacktrace at default verbosity (i.e. verbosity 1).

* The address description logic used by Memcheck and Helgrind now
  describes addresses in anonymous segments, file mmap-ed segments,
  shared memory segments and the brk data segment.

* The new option --error-markers=<begin>,<end> can be used to mark the
  begin/end of errors in textual output mode, to facilitate
  searching/extracting errors in output files that mix valgrind errors
  with program output.

* The new option --max-threads=<number> can be used to change the number
  of threads valgrind can handle. The default is 500 threads which
  should be more than enough for most applications.

* The new option --valgrind-stacksize=<number> can be used to change the
  size of the private thread stacks used by Valgrind. This is useful
  for reducing memory use or increasing the stack size if Valgrind
  segfaults due to stack overflow.

* The new option --avg-transtab-entry-size=<number> can be used to specify
  the expected instrumented block size, either to reduce memory use or
  to avoid excessive retranslation.

* Valgrind can be built with Intel's ICC compiler, version 14.0 or later.

* New and modified GDB server monitor features:

  - When a signal is reported in GDB, you can now use the GDB convenience
    variable $_siginfo to examine detailed signal information.

  - Valgrind's gdbserver now allows the user to change the signal

to deliver to the process. So, use 'signal SIGNAL' to continue execution
with SIGNAL instead of the signal reported to GDB. Use 'signal 0' to
continue without passing the signal to the process.

- With GDB >= 7.10, the command 'target remote'
  will automatically load the executable file of the process running
  under Valgrind. This means you do not need to specify the executable
  file yourself, GDB will discover it itself. See GDB documentation about
  'qXfer:exec-file:read' packet for more info.

* ==================== FIXED BUGS ====================

The following bugs have been fixed or resolved. Note that "n-i-bz"
stands for "not in bugzilla" -- that is, a bug that was reported to us
but never got a bugzilla entry. We encourage you to file bugs in
bugzilla (https://bugs.kde.org/enter_bug.cgi?product=valgrind) rather
than mailing the developers (or mailing lists) directly -- bugs that
are not entered into bugzilla tend to get forgotten about or ignored.

To see details of a given bug, visit
  https://bugs.kde.org/show_bug.cgi?id=XXXXXX
where XXXXXX is the bug number as listed below.

```
116002  VG_(printf): Problems with justification of strings and integers
155125  avoid cutting away file:lineno after long function name
197259  Unsupported arch_prtctl PR_SET_GS option
201152  ppc64: Assertion in ppc32g_dirtyhelper_MFSPR_268_269
201216  Fix Valgrind does not support pthread_sigmask() on OS X
201435  Fix Darwin: -v does not show kernel version
208217  "Warning: noted but unhandled ioctl 0x2000747b" on Mac OS X
211256  Fixed an outdated comment regarding the default platform.
211529  Incomplete call stacks for code compiled by newer versions of MSVC
211926  Avoid compilation warnings in valgrind.h with -pedantic
212291  Fix unhandled syscall: unix:132 (mkfifo) on OS X
        == 263119
226609  Crediting upstream authors in man page
231257  Valgrind omits path when executing script from shebang line
254164  OS X task_info: UNKNOWN task message [id 3405, to mach_task_self() [..]
269360  s390x: Fix addressing mode selection for compare-and-swap
302630  Memcheck: Assertion failed: 'sizeof(UWord) == sizeof(UInt)'
        == 326797
312989  ioctl handling needs to do POST handling on generic ioctls and [..]
319274  Fix unhandled syscall: unix:410 (sigsuspend_nocancel) on OS X
324181  mmap does not handle MAP_32BIT (handle it now, rather than fail it)
327745  Fix valgrind 3.9.0 build fails on Mac OS X 10.6.8
330147  libmpiwrap PMPI_Get_count returns undefined value
333051  mmap of huge pages fails due to incorrect alignment
        == 339163
334802  valgrind does not always explain why a given option is bad
335618  mov.w rN, pc/sp (ARM32)
335785  amd64->IR 0xC4 0xE2 0x75 0x2F (vmaskmovpd)
        == 307399
        == 343175
        == 342740
```

== 346912
335907 segfault when running wine's ddrawex/tests/surface.c under valgrind
338602 AVX2 bit in CPUID missing
338606 Strange message for scripts with invalid interpreter
338731 ppc: Fix testsuite build for toolchains not supporting -maltivec
338995 shmat with hugepages (SHM_HUGETLB) fails with EINVAL
339045 Getting valgrind to compile and run on OS X Yosemite (10.10)
        == 340252
339156 gdbsrv not called for fatal signal
339215 Valgrind 3.10.0 contain 2013 in copyrights notice
339288 support Cavium Octeon MIPS specific BBIT*32 instructions
339636 Use fxsave64 and fxrstor64 mnemonics instead of old-school rex64 prefix
339442 Fix testsuite build failure on OS X 10.9
339542 Enable compilation with Intel's ICC compiler
339563 The DVB demux DMX_STOP ioctl doesn't have a wrapper
339688 Mac-specific ASM does not support .version directive (cpuid,
        tronical and pushfpopf tests)
339745 Valgrind crash when check Marmalade app (partial fix)
339755 Fix known deliberate memory leak in setenv() on Mac OS X 10.9
339778 Linux/TileGx platform support for Valgrind
339780 Fix known uninitialised read in pthread_rwlock_init() on Mac OS X 10.9
339789 Fix none/tests/execve test on Mac OS X 10.9
339808 Fix none/tests/rlimit64_nofile test on Mac OS X 10.9
339820 vex amd64->IR: 0x66 0xF 0x3A 0x63 0xA 0x42 0x74 0x9 (pcmpistri $0x42)
340115 Fix none/tests/cmdline[1|2] tests on systems which define TMPDIR
340392 Allow user to select more accurate definedness checking in memcheck
        to avoid invalid complaints on optimised code
340430 Fix some grammatical weirdness in the manual.
341238 Recognize GCC5/DWARFv5 DW_LANG constants (Go, C11, C++11, C++14)
341419 Signal handler ucontext_t not filled out correctly on OS X
341539 VG_(describe_addr) should not describe address as belonging to client
        segment if it is past the heap end
341613 Enable building of manythreads and thread-exits tests on Mac OS X
341615 Fix none/tests/darwin/access_extended test on Mac OS X
341698 Valgrind's AESKEYGENASSIST gives wrong result in words 0 and 2 [..]
341789 aarch64: shmat fails with valgrind on ARMv8
341997 MIPS64: Cavium OCTEON insns - immediate operand handled incorrectly
342008 valgrind.h needs type cast [..] for clang/llvm in 64-bit mode
342038 Unhandled syscalls on aarch64 (mbind/get/set_mempolicy)
342063 wrong format specifier for test mcblocklistsearch in gdbserver_tests
342117 Hang when loading PDB file for MSVC compiled Firefox under Wine
342221 socket connect false positive uninit memory for unknown af family
342353 Allow dumping full massif output while valgrind is still running
342571 Valgrind chokes on AVX compare intrinsic with _CMP_GE_QS
        == 346476
        == 348387
        == 350593
342603 Add I2C_SMBUS ioctl support
342635 OS X 10.10 (Yosemite) - missing system calls and fcntl code
342683 Mark memory past the initial brk limit as unaddressable
342783 arm: unhandled instruction 0xEEFE1ACA = "vcvt.s32.f32 s3, s3, #12"
342795 Internal glibc __GI_mempcpy call should be intercepted
342841 s390x: Support instructions fiebr(a) and fidbr(a)
343012 Unhandled syscall 319 (memfd_create)

343069 Patch updating v4l2 API support
343173 helgrind crash during stack unwind
343219 fix GET_STARTREGS for arm
343303 Fix known deliberate memory leak in setenv() on Mac OS X 10.10
343306 OS X 10.10: UNKNOWN mach_msg unhandled MACH_SEND_TRAILER option
343332 Unhandled instruction 0x9E310021 (fcvtmu) on aarch64
343335 unhandled instruction 0x1E638400 (fccmp) aarch64
343523 OS X mach_ports_register: UNKNOWN task message [id 3403, to [..]
343525 OS X host_get_special_port: UNKNOWN host message [id 412, to [..]
343597 ppc64le: incorrect use of offseof macro
343649 OS X host_create_mach_voucher: UNKNOWN host message [id 222, to [..]
343663 OS X 10.10 Memchecj always reports a leak regardless of [..]
343732 Unhandled syscall 144 (setgid) on aarch64
343733 Unhandled syscall 187 (msgctl and related) on aarch64
343802 s390x: False positive "conditional jump or move depends on [..]
343902 --vgdb=yes doesn't break when --xml=yes is used
343967 Don't warn about setuid/setgid/setcap executable for directories
343978 Recognize DWARF5/GCC5 DW_LANG_Fortran 2003 and 2008 constants
344007 accept4 syscall unhandled on arm64 (242) and ppc64 (344)
344033 Helgrind on ARM32 loses track of mutex state in pthread_cond_wait
344054 www - update info for Solaris/illumos
344416 'make regtest' does not work cleanly on OS X
344235 Remove duplicate include of pub_core_aspacemgr.h
344279 syscall sendmmsg on arm64 (269) and ppc32/64 (349) unhandled
344295 syscall recvmmsg on arm64 (243) and ppc32/64 (343) unhandled
344307 2 unhandled syscalls on aarch64/arm64: umount2(39), mount (40)
344314 callgrind_annotate ... warnings about commands containing newlines
344318 socketcall should wrap recvmmsg and sendmmsg
344337 Fix unhandled syscall: mach:41 (_kernelrpc_mach_port_guard_trap)
344416 Fix 'make regtest' does not work cleanly on OS X
344499 Fix compilation for Linux kernel >= 4.0.0
344512 OS X: unhandled syscall: unix:348 (__pthread_chdir),
        unix:349 (__pthread_fchdir)
344559 Garbage collection of unused segment names in address space manager
344560 Fix stack traces missing penultimate frame on OS X
344621 Fix memcheck/tests/err_disable4 test on OS X
344686 Fix suppression for pthread_rwlock_init on OS X 10.10
344702 Fix missing libobjc suppressions on OS X 10.10
        == 344543
344936 Fix unhandled syscall: unix:473 (readlinkat) on OS X 10.10
344939 Fix memcheck/tests/xml1 on OS X 10.10
345016 helgrind/tests/locked_vs_unlocked2 is failing sometimes
345079 Fix build problems in VEX/useful/test_main.c
345126 Incorrect handling of VIDIOC_G_AUDIO and G_AUDOUT
345177 arm64: prfm (reg) not implemented
345215 Performance improvements for the register allocator
345248 add support for Solaris OS in valgrind
345338 TIOCGSERIAL and TIOCSSERIAL ioctl support on Linux
345394 Fix memcheck/tests/strchr on OS X
345637 Fix memcheck/tests/sendmsg on OS X
345695 Add POWERPC support for AT_DCACHESIZE and HWCAP2
345824 Fix aspacem segment mismatch: seen with none/tests/bigcode
345887 Fix an assertion in the address space manager
345928 amd64: callstack only contains current function for small stacks

345984   disInstr(arm): unhandled instruction: 0xEE193F1E
345987   MIPS64: Implement cavium LHX instruction
346031   MIPS: Implement support for the CvmCount register (rhwr %0, 31)
346185   Fix typo saving altivec register v24
346267   Compiler warnings for PPC64 code on call to LibVEX_GuestPPC64_get_XER()
         and LibVEX_GuestPPC64_get_CR()
346270   Regression tests none/tests/jm_vec/isa_2_07 and
         none/tests/test_isa_2_07_part2 have failures on PPC64 little endian
346307   fuse filesystem syscall deadlocks
346324   PPC64 missing support for lbarx, lharx, stbcx and sthcx instructions
346411   MIPS: SysRes::_valEx handling is incorrect
346416   Add support for LL_IOC_PATH2FID and LL_IOC_GETPARENT Lustre ioctls
346474   PPC64 Power 8, spr TEXASRU register not supported
346487   Compiler generates "note" about a future ABI change for PPC64
346562   MIPS64: lwl/lwr instructions are performing 64bit loads
         and causing spurious "invalid read of size 8" warnings
346801   Fix link error on OS X: _vgModuleLocal_sf_maybe_extend_stack
347151   Fix suppression for pthread_rwlock_init on OS X 10.8
347233   Fix memcheck/tests/strchr on OS X 10.10 (Haswell)
347322   Power PC regression test cleanup
347379   valgrind --leak-check=full leak errors from system libs on OS X 10.8
         == 217236
347389   unhandled syscall: 373 (Linux ARM syncfs)
347686   Patch set to cleanup PPC64 regtests
347978   Remove bash dependencies where not needed
347982   OS X: undefined symbols for architecture x86_64: "_global" [..]
347988   Memcheck: the 'impossible' happened: unexpected size for Addr (OSX/wine)
         == 345929
348102   Patch updating v4l2 API support
348247   amd64 front end: jno jumps wrongly when overflow is not set
348269   Improve mmap MAP_HUGETLB support.
348334   (ppc) valgrind does not simulate dcbfl - then my program terminates
348345   Assertion fails for negative lineno
348377   Unsupported ARM instruction: yield
348565   Fix detection of command line option availability for clang
348574   vex amd64->IR pcmpistri SSE4.2 unsupported (pcmpistri $0x18)
348728   Fix broken check for VIDIOC_G_ENC_INDEX
348748   Fix redundant condition
348890   Fix clang warning about unsupported --param inline-unit-growth=900
348949   Bogus "ERROR: --ignore-ranges: suspiciously large range"
349034   Add Lustre ioctls LL_IOC_GROUP_LOCK and LL_IOC_GROUP_UNLOCK
349086   Fix UNKNOWN task message [id 3406, to mach_task_self(), [..]
349087   Fix UNKNOWN task message [id 3410, to mach_task_self(), [..]
349626   Implemented additional Xen hypercalls
349769   Clang/osx: ld: warning: -read_only_relocs cannot be used with x86_64
349790   Clean up of the hardware capability checking utilities.
349828   memcpy intercepts memmove causing src/dst overlap error (ppc64 ld.so)
349874   Fix typos in source code
349879   memcheck: add handwritten assembly for helperc_LOADV*
349941   di_notify_mmap might create wrong start/size DebugInfoMapping
350062   vex x86->IR: 0x66 0xF 0x3A 0xB (ROUNDSD) on OS X
350202   Add limited param to 'monitor block_list'
350290   s390x: Support instructions fixbr(a)
350359   memcheck/tests/x86/fxsave hangs indefinetely on OS X

350809 Fix none/tests/async-sigs for Solaris
350811 Remove reference to --db-attach which has been removed.
350813 Memcheck/x86: enable handwritten assembly helpers for x86/Solaris too
350854 hard-to-understand code in VG_(load_ELF)()
351140 arm64 syscalls setuid (146) and setresgid (149) not implemented
351386 Solaris: Cannot run ld.so.1 under Valgrind
351474 Fix VG_(iseqsigset) as obvious
351534 Fix incorrect header guard
351632 Fix UNKNOWN fcntl 97 on OS X 10.11
351756 Intercept platform_memchr$VARIANT$Haswell on OS X
351858 ldsoexec support on Solaris
351873 Newer gcc doesn't allow __builtin_tabortdc[i] in ppc32 mode
352130 helgrind reports false races for printfs using mempcpy on FILE* state
352284 s390: Conditional jump depends on uninitialised value(s) in vfprintf
352320 arm64 crash on none/tests/nestedfs
352765 Vbit test fails on Power 6
352768 The mbar instruction is missing from the Power PC support
352769 Power PC program priority register (PPR) is not supported
n-i-bz Provide implementations of certain compiler builtins to support
       compilers that may not provide those
n-i-bz Old STABS code is still being compiled, but never used. Remove it.
n-i-bz Fix compilation on distros with glibc < 2.5
n-i-bz (vex 3098) Avoid generation of Neon insns on non-Neon hosts
n-i-bz Enable rt_sigpending syscall on ppc64 linux.
n-i-bz mremap did not work properly on shared memory
n-i-bz Fix incorrect sizeof expression in syswrap-xen.c reported by Coverity
n-i-bz In VALGRIND_PRINTF write out thread name, if any, to xml

(3.11.0.TEST1: 8 September 2015, vex r3187, valgrind r15646)
(3.11.0.TEST2: 21 September 2015, vex r3193, valgrind r15667)
(3.11.0:   22 September 2015, vex r3195, valgrind r15674)

Release 3.10.1 (25 November 2014)
~~~~~~~~~~~~~~~~~~~~~~~~~~~~~~~~~~
3.10.1 is a bug fix release. It fixes various bugs reported in 3.10.0
and backports fixes for all reported missing AArch64 ARMv8 instructions
and syscalls from the trunk. If you package or deliver 3.10.0 for others
to use, you might want to consider upgrading to 3.10.1 instead.

The following bugs have been fixed or resolved. Note that "n-i-bz"
stands for "not in bugzilla" -- that is, a bug that was reported to us
but never got a bugzilla entry. We encourage you to file bugs in
bugzilla (https://bugs.kde.org/enter_bug.cgi?product=valgrind) rather
than mailing the developers (or mailing lists) directly -- bugs that
are not entered into bugzilla tend to get forgotten about or ignored.

To see details of a given bug, visit
  https://bugs.kde.org/show_bug.cgi?id=XXXXXX
where XXXXXX is the bug number as listed below.

335440 arm64: ld1 (single structure) is not implemented
335713 arm64: unhanded instruction: prfm (immediate)

339020 ppc64: memcheck/tests/ppc64/power_ISA2_05 failing in nightly build
339182 ppc64: AvSplat ought to load destination vector register with [..]
339336 PPC64 store quad instruction (stq) is not supposed to change [..]
339433 ppc64 lxvw4x instruction uses four 32-byte loads
339645 Use correct tag names in sys_getdents/64 wrappers
339706 Fix false positive for ioctl(TIOCSIG) on linux
339721 assertion 'check_sibling == sibling' failed in readdwarf3.c ...
339853 arm64 times syscall unknown
339855 arm64 unhandled getsid/setsid syscalls
339858 arm64 dmb sy not implemented
339926 Unhandled instruction 0x1E674001 (frintx) on aarm64
339927 Unhandled instruction 0x9E7100C6 (fcvtmu) on aarch64
339938 disInstr(arm64): unhandled instruction 0x4F8010A4 (fmla)
        == 339950
339940 arm64: unhandled syscall: 83 (sys_fdatasync) + patch
340033 arm64: unhandled insn dmb ishld and some other isb-dmb-dsb variants
340028 unhandled syscalls for arm64 (msync, pread64, setreuid and setregid)
340036 arm64: Unhandled instruction ld4 (multiple structures, no offset)
340236 arm64: unhandled syscalls: mknodat, fchdir, chroot, fchownat
340509 arm64: unhandled instruction fcvtas
340630 arm64: fchmod (52) and fchown (55) syscalls not recognized
340632 arm64: unhandled instruction fcvtas
340722 Resolve "UNKNOWN attrlist flags 0.0x10000000"
340725 AVX2: Incorrect decoding of vpbroadcast{b,w} reg,reg forms
340788 warning: unhandled syscall: 318 (getrandom)
340807 disInstr(arm): unhandled instruction: 0xEE989B20
340856 disInstr(arm64): unhandled instruction 0x1E634C45 (fcsel)
340922 arm64: unhandled getgroups/setgroups syscalls
350251 Fix typo in VEX utility program (test_main.c).
350407 arm64: unhandled instruction ucvtf (vector, integer)
350809 none/tests/async-sigs breaks when run under cron on Solaris
350811 update README.solaris after r15445
350813 Use handwritten memcheck assembly helpers on x86/Solaris [..]
350854 strange code in VG_(load_ELF)()
351140 arm64 syscalls setuid (146) and setresgid (149) not implemented
n-i-bz DRD and Helgrind: Handle Imbe_CancelReservation (clrex on ARM)
n-i-bz Add missing]] to terminate CDATA.
n-i-bz Glibc versions prior to 2.5 do not define PTRACE_GETSIGINFO
n-i-bz Enable sys_fadvise64_64 on arm32.
n-i-bz Add test cases for all remaining AArch64 SIMD, FP and memory insns.
n-i-bz Add test cases for all known arm64 load/store instructions.
n-i-bz PRE(sys_openat): when checking whether ARG1 == VKI_AT_FDCWD [..]
n-i-bz Add detection of old ppc32 magic instructions from bug 278808.
n-i-bz exp-dhat: Implement missing function "dh_malloc_usable_size".
n-i-bz arm64: Implement "fcvtpu w, s".
n-i-bz arm64: implement ADDP and various others
n-i-bz arm64: Implement {S,U}CVTF (scalar, fixedpt).
n-i-bz arm64: enable FCVT{A,N}S X,S.

(3.10.1: 25 November 2014, vex r3026, valgrind r14785)

Release 3.10.0 (10 September 2014)

~~~~~~~~~~~~~~~~~~~~~~~~~~~~~~~~

3.10.0 is a feature release with many improvements and the usual
collection of bug fixes.

This release supports X86/Linux, AMD64/Linux, ARM32/Linux, ARM64/Linux,
PPC32/Linux, PPC64BE/Linux, PPC64LE/Linux, S390X/Linux, MIPS32/Linux,
MIPS64/Linux, ARM/Android, MIPS32/Android, X86/Android, X86/MacOSX 10.9
and AMD64/MacOSX 10.9. Support for MacOSX 10.8 and 10.9 is
significantly improved relative to the 3.9.0 release.

* =================== PLATFORM CHANGES =================

* Support for the 64-bit ARM Architecture (AArch64 ARMv8). This port
  is mostly complete, and is usable, but some SIMD instructions are as
  yet unsupported.

* Support for little-endian variant of the 64-bit POWER architecture.

* Support for Android on MIPS32.

* Support for 64bit FPU on MIPS32 platforms.

* Both 32- and 64-bit executables are supported on MacOSX 10.8 and 10.9.

* Configuration for and running on Android targets has changed.
  See README.android in the source tree for details.

* =================== DEPRECATED FEATURES =================

* --db-attach is now deprecated and will be removed in the next
  valgrind feature release. The built-in GDB server capabilities are
  superior and should be used instead. Learn more here:
  http://valgrind.org/docs/manual/manual-core-adv.html#manual-core-adv.gdbserver

* ===================== TOOL CHANGES ====================

* Memcheck:

  - Client code can now selectively disable and re-enable reporting of
    invalid address errors in specific ranges using the new client
    requests VALGRIND_DISABLE_ADDR_ERROR_REPORTING_IN_RANGE and
    VALGRIND_ENABLE_ADDR_ERROR_REPORTING_IN_RANGE.

  - Leak checker: there is a new leak check heuristic called
    "length64". This is used to detect interior pointers pointing 8
    bytes inside a block, on the assumption that the first 8 bytes
    holds the value "block size - 8". This is used by
    sqlite3MemMalloc, for example.

  - Checking of system call parameters: if a syscall parameter
    (e.g. bind struct sockaddr, sendmsg struct msghdr, ...) has
    several fields not initialised, an error is now reported for each
    field. Previously, an error was reported only for the first

uninitialised field.

- Mismatched alloc/free checking: a new flag
  --show-mismatched-frees=no|yes [yes] makes it possible to turn off
  such checks if necessary.

* Helgrind:

  - Improvements to error messages:

    o Race condition error message involving heap allocated blocks also
      show the thread number that allocated the raced-on block.

    o All locks referenced by an error message are now announced.
      Previously, some error messages only showed the lock addresses.

    o The message indicating where a lock was first observed now also
      describes the address/location of the lock.

  - Helgrind now understands the Ada task termination rules and
    creates a happens-before relationship between a terminated task
    and its master. This avoids some false positives and avoids a big
    memory leak when a lot of Ada tasks are created and terminated.
    The interceptions are only activated with forthcoming releases of
    gnatpro >= 7.3.0w-20140611 and gcc >= 5.0.

  - A new GDB server monitor command "info locks" giving the list of
    locks, their location, and their status.

* Callgrind:

  - callgrind_control now supports the --vgdb-prefix argument,
    which is needed if valgrind was started with this same argument.

* ==================== OTHER CHANGES ====================

* Unwinding through inlined function calls. Stack unwinding can now
  make use of Dwarf3 inlined-unwind information if it is available.
  The practical effect is that inlined calls become visible in stack
  traces. The suppression matching machinery has been adjusted
  accordingly. This is controlled by the new option
  --read-inline-info=yes|no. Currently this is enabled by default
  only on Linux and Android targets and only for the tools Memcheck,
  Helgrind and DRD.

* Valgrind can now read EXIDX unwind information on 32-bit ARM
  targets. If an object contains both CFI and EXIDX unwind
  information, Valgrind will prefer the CFI over the EXIDX. This
  facilitates unwinding through system libraries on arm-android
  targets.

* Address description logic has been improved and is now common
  between Memcheck and Helgrind, resulting in better address
  descriptions for some kinds of error messages.

* Error messages about dubious arguments (eg, to malloc or calloc) are
  output like other errors. This means that they can be suppressed
  and they have a stack trace.

* The C++ demangler has been updated for better C++11 support.

* New and modified GDB server monitor features:

  - Thread local variables/storage (__thread) can now be displayed.

  - The GDB server monitor command "v.info location <address>"
    displays information about an address. The information produced
    depends on the tool and on the options given to valgrind.
    Possibly, the following are described: global variables, local
    (stack) variables, allocated or freed blocks, ...

  - The option "--vgdb-stop-at=event1,event2,..." allows the user to
    ask the GDB server to stop at the start of program execution, at
    the end of the program execution and on Valgrind internal errors.

  - A new monitor command "v.info stats" shows various Valgrind core
    and tool statistics.

  - A new monitor command "v.set hostvisibility" allows the GDB server
    to provide access to Valgrind internal host status/memory.

* A new option "--aspace-minaddr=<address>" can in some situations
  allow the use of more memory by decreasing the address above which
  Valgrind maps memory. It can also be used to solve address
  conflicts with system libraries by increasing the default value.
  See user manual for details.

* The amount of memory used by Valgrind to store debug info (unwind
  info, line number information and symbol data) has been
  significantly reduced, even though Valgrind now reads more
  information in order to support unwinding of inlined function calls.

* Dwarf3 handling with --read-var-info=yes has been improved:

  - Ada and C struct containing VLAs no longer cause a "bad DIE" error

  - Code compiled with
    -ffunction-sections -fdata-sections -Wl,--gc-sections
    no longer causes assertion failures.

* Improved checking for the --sim-hints= and --kernel-variant=
  options. Unknown strings are now detected and reported to the user
  as a usage error.

* The semantics of stack start/end boundaries in the valgrind.h
  VALGRIND_STACK_REGISTER client request has been clarified and
  documented. The convention is that start and end are respectively
  the lowest and highest addressable bytes of the stack.

* ==================== FIXED BUGS ====================

The following bugs have been fixed or resolved. Note that "n-i-bz"
stands for "not in bugzilla" -- that is, a bug that was reported to us
but never got a bugzilla entry. We encourage you to file bugs in
bugzilla (https://bugs.kde.org/enter_bug.cgi?product=valgrind) rather
than mailing the developers (or mailing lists) directly -- bugs that
are not entered into bugzilla tend to get forgotten about or ignored.

To see details of a given bug, visit
  https://bugs.kde.org/show_bug.cgi?id=XXXXXX
where XXXXXX is the bug number as listed below.

```
175819  Support for ipv6 socket reporting with --track-fds
232510  make distcheck fails
249435  Analyzing wine programs with callgrind triggers a crash
278972  support for inlined function calls in stacktraces and suppression
          == 199144
291310  FXSAVE instruction marks memory as undefined on amd64
303536  ioctl for SIOCETHTOOL (ethtool(8)) isn't wrapped
308729  vex x86->IR: unhandled instruction bytes 0xf 0x5 (syscall)
315199  vgcore file for threaded app does not show which thread crashed
315952  tun/tap ioctls are not supported
323178  Unhandled instruction: PLDW register (ARM)
323179  Unhandled instruction: PLDW immediate (ARM)
324050  Helgrind: SEGV because of unaligned stack when using movdqa
325110  Add test-cases for Power ISA 2.06 insns: divdo/divdo. and divduo/divduo.
325124  [MIPSEL] Compilation error
325477  Phase 4 support for IBM Power ISA 2.07
325538  cavium octeon mips64, valgrind reported "dumping core" [...]
325628  Phase 5 support for IBM Power ISA 2.07
325714  Empty vgcore but RLIMIT_CORE is big enough (too big)
325751  Missing the two privileged Power PC Transactional Memory Instructions
325816  Phase 6 support for IBM Power ISA 2.07
325856  Make SGCheck fail gracefully on unsupported platforms
326026  Iop names for count leading zeros/sign bits incorrectly imply [..]
326436  DRD: False positive in libstdc++ std::list::push_back
326444  Cavium MIPS Octeon Specific Load Indexed Instructions
326462  Refactor vgdb to isolate invoker stuff into separate module
326469  amd64->IR: 0x66 0xF 0x3A 0x63 0xC1 0xE (pcmpistri 0x0E)
326623  DRD: false positive conflict report in a field assignment
326724  Valgrind does not compile on OSX 1.9 Mavericks
326816  Intercept for __strncpy_sse2_unaligned missing?
326921  coregrind fails to compile m_trampoline.S with MIPS/Linux port of V
326983  Clear direction flag after tests on amd64.
327212  Do not prepend the current directory to absolute path names.
327223  Support for Cavium MIPS Octeon Atomic and Count Instructions
327238  Callgrind Assertion 'passed <= last_bb->cjmp_count' failed
327284  s390x: Fix translation of the risbg instruction
327639  vex amd64->IR pcmpestri SSE4.2 instruction is unsupported 0x34
327837  dwz compressed alternate .debug_info and .debug_str not read correctly
327916  DW_TAG_typedef may have no name
327943  s390x: add a redirection for the 'index' function
```

328100   XABORT not implemented
328205   Implement additional Xen hypercalls
328454   add support Backtraces with ARM unwind tables (EXIDX)
328455   s390x: SIGILL after emitting wrong register pair for ldxbr
328711   valgrind.1 manpage "memcheck options" section is badly generated
328878   vex amd64->IR pcmpestri SSE4.2 instruction is unsupported 0x14
329612   Incorrect handling of AT_BASE for image execution
329694   clang warns about using uninitialized variable
329956   valgrind crashes when lmw/stmw instructions are used on ppc64
330228   mmap must align to VKI_SHMLBA on mips32
330257   LLVM does not support '-mno-dynamic-no-pic' option
330319   amd64->IR: unhandled instruction bytes: 0xF 0x1 0xD5 (xend)
330459   --track-fds=yes doesn't track eventfds
330469   Add clock_adjtime syscall support
330594   Missing sysalls on PowerPC / uClibc
330622   Add test to regression suite for POWER instruction: dcbzl
330939   Support for AMD's syscall instruction on x86
         == 308729
330941   Typo in PRE(poll) syscall wrapper
331057   unhandled instruction: 0xEEE01B20 (vfma.f64) (has patch)
331254   Fix expected output for memcheck/tests/dw4
331255   Fix race condition in test none/tests/coolo_sigaction
331257   Fix type of jump buffer in test none/tests/faultstatus
331305   configure uses bash specific syntax
331337   s390x WARNING: unhandled syscall: 326 (dup3)
331380   Syscall param timer_create(evp) points to uninitialised byte(s)
331476   Patch to handle ioctl 0x5422 on Linux (x86 and amd64)
331829   Unexpected ioctl opcode sign extension
331830   ppc64: WARNING: unhandled syscall: 96/97
331839   drd/tests/sem_open specifies invalid semaphore name
331847   outcome of drd/tests/thread_name is nondeterministic
332037   Valgrind cannot handle Thumb "add pc, reg"
332055   drd asserts on platforms with VG_STACK_REDZONE_SZB == 0 and
         consistency checks enabled
332263   intercepts for pthread_rwlock_timedrdlock and
         pthread_rwlock_timedwrlock are incorrect
332265   drd could do with post-rwlock_init and pre-rwlock_destroy
         client requests
332276   Implement additional Xen hypercalls
332658   ldrd.w r1, r2, [PC, #imm] does not adjust for 32bit alignment
332765   Fix ms_print to create temporary files in a proper directory
333072   drd: Add semaphore annotations
333145   Tests for missaligned PC+#imm access for arm
333228   AAarch64 Missing instruction encoding: mrs %[reg], ctr_el0
333230   AAarch64 missing instruction encodings: dc, ic, dsb.
333248   WARNING: unhandled syscall: unix:443
333428   ldr.w pc [rD, #imm] instruction leads to assertion
333501   cachegrind: assertion: Cache set count is not a power of two.
         == 336577
         == 292281
333666   Recognize MPX instructions and bnd prefix.
333788   Valgrind does not support the CDROM_DISC_STATUS ioctl (has patch)
333817   Valgrind reports the memory areas written to by the SG_IO
         ioctl as untouched

334049   lzcnt fails silently (x86_32)
334384   Valgrind does not have support Little Endian support for
         IBM POWER PPC 64
334585   recvmmsg unhandled (+patch) (arm)
334705   sendmsg and recvmsg should guard against bogus msghdr fields.
334727   Build fails with -Werror=format-security
334788   clarify doc about --log-file initial program directory
334834   PPC64 Little Endian support, patch 2
334836   PPC64 Little Endian support, patch 3 testcase fixes
334936   patch to fix false positives on alsa SNDRV_CTL_* ioctls
335034   Unhandled ioctl: HCIGETDEVLIST
335155   vgdb, fix error print statement.
335262   arm64: movi 8bit version is not supported
335263   arm64: dmb instruction is not implemented
335441   unhandled ioctl 0x8905 (SIOCATMARK) when running wine under valgrind
335496   arm64: sbc/abc instructions are not implemented
335554   arm64: unhandled instruction: abs
335564   arm64: unhandled instruction: fcvtpu Xn, Sn
335735   arm64: unhandled instruction: cnt
335736   arm64: unhandled instruction: uaddlv
335848   arm64: unhandled instruction: {s,u}cvtf
335902   arm64: unhandled instruction: sli
335903   arm64: unhandled instruction: umull (vector)
336055   arm64: unhandled instruction: mov (element)
336062   arm64: unhandled instruction: shrn{,2}
336139   mip64: [...] valgrind hangs and spins on a single core [...]
336189   arm64: unhandled Instruction: mvn
336435   Valgrind hangs in pthread_spin_lock consuming 100% CPU
336619   valgrind --read-var-info=yes doesn't handle DW_TAG_restrict_type
336772   Make moans about unknown ioctls more informative
336957   Add a section about the Solaris/illumos port on the webpage
337094   ifunc wrapper is broken on ppc64
337285   fcntl commands F_OFD_SETLK, F_OFD_SETLKW, and F_OFD_GETLK not supported
337528   leak check heuristic for block prefixed by length as 64bit number
337740   Implement additional Xen hypercalls
337762   guest_arm64_toIR.c:4166 (dis_ARM64_load_store): Assertion '0' failed.
337766   arm64-linux: unhandled syscalls mlock (228) and mlockall (230)
337871   deprecate --db-attach
338023   Add support for all V4L2/media ioctls
338024   inlined functions are not shown if DW_AT_ranges is used
338106   Add support for 'kcmp' syscall
338115   DRD: computed conflict set differs from actual after fork
338160   implement display of thread local storage in gdbsrv
338205   configure.ac and check for -Wno-tautological-compare
338300   coredumps are missing one byte of every segment
338445   amd64 vbit-test fails with unknown opcodes used by arm64 VEX
338499   --sim-hints parsing broken due to wrong order in tokens
338615   suppress glibc 2.20 optimized strcmp implementation for ARMv7
338681   Unable to unwind through clone thread created on i386-linux
338698   race condition between gdbsrv and vgdb on startup
338703   helgrind on arm-linux gets false positives in dynamic loader
338791   alt dwz files can be relative of debug/main file
338878   on MacOS: assertion 'VG_IS_PAGE_ALIGNED(clstack_end+1)' failed
338932   build V-trunk with gcc-trunk

338974 glibc 2.20 changed size of struct sigaction sa_flags field on s390
345079 Fix build problems in VEX/useful/test_main.c
n-i-bz Fix KVM_CREATE_IRQCHIP ioctl handling
n-i-bz s390x: Fix memory corruption for multithreaded applications
n-i-bz vex arm->IR: allow PC as basereg in some LDRD cases
n-i-bz internal error in Valgrind if vgdb transmit signals when ptrace invoked
n-i-bz Fix mingw64 support in valgrind.h (dev@, 9 May 2014)
n-i-bz drd manual: Document how to C++11 programs that use class "std::thread"
n-i-bz Add command-line option --default-suppressions
n-i-bz Add support for BLKDISCARDZEROES ioctl
n-i-bz ppc32/64: fix a regression with the mtfsb0/mtfsb1 instructions
n-i-bz Add support for sys_pivot_root and sys_unshare

(3.10.0.BETA1: 2 September 2014, vex r2940, valgrind r14428)
(3.10.0.BETA2: 8 September 2014, vex r2950, valgrind r14503)
(3.10.0:   10 September 2014, vex r2950, valgrind r14514)

Release 3.9.0 (31 October 2013)
~~~~~~~~~~~~~~~~~~~~~~~~~~~~~~~~~
3.9.0 is a feature release with many improvements and the usual
collection of bug fixes.

This release supports X86/Linux, AMD64/Linux, ARM/Linux, PPC32/Linux,
PPC64/Linux, S390X/Linux, MIPS32/Linux, MIPS64/Linux, ARM/Android,
X86/Android, X86/MacOSX 10.7 and AMD64/MacOSX 10.7. Support for
MacOSX 10.8 is significantly improved relative to the 3.8.0 release.

* ================== PLATFORM CHANGES ==================

* Support for MIPS64 LE and BE running Linux. Valgrind has been
  tested on MIPS64 Debian Squeeze and Debian Wheezy distributions.

* Support for MIPS DSP ASE on MIPS32 platforms.

* Support for s390x Decimal Floating Point instructions on hosts that
  have the DFP facility installed.

* Support for POWER8 (Power ISA 2.07) instructions

* Support for Intel AVX2 instructions. This is available only on 64
  bit code.

* Initial support for Intel Transactional Synchronization Extensions,
  both RTM and HLE.

* Initial support for Hardware Transactional Memory on POWER.

* Improved support for MacOSX 10.8 (64-bit only). Memcheck can now
  run large GUI apps tolerably well.

* ==================== TOOL CHANGES ====================

* Memcheck:

 - Improvements in handling of vectorised code, leading to
   significantly fewer false error reports. You need to use the flag
   --partial-loads-ok=yes to get the benefits of these changes.

 - Better control over the leak checker. It is now possible to
   specify which leak kinds (definite/indirect/possible/reachable)
   should be displayed, which should be regarded as errors, and which
   should be suppressed by a given leak suppression. This is done
   using the options --show-leak-kinds=kind1,kind2,..,
   --errors-for-leak-kinds=kind1,kind2,.. and an optional
   "match-leak-kinds:" line in suppression entries, respectively.

   Note that generated leak suppressions contain this new line and
   are therefore more specific than in previous releases. To get the
   same behaviour as previous releases, remove the "match-leak-kinds:"
   line from generated suppressions before using them.

 - Reduced "possible leak" reports from the leak checker by the use
   of better heuristics. The available heuristics provide detection
   of valid interior pointers to std::stdstring, to new[] allocated
   arrays with elements having destructors and to interior pointers
   pointing to an inner part of a C++ object using multiple
   inheritance. They can be selected individually using the
   option --leak-check-heuristics=heur1,heur2,...

 - Better control of stacktrace acquisition for heap-allocated
   blocks. Using the --keep-stacktraces option, it is possible to
   control independently whether a stack trace is acquired for each
   allocation and deallocation. This can be used to create better
   "use after free" errors or to decrease Valgrind's resource
   consumption by recording less information.

 - Better reporting of leak suppression usage. The list of used
   suppressions (shown when the -v option is given) now shows, for
   each leak suppressions, how many blocks and bytes it suppressed
   during the last leak search.

* Helgrind:

 - False errors resulting from the use of statically initialised
   mutexes and condition variables (PTHREAD_MUTEX_INITIALISER, etc)
   have been removed.

 - False errors resulting from the use of pthread_cond_waits that
   timeout, have been removed.

* ==================== OTHER CHANGES ====================

* Some attempt to tune Valgrind's space requirements to the expected
  capabilities of the target:

 - The default size of the translation cache has been reduced from 8 sectors to 6 on Android platforms, since each sector occupies about 40MB when using Memcheck.

- The default size of the translation cache has been increased to 16 sectors on all other platforms, reflecting the fact that large applications require instrumentation and storage of huge amounts of code. For similar reasons, the number of memory mapped segments that can be tracked has been increased by a factor of 6.

- In all cases, the maximum number of sectors in the translation cache can be controlled by the new flag --num-transtab-sectors.

* Changes in how debug info (line numbers, etc) is read:

- Valgrind no longer temporarily mmaps the entire object to read from it. Instead, reading is done through a small fixed sized buffer. This avoids virtual memory usage spikes when Valgrind reads debuginfo from large shared objects.

- A new experimental remote debug info server. Valgrind can read debug info from a different machine (typically, a build host) where debuginfo objects are stored. This can save a lot of time and hassle when running Valgrind on resource-constrained targets (phones, tablets) when the full debuginfo objects are stored somewhere else. This is enabled by the --debuginfo-server= option.

- Consistency checking between main and debug objects can be disabled using the --allow-mismatched-debuginfo option.

* Stack unwinding by stack scanning, on ARM. Unwinding by stack scanning can recover stack traces in some cases when the normal unwind mechanisms fail. Stack scanning is best described as "a nasty, dangerous and misleading hack" and so is disabled by default. Use --unw-stack-scan-thresh and --unw-stack-scan-frames to enable and control it.

* Detection and merging of recursive stack frame cycles. When your program has recursive algorithms, this limits the memory used by Valgrind for recorded stack traces and avoids recording uninteresting repeated calls. This is controlled by the command line option --merge-recursive-frame and by the monitor command "v.set merge-recursive-frames".

* File name and line numbers for used suppressions. The list of used suppressions (shown when the -v option is given) now shows, for each used suppression, the file name and line number where the suppression is defined.

* New and modified GDB server monitor features:

- valgrind.h has a new client request, VALGRIND_MONITOR_COMMAND, that can be used to execute gdbserver monitor commands from the client program.

- A new monitor command, "v.info open_fds", that gives the list of
  open file descriptors and additional details.

- An optional message in the "v.info n_errs_found" monitor command,
  for example "v.info n_errs_found test 1234 finished", allowing a
  comment string to be added to the process output, perhaps for the
  purpose of separating errors of different tests or test phases.

- A new monitor command "v.info execontext" that shows information
  about the stack traces recorded by Valgrind.

- A new monitor command "v.do expensive_sanity_check_general" to run
  some internal consistency checks.

* New flag --sigill-diagnostics to control whether a diagnostic
  message is printed when the JIT encounters an instruction it can't
  translate. The actual behavior -- delivery of SIGILL to the
  application -- is unchanged.

* The maximum amount of memory that Valgrind can use on 64 bit targets
  has been increased from 32GB to 64GB. This should make it possible
  to run applications on Memcheck that natively require up to about 35GB.

* ===================== FIXED BUGS =====================

The following bugs have been fixed or resolved. Note that "n-i-bz"
stands for "not in bugzilla" -- that is, a bug that was reported to us
but never got a bugzilla entry. We encourage you to file bugs in
bugzilla (https://bugs.kde.org/enter_bug.cgi?product=valgrind) rather
than mailing the developers (or mailing lists) directly -- bugs that
are not entered into bugzilla tend to get forgotten about or ignored.

To see details of a given bug, visit
   https://bugs.kde.org/show_bug.cgi?id=XXXXXX
where XXXXXX is the bug number as listed below.

123837   system call: 4th argument is optional, depending on cmd
135425   memcheck should tell you where Freed blocks were Mallocd
164485   VG_N_SEGNAMES and VG_N_SEGMENTS are (still) too small
207815   Adds some of the drm ioctls to syswrap-linux.c
251569   vex amd64->IR: 0xF 0x1 0xF9 0xBF 0x90 0xD0 0x3 0x0 (RDTSCP)
252955   Impossible to compile with ccache
253519   Memcheck reports auxv pointer accesses as invalid reads.
263034   Crash when loading some PPC64 binaries
269599   Increase deepest backtrace
274695   s390x: Support "compare to/from logical" instructions (z196)
275800   s390x: Autodetect cache info (part 2)
280271   Valgrind reports possible memory leaks on still-reachable std::string
284540   Memcheck shouldn't count suppressions matching still-reachable [..]
289578   Backtraces with ARM unwind tables (stack scan flags)
296311   Wrong stack traces due to -fomit-frame-pointer (x86)
304832   ppc32: build failure
305431   Use find_buildid shdr fallback for separate .debug files

305728   Add support for AVX2 instructions
305948   ppc64: code generation for ShlD64 / ShrD64 asserts
306035   s390x: Fix IR generation for LAAG and friends
306054   s390x: Condition code computation for convert-to-int/logical
306098   s390x: alternate opcode form for convert to/from fixed
306587   Fix cache line detection from auxiliary vector for PPC.
306783   Mips unhandled syscall :   4025   /   4079   / 4182
307038   DWARF2 CFI reader: unhandled DW_OP_ opcode 0x8 (DW_OP_const1u et al)
307082   HG false positive: pthread_cond_destroy: destruction of unknown CV
307101   sys_capget second argument can be NULL
307103   sys_openat: If pathname is absolute, then dirfd is ignored.
307106   amd64->IR: f0 0f c0 02 (lock xadd byte)
307113   s390x: DFP support
307141   valgrind does't work in mips-linux system
307155   filter_gdb should filter out syscall-template.S T_PSEUDO
307285   x86_amd64 feature test for avx in test suite is wrong
307290   memcheck overlap testcase needs memcpy version filter
307463   Please add "&limit=0" to the "all open bugs" link
307465   --show-possibly-lost=no should reduce the error count / exit code
307557   Leaks on Mac OS X 10.7.5 libraries at ImageLoader::recursiveInit[..]
307729   pkgconfig support broken valgrind.pc
307828   Memcheck false errors SSE optimized wcscpy, wcscmp, wcsrchr, wcschr
307955   Building valgrind 3.7.0-r4 fails in Gentoo AMD64 when using clang
308089   Unhandled syscall on ppc64: prctl
308135   PPC32 MPC8xx has 16 bytes cache size
308321   testsuite memcheck filter interferes with gdb_filter
308333   == 307106
308341   vgdb should report process exit (or fatal signal)
308427   s390 memcheck reports tsearch cjump/cmove depends on uninit
308495   Remove build dependency on installed Xen headers
308573   Internal error on 64-bit instruction executed in 32-bit mode
308626   == 308627
308627   pmovmskb validity bit propagation is imprecise
308644   vgdb command for having the info for the track-fds option
308711   give more info about aspacemgr and arenas in out_of_memory
308717   ARM: implement fixed-point VCVT.F64.[SU]32
308718   ARM implement SMLALBB family of instructions
308886   Missing support for PTRACE_SET/GETREGSET
308930   syscall name_to_handle_at (303 on amd64) not handled
309229   V-bit tester does not report number of tests generated
309323   print unrecognized instuction on MIPS
309425   Provide a --sigill-diagnostics flag to suppress illegal [..]
309427   SSE optimized stpncpy trigger uninitialised value [..] errors
309430   Self hosting ppc64 encounters a vassert error on operand type
309600   valgrind is a bit confused about 0-sized sections
309823   Generate errors for still reachable blocks
309921   PCMPISTRI validity bit propagation is imprecise
309922   none/tests/ppc64/test_dfp5 sometimes fails
310169   The Iop_CmpORD class of Iops is not supported by the vbit checker.
310424   --read-var-info does not properly describe static variables
310792   search additional path for debug symbols
310931   s390x: Message-security assist (MSA) instruction extension [..]
311100   PPC DFP implementation of the integer operands is inconsistent [..]
311318   ARM: "128-bit constant is not implemented" error message

311407 ssse3 bcopy (actually converted memcpy) causes invalid read [..]
311690 V crashes because it redirects branches inside of a redirected function
311880 x86_64: make regtest hangs at shell_valid1
311922 WARNING: unhandled syscall: 170
311933 == 251569
312171 ppc: insn selection for DFP
312571 Rounding mode call wrong for the DFP Iops [..]
312620 Change to Iop_D32toD64 [..] for s390 DFP support broke ppc [..]
312913 Dangling pointers error should also report the alloc stack trace
312980 Building on Mountain Lion generates some compiler warnings
313267 Adding MIPS64/Linux port to Valgrind
313348 == 251569
313354 == 251569
313811 Buffer overflow in assert_fail
314099 coverity pointed out error in VEX guest_ppc_toIR.c insn_suffix
314269 ppc: dead code in insn selection
314718 ARM: implement integer divide instruction (sdiv and udiv)
315345 cl-format.xml and callgrind/dump.c don't agree on using cfl= or cfi=
315441 sendmsg syscall should ignore unset msghdr msg_flags
315534 msgrcv inside a thread causes valgrind to hang (block)
315545 Assertion '(UChar*)sec->tt[tteNo].tcptr <= (UChar*)hcode' failed
315689 disInstr(thumb): unhandled instruction: 0xF852 0x0E10 (LDRT)
315738 disInstr(arm): unhandled instruction: 0xEEBE0BEE (vcvt.s32.f64)
315959 valgrind man page has bogus SGCHECK (and no BBV) OPTIONS section
316144 valgrind.1 manpage contains unknown ??? strings [..]
316145 callgrind command line options in manpage reference (unknown) [..]
316145 callgrind command line options in manpage reference [..]
316181 drd: Fixed a 4x slowdown for certain applications
316503 Valgrind does not support SSE4 "movntdqa" instruction
316535 Use of |signed int| instead of |size_t| in valgrind messages
316696   fluidanimate program of parsec 2.1 stuck
316761 syscall open_by_handle_at (304 on amd64, 342 on x86) not handled
317091 Use -Wl,-Ttext-segment when static linking if possible [..]
317186 "Impossible happens" when occurs VCVT instruction on ARM
317318 Support for Threading Building Blocks "scalable_malloc"
317444 amd64->IR: 0xC4 0x41 0x2C 0xC2 0xD2 0x8 (vcmpeq_uqps)
317461 Fix BMI assembler configure check and avx2/bmi/fma vgtest prereqs
317463 bmi testcase IR SANITY CHECK FAILURE
317506 memcheck/tests/vbit-test fails with unknown opcode after [..]
318050 libmpiwrap fails to compile with out-of-source build
318203 setsockopt handling needs to handle SOL_SOCKET/SO_ATTACH_FILTER
318643 annotate_trace_memory tests infinite loop on arm and ppc [..]
318773 amd64->IR: 0xF3 0x48 0x0F 0xBC 0xC2 0xC3 0x66 0x0F
318929 Crash with: disInstr(thumb): 0xF321 0x0001 (ssat16)
318932 Add missing PPC64 and PPC32 system call support
319235 --db-attach=yes is broken with Yama (ptrace scoping) enabled
319395 Crash with unhandled instruction on STRT (Thumb) instructions
319494 VEX Makefile-gcc standalone build update after r2702
319505 [MIPSEL] Crash: unhandled UNRAY operator.
319858 disInstr(thumb): unhandled instruction on instruction STRBT
319932 disInstr(thumb): unhandled instruction on instruction STRHT
320057 Problems when we try to mmap more than 12 memory pages on MIPS32
320063 Memory from PTRACE_GET_THREAD_AREA is reported uninitialised
320083 disInstr(thumb): unhandled instruction on instruction LDRBT

320116 bind on AF_BLUETOOTH produces warnings because of sockaddr_rc padding
320131 WARNING: unhandled syscall: 369 on ARM (prlimit64)
320211 Stack buffer overflow in ./coregrind/m_main.c with huge TMPDIR
320661 vgModuleLocal_read_elf_debug_info(): "Assertion '!di->soname'
320895 add fanotify support (patch included)
320998 vex amd64->IR pcmpestri and pcmpestrm SSE4.2 instruction
321065 Valgrind updates for Xen 4.3
321148 Unhandled instruction: PLI (Thumb 1, 2, 3)
321363 Unhandled instruction: SSAX (ARM + Thumb)
321364 Unhandled instruction: SXTAB16 (ARM + Thumb)
321466 Unhandled instruction: SHASX (ARM + Thumb)
321467 Unhandled instruction: SHSAX (ARM + Thumb)
321468 Unhandled instruction: SHSUB16 (ARM + Thumb)
321619 Unhandled instruction: SHSUB8 (ARM + Thumb)
321620 Unhandled instruction: UASX (ARM + Thumb)
321621 Unhandled instruction: USAX (ARM + Thumb)
321692 Unhandled instruction: UQADD16 (ARM + Thumb)
321693 Unhandled instruction: LDRSBT (Thumb)
321694 Unhandled instruction: UQASX (ARM + Thumb)
321696 Unhandled instruction: UQSAX (Thumb + ARM)
321697 Unhandled instruction: UHASX (ARM + Thumb)
321703 Unhandled instruction: UHSAX (ARM + Thumb)
321704 Unhandled instruction: REVSH (ARM + Thumb)
321730 Add cg_diff and cg_merge man pages
321738 Add vgdb and valgrind-listener man pages
321814 == 315545
321891 Unhandled instruction: LDRHT (Thumb)
321960 pthread_create() then alloca() causing invalid stack write errors
321969 ppc32 and ppc64 don't support [lf]setxattr
322254 Show threadname together with tid if set by application
322294 Add initial support for IBM Power ISA 2.07
322368 Assertion failure in wqthread_hijack under OS X 10.8
322563 vex mips->IR: 0x70 0x83 0xF0 0x3A
322807 VALGRIND_PRINTF_BACKTRACE writes callstack to xml and text to stderr
322851 0bXXX binary literal syntax is not standard
323035 Unhandled instruction: LDRSHT(Thumb)
323036 Unhandled instruction: SMMLS (ARM and Thumb)
323116 The memcheck/tests/ppc64/power_ISA2_05.c fails to build [..]
323175 Unhandled instruction: SMLALD (ARM + Thumb)
323177 Unhandled instruction: SMLSLD (ARM + Thumb)
323432 Calling pthread_cond_destroy() or pthread_mutex_destroy() [..]
323437 Phase 2 support for IBM Power ISA 2.07
323713 Support mmxext (integer sse) subset on i386 (athlon)
323803 Transactional memory instructions are not supported for Power
323893 SSE3 not available on amd cpus in valgrind
323905 Probable false positive from Valgrind/drd on close()
323912 valgrind.h header isn't compatible for mingw64
324047 Valgrind doesn't support [LDR,ST]{S}[B,H]T ARM instructions
324149 helgrind: When pthread_cond_timedwait returns ETIMEDOUT [..]
324181 mmap does not handle MAP_32BIT
324227 memcheck false positive leak when a thread calls exit+block [..]
324421 Support for fanotify API on ARM architecture
324514 gdbserver monitor cmd output behaviour consistency [..]
324518 ppc64: Emulation of dcbt instructions does not handle [..]

324546   none/tests/ppc32 test_isa_2_07_part2 requests -m64
324582   When access is made to freed memory, report both allocation [..]
324594   Fix overflow computation for Power ISA 2.06 insns: mulldo/mulldo.
324765   ppc64: illegal instruction when executing none/tests/ppc64/jm-misc
324816   Incorrect VEX implementation for xscvspdp/xvcvspdp for SNaN inputs
324834   Unhandled instructions in Microsoft C run-time for x86_64
324894   Phase 3 support for IBM Power ISA 2.07
326091   drd: Avoid false race reports from optimized strlen() impls
326113   valgrind libvex hwcaps error on AMD64
n-i-bz   Some wrong command line options could be ignored
n-i-bz   patch to allow fair-sched on android
n-i-bz   report error for vgdb snapshot requested before execution
n-i-bz   same as 303624 (fixed in 3.8.0), but for x86 android

(3.9.0: 31 October 2013, vex r2796, valgrind r13708)

Release 3.8.1 (19 September 2012)
~~~~~~~~~~~~~~~~~~~~~~~~~~~~~~~~~~~
3.8.1 is a bug fix release. It fixes some assertion failures in 3.8.0
that occur moderately frequently in real use cases, adds support for
some missing instructions on ARM, and fixes a deadlock condition on
MacOSX. If you package or deliver 3.8.0 for others to use, you might
want to consider upgrading to 3.8.1 instead.

The following bugs have been fixed or resolved. Note that "n-i-bz"
stands for "not in bugzilla" -- that is, a bug that was reported to us
but never got a bugzilla entry. We encourage you to file bugs in
bugzilla (https://bugs.kde.org/enter_bug.cgi?product=valgrind) rather
than mailing the developers (or mailing lists) directly -- bugs that
are not entered into bugzilla tend to get forgotten about or ignored.

To see details of a given bug, visit
   https://bugs.kde.org/show_bug.cgi?id=XXXXXX
where XXXXXX is the bug number as listed below.

284004   == 301281
289584   Unhandled instruction: 0xF 0x29 0xE5 (MOVAPS)
295808   amd64->IR: 0xF3 0xF 0xBC 0xC0 (TZCNT)
298281   wcslen causes false(?) uninitialised value warnings
301281   valgrind hangs on OS X when the process calls system()
304035   disInstr(arm): unhandled instruction 0xE1023053
304867   implement MOVBE instruction in x86 mode
304980   Assertion 'lo <= hi' failed in vgModuleLocal_find_rx_mapping
305042   amd64: implement 0F 7F encoding of movq between two registers
305199   ARM: implement QDADD and QDSUB
305321   amd64->IR: 0xF 0xD 0xC (prefetchw)
305513   killed by fatal signal: SIGSEGV
305690   DRD reporting invalid semaphore when sem_trywait fails
305926   Invalid alignment checks for some AVX instructions
306297   disInstr(thumb): unhandled instruction 0xE883 0x000C
306310   3.8.0 release tarball missing some files
306612   RHEL 6 glibc-2.X default suppressions need /lib*/libc-*patterns

306664   vex amd64->IR: 0x66 0xF 0x3A 0x62 0xD1 0x46 0x66 0xF
n-i-bz   shmat of a segment > 4Gb does not work
n-i-bz   simulate_control_c script wrong USR1 signal number on mips
n-i-bz   vgdb ptrace calls wrong on mips [...]
n-i-bz   Fixes for more MPI false positives
n-i-bz   exp-sgcheck's memcpy causes programs to segfault
n-i-bz   OSX build w/ clang: asserts at startup
n-i-bz   Incorrect undef'dness prop for Iop_DPBtoBCD and Iop_BCDtoDPB
n-i-bz   fix a couple of union tag-vs-field mixups
n-i-bz   OSX: use __NR_poll_nocancel rather than __NR_poll

The following bugs were fixed in 3.8.0 but not listed in this NEWS
file at the time:

254088   Valgrind should know about UD2 instruction
301280   == 254088
301902   == 254088
304754   NEWS blows TeX's little mind

(3.8.1: 19 September 2012, vex r2537, valgrind r12996)

Release 3.8.0 (10 August 2012)
~~~~~~~~~~~~~~~~~~~~~~~~~~~~~~~
3.8.0 is a feature release with many improvements and the usual
collection of bug fixes.

This release supports X86/Linux, AMD64/Linux, ARM/Linux, PPC32/Linux,
PPC64/Linux, S390X/Linux, MIPS/Linux, ARM/Android, X86/Android,
X86/MacOSX 10.6/10.7 and AMD64/MacOSX 10.6/10.7. Support for recent
distros and toolchain components (glibc 2.16, gcc 4.7) has been added.
There is initial support for MacOSX 10.8, but it is not usable for
serious work at present.

* ================== PLATFORM CHANGES =================

* Support for MIPS32 platforms running Linux. Valgrind has been
  tested on MIPS32 and MIPS32r2 platforms running different Debian
  Squeeze and MeeGo distributions. Both little-endian and big-endian
  cores are supported. The tools Memcheck, Massif and Lackey have
  been tested and are known to work. See README.mips for more details.

* Preliminary support for Android running on x86.

* Preliminary (as-yet largely unusable) support for MacOSX 10.8.

* Support for Intel AVX instructions and for AES instructions. This
  support is available only for 64 bit code.

* Support for POWER Decimal Floating Point instructions.

* ==================== TOOL CHANGES ====================

* Non-libc malloc implementations are now supported. This is useful
  for tools that replace malloc (Memcheck, Massif, DRD, Helgrind).
  Using the new option --soname-synonyms, such tools can be informed
  that the malloc implementation is either linked statically into the
  executable, or is present in some other shared library different
  from libc.so. This makes it possible to process statically linked
  programs, and programs using other malloc libraries, for example
  TCMalloc or JEMalloc.

* For tools that provide their own replacement for malloc et al, the
  option --redzone-size=<number> allows users to specify the size of
  the padding blocks (redzones) added before and after each client
  allocated block. Smaller redzones decrease the memory needed by
  Valgrind. Bigger redzones increase the chance to detect blocks
  overrun or underrun. Prior to this change, the redzone size was
  hardwired to 16 bytes in Memcheck.

* Memcheck:

  - The leak_check GDB server monitor command now can
    control the maximum nr of loss records to output.

  - Reduction of memory use for applications allocating
    many blocks and/or having many partially defined bytes.

  - Addition of GDB server monitor command 'block_list' that lists
    the addresses/sizes of the blocks of a leak search loss record.

  - Addition of GDB server monitor command 'who_points_at' that lists
    the locations pointing at a block.

  - If a redzone size > 0 is given, VALGRIND_MALLOCLIKE_BLOCK now will
    detect an invalid access of these redzones, by marking them
    noaccess. Similarly, if a redzone size is given for a memory
    pool, VALGRIND_MEMPOOL_ALLOC will mark the redzones no access.
    This still allows to find some bugs if the user has forgotten to
    mark the pool superblock noaccess.

  - Performance of memory leak check has been improved, especially in
    cases where there are many leaked blocks and/or many suppression
    rules used to suppress leak reports.

  - Reduced noise (false positive) level on MacOSX 10.6/10.7, due to
    more precise analysis, which is important for LLVM/Clang
    generated code. This is at the cost of somewhat reduced
    performance. Note there is no change to analysis precision or
    costs on Linux targets.

* DRD:

  - Added even more facilities that can help finding the cause of a data
    race, namely the command-line option --ptrace-addr and the macro
    DRD_STOP_TRACING_VAR(x). More information can be found in the manual.

- Fixed a subtle bug that could cause false positive data race reports.

* ==================== OTHER CHANGES ====================

* The C++ demangler has been updated so as to work well with C++
compiled by up to at least g++ 4.6.

* Tool developers can make replacement/wrapping more flexible thanks
to the new option --soname-synonyms. This was reported above, but
in fact is very general and applies to all function
replacement/wrapping, not just to malloc-family functions.

* Round-robin scheduling of threads can be selected, using the new
option --fair-sched= yes. Prior to this change, the pipe-based
thread serialisation mechanism (which is still the default) could
give very unfair scheduling. --fair-sched=yes improves
responsiveness of interactive multithreaded applications, and
improves repeatability of results from the thread checkers Helgrind
and DRD.

* For tool developers: support to run Valgrind on Valgrind has been
improved. We can now routinely Valgrind on Helgrind or Memcheck.

* gdbserver now shows the float shadow registers as integer
rather than float values, as the shadow values are mostly
used as bit patterns.

* Increased limit for the --num-callers command line flag to 500.

* Performance improvements for error matching when there are many
suppression records in use.

* Improved support for DWARF4 debugging information (bug 284184).

* Initial support for DWZ compressed Dwarf debug info.

* Improved control over the IR optimiser's handling of the tradeoff
between performance and precision of exceptions. Specifically,
--vex-iropt-precise-memory-exns has been removed and replaced by
--vex-iropt-register-updates, with extended functionality. This
allows the Valgrind gdbserver to always show up to date register
values to GDB.

* Modest performance gains through the use of translation chaining for
JIT-generated code.

* ==================== FIXED BUGS ====================

The following bugs have been fixed or resolved. Note that "n-i-bz"
stands for "not in bugzilla" -- that is, a bug that was reported to us
but never got a bugzilla entry. We encourage you to file bugs in
bugzilla (https://bugs.kde.org/enter_bug.cgi?product=valgrind) rather
than mailing the developers (or mailing lists) directly -- bugs that
are not entered into bugzilla tend to get forgotten about or ignored.

To see details of a given bug, visit
  https://bugs.kde.org/show_bug.cgi?id=XXXXXX
where XXXXXX is the bug number as listed below.

197914 Building valgrind from svn now requires automake-1.10
203877 increase to 16Mb maximum allowed alignment for memalign et al
219156 Handle statically linked malloc or other malloc lib (e.g. tcmalloc)
247386 make perf does not run all performance tests
270006 Valgrind scheduler unfair
270777 Adding MIPS/Linux port to Valgrind
270796 s390x: Removed broken support for the TS insn
271438 Fix configure for proper SSE4.2 detection
273114 s390x: Support TR, TRE, TROO, TROT, TRTO, and TRTT instructions
273475 Add support for AVX instructions
274078 improved configure logic for mpicc
276993 fix mremap 'no thrash checks'
278313 Fedora 15/x64: err read debug info with --read-var-info=yes flag
281482 memcheck incorrect byte allocation count in realloc() for silly argument
282230 group allocator for small fixed size, use it for MC_Chunk/SEc vbit
283413 Fix wrong sanity check
283671 Robustize alignment computation in LibVEX_Alloc
283961 Adding support for some HCI IOCTLs
284124 parse_type_DIE: confused by: DWARF 4
284864 == 273475 (Add support for AVX instructions)
285219 Too-restrictive constraints for Thumb2 "SP plus/minus register"
285662 (MacOSX): Memcheck needs to replace memcpy/memmove
285725 == 273475 (Add support for AVX instructions)
286261 add wrapper for linux I2C_RDWR ioctl
286270 vgpreload is not friendly to 64->32 bit execs, gives ld.so warnings
286374 Running cachegrind with --branch-sim=yes on 64-bit PowerPC program fails
286384 configure fails "checking for a supported version of gcc"
286497 == 273475 (Add support for AVX instructions)
286596 == 273475 (Add support for AVX instructions)
286917 disInstr(arm): unhandled instruction: QADD (also QSUB)
287175 ARM: scalar VFP fixed-point VCVT instructions not handled
287260 Incorrect conditional jump or move depends on uninitialised value(s)
287301 vex amd64->IR: 0x66 0xF 0x38 0x41 0xC0 0xB8 0x0 0x0 (PHMINPOSUW)
287307 == 273475 (Add support for AVX instructions)
287858 VG_(strerror): unknown error
288298 (MacOSX) unhandled syscall shm_unlink
288995 == 273475 (Add support for AVX instructions)
289470 Loading of large Mach-O thin binaries fails.
289656 == 273475 (Add support for AVX instructions)
289699 vgdb connection in relay mode erroneously closed due to buffer overrun
289823 == 293754 (PCMPxSTRx not implemented for 16-bit characters)
289839 s390x: Provide support for unicode conversion instructions
289939 monitor cmd 'leak_check' with details about leaked or reachable blocks
290006 memcheck doesn't mark %xmm as initialized after "pcmpeqw %xmm %xmm"
290655 Add support for AESKEYGENASSIST instruction
290719 valgrind-3.7.0 fails with automake-1.11.2 due to"pkglibdir" usage
290974 vgdb must align pages to VKI_SHMLBA (16KB) on ARM
291253 ES register not initialised in valgrind simulation
291568 Fix 3DNOW-related crashes with baseline x86_64 CPU (w patch)

291865 s390x: Support the "Compare Double and Swap" family of instructions
292300 == 273475 (Add support for AVX instructions)
292430 unrecognized instruction in __intel_get_new_mem_ops_cpuid
292493 == 273475 (Add support for AVX instructions)
292626 Missing fcntl F_SETOWN_EX and F_GETOWN_EX support
292627 Missing support for some SCSI ioctls
292628 none/tests/x86/bug125959-x86.c triggers undefined behavior
292841 == 273475 (Add support for AVX instructions)
292993 implement the getcpu syscall on amd64-linux
292995 Implement the "cross memory attach" syscalls introduced in Linux 3.2
293088 Add some VEX sanity checks for ppc64 unhandled instructions
293751 == 290655 (Add support for AESKEYGENASSIST instruction)
293754 PCMPxSTRx not implemented for 16-bit characters
293755 == 293754 (No tests for PCMPxSTRx on 16-bit characters)
293808 CLFLUSH not supported by latest VEX for amd64
294047 valgrind does not correctly emulate prlimit64(..., RLIMIT_NOFILE, ...)
294048 MPSADBW instruction not implemented
294055 regtest none/tests/shell fails when locale is not set to C
294185 INT 0x44 (and others) not supported on x86 guest, but used by Jikes RVM
294190 --vgdb-error=xxx can be out of sync with errors shown to the user
294191 amd64: fnsave/frstor and 0x66 size prefixes on FP instructions
294260 disInstr_AMD64: disInstr miscalculated next %rip
294523 --partial-loads-ok=yes causes false negatives
294617 vex amd64->IR: 0x66 0xF 0x3A 0xDF 0xD1 0x1 0xE8 0x6A
294736 vex amd64->IR: 0x48 0xF 0xD7 0xD6 0x48 0x83
294812 patch allowing to run (on x86 at least) helgrind/drd on tool.
295089 can not annotate source for both helgrind and drd
295221 POWER Processor decimal floating point instruction support missing
295427 building for i386 with clang on darwin11 requires "-new_linker linker"
295428 coregrind/m_main.c has incorrect x86 assembly for darwin
295590 Helgrind: Assertion 'cvi->nWaiters > 0' failed
295617 ARM - Add some missing syscalls
295799 Missing \n with get_vbits in gdbserver when line is % 80 [...]
296229 Linux user input device ioctls missing wrappers
296318 ELF Debug info improvements (more than one rx/rw mapping)
296422 Add translation chaining support
296457 vex amd64->IR: 0x66 0xF 0x3A 0xDF 0xD1 0x1 0xE8 0x6A (dup of AES)
296792 valgrind 3.7.0: add SIOCSHWTSTAMP (0x89B0) ioctl wrapper
296983 Fix build issues on x86_64/ppc64 without 32-bit toolchains
297078 gdbserver signal handling problems [..]
297147 drd false positives on newly allocated memory
297329 disallow decoding of IBM Power DFP insns on some machines
297497 POWER Processor decimal floating point instruction support missing
297701 Another alias for strncasecmp_l in libc-2.13.so
297911 'invalid write' not reported when using APIs for custom mem allocators.
297976 s390x: revisit EX implementation
297991 Valgrind interferes with mmap()+ftell()
297992 Support systems missing WIFCONTINUED (e.g. pre-2.6.10 Linux)
297993 Fix compilation of valgrind with gcc -g3.
298080 POWER Processor DFP support missing, part 3
298227 == 273475 (Add support for AVX instructions)
298335 == 273475 (Add support for AVX instructions)
298354 Unhandled ARM Thumb instruction 0xEB0D 0x0585 (streq)
298394 s390x: Don't bail out on an unknown machine model. [..]

298421 accept4() syscall (366) support is missing for ARM
298718 vex amd64->IR: 0xF 0xB1 0xCB 0x9C 0x8F 0x45
298732 valgrind installation problem in ubuntu with kernel version 3.x
298862 POWER Processor DFP instruction support missing, part 4
298864 DWARF reader mis-parses DW_FORM_ref_addr
298943 massif asserts with --pages-as-heap=yes when brk is changing [..]
299053 Support DWARF4 DW_AT_high_pc constant form
299104 == 273475 (Add support for AVX instructions)
299316 Helgrind: hg_main.c:628 (map_threads_lookup): Assertion 'thr' failed.
299629 dup3() syscall (358) support is missing for ARM
299694 POWER Processor DFP instruction support missing, part 5
299756 Ignore --free-fill for MEMPOOL_FREE and FREELIKE client requests
299803 == 273475 (Add support for AVX instructions)
299804 == 273475 (Add support for AVX instructions)
299805 == 273475 (Add support for AVX instructions)
300140 ARM - Missing (T1) SMMUL
300195 == 296318 (ELF Debug info improvements (more than one rx/rw mapping))
300389 Assertion 'are_valid_hwcaps(VexArchAMD64, [..])' failed.
300414 FCOM and FCOMP unimplemented for amd64 guest
301204 infinite loop in canonicaliseSymtab with ifunc symbol
301229 == 203877 (increase to 16Mb maximum allowed alignment for memalign etc)
301265 add x86 support to Android build
301984 configure script doesn't detect certain versions of clang
302205 Fix compiler warnings for POWER VEX code and POWER test cases
302287 Unhandled movbe instruction on Atom processors
302370 PPC: fnmadd, fnmsub, fnmadds, fnmsubs insns always negate the result
302536 Fix for the POWER Valgrind regression test: memcheck-ISA2.0.
302578 Unrecognized isntruction 0xc5 0x32 0xc2 0xca 0x09 vcmpngess
302656 == 273475 (Add support for AVX instructions)
302709 valgrind for ARM needs extra tls support for android emulator [..]
302827 add wrapper for CDROM_GET_CAPABILITY
302901 Valgrind crashes with dwz optimized debuginfo
302918 Enable testing of the vmaddfp and vnsubfp instructions in the testsuite
303116 Add support for the POWER instruction popcntb
303127 Power test suite fixes for frsqrte, vrefp, and vrsqrtefp instructions.
303250 Assertion 'instrs_in->arr_used <= 10000' failed w/ OpenSSL code
303466 == 273475 (Add support for AVX instructions)
303624 segmentation fault on Android 4.1 (e.g. on Galaxy Nexus OMAP)
303963 strstr() function produces wrong results under valgrind callgrind
304054 CALL_FN_xx macros need to enforce stack alignment
304561 tee system call not supported
715750 (MacOSX): Incorrect invalid-address errors near 0xFFFFxxxx (mozbug#)
n-i-bz Add missing gdbserver xml files for shadow registers for ppc32
n-i-bz Bypass gcc4.4/4.5 code gen bugs causing out of memory or asserts
n-i-bz Fix assert in gdbserver for watchpoints watching the same address
n-i-bz Fix false positive in sys_clone on amd64 when optional args [..]
n-i-bz s390x: Shadow registers can now be examined using vgdb

(3.8.0-TEST3: 9 August 2012, vex r2465, valgrind r12865)
(3.8.0:   10 August 2012, vex r2465, valgrind r12866)

Release 3.7.0 (5 November 2011)

~~~~~~~~~~~~~~~~~~~~~~~~~~~~~~~~

3.7.0 is a feature release with many significant improvements and the usual collection of bug fixes.

This release supports X86/Linux, AMD64/Linux, ARM/Linux, PPC32/Linux, PPC64/Linux, S390X/Linux, ARM/Android, X86/Darwin and AMD64/Darwin. Support for recent distros and toolchain components (glibc 2.14, gcc 4.6, MacOSX 10.7) has been added.

* ================== PLATFORM CHANGES ==================

* Support for IBM z/Architecture (s390x) running Linux. Valgrind can analyse 64-bit programs running on z/Architecture. Most user space instructions up to and including z10 are supported. Valgrind has been tested extensively on z9, z10, and z196 machines running SLES 10/11, RedHat 5/6m, and Fedora. The Memcheck and Massif tools are known to work well. Callgrind, Helgrind, and DRD work reasonably well on z9 and later models. See README.s390 for more details.

* Preliminary support for MacOSX 10.7 and XCode 4. Both 32- and 64-bit processes are supported. Some complex threaded applications (Firefox) are observed to hang when run as 32 bit applications, whereas 64-bit versions run OK. The cause is unknown. Memcheck will likely report some false errors. In general, expect some rough spots. This release also supports MacOSX 10.6, but drops support for 10.5.

* Preliminary support for Android (on ARM). Valgrind can now run large applications (eg, Firefox) on (eg) a Samsung Nexus S. See README.android for more details, plus instructions on how to get started.

* Support for the IBM Power ISA 2.06 (Power7 instructions)

* General correctness and performance improvements for ARM/Linux, and, by extension, ARM/Android.

* Further solidification of support for SSE 4.2 in 64-bit mode. AVX instruction set support is under development but is not available in this release.

* Support for AIX5 has been removed.

* ==================== TOOL CHANGES ====================

* Memcheck: some incremental changes:

  - reduction of memory use in some circumstances

  - improved handling of freed memory, which in some circumstances can cause detection of use-after-free that would previously have been missed

  - fix of a longstanding bug that could cause false negatives (missed errors) in programs doing vector saturated narrowing instructions.

* Helgrind: performance improvements and major memory use reductions,
  particularly for large, long running applications which perform many
  synchronisation (lock, unlock, etc) events. Plus many smaller
  changes:

  - display of locksets for both threads involved in a race

  - general improvements in formatting/clarity of error messages

  - addition of facilities and documentation regarding annotation
    of thread safe reference counted C++ classes

  - new flag --check-stack-refs=no|yes [yes], to disable race checking
    on thread stacks (a performance hack)

  - new flag --free-is-write=no|yes [no], to enable detection of races
    where one thread accesses heap memory but another one frees it,
    without any coordinating synchronisation event

* DRD: enabled XML output; added support for delayed thread deletion
  in order to detect races that occur close to the end of a thread
  (--join-list-vol); fixed a memory leak triggered by repeated client
  memory allocatation and deallocation; improved Darwin support.

* exp-ptrcheck: this tool has been renamed to exp-sgcheck

* exp-sgcheck: this tool has been reduced in scope so as to improve
  performance and remove checking that Memcheck does better.
  Specifically, the ability to check for overruns for stack and global
  arrays is unchanged, but the ability to check for overruns of heap
  blocks has been removed. The tool has accordingly been renamed to
  exp-sgcheck ("Stack and Global Array Checking").

* ==================== OTHER CHANGES ====================

* GDB server: Valgrind now has an embedded GDB server. That means it
  is possible to control a Valgrind run from GDB, doing all the usual
  things that GDB can do (single stepping, breakpoints, examining
  data, etc). Tool-specific functionality is also available. For
  example, it is possible to query the definedness state of variables
  or memory from within GDB when running Memcheck; arbitrarily large
  memory watchpoints are supported, etc. To use the GDB server, start
  Valgrind with the flag --vgdb-error=0 and follow the on-screen
  instructions.

* Improved support for unfriendly self-modifying code: a new option
  --smc-check=all-non-file is available. This adds the relevant
  consistency checks only to code that originates in non-file-backed
  mappings. In effect this confines the consistency checking only to
  code that is or might be JIT generated, and avoids checks on code
  that must have been compiled ahead of time. This significantly
  improves performance on applications that generate code at run time.

* It is now possible to build a working Valgrind using Clang-2.9 on
  Linux.

* new client requests VALGRIND_{DISABLE,ENABLE}_ERROR_REPORTING.
  These enable and disable error reporting on a per-thread, and
  nestable, basis. This is useful for hiding errors in particularly
  troublesome pieces of code. The MPI wrapper library (libmpiwrap.c)
  now uses this facility.

* Added the --mod-funcname option to cg_diff.

* ==================== FIXED BUGS ====================

The following bugs have been fixed or resolved. Note that "n-i-bz"
stands for "not in bugzilla" -- that is, a bug that was reported to us
but never got a bugzilla entry. We encourage you to file bugs in
bugzilla (http://bugs.kde.org/enter_valgrind_bug.cgi) rather than
mailing the developers (or mailing lists) directly -- bugs that are
not entered into bugzilla tend to get forgotten about or ignored.

To see details of a given bug, visit
https://bugs.kde.org/show_bug.cgi?id=XXXXXX
where XXXXXX is the bug number as listed below.

 79311   malloc silly arg warning does not give stack trace
210935   port valgrind.h (not valgrind) to win32 to support client requests
214223   valgrind SIGSEGV on startup gcc 4.4.1 ppc32 (G4) Ubuntu 9.10
243404   Port to zSeries
243935   Helgrind: incorrect handling of ANNOTATE_HAPPENS_BEFORE()/AFTER()
247223   non-x86: Suppress warning: 'regparm' attribute directive ignored
250101   huge "free" memory usage due to m_mallocfree.c fragmentation
253206   Some fixes for the faultstatus testcase
255223   capget testcase fails when running as root
256703   xlc_dbl_u32.c testcase broken
256726   Helgrind tests have broken inline asm
259977   == 214223 (Valgrind segfaults doing __builtin_longjmp)
264800   testcase compile failure on zseries
265762   make public VEX headers compilable by G++ 3.x
265771   assertion in jumps.c (r11523) fails with glibc-2.3
266753   configure script does not give the user the option to not use QtCore
266931   gen_insn_test.pl is broken
266961   ld-linux.so.2 i?86-linux strlen issues
266990   setns instruction causes false positive
267020   Make directory for temporary files configurable at run-time.
267342   == 267997 (segmentation fault on Mac OS 10.6)
267383   Assertion 'vgPlain_strlen(dir) + vgPlain_strlen(file) + 1 < 256' failed
267413   Assertion 'DRD_(g_threadinfo)[tid].synchr_nesting >= 1' failed.
267488   regtest: darwin support for 64-bit build
267552   SIGSEGV (misaligned_stack_error) with DRD, but not with other tools
267630   Add support for IBM Power ISA 2.06 -- stage 1
267769   == 267997 (Darwin: memcheck triggers segmentation fault)
267819   Add client request for informing the core about reallocation
267925   laog data structure quadratic for a single sequence of lock

267968 drd: (vgDrd_thread_set_joinable): Assertion '0 <= (int)tid ..' failed
267997 MacOSX: 64-bit V segfaults on launch when built with Xcode 4.0.1
268513 missed optimizations in fold_Expr
268619 s390x: fpr - gpr transfer facility
268620 s390x: reconsider "long displacement" requirement
268621 s390x: improve IR generation for XC
268715 s390x: FLOGR is not universally available
268792 == 267997 (valgrind seg faults on startup when compiled with Xcode 4)
268930 s390x: MHY is not universally available
269078 arm->IR: unhandled instruction SUB (SP minus immediate/register)
269079 Support ptrace system call on ARM
269144 missing "Bad option" error message
269209 conditional load and store facility (z196)
269354 Shift by zero on x86 can incorrectly clobber CC_NDEP
269641 == 267997 (valgrind segfaults immediately (segmentation fault))
269736 s390x: minor code generation tweaks
269778 == 272986 (valgrind.h: swap roles of VALGRIND_DO_CLIENT_REQUEST() ..)
269863 s390x: remove unused function parameters
269864 s390x: tweak s390_emit_load_cc
269884 == 250101 (overhead for huge blocks exhausts space too soon)
270082 s390x: Make sure to point the PSW address to the next address on SIGILL
270115 s390x: rewrite some testcases
270309 == 267997 (valgrind crash on startup)
270320 add support for Linux FIOQSIZE ioctl() call
270326 segfault while trying to sanitize the environment passed to execle
270794 IBM POWER7 support patch causes regression in none/tests
270851 IBM POWER7 fcfidus instruction causes memcheck to fail
270856 IBM POWER7 xsnmaddadp instruction causes memcheck to fail on 32bit app
270925 hyper-optimized strspn() in /lib64/libc-2.13.so needs fix
270959 s390x: invalid use of R0 as base register
271042 VSX configure check fails when it should not
271043 Valgrind build fails with assembler error on ppc64 with binutils 2.21
271259 s390x: fix code confusion
271337 == 267997 (Valgrind segfaults on MacOS X)
271385 s390x: Implement Ist_MBE
271501 s390x: misc cleanups
271504 s390x: promote likely and unlikely
271579 ppc: using wrong enum type
271615 unhandled instruction "popcnt" (arch=amd10h)
271730 Fix bug when checking ioctls: duplicate check
271776 s390x: provide STFLE instruction support
271779 s390x: provide clock instructions like STCK
271799 Darwin: ioctls without an arg report a memory error
271820 arm: fix type confusion
271917 pthread_cond_timedwait failure leads to not-locked false positive
272067 s390x: fix DISP20 macro
272615 A typo in debug output in mc_leakcheck.c
272661 callgrind_annotate chokes when run from paths containing regex chars
272893 amd64->IR: 0x66 0xF 0x38 0x2B 0xC1 0x66 0xF 0x7F == (closed as dup)
272955 Unhandled syscall error for pwrite64 on ppc64 arch
272967 make documentation build-system more robust
272986 Fix gcc-4.6 warnings with valgrind.h
273318 amd64->IR: 0x66 0xF 0x3A 0x61 0xC1 0x38 (missing PCMPxSTRx case)
273318 unhandled PCMPxSTRx case: vex amd64->IR: 0x66 0xF 0x3A 0x61 0xC1 0x38

273431   valgrind segfaults in evalCfiExpr (debuginfo.c:2039)
273465   Callgrind: jumps.c:164 (new_jcc): Assertion '(0 <= jmp) && ...'
273536   Build error: multiple definition of 'vgDrd_pthread_cond_initializer'
273640   ppc64-linux: unhandled syscalls setresuid(164) and setresgid(169)
273729   == 283000 (Illegal opcode for SSE2 "roundsd" instruction)
273778   exp-ptrcheck: unhandled sysno == 259
274089   exp-ptrcheck: unhandled sysno == 208
274378   s390x: Various dispatcher tweaks
274447   WARNING: unhandled syscall: 340
274776   amd64->IR: 0x66 0xF 0x38 0x2B 0xC5 0x66
274784   == 267997 (valgrind ls -l results in Segmentation Fault)
274926   valgrind does not build against linux-3
275148   configure FAIL with glibc-2.14
275151   Fedora 15 / glibc-2.14 'make regtest' FAIL
275168   Make Valgrind work for MacOSX 10.7 Lion
275212   == 275284 (lots of false positives from __memcpy_ssse3_back et al)
275278   valgrind does not build on Linux kernel 3.0.* due to silly
275284   Valgrind memcpy/memmove redirection stopped working in glibc 2.14/x86_64
275308   Fix implementation for ppc64 fres instruc
275339   s390x: fix testcase compile warnings
275517   s390x: Provide support for CKSM instruction
275710   s390x: get rid of redundant address mode calculation
275815   == 247894 (Valgrind doesn't know about Linux readahead(2) syscall)
275852   == 250101 (valgrind uses all swap space and is killed)
276784   Add support for IBM Power ISA 2.06 -- stage 3
276987   gdbsrv: fix tests following recent commits
277045   Valgrind crashes with unhandled DW_OP_ opcode 0x2a
277199   The test_isa_2_06_part1.c in none/tests/ppc64 should be a symlink
277471   Unhandled syscall: 340
277610   valgrind crashes in VG_(lseek)(core_fd, phdrs[idx].p_offset, ...)
277653   ARM: support Thumb2 PLD instruction
277663   ARM: NEON float VMUL by scalar incorrect
277689   ARM: tests for VSTn with register post-index are broken
277694   ARM: BLX LR instruction broken in ARM mode
277780   ARM: VMOV.F32 (immediate) instruction is broken
278057   fuse filesystem syscall deadlocks
278078   Unimplemented syscall 280 on ppc32
278349   F_GETPIPE_SZ and F_SETPIPE_SZ Linux fcntl commands
278454   VALGRIND_STACK_DEREGISTER has wrong output type
278502   == 275284 (Valgrind confuses memcpy() and memmove())
278892   gdbsrv: factorize gdb version handling, fix doc and typos
279027   Support for MVCL and CLCL instruction
279027   s390x: Provide support for CLCL and MVCL instructions
279062   Remove a redundant check in the insn selector for ppc.
279071   JDK creates PTEST with redundant REX.W prefix
279212   gdbsrv: add monitor cmd v.info scheduler.
279378   exp-ptrcheck: the 'impossible' happened on mkfifo call
279698   memcheck discards valid-bits for packuswb
279795   memcheck reports uninitialised values for mincore on amd64
279994   Add support for IBM Power ISA 2.06 -- stage 3
280083   mempolicy syscall check errors
280290   vex amd64->IR: 0x66 0xF 0x38 0x28 0xC1 0x66 0xF 0x6F
280710   s390x: config files for nightly builds
280757   /tmp dir still used by valgrind even if TMPDIR is specified

280965 Valgrind breaks fcntl locks when program does mmap
281138 WARNING: unhandled syscall: 340
281241 == 275168 (valgrind useless on Macos 10.7.1 Lion)
281304 == 275168 (Darwin: dyld "cannot load inserted library")
281305 == 275168 (unhandled syscall: unix:357 on Darwin 11.1)
281468 s390x: handle do_clone and gcc clones in call traces
281488 ARM: VFP register corruption
281828 == 275284 (false memmove warning: "Source and destination overlap")
281883 s390x: Fix system call wrapper for "clone".
282105 generalise 'reclaimSuperBlock' to also reclaim splittable superblock
282112 Unhandled instruction bytes: 0xDE 0xD9 0x9B 0xDF (fcompp)
282238 SLES10: make check fails
282979 strcasestr needs replacement with recent(>=2.12) glibc
283000 vex amd64->IR: 0x66 0xF 0x3A 0xA 0xC0 0x9 0xF3 0xF
283243 Regression in ppc64 memcheck tests
283325 == 267997 (Darwin: V segfaults on startup when built with Xcode 4.0)
283427 re-connect epoll_pwait syscall on ARM linux
283600 gdbsrv: android: port vgdb.c
283709 none/tests/faultstatus needs to account for page size
284305 filter_gdb needs enhancement to work on ppc64
284384 clang 3.1 -Wunused-value warnings in valgrind.h, memcheck.h
284472 Thumb2 ROR.W encoding T2 not implemented
284621 XML-escape process command line in XML output
n-i-bz cachegrind/callgrind: handle CPUID information for Core iX Intel CPUs
        that have non-power-of-2 sizes (also AMDs)
n-i-bz don't be spooked by libraries mashed by elfhack
n-i-bz don't be spooked by libxul.so linked with gold
n-i-bz improved checking for VALGRIND_CHECK_MEM_IS_DEFINED

(3.7.0-TEST1: 27 October 2011, vex r2228, valgrind r12245)
(3.7.0.RC1:   1 November 2011, vex r2231, valgrind r12257)
(3.7.0:   5 November 2011, vex r2231, valgrind r12258)

Release 3.6.1 (16 February 2011)
~~~~~~~~~~~~~~~~~~~~~~~~~~~~~~~~~~
3.6.1 is a bug fix release. It adds support for some SSE4
instructions that were omitted in 3.6.0 due to lack of time. Initial
support for glibc-2.13 has been added. A number of bugs causing
crashing or assertion failures have been fixed.

The following bugs have been fixed or resolved. Note that "n-i-bz"
stands for "not in bugzilla" -- that is, a bug that was reported to us
but never got a bugzilla entry. We encourage you to file bugs in
bugzilla (http://bugs.kde.org/enter_valgrind_bug.cgi) rather than
mailing the developers (or mailing lists) directly -- bugs that are
not entered into bugzilla tend to get forgotten about or ignored.

To see details of a given bug, visit
https://bugs.kde.org/show_bug.cgi?id=XXXXXX
where XXXXXX is the bug number as listed below.

188572 Valgrind on Mac should suppress setenv() mem leak

194402   vex amd64->IR: 0x48 0xF 0xAE 0x4 (proper FX{SAVE,RSTOR} support)
210481   vex amd64->IR: Assertion 'sz == 2 || sz == 4' failed (REX.W POPQ)
246152   callgrind internal error after pthread_cancel on 32 Bit Linux
250038   ppc64: Altivec LVSR and LVSL instructions fail their regtest
254420   memory pool tracking broken
254957   Test code failing to compile due to changes in memcheck.h
255009   helgrind/drd: crash on chmod with invalid parameter
255130   readdwarf3.c parse_type_DIE confused by GNAT Ada types
255355   helgrind/drd: crash on threaded programs doing fork
255358   == 255355
255418   (SSE4.x) rint call compiled with ICC
255822   --gen-suppressions can create invalid files: "too many callers [...]"
255888   closing valgrindoutput tag outputted to log-stream on error
255963   (SSE4.x) vex amd64->IR: 0x66 0xF 0x3A 0x9 0xDB 0x0 (ROUNDPD)
255966   Slowness when using mempool annotations
256387   vex x86->IR: 0xD4 0xA 0x2 0x7 (AAD and AAM)
256600   super-optimized strcasecmp() false positive
256669   vex amd64->IR: Unhandled LOOPNEL insn on amd64
256968   (SSE4.x) vex amd64->IR: 0x66 0xF 0x38 0x10 0xD3 0x66 (BLENDVPx)
257011   (SSE4.x) vex amd64->IR: 0x66 0xF 0x3A 0xE 0xFD 0xA0 (PBLENDW)
257063   (SSE4.x) vex amd64->IR: 0x66 0xF 0x3A 0x8 0xC0 0x0 (ROUNDPS)
257276   Missing case in memcheck --track-origins=yes
258870   (SSE4.x) Add support for EXTRACTPS SSE 4.1 instruction
261966   (SSE4.x) support for CRC32B and CRC32Q is lacking (also CRC32{W,L})
262985   VEX regression in valgrind 3.6.0 in handling PowerPC VMX
262995   (SSE4.x) crash when trying to valgrind gcc-snapshot (PCMPxSTRx $0)
263099   callgrind_annotate counts Ir improperly [...]
263877   undefined coprocessor instruction on ARMv7
265964   configure FAIL with glibc-2.13
n-i-bz   Fix compile error w/ icc-12.x in guest_arm_toIR.c
n-i-bz   Docs: fix bogus descriptions for VALGRIND_CREATE_BLOCK et al
n-i-bz   Massif: don't assert on shmat() with --pages-as-heap=yes
n-i-bz   Bug fixes and major speedups for the exp-DHAT space profiler
n-i-bz   DRD: disable --free-is-write due to implementation difficulties

(3.6.1: 16 February 2011, vex r2103, valgrind r11561).

Release 3.6.0 (21 October 2010)
~~~~~~~~~~~~~~~~~~~~~~~~~~~~~~~
3.6.0 is a feature release with many significant improvements and the
usual collection of bug fixes.

This release supports X86/Linux, AMD64/Linux, ARM/Linux, PPC32/Linux,
PPC64/Linux, X86/Darwin and AMD64/Darwin. Support for recent distros
and toolchain components (glibc 2.12, gcc 4.5, OSX 10.6) has been added.

Here are some highlights. Details are shown further down:

* Support for ARM/Linux.

* Support for recent Linux distros: Ubuntu 10.10 and Fedora 14.

* Support for Mac OS X 10.6, both 32- and 64-bit executables.

* Support for the SSE4.2 instruction set.

* Enhancements to the Callgrind profiler, including the ability to
  handle CPUs with three levels of cache.

* A new experimental heap profiler, DHAT.

* A huge number of bug fixes and small enhancements.

Here are details of the above changes, together with descriptions of
many other changes, and a list of fixed bugs.

* =================== PLATFORM CHANGES =================

* Support for ARM/Linux. Valgrind now runs on ARMv7 capable CPUs
  running Linux. It is known to work on Ubuntu 10.04, Ubuntu 10.10,
  and Maemo 5, so you can run Valgrind on your Nokia N900 if you want.

  This requires a CPU capable of running the ARMv7-A instruction set
  (Cortex A5, A8 and A9). Valgrind provides fairly complete coverage
  of the user space instruction set, including ARM and Thumb integer
  code, VFPv3, NEON and V6 media instructions. The Memcheck,
  Cachegrind and Massif tools work properly; other tools work to
  varying degrees.

* Support for recent Linux distros (Ubuntu 10.10 and Fedora 14), along
  with support for recent releases of the underlying toolchain
  components, notably gcc-4.5 and glibc-2.12.

* Support for Mac OS X 10.6, both 32- and 64-bit executables. 64-bit
  support also works much better on OS X 10.5, and is as solid as
  32-bit support now.

* Support for the SSE4.2 instruction set. SSE4.2 is supported in
  64-bit mode. In 32-bit mode, support is only available up to and
  including SSSE3. Some exceptions: SSE4.2 AES instructions are not
  supported in 64-bit mode, and 32-bit mode does in fact support the
  bare minimum SSE4 instructions to needed to run programs on Mac OS X
  10.6 on 32-bit targets.

* Support for IBM POWER6 cpus has been improved. The Power ISA up to
  and including version 2.05 is supported.

* ==================== TOOL CHANGES ====================

* Cachegrind has a new processing script, cg_diff, which finds the
  difference between two profiles. It's very useful for evaluating
  the performance effects of a change in a program.

Related to this change, the meaning of cg_annotate's (rarely-used)
--threshold option has changed; this is unlikely to affect many
people, if you do use it please see the user manual for details.

* Callgrind now can do branch prediction simulation, similar to
  Cachegrind. In addition, it optionally can count the number of
  executed global bus events. Both can be used for a better
  approximation of a "Cycle Estimation" as derived event (you need to
  update the event formula in KCachegrind yourself).

* Cachegrind and Callgrind now refer to the LL (last-level) cache
  rather than the L2 cache. This is to accommodate machines with
  three levels of caches -- if Cachegrind/Callgrind auto-detects the
  cache configuration of such a machine it will run the simulation as
  if the L2 cache isn't present. This means the results are less
  likely to match the true result for the machine, but
  Cachegrind/Callgrind's results are already only approximate, and
  should not be considered authoritative. The results are still
  useful for giving a general idea about a program's locality.

* Massif has a new option, --pages-as-heap, which is disabled by
  default. When enabled, instead of tracking allocations at the level
  of heap blocks (as allocated with malloc/new/new[]), it instead
  tracks memory allocations at the level of memory pages (as mapped by
  mmap, brk, etc). Each mapped page is treated as its own block.
  Interpreting the page-level output is harder than the heap-level
  output, but this option is useful if you want to account for every
  byte of memory used by a program.

* DRD has two new command-line options: --free-is-write and
  --trace-alloc. The former allows to detect reading from already freed
  memory, and the latter allows tracing of all memory allocations and
  deallocations.

* DRD has several new annotations. Custom barrier implementations can
  now be annotated, as well as benign races on static variables.

* DRD's happens before / happens after annotations have been made more
  powerful, so that they can now also be used to annotate e.g. a smart
  pointer implementation.

* Helgrind's annotation set has also been drastically improved, so as
  to provide to users a general set of annotations to describe locks,
  semaphores, barriers and condition variables. Annotations to
  describe thread-safe reference counted heap objects have also been
  added.

* Memcheck has a new command-line option, --show-possibly-lost, which
  is enabled by default. When disabled, the leak detector will not
  show possibly-lost blocks.

* A new experimental heap profiler, DHAT (Dynamic Heap Analysis Tool),
  has been added. DHAT keeps track of allocated heap blocks, and also

inspects every memory reference to see which block (if any) is being accessed. This gives a lot of insight into block lifetimes, utilisation, turnover, liveness, and the location of hot and cold fields. You can use DHAT to do hot-field profiling.

* ==================== OTHER CHANGES ====================

* Improved support for unfriendly self-modifying code: the extra overhead incurred by --smc-check=all has been reduced by approximately a factor of 5 as compared with 3.5.0.

* Ability to show directory names for source files in error messages. This is combined with a flexible mechanism for specifying which parts of the paths should be shown. This is enabled by the new flag --fullpath-after.

* A new flag, --require-text-symbol, which will stop the run if a specified symbol is not found it a given shared object when it is loaded into the process. This makes advanced working with function intercepting and wrapping safer and more reliable.

* Improved support for the Valkyrie GUI, version 2.0.0. GUI output and control of Valgrind is now available for the tools Memcheck and Helgrind. XML output from Valgrind is available for Memcheck, Helgrind and exp-Ptrcheck.

* More reliable stack unwinding on amd64-linux, particularly in the presence of function wrappers, and with gcc-4.5 compiled code.

* Modest scalability (performance improvements) for massive long-running applications, particularly for those with huge amounts of code.

* Support for analyzing programs running under Wine with has been improved. The header files <valgrind/valgrind.h>, <valgrind/memcheck.h> and <valgrind/drd.h> can now be used in Windows-programs compiled with MinGW or one of the Microsoft Visual Studio compilers.

* A rare but serious error in the 64-bit x86 CPU simulation was fixed. The 32-bit simulator was not affected. This did not occur often, but when it did would usually crash the program under test. Bug 245925.

* A large number of bugs were fixed. These are shown below.

* A number of bugs were investigated, and were candidates for fixing, but are not fixed in 3.6.0, due to lack of developer time. They may get fixed in later releases. They are:

194402   vex amd64->IR: 0x48 0xF 0xAE 0x4 0x24 0x49   (FXSAVE64)
212419   false positive "lock order violated" (A+B vs A)
213685   Undefined value propagates past dependency breaking instruction
216837   Incorrect instrumentation of NSOperationQueue on Darwin

237920 valgrind segfault on fork failure
242137 support for code compiled by LLVM-2.8
242423 Another unknown Intel cache config value
243232 Inconsistent Lock Orderings report with trylock
243483 ppc: callgrind triggers VEX assertion failure
243935 Helgrind: implementation of ANNOTATE_HAPPENS_BEFORE() is wrong
244677 Helgrind crash hg_main.c:616 (map_threads_lookup): Assertion
        'thr' failed.
246152 callgrind internal error after pthread_cancel on 32 Bit Linux
249435 Analyzing wine programs with callgrind triggers a crash
250038 ppc64: Altivec lvsr and lvsl instructions fail their regtest
250065 Handling large allocations
250101 huge "free" memory usage due to m_mallocfree.c
        "superblocks fragmentation"
251569 vex amd64->IR: 0xF 0x1 0xF9 0x8B 0x4C 0x24 (RDTSCP)
252091 Callgrind on ARM does not detect function returns correctly
252600 [PATCH] Allow lhs to be a pointer for shl/shr
254420 memory pool tracking broken
n-i-bz support for adding symbols for JIT generated code

The following bugs have been fixed or resolved. Note that "n-i-bz"
stands for "not in bugzilla" -- that is, a bug that was reported to us
but never got a bugzilla entry. We encourage you to file bugs in
bugzilla (http://bugs.kde.org/enter_valgrind_bug.cgi) rather than
mailing the developers (or mailing lists) directly -- bugs that are
not entered into bugzilla tend to get forgotten about or ignored.

To see details of a given bug, visit
https://bugs.kde.org/show_bug.cgi?id=XXXXXX
where XXXXXX is the bug number as listed below.

135264 dcbzl instruction missing
142688 == 250799
153699 Valgrind should report unaligned reads with movdqa
180217 == 212335
190429 Valgrind reports lost of errors in ld.so
        with x86_64 2.9.90 glibc
197266 valgrind appears to choke on the xmms instruction
        "roundsd" on x86_64
197988 Crash when demangling very large symbol names
202315 unhandled syscall: 332 (inotify_init1)
203256 Add page-level profiling to Massif
205093 dsymutil=yes needs quotes, locking (partial fix)
205241 Snow Leopard 10.6 support (partial fix)
206600 Leak checker fails to upgrade indirect blocks when their
        parent becomes reachable
210935 port valgrind.h (not valgrind) to win32 so apps run under
        wine can make client requests
211410 vex amd64->IR: 0x15 0xFF 0xFF 0x0 0x0 0x89
        within Linux ip-stack checksum functions
212335 unhandled instruction bytes: 0xF3 0xF 0xBD 0xC0
        (lzcnt %eax,%eax)
213685 Undefined value propagates past dependency breaking instruction

(partial fix)
215914   Valgrind inserts bogus empty environment variable
217863   == 197988
219538   adjtimex syscall wrapper wrong in readonly adjtime mode
222545   shmat fails under valgind on some arm targets
222560   ARM NEON support
230407   == 202315
231076   == 202315
232509   Docs build fails with formatting inside <title></title> elements
232793   == 202315
235642   [PATCH] syswrap-linux.c: support evdev EVIOCG* ioctls
236546   vex x86->IR: 0x66 0xF 0x3A 0xA
237202   vex amd64->IR: 0xF3 0xF 0xB8 0xC0 0x49 0x3B
237371   better support for VALGRIND_MALLOCLIKE_BLOCK
237485   symlink (syscall 57) is not supported on Mac OS
237723   sysno == 101 exp-ptrcheck: the 'impossible' happened:
         unhandled syscall
238208   is_just_below_ESP doesn't take into account red-zone
238345   valgrind passes wrong $0 when executing a shell script
238679   mq_timedreceive syscall doesn't flag the reception buffer
         as "defined"
238696   fcntl command F_DUPFD_CLOEXEC not supported
238713   unhandled instruction bytes: 0x66 0xF 0x29 0xC6
238713   unhandled instruction bytes: 0x66 0xF 0x29 0xC6
238745   3.5.0 Make fails on PPC Altivec opcodes, though configure
         says "Altivec off"
239992   vex amd64->IR: 0x48 0xF 0xC4 0xC1 0x0 0x48
240488   == 197988
240639   == 212335
241377   == 236546
241903   == 202315
241920   == 212335
242606   unhandled syscall: setegid (in Ptrcheck)
242814   Helgrind "Impossible has happened" during
         QApplication::initInstance();
243064   Valgrind attempting to read debug information from iso
243270   Make stack unwinding in Valgrind wrappers more reliable
243884   exp-ptrcheck: the 'impossible happened: unhandled syscall
         sysno = 277 (mq_open)
244009   exp-ptrcheck unknown syscalls in analyzing lighttpd
244493   ARM VFP d16-d31 registers support
244670   add support for audit_session_self syscall on Mac OS 10.6
244921   The xml report of helgrind tool is not well format
244923   In the xml report file, the <preamble> not escape the
         xml char, eg '<','&','>'
245535   print full path names in plain text reports
245925   x86-64 red zone handling problem
246258   Valgrind not catching integer underruns + new [] s
246311   reg/reg cmpxchg doesn't work on amd64
246549   unhandled syscall unix:277 while testing 32-bit Darwin app
246888   Improve Makefile.vex.am
247510   [OS X 10.6] Memcheck reports unaddressable bytes passed
         to [f]chmod_extended
247526   IBM POWER6 (ISA 2.05) support is incomplete

247561   Some leak testcases fails due to reachable addresses in
         caller save regs
247875   sizeofIRType to handle Ity_I128
247894   [PATCH] unhandled syscall sys_readahead
247980   Doesn't honor CFLAGS passed to configure
248373   darwin10.supp is empty in the trunk
248822   Linux FIBMAP ioctl has int parameter instead of long
248893   [PATCH] make readdwarf.c big endianess safe to enable
         unwinding on big endian systems
249224   Syscall 336 not supported (SYS_proc_info)
249359   == 245535
249775   Incorrect scheme for detecting NEON capabilities of host CPU
249943   jni JVM init fails when using valgrind
249991   Valgrind incorrectly declares AESKEYGENASSIST support
         since VEX r2011
249996   linux/arm: unhandled syscall: 181 (__NR_pwrite64)
250799   frexp$fenv_access_off function generates SIGILL
250998   vex x86->IR: unhandled instruction bytes: 0x66 0x66 0x66 0x2E
251251   support pclmulqdq insn
251362   valgrind: ARM: attach to debugger either fails or provokes
         kernel oops
251674   Unhandled syscall 294
251818   == 254550

254257   Add support for debugfiles found by build-id
254550   [PATCH] Implement DW_ATE_UTF (DWARF4)
254646   Wrapped functions cause stack misalignment on OS X
         (and possibly Linux)
254556   ARM: valgrinding anything fails with SIGSEGV for 0xFFFF0FA0

(3.6.0: 21 October 2010, vex r2068, valgrind r11471).

Release 3.5.0 (19 August 2009)
~~~~~~~~~~~~~~~~~~~~~~~~~~~~~~
3.5.0 is a feature release with many significant improvements and the
usual collection of bug fixes. The main improvement is that Valgrind
now works on Mac OS X.

This release supports X86/Linux, AMD64/Linux, PPC32/Linux, PPC64/Linux
and X86/Darwin. Support for recent distros and toolchain components
(glibc 2.10, gcc 4.5) has been added.

Here is a short summary of the changes. Details are shown further
down:

* Support for Mac OS X (10.5.x).

* Improvements and simplifications to Memcheck's leak checker.

* Clarification and simplifications in various aspects of Valgrind's

text output.

* XML output for Helgrind and Ptrcheck.

* Performance and stability improvements for Helgrind and DRD.

* Genuinely atomic support for x86/amd64/ppc atomic instructions.

* A new experimental tool, BBV, useful for computer architecture
  research.

* Improved Wine support, including ability to read Windows PDB
  debuginfo.

Here are details of the above changes, followed by descriptions of
many other minor changes, and a list of fixed bugs.

* Valgrind now runs on Mac OS X. (Note that Mac OS X is sometimes
  called "Darwin" because that is the name of the OS core, which is the
  level that Valgrind works at.)

  Supported systems:

  - It requires OS 10.5.x (Leopard). Porting to 10.4.x is not planned
    because it would require work and 10.4 is only becoming less common.

  - 32-bit programs on x86 and AMD64 (a.k.a x86-64) machines are supported
    fairly well. For 10.5.x, 32-bit programs are the default even on
    64-bit machines, so it handles most current programs.

  - 64-bit programs on x86 and AMD64 (a.k.a x86-64) machines are not
    officially supported, but simple programs at least will probably work.
    However, start-up is slow.

  - PowerPC machines are not supported.

  Things that don't work:

  - The Ptrcheck tool.

  - Objective-C garbage collection.

  - --db-attach=yes.

  - If you have Rogue Amoeba's "Instant Hijack" program installed,
    Valgrind will fail with a SIGTRAP at start-up. See
    https://bugs.kde.org/show_bug.cgi?id=193917 for details and a
    simple work-around.

  Usage notes:

- You will likely find --dsymutil=yes a useful option, as error
  messages may be imprecise without it.

- Mac OS X support is new and therefore will be less robust than the
  Linux support. Please report any bugs you find.

- Threaded programs may run more slowly than on Linux.

Many thanks to Greg Parker for developing this port over several years.

* Memcheck's leak checker has been improved.

  - The results for --leak-check=summary now match the summary results
    for --leak-check=full. Previously they could differ because
    --leak-check=summary counted "indirectly lost" blocks and
    "suppressed" blocks as "definitely lost".

  - Blocks that are only reachable via at least one interior-pointer,
    but are directly pointed to by a start-pointer, were previously
    marked as "still reachable". They are now correctly marked as
    "possibly lost".

  - The default value for the --leak-resolution option has been
    changed from "low" to "high". In general, this means that more
    leak reports will be produced, but each leak report will describe
    fewer leaked blocks.

  - With --leak-check=full, "definitely lost" and "possibly lost"
    leaks are now considered as proper errors, ie. they are counted
    for the "ERROR SUMMARY" and affect the behaviour of
    --error-exitcode. These leaks are not counted as errors if
    --leak-check=summary is specified, however.

  - Documentation for the leak checker has been improved.

* Various aspects of Valgrind's text output have changed.

  - Valgrind's start-up message has changed. It is shorter but also
    includes the command being run, which makes it easier to use
    --trace-children=yes. An example:

  - Valgrind's shut-down messages have also changed. This is most
    noticeable with Memcheck, where the leak summary now occurs before
    the error summary. This change was necessary to allow leaks to be
    counted as proper errors (see the description of the leak checker
    changes above for more details). This was also necessary to fix a
    longstanding bug in which uses of suppressions against leaks were
    not "counted", leading to difficulties in maintaining suppression
    files (see https://bugs.kde.org/show_bug.cgi?id=186790).

  - Behavior of -v has changed. In previous versions, -v printed out
    a mixture of marginally-user-useful information, and tool/core

statistics. The statistics printing has now been moved to its own
flag, --stats=yes. This means -v is less verbose and more likely
to convey useful end-user information.

- The format of some (non-XML) stack trace entries has changed a
  little. Previously there were six possible forms:

    0x80483BF: really (a.c:20)
    0x80483BF: really (in /foo/a.out)
    0x80483BF: really
    0x80483BF: (within /foo/a.out)
    0x80483BF: ??? (a.c:20)
    0x80483BF: ???

  The third and fourth of these forms have been made more consistent
  with the others. The six possible forms are now:

    0x80483BF: really (a.c:20)
    0x80483BF: really (in /foo/a.out)
    0x80483BF: really (in ???)
    0x80483BF: ??? (in /foo/a.out)
    0x80483BF: ??? (a.c:20)
    0x80483BF: ???

  Stack traces produced when --xml=yes is specified are different
  and unchanged.

* Helgrind and Ptrcheck now support XML output, so they can be used
  from GUI tools. Also, the XML output mechanism has been
  overhauled.

  - The XML format has been overhauled and generalised, so it is more
    suitable for error reporting tools in general. The Memcheck
    specific aspects of it have been removed. The new format, which
    is an evolution of the old format, is described in
    docs/internals/xml-output-protocol4.txt.

  - Memcheck has been updated to use the new format.

  - Helgrind and Ptrcheck are now able to emit output in this format.

  - The XML output mechanism has been overhauled. XML is now output
    to its own file descriptor, which means that:

    * Valgrind can output text and XML independently.

    * The longstanding problem of XML output being corrupted by
      unexpected un-tagged text messages is solved.

    As before, the destination for text output is specified using
    --log-file=, --log-fd= or --log-socket=.

    As before, XML output for a tool is enabled using --xml=yes.

Because there's a new XML output channel, the XML output destination is now specified by --xml-file=, --xml-fd= or --xml-socket=.

Initial feedback has shown this causes some confusion. To clarify, the two envisaged usage scenarios are:

(1) Normal text output. In this case, do not specify --xml=yes nor any of --xml-file=, --xml-fd= or --xml-socket=.

(2) XML output. In this case, specify --xml=yes, and one of --xml-file=, --xml-fd= or --xml-socket= to select the XML destination, one of --log-file=, --log-fd= or --log-socket= to select the destination for any remaining text messages, and, importantly, -q.

   -q makes Valgrind completely silent on the text channel, except in the case of critical failures, such as Valgrind itself segfaulting, or failing to read debugging information. Hence, in this scenario, it suffices to check whether or not any output appeared on the text channel. If yes, then it is likely to be a critical error which should be brought to the attention of the user. If no (the text channel produced no output) then it can be assumed that the run was successful.

   This allows GUIs to make the critical distinction they need to make (did the run fail or not?) without having to search or filter the text output channel in any way.

It is also recommended to use --child-silent-after-fork=yes in scenario (2).

* Improvements and changes in Helgrind:

  - XML output, as described above

  - Checks for consistent association between pthread condition variables and their associated mutexes are now performed.

  - pthread_spinlock functions are supported.

  - Modest performance improvements.

  - Initial (skeletal) support for describing the behaviour of non-POSIX synchronisation objects through ThreadSanitizer compatible ANNOTATE_* macros.

  - More controllable tradeoffs between performance and the level of detail of "previous" accesses in a race. There are now three settings:

    * --history-level=full. This is the default, and was also the

default in 3.4.x. It shows both stacks involved in a race, but requires a lot of memory and can be very slow in programs that do many inter-thread synchronisation events.

* --history-level=none. This only shows the later stack involved in a race. This can be much faster than --history-level=full, but makes it much more difficult to find the other access involved in the race.

The new intermediate setting is

* --history-level=approx

For the earlier (other) access, two stacks are presented. The earlier access is guaranteed to be somewhere in between the two program points denoted by those stacks. This is not as useful as showing the exact stack for the previous access (as per --history-level=full), but it is better than nothing, and it's almost as fast as --history-level=none.

* New features and improvements in DRD:

- The error messages printed by DRD are now easier to interpret. Instead of using two different numbers to identify each thread (Valgrind thread ID and DRD thread ID), DRD does now identify threads via a single number (the DRD thread ID). Furthermore "first observed at" information is now printed for all error messages related to synchronization objects.

- Added support for named semaphores (sem_open() and sem_close()).

- Race conditions between pthread_barrier_wait() and pthread_barrier_destroy() calls are now reported.

- Added support for custom allocators through the macros VALGRIND_MALLOCLIKE_BLOCK() VALGRIND_FREELIKE_BLOCK() (defined in in <valgrind/valgrind.h>). An alternative for these two macros is the new client request VG_USERREQ__DRD_CLEAN_MEMORY (defined in <valgrind/drd.h>).

- Added support for annotating non-POSIX synchronization objects through several new ANNOTATE_*() macros.

- OpenMP: added support for the OpenMP runtime (libgomp) included with gcc versions 4.3.0 and 4.4.0.

- Faster operation.

- Added two new command-line options (--first-race-only and --segment-merging-interval).

* Genuinely atomic support for x86/amd64/ppc atomic instructions

Valgrind will now preserve (memory-access) atomicity of LOCK-prefixed x86/amd64 instructions, and any others implying a global bus lock. Ditto for PowerPC l{w,d}arx/st{w,d}cx. instructions.

This means that Valgrinded processes will "play nicely" in situations where communication with other processes, or the kernel, is done through shared memory and coordinated with such atomic instructions. Prior to this change, such arrangements usually resulted in hangs, races or other synchronisation failures, because Valgrind did not honour atomicity of such instructions.

* A new experimental tool, BBV, has been added. BBV generates basic block vectors for use with the SimPoint analysis tool, which allows a program's overall behaviour to be approximated by running only a fraction of it. This is useful for computer architecture researchers. You can run BBV by specifying --tool=exp-bbv (the "exp-" prefix is short for "experimental"). BBV was written by Vince Weaver.

* Modestly improved support for running Windows applications under Wine. In particular, initial support for reading Windows .PDB debug information has been added.

* A new Memcheck client request VALGRIND_COUNT_LEAK_BLOCKS has been added. It is similar to VALGRIND_COUNT_LEAKS but counts blocks instead of bytes.

* The Valgrind client requests VALGRIND_PRINTF and VALGRIND_PRINTF_BACKTRACE have been changed slightly. Previously, the string was always printed immediately on its own line. Now, the string will be added to a buffer but not printed until a newline is encountered, or other Valgrind output is printed (note that for VALGRIND_PRINTF_BACKTRACE, the back-trace itself is considered "other Valgrind output"). This allows you to use multiple VALGRIND_PRINTF calls to build up a single output line, and also to print multiple output lines with a single request (by embedding multiple newlines in the string).

* The graphs drawn by Massif's ms_print program have changed slightly:

  - The half-height chars '.' and ',' are no longer drawn, because they are confusing. The --y option can be used if the default y-resolution is not high enough.

  - Horizontal lines are now drawn after the top of a snapshot if there is a gap until the next snapshot. This makes it clear that the memory usage has not dropped to zero between snapshots.

* Something that happened in 3.4.0, but wasn't clearly announced: the
  option --read-var-info=yes can be used by some tools (Memcheck,
  Helgrind and DRD). When enabled, it causes Valgrind to read DWARF3
  variable type and location information. This makes those tools
  start up more slowly and increases memory consumption, but
  descriptions of data addresses in error messages become more
  detailed.

* exp-Omega, an experimental instantaneous leak-detecting tool, was
  disabled in 3.4.0 due to a lack of interest and maintenance,
  although the source code was still in the distribution. The source
  code has now been removed from the distribution. For anyone
  interested, the removal occurred in SVN revision r10247.

* Some changes have been made to the build system.

  - VEX/ is now integrated properly into the build system. This means
    that dependency tracking within VEX/ now works properly, "make
    install" will work without requiring "make" before it, and
    parallel builds (ie. 'make -j') now work (previously a
    .NOTPARALLEL directive was used to serialize builds, ie. 'make -j'
    was effectively ignored).

  - The --with-vex configure option has been removed. It was of
    little use and removing it simplified the build system.

  - The location of some install files has changed. This should not
    affect most users. Those who might be affected:

    * For people who use Valgrind with MPI programs, the installed
      libmpiwrap.so library has moved from
      $(INSTALL)/<platform>/libmpiwrap.so to
      $(INSTALL)/libmpiwrap-<platform>.so.

    * For people who distribute standalone Valgrind tools, the
      installed libraries such as $(INSTALL)/<platform>/libcoregrind.a
      have moved to $(INSTALL)/libcoregrind-<platform>.a.

    These changes simplify the build system.

  - Previously, all the distributed suppression (*.supp) files were
    installed. Now, only default.supp is installed. This should not
    affect users as the other installed suppression files were not
    read; the fact that they were installed was a mistake.

* KNOWN LIMITATIONS:

  - Memcheck is unusable with the Intel compiler suite version 11.1,
    when it generates code for SSE2-and-above capable targets. This
    is because of icc's use of highly optimised inlined strlen

implementations. It causes Memcheck to report huge numbers of false errors even in simple programs. Helgrind and DRD may also have problems.

Versions 11.0 and earlier may be OK, but this has not been properly tested.

The following bugs have been fixed or resolved. Note that "n-i-bz" stands for "not in bugzilla" -- that is, a bug that was reported to us but never got a bugzilla entry. We encourage you to file bugs in bugzilla (http://bugs.kde.org/enter_valgrind_bug.cgi) rather than mailing the developers (or mailing lists) directly -- bugs that are not entered into bugzilla tend to get forgotten about or ignored.

To see details of a given bug, visit
https://bugs.kde.org/show_bug.cgi?id=XXXXXX
where XXXXXX is the bug number as listed below.

84303   How about a LockCheck tool?
91633   dereference of null ptr in vgPlain_st_basetype
97452   Valgrind doesn't report any pthreads problems
100628 leak-check gets assertion failure when using
        VALGRIND_MALLOCLIKE_BLOCK on malloc()ed memory
108528 NPTL pthread cleanup handlers not called
110126 Valgrind 2.4.1 configure.in tramples CFLAGS
110128 mallinfo is not implemented...
110770 VEX: Generated files not always updated when making valgrind
111102 Memcheck: problems with large (memory footprint) applications
115673 Vex's decoder should never assert
117564 False positive: Syscall param clone(child_tidptr) contains
        uninitialised byte(s)
119404 executing ssh from inside valgrind fails
133679 Callgrind does not write path names to sources with dwarf debug
        info
135847 configure.in problem with non gnu compilers (and possible fix)
136154 threads.c:273 (vgCallgrind_post_signal): Assertion
        '*(vgCallgrind_current_fn_stack.top) == 0' failed.
136230 memcheck reports "possibly lost", should be "still reachable"
137073 NULL arg to MALLOCLIKE_BLOCK causes crash
137904 Valgrind reports a memory leak when using POSIX threads,
        while it shouldn't
139076 valgrind VT_GETSTATE error
142228 complaint of elf_dynamic_do_rela in trivial usage
145347 spurious warning with USBDEVFS_REAPURB
148441 (wine) can't find memory leak in Wine, win32 binary
        executable file.
148742 Leak-check fails assert on exit
149878 add (proper) check for calloc integer overflow
150606 Call graph is broken when using callgrind control
152393 leak errors produce an exit code of 0. I need some way to
        cause leak errors to result in a nonzero exit code.
157154 documentation (leak-resolution doc speaks about num-callers
        def=4) + what is a loss record

159501 incorrect handling of ALSA ioctls
162020 Valgrinding an empty/zero-byte file crashes valgrind
162482 ppc: Valgrind crashes while reading stabs information
162718 x86: avoid segment selector 0 in sys_set_thread_area()
163253 (wine) canonicaliseSymtab forgot some fields in DiSym
163560 VEX/test_main.c is missing from valgrind-3.3.1
164353 malloc_usable_size() doesn't return a usable size
165468 Inconsistent formatting in memcheck manual -- please fix
169505 main.c:286 (endOfInstr):
        Assertion 'ii->cost_offset == *cost_offset' failed
177206 Generate default.supp during compile instead of configure
177209 Configure valt_load_address based on arch+os
177305 eventfd / syscall 323 patch lost
179731 Tests fail to build because of inlining of non-local asm labels
181394 helgrind: libhb_core.c:3762 (msm_write): Assertion
        'ordxx == POrd_EQ || ordxx == POrd_LT' failed.
181594 Bogus warning for empty text segment
181707 dwarf doesn't require enumerations to have name
185038 exp-ptrcheck: "unhandled syscall: 285" (fallocate) on x86_64
185050 exp-ptrcheck: sg_main.c:727 (add_block_to_GlobalTree):
        Assertion '!already present' failed.
185359 exp-ptrcheck: unhandled syscall getresuid()
185794 "WARNING: unhandled syscall: 285" (fallocate) on x86_64
185816 Valgrind is unable to handle debug info for files with split
        debug info that are prelinked afterwards
185980 [darwin] unhandled syscall: sem_open
186238 bbToIR_AMD64: disInstr miscalculated next %rip
186507 exp-ptrcheck unhandled syscalls prctl, etc.
186790 Suppression pattern used for leaks are not reported
186796 Symbols with length>200 in suppression files are ignored
187048 drd: mutex PTHREAD_PROCESS_SHARED attribute missinterpretation
187416 exp-ptrcheck: support for __NR_{setregid,setreuid,setresuid}
188038 helgrind: hg_main.c:926: mk_SHVAL_fail: the 'impossible' happened
188046 bashisms in the configure script
188127 amd64->IR: unhandled instruction bytes: 0xF0 0xF 0xB0 0xA
188161 memcheck: --track-origins=yes asserts "mc_machine.c:672
        (get_otrack_shadow_offset_wrk): the 'impossible' happened."
188248 helgrind: pthread_cleanup_push, pthread_rwlock_unlock,
        assertion fail "!lock->heldBy"
188427 Add support for epoll_create1 (with patch)
188530 Support for SIOCGSTAMPNS
188560 Include valgrind.spec in the tarball
188572 Valgrind on Mac should suppress setenv() mem leak
189054 Valgrind fails to build because of duplicate non-local asm labels
189737 vex amd64->IR: unhandled instruction bytes: 0xAC
189762 epoll_create syscall not handled (--tool=exp-ptrcheck)
189763 drd assertion failure: s_threadinfo[tid].is_recording
190219 unhandled syscall: 328 (x86-linux)
190391 dup of 181394; see above
190429 Valgrind reports lots of errors in ld.so with x86_64 2.9.90 glibc
190820 No debug information on powerpc-linux
191095 PATCH: Improve usbdevfs ioctl handling
191182 memcheck: VALGRIND_LEAK_CHECK quadratic when big nr of chunks
        or big nr of errors

191189 --xml=yes should obey --gen-suppressions=all
191192 syslog() needs a suppression on macosx
191271 DARWIN: WARNING: unhandled syscall: 33554697 a.k.a.: 265
191761 getrlimit on MacOSX
191992 multiple --fn-skip only works sometimes; dependent on order
192634 V. reports "aspacem sync_check_mapping_callback:
        segment mismatch" on Darwin
192954 __extension__ missing on 2 client requests
194429 Crash at start-up with glibc-2.10.1 and linux-2.6.29
194474 "INSTALL" file has different build instructions than "README"
194671 Unhandled syscall (sem_wait?) from mac valgrind
195069 memcheck: reports leak (memory still reachable) for
        printf("%d', x)
195169 drd: (vgDrd_barrier_post_wait):
        Assertion 'r->sg[p->post_iteration]' failed.
195268 valgrind --log-file doesn't accept ~/...
195838 VEX abort: LibVEX_N_SPILL_BYTES too small for CPUID boilerplate
195860 WARNING: unhandled syscall: unix:223
196528 need a error suppression for pthread_rwlock_init under os x?
197227 Support aio_* syscalls on Darwin
197456 valgrind should reject --suppressions=(directory)
197512 DWARF2 CFI reader: unhandled CFI instruction 0:10
197591 unhandled syscall 27 (mincore)
197793 Merge DCAS branch to the trunk == 85756, 142103
197794 Avoid duplicate filenames in Vex
197898 make check fails on current SVN
197901 make check fails also under exp-ptrcheck in current SVN
197929 Make --leak-resolution=high the default
197930 Reduce spacing between leak reports
197933 Print command line of client at start-up, and shorten preamble
197966 unhandled syscall 205 (x86-linux, --tool=exp-ptrcheck)
198395 add BBV to the distribution as an experimental tool
198624 Missing syscalls on Darwin: 82, 167, 281, 347
198649 callgrind_annotate doesn't cumulate counters
199338 callgrind_annotate sorting/thresholds are broken for all but Ir
199977 Valgrind complains about an unrecognized instruction in the
        atomic_incs test program
200029 valgrind isn't able to read Fedora 12 debuginfo
200760 darwin unhandled syscall: unix:284
200827 DRD doesn't work on Mac OS X
200990 VG_(read_millisecond_timer)() does not work correctly
201016 Valgrind does not support pthread_kill() on Mac OS
201169 Document --read-var-info
201323 Pre-3.5.0 performance sanity checking
201384 Review user manual for the 3.5.0 release
201585 mfpvr not implemented on ppc
201708 tests failing because x86 direction flag is left set
201757 Valgrind doesn't handle any recent sys_futex additions
204377 64-bit valgrind can not start a shell script
        (with #!/path/to/shell) if the shell is a 32-bit executable
n-i-bz drd: fixed assertion failure triggered by mutex reinitialization.
n-i-bz drd: fixed a bug that caused incorrect messages to be printed
        about memory allocation events with memory access tracing enabled
n-i-bz drd: fixed a memory leak triggered by vector clock deallocation

(3.5.0: 19 Aug 2009, vex r1913, valgrind r10846).

Release 3.4.1 (28 February 2009)
~~~~~~~~~~~~~~~~~~~~~~~~~~~~~~~~
3.4.1 is a bug-fix release that fixes some regressions and assertion
failures in debug info reading in 3.4.0, most notably incorrect stack
traces on amd64-linux on older (glibc-2.3 based) systems. Various
other debug info problems are also fixed. A number of bugs in the
exp-ptrcheck tool introduced in 3.4.0 have been fixed.

In view of the fact that 3.4.0 contains user-visible regressions
relative to 3.3.x, upgrading to 3.4.1 is recommended. Packagers are
encouraged to ship 3.4.1 in preference to 3.4.0.

The fixed bugs are as follows. Note that "n-i-bz" stands for "not in
bugzilla" -- that is, a bug that was reported to us but never got a
bugzilla entry. We encourage you to file bugs in bugzilla
(http://bugs.kde.org/enter_valgrind_bug.cgi) rather than mailing the
developers (or mailing lists) directly -- bugs that are not entered
into bugzilla tend to get forgotten about or ignored.

n-i-bz   Fix various bugs reading icc-11 generated debug info
n-i-bz   Fix various bugs reading gcc-4.4 generated debug info
n-i-bz   Preliminary support for glibc-2.10 / Fedora 11
n-i-bz   Cachegrind and Callgrind: handle non-power-of-two cache sizes,
         so as to support (eg) 24k Atom D1 and Core2 with 3/6/12MB L2.
179618   exp-ptrcheck crashed / exit prematurely
179624   helgrind: false positive races with pthread_create and
         recv/open/close/read
134207   pkg-config output contains @VG_PLATFORM@
176926   floating point exception at valgrind startup with PPC 440EPX
181594   Bogus warning for empty text segment
173751   amd64->IR: 0x48 0xF 0x6F 0x45 (even more redundant rex prefixes)
181707   Dwarf3 doesn't require enumerations to have name
185038   exp-ptrcheck: "unhandled syscall: 285" (fallocate) on x86_64
185050   exp-ptrcheck: sg_main.c:727 (add_block_to_GlobalTree):
         Assertion '!already_present' failed.
185359   exp-ptrcheck unhandled syscall getresuid()

(3.4.1.RC1: 24 Feb 2008, vex r1884, valgrind r9253).
(3.4.1:   28 Feb 2008, vex r1884, valgrind r9293).

Release 3.4.0 (2 January 2009)
~~~~~~~~~~~~~~~~~~~~~~~~~~~~~~~
3.4.0 is a feature release with many significant improvements and the
usual collection of bug fixes. This release supports X86/Linux,
AMD64/Linux, PPC32/Linux and PPC64/Linux. Support for recent distros
(using gcc 4.4, glibc 2.8 and 2.9) has been added.

3.4.0 brings some significant tool improvements. Memcheck can now report the origin of uninitialised values, the thread checkers Helgrind and DRD are much improved, and we have a new experimental tool, exp-Ptrcheck, which is able to detect overruns of stack and global arrays. In detail:

* Memcheck is now able to track the origin of uninitialised values. When it reports an uninitialised value error, it will try to show the origin of the value, as either a heap or stack allocation. Origin tracking is expensive and so is not enabled by default. To use it, specify --track-origins=yes. Memcheck's speed will be essentially halved, and memory usage will be significantly increased. Nevertheless it can drastically reduce the effort required to identify the root cause of uninitialised value errors, and so is often a programmer productivity win, despite running more slowly.

* A version (1.4.0) of the Valkyrie GUI, that works with Memcheck in 3.4.0, will be released shortly.

* Helgrind's race detection algorithm has been completely redesigned and reimplemented, to address usability and scalability concerns:

  - The new algorithm has a lower false-error rate: it is much less likely to report races that do not really exist.

  - Helgrind will display full call stacks for both accesses involved in a race. This makes it easier to identify the root causes of races.

  - Limitations on the size of program that can run have been removed.

  - Performance has been modestly improved, although that is very workload-dependent.

  - Direct support for Qt4 threading has been added.

  - pthread_barriers are now directly supported.

  - Helgrind works well on all supported Linux targets.

* The DRD thread debugging tool has seen major improvements:

  - Greatly improved performance and significantly reduced memory usage.

  - Support for several major threading libraries (Boost.Thread, Qt4, glib, OpenMP) has been added.

  - Support for atomic instructions, POSIX semaphores, barriers and reader-writer locks has been added.

  - Works now on PowerPC CPUs too.

- Added support for printing thread stack usage at thread exit time.

- Added support for debugging lock contention.

- Added a manual for Drd.

* A new experimental tool, exp-Ptrcheck, has been added. Ptrcheck
  checks for misuses of pointers. In that sense it is a bit like
  Memcheck. However, Ptrcheck can do things Memcheck can't: it can
  detect overruns of stack and global arrays, it can detect
  arbitrarily far out-of-bounds accesses to heap blocks, and it can
  detect accesses heap blocks that have been freed a very long time
  ago (millions of blocks in the past).

  Ptrcheck currently works only on x86-linux and amd64-linux. To use
  it, use --tool=exp-ptrcheck. A simple manual is provided, as part
  of the main Valgrind documentation. As this is an experimental
  tool, we would be particularly interested in hearing about your
  experiences with it.

* exp-Omega, an experimental instantaneous leak-detecting tool, is no
  longer built by default, although the code remains in the repository
  and the tarball. This is due to three factors: a perceived lack of
  users, a lack of maintenance, and concerns that it may not be
  possible to achieve reliable operation using the existing design.

* As usual, support for the latest Linux distros and toolchain
  components has been added. It should work well on Fedora Core 10,
  OpenSUSE 11.1 and Ubuntu 8.10. gcc-4.4 (in its current pre-release
  state) is supported, as is glibc-2.9. The C++ demangler has been
  updated so as to work well with C++ compiled by even the most recent
  g++'s.

* You can now use frame-level wildcards in suppressions. This was a
  frequently-requested enhancement. A line "..." in a suppression now
  matches zero or more frames. This makes it easier to write
  suppressions which are precise yet insensitive to changes in
  inlining behaviour.

* 3.4.0 adds support on x86/amd64 for the SSSE3 instruction set.

* Very basic support for IBM Power6 has been added (64-bit processes only).

* Valgrind is now cross-compilable. For example, it is possible to
  cross compile Valgrind on an x86/amd64-linux host, so that it runs
  on a ppc32/64-linux target.

* You can set the main thread's stack size at startup using the
  new --main-stacksize= flag (subject of course to ulimit settings).
  This is useful for running apps that need a lot of stack space.

* The limitation that you can't use --trace-children=yes together
  with --db-attach=yes has been removed.

* The following bugs have been fixed. Note that "n-i-bz" stands for
  "not in bugzilla" -- that is, a bug that was reported to us but
  never got a bugzilla entry. We encourage you to file bugs in
  bugzilla (http://bugs.kde.org/enter_valgrind_bug.cgi) rather than
  mailing the developers (or mailing lists) directly.

  n-i-bz   Make return types for some client requests 64-bit clean
  n-i-bz   glibc 2.9 support
  n-i-bz   ignore unsafe .valgrindrc's (CVE-2008-4865)
  n-i-bz   MPI_Init(0,0) is valid but libmpiwrap.c segfaults
  n-i-bz   Building in an env without gdb gives bogus gdb attach
  92456   Tracing the origin of uninitialised memory
  106497   Valgrind does not demangle some C++ template symbols
  162222   ==106497
  151612   Suppression with "..." (frame-level wildcards in .supp files)
  156404   Unable to start oocalc under memcheck on openSUSE 10.3 (64-bit)
  159285   unhandled syscall:25 (stime, on x86-linux)
  159452   unhandled ioctl 0x8B01 on "valgrind iwconfig"
  160954   ppc build of valgrind crashes with illegal instruction (isel)
  160956   mallinfo implementation, w/ patch
  162092   Valgrind fails to start gnome-system-monitor
  162819   malloc_free_fill test doesn't pass on glibc2.8 x86
  163794   assertion failure with "--track-origins=yes"
  163933   sigcontext.err and .trapno must be set together
  163955   remove constraint !(--db-attach=yes && --trace-children=yes)
  164476   Missing kernel module loading system calls
  164669   SVN regression: mmap() drops posix file locks
  166581   Callgrind output corruption when program forks
  167288   Patch file for missing system calls on Cell BE
  168943   unsupported scas instruction pentium
  171645   Unrecognised instruction (MOVSD, non-binutils encoding)
  172417   x86->IR: 0x82 ...
  172563   amd64->IR: 0xD9 0xF5 - fprem1
  173099   .lds linker script generation error
  173177   [x86_64] syscalls: 125/126/179 (capget/capset/quotactl)
  173751   amd64->IR: 0x48 0xF 0x6F 0x45 (even more redundant prefixes)
  174532   == 173751
  174908   --log-file value not expanded correctly for core file
  175044   Add lookup_dcookie for amd64
  175150   x86->IR: 0xF2 0xF 0x11 0xC1 (movss non-binutils encoding)

Developer-visible changes:

* Valgrind's debug-info reading machinery has been majorly overhauled.
  It can now correctly establish the addresses for ELF data symbols,
  which is something that has never worked properly before now.

  Also, Valgrind can now read DWARF3 type and location information for
  stack and global variables. This makes it possible to use the
  framework to build tools that rely on knowing the type and locations
  of stack and global variables, for example exp-Ptrcheck.

  Reading of such information is disabled by default, because most
  tools don't need it, and because it is expensive in space and time.

However, you can force Valgrind to read it, using the
--read-var-info=yes flag. Memcheck, Helgrind and DRD are able to
make use of such information, if present, to provide source-level
descriptions of data addresses in the error messages they create.

(3.4.0.RC1: 24 Dec 2008, vex r1878, valgrind r8882).
(3.4.0:   3 Jan 2009, vex r1878, valgrind r8899).

3. OLDER NEWS

Release 3.3.1 (4 June 2008)
~~~~~~~~~~~~~~~~~~~~~~~~~~~

3.3.1 fixes a bunch of bugs in 3.3.0, adds support for glibc-2.8 based systems (openSUSE 11, Fedora Core 9), improves the existing glibc-2.7 support, and adds support for the SSSE3 (Core 2) instruction set.

3.3.1 will likely be the last release that supports some very old systems. In particular, the next major release, 3.4.0, will drop support for the old LinuxThreads threading library, and for gcc versions prior to 3.0.

The fixed bugs are as follows. Note that "n-i-bz" stands for "not in bugzilla" -- that is, a bug that was reported to us but never got a bugzilla entry. We encourage you to file bugs in bugzilla (http://bugs.kde.org/enter_valgrind_bug.cgi) rather than mailing the developers (or mailing lists) directly -- bugs that are not entered into bugzilla tend to get forgotten about or ignored.

```
n-i-bz   Massif segfaults at exit
n-i-bz   Memcheck asserts on Altivec code
n-i-bz   fix sizeof bug in Helgrind
n-i-bz   check fd on sys_llseek
n-i-bz   update syscall lists to kernel 2.6.23.1
n-i-bz   support sys_sync_file_range
n-i-bz   handle sys_sysinfo, sys_getresuid, sys_getresgid on ppc64-linux
n-i-bz   intercept memcpy in 64-bit ld.so's
n-i-bz   Fix wrappers for sys_{futimesat,utimensat}
n-i-bz   Minor false-error avoidance fixes for Memcheck
n-i-bz   libmpiwrap.c: add a wrapper for MPI_Waitany
n-i-bz   helgrind support for glibc-2.8
n-i-bz   partial fix for mc_leakcheck.c:698 assert:
         'lc_shadows[i]->data + lc_shadows[i] ...
n-i-bz   Massif/Cachegrind output corruption when programs fork
n-i-bz   register allocator fix: handle spill stores correctly
n-i-bz   add support for PA6T PowerPC CPUs
126389   vex x86->IR: 0xF 0xAE (FXRSTOR)
158525   ==126389
152818   vex x86->IR: 0xF3 0xAC (repz lodsb)
153196   vex x86->IR: 0xF2 0xA6 (repnz cmpsb)
155011   vex x86->IR: 0xCF (iret)
155091   Warning [...] unhandled DW_OP_ opcode 0x23
156960   ==155901
155528   support Core2/SSSE3 insns on x86/amd64
155929   ms_print fails on massif outputs containing long lines
157665   valgrind fails on shmdt(0) after shmat to 0
157748   support x86 PUSHFW/POPFW
158212   helgrind: handle pthread_rwlock_try{rd,wr}lock.
158425   sys_poll incorrectly emulated when RES==0
158744   vex amd64->IR: 0xF0 0x41 0xF 0xC0 (xaddb)
160907   Support for a couple of recent Linux syscalls
```

161285 Patch -- support for eventfd() syscall
161378 illegal opcode in debug libm (FUCOMPP)
160136 ==161378
161487 number of suppressions files is limited to 10
162386 ms_print typo in milliseconds time unit for massif
161036 exp-drd: client allocated memory was never freed
162663 signalfd_wrapper fails on 64bit linux

(3.3.1.RC1: 2 June 2008, vex r1854, valgrind r8169).
(3.3.1:   4 June 2008, vex r1854, valgrind r8180).

Release 3.3.0 (7 December 2007)
~~~~~~~~~~~~~~~~~~~~~~~~~~~~~~~~~
3.3.0 is a feature release with many significant improvements and the
usual collection of bug fixes. This release supports X86/Linux,
AMD64/Linux, PPC32/Linux and PPC64/Linux. Support for recent distros
(using gcc 4.3, glibc 2.6 and 2.7) has been added.

The main excitement in 3.3.0 is new and improved tools. Helgrind
works again, Massif has been completely overhauled and much improved,
Cachegrind now does branch-misprediction profiling, and a new category
of experimental tools has been created, containing two new tools:
Omega and DRD. There are many other smaller improvements. In detail:

- Helgrind has been completely overhauled and works for the first time
  since Valgrind 2.2.0. Supported functionality is: detection of
  misuses of the POSIX PThreads API, detection of potential deadlocks
  resulting from cyclic lock dependencies, and detection of data
  races. Compared to the 2.2.0 Helgrind, the race detection algorithm
  has some significant improvements aimed at reducing the false error
  rate. Handling of various kinds of corner cases has been improved.
  Efforts have been made to make the error messages easier to
  understand. Extensive documentation is provided.

- Massif has been completely overhauled. Instead of measuring
  space-time usage -- which wasn't always useful and many people found
  confusing -- it now measures space usage at various points in the
  execution, including the point of peak memory allocation. Its
  output format has also changed: instead of producing PostScript
  graphs and HTML text, it produces a single text output (via the new
  'ms_print' script) that contains both a graph and the old textual
  information, but in a more compact and readable form. Finally, the
  new version should be more reliable than the old one, as it has been
  tested more thoroughly.

- Cachegrind has been extended to do branch-misprediction profiling.
  Both conditional and indirect branches are profiled. The default
  behaviour of Cachegrind is unchanged. To use the new functionality,
  give the option --branch-sim=yes.

- A new category of "experimental tools" has been created. Such tools
  may not work as well as the standard tools, but are included because

some people will find them useful, and because exposure to a wider
user group provides tool authors with more end-user feedback. These
tools have a "exp-" prefix attached to their names to indicate their
experimental nature. Currently there are two experimental tools:

* exp-Omega: an instantaneous leak detector. See
  exp-omega/docs/omega_introduction.txt.

* exp-DRD: a data race detector based on the happens-before
  relation. See exp-drd/docs/README.txt.

- Scalability improvements for very large programs, particularly those
  which have a million or more malloc'd blocks in use at once. These
  improvements mostly affect Memcheck. Memcheck is also up to 10%
  faster for all programs, with x86-linux seeing the largest
  improvement.

- Works well on the latest Linux distros. Has been tested on Fedora
  Core 8 (x86, amd64, ppc32, ppc64) and openSUSE 10.3. glibc 2.6 and
  2.7 are supported. gcc-4.3 (in its current pre-release state) is
  supported. At the same time, 3.3.0 retains support for older
  distros.

- The documentation has been modestly reorganised with the aim of
  making it easier to find information on common-usage scenarios.
  Some advanced material has been moved into a new chapter in the main
  manual, so as to unclutter the main flow, and other tidying up has
  been done.

- There is experimental support for AIX 5.3, both 32-bit and 64-bit
  processes. You need to be running a 64-bit kernel to use Valgrind
  on a 64-bit executable.

- There have been some changes to command line options, which may
  affect you:

  * --log-file-exactly and
    --log-file-qualifier options have been removed.

    To make up for this --log-file option has been made more powerful.
    It now accepts a %p format specifier, which is replaced with the
    process ID, and a %q{FOO} format specifier, which is replaced with
    the contents of the environment variable FOO.

  * --child-silent-after-fork=yes|no [no]

    Causes Valgrind to not show any debugging or logging output for
    the child process resulting from a fork() call. This can make the
    output less confusing (although more misleading) when dealing with
    processes that create children.

  * --cachegrind-out-file, --callgrind-out-file and --massif-out-file

    These control the names of the output files produced by

      Cachegrind, Callgrind and Massif. They accept the same %p and %q
      format specifiers that --log-file accepts. --callgrind-out-file
      replaces Callgrind's old --base option.

  * Cachegrind's 'cg_annotate' script no longer uses the --<pid>
    option to specify the output file. Instead, the first non-option
    argument is taken to be the name of the output file, and any
    subsequent non-option arguments are taken to be the names of
    source files to be annotated.

  * Cachegrind and Callgrind now use directory names where possible in
    their output files. This means that the -I option to
    'cg_annotate' and 'callgrind_annotate' should not be needed in
    most cases. It also means they can correctly handle the case
    where two source files in different directories have the same
    name.

- Memcheck offers a new suppression kind: "Jump". This is for
  suppressing jump-to-invalid-address errors. Previously you had to
  use an "Addr1" suppression, which didn't make much sense.

- Memcheck has new flags --malloc-fill=<hexnum> and
  --free-fill=<hexnum> which free malloc'd / free'd areas with the
  specified byte. This can help shake out obscure memory corruption
  problems. The definedness and addressability of these areas is
  unchanged -- only the contents are affected.

- The behaviour of Memcheck's client requests VALGRIND_GET_VBITS and
  VALGRIND_SET_VBITS have changed slightly. They no longer issue
  addressability errors -- if either array is partially unaddressable,
  they just return 3 (as before). Also, SET_VBITS doesn't report
  definedness errors if any of the V bits are undefined.

- The following Memcheck client requests have been removed:
    VALGRIND_MAKE_NOACCESS
    VALGRIND_MAKE_WRITABLE
    VALGRIND_MAKE_READABLE
    VALGRIND_CHECK_WRITABLE
    VALGRIND_CHECK_READABLE
    VALGRIND_CHECK_DEFINED
  They were deprecated in 3.2.0, when equivalent but better-named client
  requests were added. See the 3.2.0 release notes for more details.

- The behaviour of the tool Lackey has changed slightly. First, the output
  from --trace-mem has been made more compact, to reduce the size of the
  traces. Second, a new option --trace-superblocks has been added, which
  shows the addresses of superblocks (code blocks) as they are executed.

- The following bugs have been fixed. Note that "n-i-bz" stands for
  "not in bugzilla" -- that is, a bug that was reported to us but
  never got a bugzilla entry. We encourage you to file bugs in
  bugzilla (http://bugs.kde.org/enter_valgrind_bug.cgi) rather than
  mailing the developers (or mailing lists) directly.

n-i-bz   x86_linux_REDIR_FOR_index() broken
n-i-bz   guest-amd64/toIR.c:2512 (dis_op2_E_G): Assertion '0' failed.
n-i-bz   Support x86 INT insn (INT (0xCD) 0x40 - 0x43)
n-i-bz   Add sys_utimensat system call for Linux x86 platform
 79844   Helgrind complains about race condition which does not exist
 82871   Massif output function names too short
 89061   Massif: ms_main.c:485 (get_XCon): Assertion 'xpt->max_chi...'
 92615   Write output from Massif at crash
 95483   massif feature request: include peak allocation in report
112163   MASSIF crashed with signal 7 (SIGBUS) after running 2 days
119404   problems running setuid executables (partial fix)
121629   add instruction-counting mode for timing
127371   java vm giving unhandled instruction bytes: 0x26 0x2E 0x64 0x65
129937   ==150380
129576   Massif loses track of memory, incorrect graphs
132132   massif --format=html output does not do html entity escaping
132950   Heap alloc/usage summary
133962   unhandled instruction bytes: 0xF2 0x4C 0xF 0x10
134990   use -fno-stack-protector if possible
136382   ==134990
137396   I would really like helgrind to work again...
137714   x86/amd64->IR: 0x66 0xF 0xF7 0xC6 (maskmovq, maskmovdq)
141631   Massif: percentages don't add up correctly
142706   massif numbers don't seem to add up
143062   massif crashes on app exit with signal 8 SIGFPE
144453   (get_XCon): Assertion 'xpt->max_children != 0' failed.
145559   valgrind aborts when malloc_stats is called
145609   valgrind aborts all runs with 'repeated section!'
145622   --db-attach broken again on x86-64
145837   ==149519
145887   PPC32: getitimer() system call is not supported
146252   ==150678
146456   (update_XCon): Assertion 'xpt->curr_space >= -space_delta'...
146701   ==134990
146781   Adding support for private futexes
147325   valgrind internal error on syscall (SYS_io_destroy, 0)
147498   amd64->IR: 0xF0 0xF 0xB0 0xF (lock cmpxchg %cl,(%rdi))
147545   Memcheck: mc_main.c:817 (get_sec_vbits8): Assertion 'n' failed.
147628   SALC opcode 0xd6 unimplemented
147825   crash on amd64-linux with gcc 4.2 and glibc 2.6 (CFI)
148174   Incorrect type of freed_list_volume causes assertion [...]
148447   x86_64 : new NOP codes: 66 66 66 66 2e 0f 1f
149182   PPC Trap instructions not implemented in valgrind
149504   Assertion hit on alloc_xpt->curr_space >= -space_delta
149519   ppc32: V aborts with SIGSEGV on execution of a signal handler
149892   ==137714
150044   SEGV during stack deregister
150380   dwarf/gcc interoperation (dwarf3 read problems)
150408   ==148447
150678   guest-amd64/toIR.c:3741 (dis_Grp5): Assertion 'sz == 4' failed
151209   V unable to execute programs for users with UID > 2^16
151938   help on --db-command= misleading
152022   subw $0x28, %%sp causes assertion failure in memcheck
152357   inb and outb not recognized in 64-bit mode

```
152501   vex x86->IR: 0x27 0x66 0x89 0x45 (daa)
152818   vex x86->IR: 0xF3 0xAC 0xFC 0x9C (rep lodsb)
```

Developer-visible changes:

- The names of some functions and types within the Vex IR have
  changed. Run 'svn log -r1689 VEX/pub/libvex_ir.h' for full details.
  Any existing standalone tools will have to be updated to reflect
  these changes. The new names should be clearer. The file
  VEX/pub/libvex_ir.h is also much better commented.

- A number of new debugging command line options have been added.
  These are mostly of use for debugging the symbol table and line
  number readers:

  --trace-symtab-patt=<patt> limit debuginfo tracing to obj name <patt>
  --trace-cfi=no|yes   show call-frame-info details? [no]
  --debug-dump=syms   mimic /usr/bin/readelf --syms
  --debug-dump=line   mimic /usr/bin/readelf --debug-dump=line
  --debug-dump=frames   mimic /usr/bin/readelf --debug-dump=frames
  --sym-offsets=yes|no   show syms in form 'name+offset' ? [no]

- Internally, the code base has been further factorised and
  abstractified, particularly with respect to support for non-Linux
  OSs.

(3.3.0.RC1: 2 Dec 2007, vex r1803, valgrind r7268).
(3.3.0.RC2: 5 Dec 2007, vex r1804, valgrind r7282).
(3.3.0.RC3: 9 Dec 2007, vex r1804, valgrind r7288).
(3.3.0:   10 Dec 2007, vex r1804, valgrind r7290).

Release 3.2.3 (29 Jan 2007)
~~~~~~~~~~~~~~~~~~~~~~~~~~~~
Unfortunately 3.2.2 introduced a regression which can cause an
assertion failure ("vex: the 'impossible' happened: eqIRConst") when
running obscure pieces of SSE code. 3.2.3 fixes this and adds one
more glibc-2.5 intercept. In all other respects it is identical to
3.2.2. Please do not use (or package) 3.2.2; instead use 3.2.3.

n-i-bz   vex: the 'impossible' happened: eqIRConst
n-i-bz   Add an intercept for glibc-2.5 __stpcpy_chk

(3.2.3: 29 Jan 2007, vex r1732, valgrind r6560).

Release 3.2.2 (22 Jan 2007)
~~~~~~~~~~~~~~~~~~~~~~~~~~~~
3.2.2 fixes a bunch of bugs in 3.2.1, adds support for glibc-2.5 based
systems (openSUSE 10.2, Fedora Core 6), improves support for icc-9.X
compiled code, and brings modest performance improvements in some
areas, including amd64 floating point, powerpc support, and startup
responsiveness on all targets.

The fixed bugs are as follows. Note that "n-i-bz" stands for "not in bugzilla" -- that is, a bug that was reported to us but never got a bugzilla entry. We encourage you to file bugs in bugzilla (http://bugs.kde.org/enter_valgrind_bug.cgi) rather than mailing the developers (or mailing lists) directly.

129390	ppc?->IR: some kind of VMX prefetch (dstt)
129968	amd64->IR: 0xF 0xAE 0x0 (fxsave)
134319	==129968
133054	'make install' fails with syntax errors
118903	==133054
132998	startup fails in when running on UML
134207	pkg-config output contains @VG_PLATFORM@
134727	valgrind exits with "Value too large for defined data type"
n-i-bz	ppc32/64: support mcrfs
n-i-bz	Cachegrind/Callgrind: Update cache parameter detection
135012	x86->IR: 0xD7 0x8A 0xE0 0xD0 (xlat)
125959	==135012
126147	x86->IR: 0xF2 0xA5 0xF 0x77 (repne movsw)
136650	amd64->IR: 0xC2 0x8 0x0
135421	x86->IR: unhandled Grp5(R) case 6
n-i-bz	Improved documentation of the IR intermediate representation
n-i-bz	jcxz (x86) (users list, 8 Nov)
n-i-bz	ExeContext hashing fix
n-i-bz	fix CFI reading failures ("Dwarf CFI 0:24 0:32 0:48 0:7")
n-i-bz	fix Cachegrind/Callgrind simulation bug
n-i-bz	libmpiwrap.c: fix handling of MPI_LONG_DOUBLE
n-i-bz	make User errors suppressible
136844	corrupted malloc line when using --gen-suppressions=yes
138507	==136844
n-i-bz	Speed up the JIT's register allocator
n-i-bz	Fix confusing leak-checker flag hints
n-i-bz	Support recent autoswamp versions
n-i-bz	ppc32/64 dispatcher speedups
n-i-bz	ppc64 front end rld/rlw improvements
n-i-bz	ppc64 back end imm64 improvements
136300	support 64K pages on ppc64-linux
139124	== 136300
n-i-bz	fix ppc insn set tests for gcc >= 4.1
137493	x86->IR: recent binutils no-ops
137714	x86->IR: 0x66 0xF 0xF7 0xC6 (maskmovdqu)
138424	"failed in UME with error 22" (produce a better error msg)
138856	==138424
138627	Enhancement support for prctl ioctls
138896	Add support for usb ioctls
136059	==138896
139050	ppc32->IR: mfspr 268/269 instructions not handled
n-i-bz	ppc32->IR: lvxl/stvxl
n-i-bz	glibc-2.5 support
n-i-bz	memcheck: provide replacement for mempcpy
n-i-bz	memcheck: replace bcmp in ld.so
n-i-bz	Use 'ifndef' in VEX's Makefile correctly
n-i-bz	Suppressions for MVL 4.0.1 on ppc32-linux

n-i-bz   libmpiwrap.c: Fixes for MPICH
n-i-bz   More robust handling of hinted client mmaps
139776   Invalid read in unaligned memcpy with Intel compiler v9
n-i-bz   Generate valid XML even for very long fn names
n-i-bz   Don't prompt about suppressions for unshown reachable leaks
139910   amd64 rcl is not supported
n-i-bz   DWARF CFI reader: handle DW_CFA_undefined
n-i-bz   DWARF CFI reader: handle icc9 generated CFI info better
n-i-bz   fix false uninit-value errs in icc9 generated FP code
n-i-bz   reduce extraneous frames in libmpiwrap.c
n-i-bz   support pselect6 on amd64-linux

(3.2.2: 22 Jan 2007, vex r1729, valgrind r6545).

Release 3.2.1 (16 Sept 2006)
~~~~~~~~~~~~~~~~~~~~~~~~~~~~~
3.2.1 adds x86/amd64 support for all SSE3 instructions except monitor
and mwait, further reduces memcheck's false error rate on all
platforms, adds support for recent binutils (in OpenSUSE 10.2 and
Fedora Rawhide) and fixes a bunch of bugs in 3.2.0. Some of the fixed
bugs were causing large programs to segfault with --tool=callgrind and
--tool=cachegrind, so an upgrade is recommended.

In view of the fact that any 3.3.0 release is unlikely to happen until
well into 1Q07, we intend to keep the 3.2.X line alive for a while
yet, and so we tentatively plan a 3.2.2 release sometime in December
06.

The fixed bugs are as follows. Note that "n-i-bz" stands for "not in
bugzilla" -- that is, a bug that was reported to us but never got a
bugzilla entry.

n-i-bz   Expanding brk() into last available page asserts
n-i-bz   ppc64-linux stack RZ fast-case snafu
n-i-bz   'c' in --gen-supps=yes doesn't work
n-i-bz   VG_N_SEGMENTS too low (users, 28 June)
n-i-bz   VG_N_SEGNAMES too low (Stu Robinson)
106852   x86->IR: fisttp (SSE3)
117172   FUTEX_WAKE does not use uaddr2
124039   Lacks support for VKI_[GP]IO_UNIMAP*
127521   amd64->IR: 0xF0 0x48 0xF 0xC7 (cmpxchg8b)
128917   amd64->IR: 0x66 0xF 0xF6 0xC4 (psadbw,SSE2)
129246   JJ: ppc32/ppc64 syscalls, w/ patch
129358   x86->IR: fisttpl (SSE3)
129866   cachegrind/callgrind causes executable to die
130020   Can't stat .so/.exe error while reading symbols
130388   Valgrind aborts when process calls malloc_trim()
130638   PATCH: ppc32 missing system calls
130785   amd64->IR: unhandled instruction "pushfq"
131481:   (HINT_NOP) vex x86->IR: 0xF 0x1F 0x0 0xF
131298   ==131481
132146   Programs with long sequences of bswap[l,q]s
132918   vex amd64->IR: 0xD9 0xF8 (fprem)

132813   Assertion at priv/guest-x86/toIR.c:652 fails
133051   'cfsi->len > 0 && cfsi->len < 2000000' failed
132722   valgrind header files are not standard C
n-i-bz   Livelocks entire machine (users list, Timothy Terriberry)
n-i-bz   Alex Bennee mmap problem (9 Aug)
n-i-bz   BartV: Don't print more lines of a stack-trace than were obtained.
n-i-bz   ppc32 SuSE 10.1 redir
n-i-bz   amd64 padding suppressions
n-i-bz   amd64 insn printing fix.
n-i-bz   ppc cmp reg,reg fix
n-i-bz   x86/amd64 iropt e/rflag reduction rules
n-i-bz   SuSE 10.1 (ppc32) minor fixes
133678   amd64->IR: 0x48 0xF 0xC5 0xC0 (pextrw?)
133694   aspacem assertion: aspacem_minAddr <= holeStart
n-i-bz   callgrind: fix warning about malformed creator line
n-i-bz   callgrind: fix annotate script for data produced with
          --dump-instr=yes
n-i-bz   callgrind: fix failed assertion when toggling
          instrumentation mode
n-i-bz   callgrind: fix annotate script fix warnings with
          --collect-jumps=yes
n-i-bz   docs path hardwired (Dennis Lubert)

The following bugs were not fixed, due primarily to lack of developer
time, and also because bug reporters did not answer requests for
feedback in time for the release:

129390   ppc?->IR: some kind of VMX prefetch (dstt)
129968   amd64->IR: 0xF 0xAE 0x0 (fxsave)
133054   'make install' fails with syntax errors
n-i-bz   Signal race condition (users list, 13 June, Johannes Berg)
n-i-bz   Unrecognised instruction at address 0x70198EC2 (users list,
          19 July, Bennee)
132998   startup fails in when running on UML

The following bug was tentatively fixed on the mainline but the fix
was considered too risky to push into 3.2.X:

133154   crash when using client requests to register/deregister stack

(3.2.1: 16 Sept 2006, vex r1658, valgrind r6070).

Release 3.2.0 (7 June 2006)
~~~~~~~~~~~~~~~~~~~~~~~~~~~~~
3.2.0 is a feature release with many significant improvements and the
usual collection of bug fixes. This release supports X86/Linux,
AMD64/Linux, PPC32/Linux and PPC64/Linux.

Performance, especially of Memcheck, is improved, Addrcheck has been
removed, Callgrind has been added, PPC64/Linux support has been added,
Lackey has been improved, and MPI support has been added. In detail:

- Memcheck has improved speed and reduced memory use. Run times are

typically reduced by 15-30%, averaging about 24% for SPEC CPU2000.
The other tools have smaller but noticeable speed improvements. We
are interested to hear what improvements users get.

Memcheck uses less memory due to the introduction of a compressed
representation for shadow memory. The space overhead has been
reduced by a factor of up to four, depending on program behaviour.
This means you should be able to run programs that use more memory
than before without hitting problems.

- Addrcheck has been removed. It has not worked since version 2.4.0,
  and the speed and memory improvements to Memcheck make it redundant.
  If you liked using Addrcheck because it didn't give undefined value
  errors, you can use the new Memcheck option --undef-value-errors=no
  to get the same behaviour.

- The number of undefined-value errors incorrectly reported by
  Memcheck has been reduced (such false reports were already very
  rare). In particular, efforts have been made to ensure Memcheck
  works really well with gcc 4.0/4.1-generated code on X86/Linux and
  AMD64/Linux.

- Josef Weidendorfer's popular Callgrind tool has been added. Folding
  it in was a logical step given its popularity and usefulness, and
  makes it easier for us to ensure it works "out of the box" on all
  supported targets. The associated KDE KCachegrind GUI remains a
  separate project.

- A new release of the Valkyrie GUI for Memcheck, version 1.2.0,
  accompanies this release. Improvements over previous releases
  include improved robustness, many refinements to the user interface,
  and use of a standard autoconf/automake build system. You can get
  it from http://www.valgrind.org/downloads/guis.html.

- Valgrind now works on PPC64/Linux. As with the AMD64/Linux port,
  this supports programs using to 32G of address space. On 64-bit
  capable PPC64/Linux setups, you get a dual architecture build so
  that both 32-bit and 64-bit executables can be run. Linux on POWER5
  is supported, and POWER4 is also believed to work. Both 32-bit and
  64-bit DWARF2 is supported. This port is known to work well with
  both gcc-compiled and xlc/xlf-compiled code.

- Floating point accuracy has been improved for PPC32/Linux.
  Specifically, the floating point rounding mode is observed on all FP
  arithmetic operations, and multiply-accumulate instructions are
  preserved by the compilation pipeline. This means you should get FP
  results which are bit-for-bit identical to a native run. These
  improvements are also present in the PPC64/Linux port.

- Lackey, the example tool, has been improved:

  * It has a new option --detailed-counts (off by default) which
    causes it to print out a count of loads, stores and ALU operations
    done, and their sizes.

  * It has a new option --trace-mem (off by default) which causes it
    to print out a trace of all memory accesses performed by a
    program. It's a good starting point for building Valgrind tools
    that need to track memory accesses. Read the comments at the top
    of the file lackey/lk_main.c for details.

  * The original instrumentation (counting numbers of instructions,
    jumps, etc) is now controlled by a new option --basic-counts. It
    is on by default.

- MPI support: partial support for debugging distributed applications
  using the MPI library specification has been added. Valgrind is
  aware of the memory state changes caused by a subset of the MPI
  functions, and will carefully check data passed to the (P)MPI_
  interface.

- A new flag, --error-exitcode=, has been added. This allows changing
  the exit code in runs where Valgrind reported errors, which is
  useful when using Valgrind as part of an automated test suite.

- Various segfaults when reading old-style "stabs" debug information
  have been fixed.

- A simple performance evaluation suite has been added. See
  perf/README and README_DEVELOPERS for details. There are
  various bells and whistles.

- New configuration flags:
    --enable-only32bit
    --enable-only64bit
  By default, on 64 bit platforms (ppc64-linux, amd64-linux) the build
  system will attempt to build a Valgrind which supports both 32-bit
  and 64-bit executables. This may not be what you want, and you can
  override the default behaviour using these flags.

Please note that Helgrind is still not working. We have made an
important step towards making it work again, however, with the
addition of function wrapping (see below).

Other user-visible changes:

- Valgrind now has the ability to intercept and wrap arbitrary
  functions. This is a preliminary step towards making Helgrind work
  again, and was required for MPI support.

- There are some changes to Memcheck's client requests. Some of them
  have changed names:

      MAKE_NOACCESS   --> MAKE_MEM_NOACCESS
      MAKE_WRITABLE   --> MAKE_MEM_UNDEFINED
      MAKE_READABLE   --> MAKE_MEM_DEFINED

      CHECK_WRITABLE --> CHECK_MEM_IS_ADDRESSABLE

CHECK_READABLE --> CHECK_MEM_IS_DEFINED
CHECK_DEFINED --> CHECK_VALUE_IS_DEFINED

The reason for the change is that the old names are subtly
misleading. The old names will still work, but they are deprecated
and may be removed in a future release.

We also added a new client request:

MAKE_MEM_DEFINED_IF_ADDRESSABLE(a, len)

which is like MAKE_MEM_DEFINED but only affects a byte if the byte is
already addressable.

- The way client requests are encoded in the instruction stream has
changed. Unfortunately, this means 3.2.0 will not honour client
requests compiled into binaries using headers from earlier versions
of Valgrind. We will try to keep the client request encodings more
stable in future.

BUGS FIXED:

108258   NPTL pthread cleanup handlers not called
117290   valgrind is sigKILL'd on startup
117295   == 117290
118703   m_signals.c:1427 Assertion 'tst->status == VgTs_WaitSys'
118466   add %reg, %reg generates incorrect validity for bit 0
123210   New: strlen from ld-linux on amd64
123244   DWARF2 CFI reader: unhandled CFI instruction 0:18
123248   syscalls in glibc-2.4: openat, fstatat, symlinkat
123258   socketcall.recvmsg(msg.msg_iov[i] points to uninit
123535   mremap(new_addr) requires MREMAP_FIXED in 4th arg
123836   small typo in the doc
124029   ppc compile failed: 'vor' gcc 3.3.5
124222   Segfault: @@don't know what type ':' is
124475   ppc32: crash (syscall?) timer_settime()
124499   amd64->IR: 0xF 0xE 0x48 0x85 (femms)
124528   FATAL: aspacem assertion failed: segment_is_sane
124697   vex x86->IR: 0xF 0x70 0xC9 0x0 (pshufw)
124892   vex x86->IR: 0xF3 0xAE (REPx SCASB)
126216   == 124892
124808   ppc32: sys_sched_getaffinity() not handled
n-i-bz   Very long stabs strings crash m_debuginfo
n-i-bz   amd64->IR: 0x66 0xF 0xF5 (pmaddwd)
125492   ppc32: support a bunch more syscalls
121617   ppc32/64: coredumping gives assertion failure
121814   Coregrind return error as exitcode patch
126517   == 121814
125607   amd64->IR: 0x66 0xF 0xA3 0x2 (btw etc)
125651   amd64->IR: 0xF8 0x49 0xFF 0xE3 (clc?)
126253   x86 movx is wrong
126451   3.2 SVN doesn't work on ppc32 CPU's without FPU
126217   increase # threads
126243   vex x86->IR: popw mem

126583   amd64->IR: 0x48 0xF 0xA4 0xC2 (shld $1,%rax,%rdx)
126668   amd64->IR: 0x1C 0xFF (sbb $0xff,%al)
126696   support for CDROMREADRAW ioctl and CDROMREADTOCENTRY fix
126722   assertion: segment_is_sane at m_aspacemgr/aspacemgr.c:1624
126938   bad checking for syscalls linkat, renameat, symlinkat

(3.2.0RC1: 27 May 2006, vex r1626, valgrind r5947).
(3.2.0:   7 June 2006, vex r1628, valgrind r5957).

Release 3.1.1 (15 March 2006)
~~~~~~~~~~~~~~~~~~~~~~~~~~~~~
3.1.1 fixes a bunch of bugs reported in 3.1.0. There is no new
functionality. The fixed bugs are:

(note: "n-i-bz" means "not in bugzilla" -- this bug does not have
 a bugzilla entry).

n-i-bz   ppc32: fsub 3,3,3 in dispatcher doesn't clear NaNs
n-i-bz   ppc32: __NR_{set,get}priority
117332   x86: missing line info with icc 8.1
117366   amd64: 0xDD 0x7C fnstsw
118274   == 117366
117367   amd64: 0xD9 0xF4 fxtract
117369   amd64: __NR_getpriority (140)
117419   ppc32: lfsu f5, -4(r11)
117419   ppc32: fsqrt
117936   more stabs problems (segfaults while reading debug info)
119914   == 117936
120345   == 117936
118239   amd64: 0xF 0xAE 0x3F (clflush)
118939   vm86old system call
n-i-bz   memcheck/tests/mempool reads freed memory
n-i-bz   AshleyP's custom-allocator assertion
n-i-bz   Dirk strict-aliasing stuff
n-i-bz   More space for debugger cmd line (Dan Thaler)
n-i-bz   Clarified leak checker output message
n-i-bz   AshleyP's --gen-suppressions output fix
n-i-bz   cg_annotate's --sort option broken
n-i-bz   OSet 64-bit fastcmp bug
n-i-bz   VG_(getgroups) fix (Shinichi Noda)
n-i-bz   ppc32: allocate from callee-saved FP/VMX regs
n-i-bz   misaligned path word-size bug in mc_main.c
119297   Incorrect error message for sse code
120410   x86: prefetchw (0xF 0xD 0x48 0x4)
120728   TIOCSERGETLSR, TIOCGICOUNT, HDIO_GET_DMA ioctls
120658   Build fixes for gcc 2.96
120734   x86: Support for changing EIP in signal handler
n-i-bz   memcheck/tests/zeropage de-looping fix
n-i-bz   x86: fxtract doesn't work reliably
121662   x86: lock xadd (0xF0 0xF 0xC0 0x2)
121893   calloc does not always return zeroed memory
121901   no support for syscall tkill
n-i-bz   Suppression update for Debian unstable

122067   amd64: fcmovnu (0xDB 0xD9)
n-i-bz   ppc32: broken signal handling in cpu feature detection
n-i-bz   ppc32: rounding mode problems (improved, partial fix only)
119482   ppc32: mtfsb1
n-i-bz   ppc32: mtocrf/mfocrf

(3.1.1: 15 March 2006, vex r1597, valgrind r5771).

Release 3.1.0 (25 November 2005)
~~~~~~~~~~~~~~~~~~~~~~~~~~~~~~~~~
3.1.0 is a feature release with a number of significant improvements:
AMD64 support is much improved, PPC32 support is good enough to be
usable, and the handling of memory management and address space is
much more robust. In detail:

- AMD64 support is much improved. The 64-bit vs. 32-bit issues in
  3.0.X have been resolved, and it should "just work" now in all
  cases. On AMD64 machines both 64-bit and 32-bit versions of
  Valgrind are built. The right version will be invoked
  automatically, even when using --trace-children and mixing execution
  between 64-bit and 32-bit executables. Also, many more instructions
  are supported.

- PPC32 support is now good enough to be usable. It should work with
  all tools, but please let us know if you have problems. Three
  classes of CPUs are supported: integer only (no FP, no Altivec),
  which covers embedded PPC uses, integer and FP but no Altivec
  (G3-ish), and CPUs capable of Altivec too (G4, G5).

- Valgrind's address space management has been overhauled. As a
  result, Valgrind should be much more robust with programs that use
  large amounts of memory. There should be many fewer "memory
  exhausted" messages, and debug symbols should be read correctly on
  large (eg. 300MB+) executables. On 32-bit machines the full address
  space available to user programs (usually 3GB or 4GB) can be fully
  utilised. On 64-bit machines up to 32GB of space is usable; when
  using Memcheck that means your program can use up to about 14GB.

  A side effect of this change is that Valgrind is no longer protected
  against wild writes by the client. This feature was nice but relied
  on the x86 segment registers and so wasn't portable.

- Most users should not notice, but as part of the address space
  manager change, the way Valgrind is built has been changed. Each
  tool is now built as a statically linked stand-alone executable,
  rather than as a shared object that is dynamically linked with the
  core. The "valgrind" program invokes the appropriate tool depending
  on the --tool option. This slightly increases the amount of disk
  space used by Valgrind, but it greatly simplified many things and
  removed Valgrind's dependence on glibc.

Please note that Addrcheck and Helgrind are still not working. Work
is underway to reinstate them (or equivalents). We apologise for the

inconvenience.

Other user-visible changes:

- The --weird-hacks option has been renamed --sim-hints.

- The --time-stamp option no longer gives an absolute date and time.
  It now prints the time elapsed since the program began.

- It should build with gcc-2.96.

- Valgrind can now run itself (see README_DEVELOPERS for how).
  This is not much use to you, but it means the developers can now
  profile Valgrind using Cachegrind. As a result a couple of
  performance bad cases have been fixed.

- The XML output format has changed slightly. See
  docs/internals/xml-output.txt.

- Core dumping has been reinstated (it was disabled in 3.0.0 and 3.0.1).
  If your program crashes while running under Valgrind, a core file with
  the name "vgcore.<pid>" will be created (if your settings allow core
  file creation). Note that the floating point information is not all
  there. If Valgrind itself crashes, the OS will create a normal core
  file.

The following are some user-visible changes that occurred in earlier
versions that may not have been announced, or were announced but not
widely noticed. So we're mentioning them now.

- The --tool flag is optional once again; if you omit it, Memcheck
  is run by default.

- The --num-callers flag now has a default value of 12. It was
  previously 4.

- The --xml=yes flag causes Valgrind's output to be produced in XML
  format. This is designed to make it easy for other programs to
  consume Valgrind's output. The format is described in the file
  docs/internals/xml-format.txt.

- The --gen-suppressions flag supports an "all" value that causes every
  suppression to be printed without asking.

- The --log-file option no longer puts "pid" in the filename, eg. the
  old name "foo.pid12345" is now "foo.12345".

- There are several graphical front-ends for Valgrind, such as Valkyrie,
  Alleyoop and Valgui. See http://www.valgrind.org/downloads/guis.html
  for a list.

BUGS FIXED:

109861   amd64 hangs at startup

110301   ditto
111554   valgrind crashes with Cannot allocate memory
111809   Memcheck tool doesn't start java
111901   cross-platform run of cachegrind fails on opteron
113468   (vgPlain_mprotect_range): Assertion 'r != -1' failed.
 92071   Reading debugging info uses too much memory
109744   memcheck loses track of mmap from direct ld-linux.so.2
110183   tail of page with _end
 82301   FV memory layout too rigid
 98278   Infinite recursion possible when allocating memory
108994   Valgrind runs out of memory due to 133x overhead
115643   valgrind cannot allocate memory
105974   vg_hashtable.c static hash table
109323   ppc32: dispatch.S uses Altivec insn, which doesn't work on POWER.
109345   ptrace_setregs not yet implemented for ppc
110831   Would like to be able to run against both 32 and 64 bit
         binaries on AMD64
110829   == 110831
111781   compile of valgrind-3.0.0 fails on my linux (gcc 2.X prob)
112670   Cachegrind: cg_main.c:486 (handleOneStatement ...
112941   vex x86: 0xD9 0xF4 (fxtract)
110201   == 112941
113015   vex amd64->IR: 0xE3 0x14 0x48 0x83 (jrcxz)
113126   Crash with binaries built with -gstabs+/-ggdb
104065   == 113126
115741   == 113126
113403   Partial SSE3 support on x86
113541   vex: Grp5(x86) (alt encoding inc/dec) case 1
113642   valgrind crashes when trying to read debug information
113810   vex x86->IR: 66 0F F6 (66 + PSADBW == SSE PSADBW)
113796   read() and write() do not work if buffer is in shared memory
113851   vex x86->IR: (pmaddwd): 0x66 0xF 0xF5 0xC7
114366   vex amd64 cannnot handle __asm__("fninit")
114412   vex amd64->IR: 0xF 0xAD 0xC2 0xD3 (128-bit shift, shrdq?)
114455   vex amd64->IR: 0xF 0xAC 0xD0 0x1 (also shrdq)
115590: amd64->IR: 0x67 0xE3 0x9 0xEB (address size override)
115953   valgrind svn r5042 does not build with parallel make (-j3)
116057   maximum instruction size - VG_MAX_INSTR_SZB too small?
116483   shmat failes with invalid argument
102202   valgrind crashes when realloc'ing until out of memory
109487   == 102202
110536   == 102202
112687   == 102202
111724   vex amd64->IR: 0x41 0xF 0xAB (more BT{,S,R,C} fun n games)
111748   vex amd64->IR: 0xDD 0xE2 (fucom)
111785   make fails if CC contains spaces
111829   vex x86->IR: sbb AL, Ib
111851   vex x86->IR: 0x9F 0x89 (lahf/sahf)
112031   iopl on AMD64 and README_MISSING_SYSCALL_OR_IOCTL update
112152   code generation for Xin_MFence on x86 with SSE0 subarch
112167   == 112152
112789   == 112152
112199   naked ar tool is used in vex makefile
112501   vex x86->IR: movq (0xF 0x7F 0xC1 0xF) (mmx MOVQ)

113583   == 112501
112538   memalign crash
113190   Broken links in docs/html/
113230   Valgrind sys_pipe on x86-64 wrongly thinks file descriptors
             should be 64bit
113996   vex amd64->IR: fucomp (0xDD 0xE9)
114196   vex x86->IR: out %eax,(%dx) (0xEF 0xC9 0xC3 0x90)
114289   Memcheck fails to intercept malloc when used in an uclibc environment
114756   mbind syscall support
114757   Valgrind dies with assertion: Assertion 'noLargerThan > 0' failed
114563   stack tracking module not informed when valgrind switches threads
114564   clone() and stacks
114565   == 114564
115496   glibc crashes trying to use sysinfo page
116200   enable fsetxattr, fgetxattr, and fremovexattr for amd64

(3.1.0RC1: 20 November 2005, vex r1466, valgrind r5224).
(3.1.0:   26 November 2005, vex r1471, valgrind r5235).

Release 3.0.1 (29 August 2005)
~~~~~~~~~~~~~~~~~~~~~~~~~~~~~~~~
3.0.1 fixes a bunch of bugs reported in 3.0.0. There is no new
functionality. Some of the fixed bugs are critical, so if you
use/distribute 3.0.0, an upgrade to 3.0.1 is recommended. The fixed
bugs are:

(note: "n-i-bz" means "not in bugzilla" -- this bug does not have
 a bugzilla entry).

109313   (== 110505) x86 cmpxchg8b
n-i-bz   x86: track but ignore changes to %eflags.AC (alignment check)
110102   dis_op2_E_G(amd64)
110202   x86 sys_waitpid(#286)
110203   clock_getres(,0)
110208   execve fail wrong retval
110274   SSE1 now mandatory for x86
110388   amd64 0xDD 0xD1
110464   amd64 0xDC 0x1D FCOMP
110478   amd64 0xF 0xD PREFETCH
n-i-bz   XML <unique> printing wrong
n-i-bz   Dirk r4359 (amd64 syscalls from trunk)
110591   amd64 and x86: rdtsc not implemented properly
n-i-bz   Nick r4384 (stub implementations of Addrcheck and Helgrind)
110652   AMD64 valgrind crashes on cwtd instruction
110653   AMD64 valgrind crashes on sarb $0x4,foo(%rip) instruction
110656   PATH=/usr/bin::/bin valgrind foobar stats ./fooba
110657   Small test fixes
110671   vex x86->IR: unhandled instruction bytes: 0xF3 0xC3 (rep ret)
n-i-bz   Nick (Cachegrind should not assert when it encounters a client
             request.)
110685   amd64->IR: unhandled instruction bytes: 0xE1 0x56 (loope Jb)
110830   configuring with --host fails to build 32 bit on 64 bit target
110875   Assertion when execve fails

n-i-bz   Updates to Memcheck manual
n-i-bz   Fixed broken malloc_usable_size()
110898   opteron instructions missing: btq btsq btrq bsfq
110954   x86->IR: unhandled instruction bytes: 0xE2 0xF6 (loop Jb)
n-i-bz   Make suppressions work for "???" lines in stacktraces.
111006   bogus warnings from linuxthreads
111092   x86: dis_Grp2(Reg): unhandled case(x86)
111231   sctp_getladdrs() and sctp_getpaddrs() returns uninitialized
         memory
111102   (comment #4)   Fixed 64-bit unclean "silly arg" message
n-i-bz   vex x86->IR: unhandled instruction bytes: 0x14 0x0
n-i-bz   minor umount/fcntl wrapper fixes
111090   Internal Error running Massif
101204   noisy warning
111513   Illegal opcode for SSE instruction (x86 movups)
111555   VEX/Makefile: CC is set to gcc
n-i-bz   Fix XML bugs in FAQ

(3.0.1: 29 August 05,
        vex/branches/VEX_3_0_BRANCH r1367,
        valgrind/branches/VALGRIND_3_0_BRANCH r4574).

Release 3.0.0 (3 August 2005)
~~~~~~~~~~~~~~~~~~~~~~~~~~~~~~
3.0.0 is a major overhaul of Valgrind. The most significant user
visible change is that Valgrind now supports architectures other than
x86. The new architectures it supports are AMD64 and PPC32, and the
infrastructure is present for other architectures to be added later.

AMD64 support works well, but has some shortcomings:

- It generally won't be as solid as the x86 version. For example,
  support for more obscure instructions and system calls may be missing.
  We will fix these as they arise.

- Address space may be limited; see the point about
  position-independent executables below.

- If Valgrind is built on an AMD64 machine, it will only run 64-bit
  executables. If you want to run 32-bit x86 executables under Valgrind
  on an AMD64, you will need to build Valgrind on an x86 machine and
  copy it to the AMD64 machine. And it probably won't work if you do
  something tricky like exec'ing a 32-bit program from a 64-bit program
  while using --trace-children=yes. We hope to improve this situation
  in the future.

The PPC32 support is very basic. It may not work reliably even for
small programs, but it's a start. Many thanks to Paul Mackerras for
his great work that enabled this support. We are working to make
PPC32 usable as soon as possible.

Other user-visible changes:

- Valgrind is no longer built by default as a position-independent
  executable (PIE), as this caused too many problems.

  Without PIE enabled, AMD64 programs will only be able to access 2GB of
  address space. We will fix this eventually, but not for the moment.

  Use --enable-pie at configure-time to turn this on.

- Support for programs that use stack-switching has been improved. Use
  the --max-stackframe flag for simple cases, and the
  VALGRIND_STACK_REGISTER, VALGRIND_STACK_DEREGISTER and
  VALGRIND_STACK_CHANGE client requests for trickier cases.

- Support for programs that use self-modifying code has been improved,
  in particular programs that put temporary code fragments on the stack.
  This helps for C programs compiled with GCC that use nested functions,
  and also Ada programs. This is controlled with the --smc-check
  flag, although the default setting should work in most cases.

- Output can now be printed in XML format. This should make it easier
  for tools such as GUI front-ends and automated error-processing
  schemes to use Valgrind output as input. The --xml flag controls this.
  As part of this change, ELF directory information is read from executables,
  so absolute source file paths are available if needed.

- Programs that allocate many heap blocks may run faster, due to
  improvements in certain data structures.

- Addrcheck is currently not working. We hope to get it working again
  soon. Helgrind is still not working, as was the case for the 2.4.0
  release.

- The JITter has been completely rewritten, and is now in a separate
  library, called Vex. This enabled a lot of the user-visible changes,
  such as new architecture support. The new JIT unfortunately translates
  more slowly than the old one, so programs may take longer to start.
  We believe the code quality is produces is about the same, so once
  started, programs should run at about the same speed. Feedback about
  this would be useful.

  On the plus side, Vex and hence Memcheck tracks value flow properly
  through floating point and vector registers, something the 2.X line
  could not do. That means that Memcheck is much more likely to be
  usably accurate on vectorised code.

- There is a subtle change to the way exiting of threaded programs
  is handled. In 3.0, Valgrind's final diagnostic output (leak check,
  etc) is not printed until the last thread exits. If the last thread
  to exit was not the original thread which started the program, any
  other process wait()-ing on this one to exit may conclude it has
  finished before the diagnostic output is printed. This may not be
  what you expect. 2.X had a different scheme which avoided this
  problem, but caused deadlocks under obscure circumstances, so we

are trying something different for 3.0.

- Small changes in control log file naming which make it easier to
  use valgrind for debugging MPI-based programs. The relevant
  new flags are --log-file-exactly= and --log-file-qualifier=.

- As part of adding AMD64 support, DWARF2 CFI-based stack unwinding
  support was added. In principle this means Valgrind can produce
  meaningful backtraces on x86 code compiled with -fomit-frame-pointer
  providing you also compile your code with -fasynchronous-unwind-tables.

- The documentation build system has been completely redone.
  The documentation masters are now in XML format, and from that
  HTML, PostScript and PDF documentation is generated. As a result
  the manual is now available in book form. Note that the
  documentation in the source tarballs is pre-built, so you don't need
  any XML processing tools to build Valgrind from a tarball.

Changes that are not user-visible:

- The code has been massively overhauled in order to modularise it.
  As a result we hope it is easier to navigate and understand.

- Lots of code has been rewritten.

BUGS FIXED:

110046 sz == 4 assertion failed
109810 vex amd64->IR: unhandled instruction bytes: 0xA3 0x4C 0x70 0xD7
109802 Add a plausible_stack_size command-line parameter ?
109783 unhandled ioctl TIOCMGET (running hw detection tool discover)
109780 unhandled ioctl BLKSSZGET (running fdisk -l /dev/hda)
109718 vex x86->IR: unhandled instruction: ffreep
109429 AMD64 unhandled syscall: 127 (sigpending)
109401 false positive uninit in strchr from ld-linux.so.2
109385 "stabs" parse failure
109378 amd64: unhandled instruction REP NOP
109376 amd64: unhandled instruction LOOP Jb
109363 AMD64 unhandled instruction bytes
109362 AMD64 unhandled syscall: 24 (sched_yield)
109358 fork() won't work with valgrind-3.0 SVN
109332 amd64 unhandled instruction: ADC Ev, Gv
109314 Bogus memcheck report on amd64
108883 Crash; vg_memory.c:905 (vgPlain_init_shadow_range):
        Assertion 'vgPlain_defined_init_shadow_page()' failed.
108349 mincore syscall parameter checked incorrectly
108059 build infrastructure: small update
107524 epoll_ctl event parameter checked on EPOLL_CTL_DEL
107123 Vex dies with unhandled instructions: 0xD9 0x31 0xF 0xAE
106841 auxmap & openGL problems
106713 SDL_Init causes valgrind to exit
106352 setcontext and makecontext not handled correctly
106293 addresses beyond initial client stack allocation
        not checked in VALGRIND_DO_LEAK_CHECK

106283 PIE client programs are loaded at address 0
105831 Assertion 'vgPlain_defined_init_shadow_page()' failed.
105039 long run-times probably due to memory manager
104797 valgrind needs to be aware of BLKGETSIZE64
103594 unhandled instruction: FICOM
103320 Valgrind 2.4.0 fails to compile with gcc 3.4.3 and -O0
103168 potentially memory leak in coregrind/ume.c
102039 bad permissions for mapped region at address 0xB7C73680
101881 weird assertion problem
101543 Support fadvise64 syscalls
75247   x86_64/amd64 support (the biggest "bug" we have ever fixed)

(3.0RC1: 27 July   05, vex r1303, valgrind r4283).
(3.0.0:   3 August 05, vex r1313, valgrind r4316).

Stable release 2.4.1 (1 August 2005)
~~~~~~~~~~~~~~~~~~~~~~~~~~~~~~~~~~~~~~
(The notes for this release have been lost. Sorry! It would have
contained various bug fixes but no new features.)

Stable release 2.4.0 (March 2005) -- CHANGES RELATIVE TO 2.2.0
~~~~~~
2.4.0 brings many significant changes and bug fixes. The most
significant user-visible change is that we no longer supply our own
pthread implementation. Instead, Valgrind is finally capable of
running the native thread library, either LinuxThreads or NPTL.

This means our libpthread has gone, along with the bugs associated
with it. Valgrind now supports the kernel's threading syscalls, and
lets you use your standard system libpthread. As a result:

* There are many fewer system dependencies and strange library-related
  bugs. There is a small performance improvement, and a large
  stability improvement.

* On the downside, Valgrind can no longer report misuses of the POSIX
  PThreads API. It also means that Helgrind currently does not work.
  We hope to fix these problems in a future release.

Note that running the native thread libraries does not mean Valgrind
is able to provide genuine concurrent execution on SMPs. We still
impose the restriction that only one thread is running at any given
time.

There are many other significant changes too:

* Memcheck is (once again) the default tool.

* The default stack backtrace is now 12 call frames, rather than 4.

* Suppressions can have up to 25 call frame matches, rather than 4.

* Memcheck and Addrcheck use less memory. Under some circumstances, they no longer allocate shadow memory if there are large regions of memory with the same A/V states - such as an mmaped file.

* The memory-leak detector in Memcheck and Addrcheck has been improved. It now reports more types of memory leak, including leaked cycles. When reporting leaked memory, it can distinguish between directly leaked memory (memory with no references), and indirectly leaked memory (memory only referred to by other leaked memory).

* Memcheck's confusion over the effect of mprotect() has been fixed: previously mprotect could erroneously mark undefined data as defined.

* Signal handling is much improved and should be very close to what you get when running natively.

  One result of this is that Valgrind observes changes to sigcontexts passed to signal handlers. Such modifications will take effect when the signal returns. You will need to run with --single-step–yes to make this useful.

* Valgrind is built in Position Independent Executable (PIE) format if your toolchain supports it. This allows it to take advantage of all the available address space on systems with 4Gbyte user address spaces.

* Valgrind can now run itself (requires PIE support).

* Syscall arguments are now checked for validity. Previously all memory used by syscalls was checked, but now the actual values passed are also checked.

* Syscall wrappers are more robust against bad addresses being passed to syscalls: they will fail with EFAULT rather than killing Valgrind with SIGSEGV.

* Because clone() is directly supported, some non-pthread uses of it will work. Partial sharing (where some resources are shared, and some are not) is not supported.

* open() and readlink() on /proc/self/exe are supported.

BUGS FIXED:

88520   pipe+fork+dup2 kills the main program
88604 Valgrind Aborts when using $VALGRIND_OPTS and user progra...
88614 valgrind: vg_libpthread.c:2323 (read): Assertion 'read_pt...
88703 Stabs parser fails to handle ";"
88886 ioctl wrappers for TIOCMBIS and TIOCMBIC
89032 valgrind pthread_cond_timedwait fails

89106 the 'impossible' happened
89139 Missing sched_setaffinity & sched_getaffinity
89198 valgrind lacks support for SIOCSPGRP and SIOCGPGRP
89263 Missing ioctl translations for scsi-generic and CD playing
89440 tests/deadlock.c line endings
89481 'impossible' happened: EXEC FAILED
89663 valgrind 2.2.0 crash on Redhat 7.2
89792 Report pthread_mutex_lock() deadlocks instead of returnin...
90111 statvfs64 gives invalid error/warning
90128 crash+memory fault with stabs generated by gnat for a run...
90778 VALGRIND_CHECK_DEFINED() not as documented in memcheck.h
90834 cachegrind crashes at end of program without reporting re...
91028 valgrind: vg_memory.c:229 (vgPlain_unmap_range): Assertio...
91162 valgrind crash while debugging drivel 1.2.1
91199 Unimplemented function
91325 Signal routing does not propagate the siginfo structure
91599 Assertion 'cv == ((void *)0)'
91604 rw_lookup clears orig and sends the NULL value to rw_new
91821 Small problems building valgrind with $top_builddir ne $t...
91844 signal 11 (SIGSEGV) at get_tcb (libpthread.c:86) in corec...
92264 UNIMPLEMENTED FUNCTION: pthread_condattr_setpshared
92331 per-target flags necessitate AM_PROG_CC_C_O
92420 valgrind doesn't compile with linux 2.6.8.1/9
92513 Valgrind 2.2.0 generates some warning messages
92528 vg_symtab2.c:170 (addLoc): Assertion 'loc->size > 0' failed.
93096 unhandled ioctl 0x4B3A and 0x5601
93117 Tool and core interface versions do not match
93128 Can't run valgrind --tool=memcheck because of unimplement...
93174 Valgrind can crash if passed bad args to certain syscalls
93309 Stack frame in new thread is badly aligned
93328 Wrong types used with sys_sigprocmask()
93763 /usr/include/asm/msr.h is missing
93776 valgrind: vg_memory.c:508 (vgPlain_find_map_space): Asser...
93810 fcntl() argument checking a bit too strict
94378 Assertion 'tst->sigqueue_head != tst->sigqueue_tail' failed.
94429 valgrind 2.2.0 segfault with mmap64 in glibc 2.3.3
94645 Impossible happened: PINSRW mem
94953 valgrind: the 'impossible' happened: SIGSEGV
95667 Valgrind does not work with any KDE app
96243 Assertion 'res==0' failed
96252 stage2 loader of valgrind fails to allocate memory
96520 All programs crashing at _dl_start (in /lib/ld-2.3.3.so) ...
96660 ioctl CDROMREADTOCENTRY causes bogus warnings
96747 After looping in a segfault handler, the impossible happens
96923 Zero sized arrays crash valgrind trace back with SIGFPE
96948 valgrind stops with assertion failure regarding mmap2
96966 valgrind fails when application opens more than 16 sockets
97398 valgrind: vg_libpthread.c:2667 Assertion failed
97407 valgrind: vg_mylibc.c:1226 (vgPlain_safe_fd): Assertion '...
97427 "Warning: invalid file descriptor -1 in syscall close()" ...
97785 missing backtrace
97792 build in obj dir fails - autoconf / makefile cleanup
97880 pthread_mutex_lock fails from shared library (special ker...
97975 program aborts without ang VG messages

98129 Failed when open and close file 230000 times using stdio
98175 Crashes when using valgrind-2.2.0 with a program using al...
98288 Massif broken
98303 UNIMPLEMENTED FUNCTION pthread_condattr_setpshared
98630 failed--compilation missing warnings.pm, fails to make he...
98756 Cannot valgrind signal-heavy kdrive X server
98966 valgrinding the JVM fails with a sanity check assertion
99035 Valgrind crashes while profiling
99142 loops with message "Signal 11 being dropped from thread 0...
99195 threaded apps crash on thread start (using QThread::start...
99348 Assertion 'vgPlain_lseek(core_fd, 0, 1) == phdrs[i].p_off...
99568 False negative due to mishandling of mprotect
99738 valgrind memcheck crashes on program that uses sigitimer
99923 0-sized allocations are reported as leaks
99949 program seg faults after exit()
100036 "newSuperblock's request for 1048576 bytes failed"
100116 valgrind: (pthread_cond_init): Assertion 'sizeof(* cond) ...
100486 memcheck reports "valgrind: the 'impossible' happened: V...
100833 second call to "mremap" fails with EINVAL
101156 (vgPlain_find_map_space): Assertion '(addr & ((1 << 12)-1...
101173 Assertion 'recDepth >= 0 && recDepth < 500' failed
101291 creating threads in a forked process fails
101313 valgrind causes different behavior when resizing a window...
101423 segfault for c++ array of floats
101562 valgrind massif dies on SIGINT even with signal handler r...

Stable release 2.2.0 (31 August 2004) -- CHANGES RELATIVE TO 2.0.0
~~~~~~

2.2.0 brings nine months worth of improvements and bug fixes. We
believe it to be a worthy successor to 2.0.0. There are literally
hundreds of bug fixes and minor improvements. There are also some
fairly major user-visible changes:

* A complete overhaul of handling of system calls and signals, and
  their interaction with threads. In general, the accuracy of the
  system call, thread and signal simulations is much improved:

  - Blocking system calls behave exactly as they do when running
    natively (not on valgrind). That is, if a syscall blocks only the
    calling thread when running natively, than it behaves the same on
    valgrind. No more mysterious hangs because V doesn't know that some
    syscall or other, should block only the calling thread.

  - Interrupted syscalls should now give more faithful results.

  - Signal contexts in signal handlers are supported.

* Improvements to NPTL support to the extent that V now works
  properly on NPTL-only setups.

* Greater isolation between Valgrind and the program being run, so
  the program is less likely to inadvertently kill Valgrind by
  doing wild writes.

* Massif: a new space profiling tool. Try it! It's cool, and it'll
  tell you in detail where and when your C/C++ code is allocating heap.
  Draws pretty .ps pictures of memory use against time. A potentially
  powerful tool for making sense of your program's space use.

* File descriptor leakage checks. When enabled, Valgrind will print out
  a list of open file descriptors on exit.

* Improved SSE2/SSE3 support.

* Time-stamped output; use --time-stamp=yes

Stable release 2.2.0 (31 August 2004) -- CHANGES RELATIVE TO 2.1.2
~~~~~~
2.2.0 is not much different from 2.1.2, released seven weeks ago.
A number of bugs have been fixed, most notably #85658, which gave
problems for quite a few people. There have been many internal
cleanups, but those are not user visible.

The following bugs have been fixed since 2.1.2:

85658   Assert in coregrind/vg_libpthread.c:2326 (open64) !=
         (void*)0 failed
         This bug was reported multiple times, and so the following
         duplicates of it are also fixed: 87620, 85796, 85935, 86065,
         86919, 86988, 87917, 88156

80716   Semaphore mapping bug caused by unmap (sem_destroy)
         (Was fixed prior to 2.1.2)

86987   semctl and shmctl syscalls family is not handled properly

86696   valgrind 2.1.2 + RH AS2.1 + librt

86730   valgrind locks up at end of run with assertion failure
         in __pthread_unwind

86641   memcheck doesn't work with Mesa OpenGL/ATI on Suse 9.1
         (also fixes 74298, a duplicate of this)

85947   MMX/SSE unhandled instruction 'sfence'

84978   Wrong error "Conditional jump or move depends on
         uninitialised value" resulting from "sbbl %reg, %reg"

86254   ssort() fails when signed int return type from comparison is
         too small to handle result of unsigned int subtraction

87089   memalign(4, xxx) makes valgrind assert

86407   Add support for low-level parallel port driver ioctls.

70587   Add timestamps to Valgrind output? (wishlist)

84937   vg_libpthread.c:2505 (se_remap): Assertion 'res == 0'
         (fixed prior to 2.1.2)

86317   cannot load libSDL-1.2.so.0 using valgrind

86989   memcpy from mac_replace_strmem.c complains about
         uninitialized pointers passed when length to copy is zero

85811   gnu pascal symbol causes segmentation fault; ok in 2.0.0

79138   writing to sbrk()'d memory causes segfault

77369   sched deadlock while signal received during pthread_join
         and the joined thread exited

88115   In signal handler for SIGFPE, siginfo->si_addr is wrong
         under Valgrind

78765   Massif crashes on app exit if FP exceptions are enabled

Additionally there are the following changes, which are not
connected to any bug report numbers, AFAICS:

* Fix scary bug causing mis-identification of SSE stores vs
  loads and so causing memcheck to sometimes give nonsense results
  on SSE code.

* Add support for the POSIX message queue system calls.

* Fix to allow 32-bit Valgrind to run on AMD64 boxes. Note: this does
  NOT allow Valgrind to work with 64-bit executables - only with 32-bit
  executables on an AMD64 box.

* At configure time, only check whether linux/mii.h can be processed
  so that we don't generate ugly warnings by trying to compile it.

* Add support for POSIX clocks and timers.

Developer (cvs head) release 2.1.2 (18 July 2004)
~~~~~~
2.1.2 contains four months worth of bug fixes and refinements.
Although officially a developer release, we believe it to be stable
enough for widespread day-to-day use. 2.1.2 is pretty good, so try it
first, although there is a chance it won't work. If so then try 2.0.0
and tell us what went wrong." 2.1.2 fixes a lot of problems present
in 2.0.0 and is generally a much better product.

Relative to 2.1.1, a large number of minor problems with 2.1.1 have
been fixed, and so if you use 2.1.1 you should try 2.1.2. Users of

the last stable release, 2.0.0, might also want to try this release.

The following bugs, and probably many more, have been fixed. These are listed at http://bugs.kde.org. Reporting a bug for valgrind in the http://bugs.kde.org is much more likely to get you a fix than mailing developers directly, so please continue to keep sending bugs there.

76869   Crashes when running any tool under Fedora Core 2 test1
        This fixes the problem with returning from a signal handler
        when VDSOs are turned off in FC2.

69508   java 1.4.2 client fails with erroneous "stack size too small".
        This fix makes more of the pthread stack attribute related
        functions work properly. Java still doesn't work though.

71906   malloc alignment should be 8, not 4
        All memory returned by malloc/new etc is now at least
        8-byte aligned.

81970   vg_alloc_ThreadState: no free slots available
        (closed because the workaround is simple: increase
        VG_N_THREADS, rebuild and try again.)

78514   Conditional jump or move depends on uninitialized value(s)
        (a slight mishanding of FP code in memcheck)

77952   pThread Support (crash) (due to initialisation-ordering probs)
        (also 85118)

80942   Addrcheck wasn't doing overlap checking as it should.
78048   return NULL on malloc/new etc failure, instead of asserting
73655   operator new() override in user .so files often doesn't get picked up
83060   Valgrind does not handle native kernel AIO
69872   Create proper coredumps after fatal signals
82026   failure with new glibc versions: __libc_* functions are not exported
70344   UNIMPLEMENTED FUNCTION: tcdrain
81297   Cancellation of pthread_cond_wait does not require mutex
82872   Using debug info from additional packages (wishlist)
83025   Support for ioctls FIGETBSZ and FIBMAP
83340   Support for ioctl HDIO_GET_IDENTITY
79714   Support for the semtimedop system call.
77022   Support for ioctls FBIOGET_VSCREENINFO and FBIOGET_FSCREENINFO
82098   hp2ps ansification (wishlist)
83573   Valgrind SIGSEGV on execve
82999   show which cmdline option was erroneous (wishlist)
83040   make valgrind VPATH and distcheck-clean (wishlist)
83998   Assertion 'newfd > vgPlain_max_fd' failed (see below)
82722   Unchecked mmap in as_pad leads to mysterious failures later
78958   memcheck seg faults while running Mozilla
85416   Arguments with colon (e.g. --logsocket) ignored

Additionally there are the following changes, which are not

connected to any bug report numbers, AFAICS:

* Rearranged address space layout relative to 2.1.1, so that
  Valgrind/tools will run out of memory later than currently in many
  circumstances. This is good news esp. for Calltree. It should
  be possible for client programs to allocate over 800MB of
  memory when using memcheck now.

* Improved checking when laying out memory. Should hopefully avoid
  the random segmentation faults that 2.1.1 sometimes caused.

* Support for Fedora Core 2 and SuSE 9.1. Improvements to NPTL
  support to the extent that V now works properly on NPTL-only setups.

* Renamed the following options:
  --logfile-fd   --> --log-fd
  --logfile   --> --log-file
  --logsocket   --> --log-socket
  to be consistent with each other and other options (esp. --input-fd).

* Add support for SIOCGMIIPHY, SIOCGMIIREG and SIOCSMIIREG ioctls and
  improve the checking of other interface related ioctls.

* Fix building with gcc-3.4.1.

* Remove limit on number of semaphores supported.

* Add support for syscalls: set_tid_address (258), acct (51).

* Support instruction "repne movs" -- not official but seems to occur.

* Implement an emulated soft limit for file descriptors in addition to
  the current reserved area, which effectively acts as a hard limit. The
  setrlimit system call now simply updates the emulated limits as best
  as possible - the hard limit is not allowed to move at all and just
  returns EPERM if you try and change it. This should stop reductions
  in the soft limit causing assertions when valgrind tries to allocate
  descriptors from the reserved area.
  (This actually came from bug #83998).

* Major overhaul of Cachegrind implementation. First user-visible change
  is that cachegrind.out files are now typically 90% smaller than they
  used to be; code annotation times are correspondingly much smaller.
  Second user-visible change is that hit/miss counts for code that is
  unloaded at run-time is no longer dumped into a single "discard" pile,
  but accurately preserved.

* Client requests for telling valgrind about memory pools.

Developer (cvs head) release 2.1.1 (12 March 2004)
~~~~~~
2.1.1 contains some internal structural changes needed for V's

long-term future. These don't affect end-users. Most notable
user-visible changes are:

* Greater isolation between Valgrind and the program being run, so
  the program is less likely to inadvertently kill Valgrind by
  doing wild writes.

* Massif: a new space profiling tool. Try it! It's cool, and it'll
  tell you in detail where and when your C/C++ code is allocating heap.
  Draws pretty .ps pictures of memory use against time. A potentially
  powerful tool for making sense of your program's space use.

* Fixes for many bugs, including support for more SSE2/SSE3 instructions,
  various signal/syscall things, and various problems with debug
  info readers.

* Support for glibc-2.3.3 based systems.

We are now doing automatic overnight build-and-test runs on a variety
of distros. As a result, we believe 2.1.1 builds and runs on:
Red Hat 7.2, 7.3, 8.0, 9, Fedora Core 1, SuSE 8.2, SuSE 9.

The following bugs, and probably many more, have been fixed. These
are listed at http://bugs.kde.org. Reporting a bug for valgrind in
the http://bugs.kde.org is much more likely to get you a fix than
mailing developers directly, so please continue to keep sending bugs
there.

69616	glibc 2.3.2 w/NPTL is massively different than what valgrind expects
69856	I don't know how to instrument MMXish stuff (Helgrind)
73892	valgrind segfaults starting with Objective-C debug info
	(fix for S-type stabs)
73145	Valgrind complains too much about close(<reserved fd>)
73902	Shadow memory allocation seems to fail on RedHat 8.0
68633	VG_N_SEMAPHORES too low (V itself was leaking semaphores)
75099	impossible to trace multiprocess programs
76839	the 'impossible' happened: disInstr: INT but not 0x80 !
76762	vg_to_ucode.c:3748 (dis_push_segreg): Assertion 'sz == 4' failed.
76747	cannot include valgrind.h in c++ program
76223	parsing B(3,10) gave NULL type => impossible happens
75604	shmdt handling problem
76416	Problems with gcc 3.4 snap 20040225
75614	using -gstabs when building your programs the 'impossible' happened
75787	Patch for some CDROM ioctls CDORM_GET_MCN, CDROM_SEND_PACKET,
75294	gcc 3.4 snapshot's libstdc++ have unsupported instructions.
	(REP RET)
73326	vg_symtab2.c:272 (addScopeRange): Assertion 'range->size > 0' failed.
72596	not recognizing __libc_malloc
69489	Would like to attach ddd to running program
72781	Cachegrind crashes with kde programs
73055	Illegal operand at DXTCV11CompressBlockSSE2 (more SSE opcodes)
73026	Descriptor leak check reports port numbers wrongly
71705	README_MISSING_SYSCALL_OR_IOCTL out of date

72643	Improve support for SSE/SSE2 instructions
72484	valgrind leaves it's own signal mask in place when execing
72650	Signal Handling always seems to restart system calls
72006	The mmap system call turns all errors in ENOMEM
71781	gdb attach is pretty useless
71180	unhandled instruction bytes: 0xF 0xAE 0x85 0xE8
69886	writes to zero page cause valgrind to assert on exit
71791	crash when valgrinding gimp 1.3 (stabs reader problem)
69783	unhandled syscall: 218
69782	unhandled instruction bytes: 0x66 0xF 0x2B 0x80
70385	valgrind fails if the soft file descriptor limit is less than about 828
69529	"rep; nop" should do a yield
70827	programs with lots of shared libraries report "mmap failed" for some of them when reading symbols
71028	glibc's strnlen is optimised enough to confuse valgrind

Unstable (cvs head) release 2.1.0 (15 December 2003)
~~~~~~
For whatever it's worth, 2.1.0 actually seems pretty darn stable to me
(Julian). It looks eminently usable, and given that it fixes some
significant bugs, may well be worth using on a day-to-day basis.
2.1.0 is known to build and pass regression tests on: SuSE 9, SuSE
8.2, RedHat 8.

2.1.0 most notably includes Jeremy Fitzhardinge's complete overhaul of
handling of system calls and signals, and their interaction with
threads. In general, the accuracy of the system call, thread and
signal simulations is much improved. Specifically:

- Blocking system calls behave exactly as they do when running
  natively (not on valgrind). That is, if a syscall blocks only the
  calling thread when running natively, than it behaves the same on
  valgrind. No more mysterious hangs because V doesn't know that some
  syscall or other, should block only the calling thread.

- Interrupted syscalls should now give more faithful results.

- Finally, signal contexts in signal handlers are supported. As a
  result, konqueror on SuSE 9 no longer segfaults when notified of
  file changes in directories it is watching.

Other changes:

- Robert Walsh's file descriptor leakage checks. When enabled,
  Valgrind will print out a list of open file descriptors on
  exit. Along with each file descriptor, Valgrind prints out a stack
  backtrace of where the file was opened and any details relating to the
  file descriptor such as the file name or socket details.
  To use, give: --track-fds=yes

- Implemented a few more SSE/SSE2 instructions.

- Less crud on the stack when you do 'where' inside a GDB attach.

- Fixed the following bugs:
    68360: Valgrind does not compile against 2.6.0-testX kernels
    68525: CVS head doesn't compile on C90 compilers
    68566: pkgconfig support (wishlist)
    68588: Assertion 'sz == 4' failed in vg_to_ucode.c (disInstr)
    69140: valgrind not able to explicitly specify a path to a binary.
    69432: helgrind asserts encountering a MutexErr when there are
           EraserErr suppressions

- Increase the max size of the translation cache from 200k average bbs
  to 300k average bbs. Programs on the size of OOo (680m17) are
  thrashing the cache at the smaller size, creating large numbers of
  retranslations and wasting significant time as a result.

Stable release 2.0.0 (5 Nov 2003)
~~~~~~~~~~~~~~~~~~~~~~~~~~~~~~~~~~~

2.0.0 improves SSE/SSE2 support, fixes some minor bugs, and
improves support for SuSE 9 and the Red Hat "Severn" beta.

- Further improvements to SSE/SSE2 support. The entire test suite of
  the GNU Scientific Library (gsl-1.4) compiled with Intel Icc 7.1
  20030307Z '-g -O -xW' now works. I think this gives pretty good
  coverage of SSE/SSE2 floating point instructions, or at least the
  subset emitted by Icc.

- Also added support for the following instructions:
    MOVNTDQ UCOMISD UNPCKLPS UNPCKHPS SQRTSS
    PUSH/POP %{FS,GS}, and PUSH %CS (Nb: there is no POP %CS).

- CFI support for GDB version 6. Needed to enable newer GDBs
  to figure out where they are when using --gdb-attach=yes.

- Fix this:
      mc_translate.c:1091 (memcheck_instrument): Assertion
      'u_in->size == 4 || u_in->size == 16' failed.

- Return an error rather than panicing when given a bad socketcall.

- Fix checking of syscall rt_sigtimedwait().

- Implement __NR_clock_gettime (syscall 265). Needed on Red Hat Severn.

- Fixed bug in overlap check in strncpy() -- it was assuming the src was 'n'
  bytes long, when it could be shorter, which could cause false
  positives.

- Support use of select() for very large numbers of file descriptors.

- Don't fail silently if the executable is statically linked, or is
  setuid/setgid. Print an error message instead.

- Support for old DWARF-1 format line number info.

Snapshot 20031012 (12 October 2003)
~~~~~~~~~~~~~~~~~~~~~~~~~~~~~~~~~~~~

Three months worth of bug fixes, roughly. Most significant single
change is improved SSE/SSE2 support, mostly thanks to Dirk Mueller.

20031012 builds on Red Hat Fedora ("Severn") but doesn't really work
(curiously, mozilla runs OK, but a modest "ls -l" bombs). I hope to
get a working version out soon. It may or may not work ok on the
forthcoming SuSE 9; I hear positive noises about it but haven't been
able to verify this myself (not until I get hold of a copy of 9).

A detailed list of changes, in no particular order:

- Describe --gen-suppressions in the FAQ.

- Syscall __NR_waitpid supported.

- Minor MMX bug fix.

- -v prints program's argv[] at startup.

- More glibc-2.3 suppressions.

- Suppressions for stack underrun bug(s) in the c++ support library
  distributed with Intel Icc 7.0.

- Fix problems reading /proc/self/maps.

- Fix a couple of messages that should have been suppressed by -q,
  but weren't.

- Make Addrcheck understand "Overlap" suppressions.

- At startup, check if program is statically linked and bail out if so.

- Cachegrind: Auto-detect Intel Pentium-M, also VIA Nehemiah

- Memcheck/addrcheck: minor speed optimisations

- Handle syscall __NR_brk more correctly than before.

- Fixed incorrect allocate/free mismatch errors when using
  operator new(unsigned, std::nothrow_t const&)
  operator new[](unsigned, std::nothrow_t const&)

- Support POSIX pthread spinlocks.

- Fixups for clean compilation with gcc-3.3.1.

- Implemented more opcodes:
    - push %es
    - push %ds
    - pop %es
    - pop %ds
    - movntq
    - sfence
    - pshufw
    - pavgb
    - ucomiss
    - enter
    - mov imm32, %esp
    - all "in" and "out" opcodes
    - inc/dec %esp
    - A whole bunch of SSE/SSE2 instructions

- Memcheck: don't bomb on SSE/SSE2 code.

Snapshot 20030725 (25 July 2003)
~~~~~~~~~~~~~~~~~~~~~~~~~~~~~~~~

Fixes some minor problems in 20030716.

- Fix bugs in overlap checking for strcpy/memcpy etc.

- Do overlap checking with Addrcheck as well as Memcheck.

- Fix this:
      Memcheck: the 'impossible' happened:
      get_error_name: unexpected type

- Install headers needed to compile new skins.

- Remove leading spaces and colon in the LD_LIBRARY_PATH / LD_PRELOAD
  passed to non-traced children.

- Fix file descriptor leak in valgrind-listener.

- Fix longstanding bug in which the allocation point of a
  block resized by realloc was not correctly set. This may
  have caused confusing error messages.

Snapshot 20030716 (16 July 2003)
~~~~~~~~~~~~~~~~~~~~~~~~~~~~~~~~

20030716 is a snapshot of our current CVS head (development) branch.
This is the branch which will become valgrind-2.0. It contains
significant enhancements over the 1.9.X branch.

Despite this being a snapshot of the CVS head, it is believed to be quite stable -- at least as stable as 1.9.6 or 1.0.4, if not more so -- and therefore suitable for widespread use. Please let us know asap if it causes problems for you.

Two reasons for releasing a snapshot now are:

- It's been a while since 1.9.6, and this snapshot fixes various problems that 1.9.6 has with threaded programs on glibc-2.3.X based systems.

- So as to make available improvements in the 2.0 line.

Major changes in 20030716, as compared to 1.9.6:

- More fixes to threading support on glibc-2.3.1 and 2.3.2-based systems (SuSE 8.2, Red Hat 9). If you have had problems with inconsistent/illogical behaviour of errno, h_errno or the DNS resolver functions in threaded programs, 20030716 should improve matters. This snapshot seems stable enough to run OpenOffice.org 1.1rc on Red Hat 7.3, SuSE 8.2 and Red Hat 9, and that's a big threaded app it ever I saw one.

- Automatic generation of suppression records; you no longer need to write them by hand. Use --gen-suppressions=yes.

- strcpy/memcpy/etc check their arguments for overlaps, when running with the Memcheck or Addrcheck skins.

- malloc_usable_size() is now supported.

- new client requests:
    - VALGRIND_COUNT_ERRORS, VALGRIND_COUNT_LEAKS: useful with regression testing
    - VALGRIND_NON_SIMD_CALL[0123]: for running arbitrary functions on real CPU (use with caution!)

- The GDB attach mechanism is more flexible. Allow the GDB to be run to be specified by --gdb-path=/path/to/gdb, and specify which file descriptor V will read its input from with --input-fd=<number>.

- Cachegrind gives more accurate results (wasn't tracking instructions in malloc() and friends previously, is now).

- Complete support for the MMX instruction set.

- Partial support for the SSE and SSE2 instruction sets. Work for this is ongoing. About half the SSE/SSE2 instructions are done, so some SSE based programs may work. Currently you need to specify --skin=addrcheck. Basically not suitable for real use yet.

- Significant speedups (10%-20%) for standard memory checking.

- Fix assertion failure in pthread_once().

- Fix this:
    valgrind: vg_intercept.c:598 (vgAllRoadsLeadToRome_select):
            Assertion 'ms_end >= ms_now' failed.

- Implement pthread_mutexattr_setpshared.

- Understand Pentium 4 branch hints. Also implemented a couple more
  obscure x86 instructions.

- Lots of other minor bug fixes.

- We have a decent regression test system, for the first time.
  This doesn't help you directly, but it does make it a lot easier
  for us to track the quality of the system, especially across
  multiple linux distributions.

  You can run the regression tests with 'make regtest' after 'make
  install' completes. On SuSE 8.2 and Red Hat 9 I get this:

      == 84 tests, 0 stderr failures, 0 stdout failures ==

  On Red Hat 8, I get this:

      == 84 tests, 2 stderr failures, 1 stdout failure ==
      corecheck/tests/res_search   (stdout)
      memcheck/tests/sigaltstack   (stderr)

  sigaltstack is probably harmless. res_search doesn't work
  on R H 8 even running natively, so I'm not too worried.

  On Red Hat 7.3, a glibc-2.2.5 system, I get these harmless failures:

      == 84 tests, 2 stderr failures, 1 stdout failure ==
      corecheck/tests/pth_atfork1   (stdout)
      corecheck/tests/pth_atfork1   (stderr)
      memcheck/tests/sigaltstack   (stderr)

  You need to run on a PII system, at least, since some tests
  contain P6-specific instructions, and the test machine needs
  access to the internet so that corecheck/tests/res_search
  (a test that the DNS resolver works) can function.

As ever, thanks for the vast amount of feedback :) and bug reports :(
We may not answer all messages, but we do at least look at all of
them, and tend to fix the most frequently reported bugs.

Version 1.9.6 (7 May 2003 or thereabouts)
~~~~~~

Major changes in 1.9.6:

- Improved threading support for glibc >= 2.3.2 (SuSE 8.2,
  RedHat 9, to name but two ...) It turned out that 1.9.5
  had problems with threading support on glibc >= 2.3.2,
  usually manifested by threaded programs deadlocking in system calls,
  or running unbelievably slowly. Hopefully these are fixed now. 1.9.6
  is the first valgrind which gives reasonable support for
  glibc-2.3.2. Also fixed a 2.3.2 problem with pthread_atfork().

- Majorly expanded FAQ.txt. We've added workarounds for all
  common problems for which a workaround is known.

Minor changes in 1.9.6:

- Fix identification of the main thread's stack. Incorrect
  identification of it was causing some on-stack addresses to not get
  identified as such. This only affected the usefulness of some error
  messages; the correctness of the checks made is unchanged.

- Support for kernels >= 2.5.68.

- Dummy implementations of __libc_current_sigrtmin,
  __libc_current_sigrtmax and __libc_allocate_rtsig, hopefully
  good enough to keep alive programs which previously died for lack of
  them.

- Fix bug in the VALGRIND_DISCARD_TRANSLATIONS client request.

- Fix bug in the DWARF2 debug line info loader, when instructions
  following each other have source lines far from each other
  (e.g. with inlined functions).

- Debug info reading: read symbols from both "symtab" and "dynsym"
  sections, rather than merely from the one that comes last in the
  file.

- New syscall support: prctl(), creat(), lookup_dcookie().

- When checking calls to accept(), recvfrom(), getsocketopt(),
  don't complain if buffer values are NULL.

- Try and avoid assertion failures in
  mash_LD_PRELOAD_and_LD_LIBRARY_PATH.

- Minor bug fixes in cg_annotate.

Version 1.9.5 (7 April 2003)
~~~~~~~~~~~~~~~~~~~~~~~~~~~~~

It occurs to me that it would be helpful for valgrind users to record
in the source distribution the changes in each release. So I now

attempt to mend my errant ways :-) Changes in this and future releases will be documented in the NEWS file in the source distribution.

Major changes in 1.9.5:

- (Critical bug fix): Fix a bug in the FPU simulation. This was causing some floating point conditional tests not to work right. Several people reported this. If you had floating point code which didn't work right on 1.9.1 to 1.9.4, it's worth trying 1.9.5.

- Partial support for Red Hat 9. RH9 uses the new Native Posix Threads Library (NPTL), instead of the older LinuxThreads. This potentially causes problems with V which will take some time to correct. In the meantime we have partially worked around this, and so 1.9.5 works on RH9. Threaded programs still work, but they may deadlock, because some system calls (accept, read, write, etc) which should be nonblocking, in fact do block. This is a known bug which we are looking into.

  If you can, your best bet (unfortunately) is to avoid using 1.9.5 on a Red Hat 9 system, or on any NPTL-based distribution. If your glibc is 2.3.1 or earlier, you're almost certainly OK.

Minor changes in 1.9.5:

- Added some #errors to valgrind.h to ensure people don't include it accidentally in their sources. This is a change from 1.0.X which was never properly documented. The right thing to include is now memcheck.h. Some people reported problems and strange behaviour when (incorrectly) including valgrind.h in code with 1.9.1 -- 1.9.4. This is no longer possible.

- Add some __extension__ bits and pieces so that gcc configured for valgrind-checking compiles even with -Werror. If you don't understand this, ignore it. Of interest to gcc developers only.

- Removed a pointless check which caused problems interworking with Clearcase. V would complain about shared objects whose names did not end ".so", and refuse to run. This is now fixed. In fact it was fixed in 1.9.4 but not documented.

- Fixed a bug causing an assertion failure of "waiters == 1" somewhere in vg_scheduler.c, when running large threaded apps, notably MySQL.

- Add support for the munlock system call (124).

Some comments about future releases:

1.9.5 is, we hope, the most stable Valgrind so far. It pretty much supersedes the 1.0.X branch. If you are a valgrind packager, please consider making 1.9.5 available to your users. You can regard the 1.0.X branch as obsolete: 1.9.5 is stable and vastly superior. There are no plans at all for further releases of the 1.0.X branch.

If you want a leading-edge valgrind, consider building the cvs head (from SourceForge), or getting a snapshot of it. Current cool stuff going in includes MMX support (done); SSE/SSE2 support (in progress), a significant (10-20%) performance improvement (done), and the usual large collection of minor changes. Hopefully we will be able to improve our NPTL support, but no promises.

4. README

Release notes for Valgrind
~~~~~~~~~~~~~~~~~~~~~~~~~~~~~~

If you are building a binary package of Valgrind for distribution,
please read README_PACKAGERS. It contains some important information.

If you are developing Valgrind, please read README_DEVELOPERS. It contains
some useful information.

For instructions on how to build/install, see the end of this file.

If you have problems, consult the FAQ to see if there are workarounds.

Executive Summary
~~~~~~~~~~~~~~~~~~

Valgrind is a framework for building dynamic analysis tools. There are
Valgrind tools that can automatically detect many memory management
and threading bugs, and profile your programs in detail. You can also
use Valgrind to build new tools.

The Valgrind distribution currently includes six production-quality
tools: a memory error detector, two thread error detectors, a cache
and branch-prediction profiler, a call-graph generating cache abd
branch-prediction profiler, and a heap profiler. It also includes
three experimental tools: a heap/stack/global array overrun detector,
a different kind of heap profiler, and a SimPoint basic block vector
generator.

Valgrind is closely tied to details of the CPU, operating system and to
a lesser extent, compiler and basic C libraries. This makes it difficult
to make it portable. Nonetheless, it is available for the following
platforms:

- X86/Linux
- AMD64/Linux
- PPC32/Linux
- PPC64/Linux
- ARM/Linux
- x86/MacOSX
- AMD64/MacOSX
- S390X/Linux
- MIPS32/Linux
- MIPS64/Linux

Note that AMD64 is just another name for x86_64, and Valgrind runs fine
on Intel processors. Also note that the core of MacOSX is called
"Darwin" and this name is used sometimes.

Valgrind is licensed under the GNU General Public License, version 2.

Read the file COPYING in the source distribution for details.

However: if you contribute code, you need to make it available as GPL version 2 or later, and not 2-only.

Documentation
~~~~~~~~~~~~~
A comprehensive user guide is supplied. Point your browser at $PREFIX/share/doc/valgrind/manual.html, where $PREFIX is whatever you specified with --prefix= when building.

Building and installing it
~~~~~~~~~~~~~~~~~~~~~~~~~~~
To install from the Subversion repository :

  0. Check out the code from SVN, following the instructions at
     http://www.valgrind.org/downloads/repository.html.

  1. cd into the source directory.

  2. Run ./autogen.sh to setup the environment (you need the standard
     autoconf tools to do so).

  3. Continue with the following instructions...

To install from a tar.bz2 distribution:

  4. Run ./configure, with some options if you wish. The only interesting
     one is the usual --prefix=/where/you/want/it/installed.

  5. Run "make".

  6. Run "make install", possibly as root if the destination permissions
     require that.

  7. See if it works. Try "valgrind ls -l". Either this works, or it
     bombs out with some complaint. In that case, please let us know
     (see www.valgrind.org).

Important! Do not move the valgrind installation into a place different from that specified by --prefix at build time. This will cause things to break in subtle ways, mostly when Valgrind handles fork/exec calls.

The Valgrind Developers

5. README_MISSING_SYSCALL_OR_IOCT

Dealing with missing system call or ioctl wrappers in Valgrind
~~~~~~
You're probably reading this because Valgrind bombed out whilst
running your program, and advised you to read this file. The good
news is that, in general, it's easy to write the missing syscall or
ioctl wrappers you need, so that you can continue your debugging. If
you send the resulting patches to me, then you'll be doing a favour to
all future Valgrind users too.

Note that an "ioctl" is just a special kind of system call, really; so
there's not a lot of need to distinguish them (at least conceptually)
in the discussion that follows.

All this machinery is in coregrind/m_syswrap.

What are syscall/ioctl wrappers? What do they do?
~~~~~~
Valgrind does what it does, in part, by keeping track of everything your
program does. When a system call happens, for example a request to read
part of a file, control passes to the Linux kernel, which fulfills the
request, and returns control to your program. The problem is that the
kernel will often change the status of some part of your program's memory
as a result, and tools (instrumentation plug-ins) may need to know about
this.

Syscall and ioctl wrappers have two jobs:

1. Tell a tool what's about to happen, before the syscall takes place. A
   tool could perform checks beforehand, eg. if memory about to be written
   is actually writeable. This part is useful, but not strictly
   essential.

2. Tell a tool what just happened, after a syscall takes place. This is
   so it can update its view of the program's state, eg. that memory has
   just been written to. This step is essential.

The "happenings" mostly involve reading/writing of memory.

So, let's look at an example of a wrapper for a system call which
should be familiar to many Unix programmers.

The syscall wrapper for time()
~~~~~~~~~~~~~~~~~~~~~~~~~~~~~~~~
The wrapper for the time system call looks like this:

```
  PRE(sys_time)
  {
```

```
    /* time_t time(time_t *t); */
    PRINT("sys_time ( %p )",ARG1);
    PRE_REG_READ1(long, "time", int *, t);
    if (ARG1 != 0) {
        PRE_MEM_WRITE( "time(t)", ARG1, sizeof(vki_time_t) );
    }
}

POST(sys_time)
{
    if (ARG1 != 0) {
        POST_MEM_WRITE( ARG1, sizeof(vki_time_t) );
    }
}
```

The first thing we do happens before the syscall occurs, in the PRE() function.
The PRE() function typically starts with invoking to the PRINT() macro. This
PRINT() macro implements support for the --trace-syscalls command line option.
Next, the tool is told the return type of the syscall, that the syscall has
one argument, the type of the syscall argument and that the argument is being
read from a register:

```
    PRE_REG_READ1(long, "time", int *, t);
```

Next, if a non-NULL buffer is passed in as the argument, tell the tool that the
buffer is about to be written to:

```
    if (ARG1 != 0) {
        PRE_MEM_WRITE( "time", ARG1, sizeof(vki_time_t) );
    }
```

Finally, the really important bit, after the syscall occurs, in the POST()
function: if, and only if, the system call was successful, tell the tool that
the memory was written:

```
    if (ARG1 != 0) {
        POST_MEM_WRITE( ARG1, sizeof(vki_time_t) );
    }
```

The POST() function won't be called if the syscall failed, so you
don't need to worry about checking that in the POST() function.
(Note: this is sometimes a bug; some syscalls do return results when
they "fail" - for example, nanosleep returns the amount of unslept
time if interrupted. TODO: add another per-syscall flag for this
case.)

Note that we use the type 'vki_time_t'. This is a copy of the kernel
type, with 'vki_' prefixed. Our copies of such types are kept in the
appropriate vki*.h file(s). We don't include kernel headers or glibc headers
directly.

Writing your own syscall wrappers (see below for ioctl wrappers)
~~~~~~

If Valgrind tells you that system call NNN is unimplemented, do the following:

1. Find out the name of the system call:

       grep NNN /usr/include/asm/unistd*.h

   This should tell you something like __NR_mysyscallname.
   Copy this entry to include/vki/vki-scnums-$(VG_PLATFORM).h.

2. Do 'man 2 mysyscallname' to get some idea of what the syscall
   does. Note that the actual kernel interface can differ from this,
   so you might also want to check a version of the Linux kernel
   source.

   NOTE: any syscall which has something to do with signals or
   threads is probably "special", and needs more careful handling.
   Post something to valgrind-developers if you aren't sure.

3. Add a case to the already-huge collection of wrappers in
   the coregrind/m_syswrap/syswrap-*.c files.
   For each in-memory parameter which is read or written by
   the syscall, do one of

       PRE_MEM_READ(...)
       PRE_MEM_RASCIIZ(...)
       PRE_MEM_WRITE(...)

   for that parameter. Then do the syscall. Then, if the syscall
   succeeds, issue suitable POST_MEM_WRITE(...) calls.
   (There's no need for POST_MEM_READ calls.)

   Also, add it to the syscall_table[] array; use one of GENX_, GENXY
   LINX_, LINXY, PLAX_, PLAXY.
   GEN* for generic syscalls (in syswrap-generic.c), LIN* for linux
   specific ones (in syswrap-linux.c) and PLA* for the platform
   dependant ones (in syswrap-$(PLATFORM)-linux.c).
   The *XY variant if it requires a PRE() and POST() function, and
   the *X_ variant if it only requires a PRE()
   function.

   If you find this difficult, read the wrappers for other syscalls
   for ideas. A good tip is to look for the wrapper for a syscall
   which has a similar behaviour to yours, and use it as a
   starting point.

   If you need structure definitions and/or constants for your syscall,
   copy them from the kernel headers into include/vki.h and co., with
   the appropriate vki_*/VKI_* name mangling. Don't #include any
   kernel headers. And certainly don't #include any glibc headers.

   Test it.

Note that a common error is to call POST_MEM_WRITE(...)
with 0 (NULL) as the first (address) argument. This usually means
your logic is slightly inadequate. It's a sufficiently common bug
that there's a built-in check for it, and you'll get a "probably
sanity check failure" for the syscall wrapper you just made, if this
is the case.

4. Once happy, send us the patch. Pretty please.

Writing your own ioctl wrappers
~~~~~~~~~~~~~~~~~~~~~~~~~~~~~~~~

Is pretty much the same as writing syscall wrappers, except that all
the action happens within PRE(ioctl) and POST(ioctl).

There's a default case, sometimes it isn't correct and you have to write a
more specific case to get the right behaviour.

As above, please create a bug report and attach the patch as described
on http://www.valgrind.org.

Writing your own door call wrappers (Solaris only)
~~~~~~

Unlike syscalls or ioctls, door calls transfer data between two userspace
programs, albeit through a kernel interface. Programs may use completely
proprietary semantics in the data buffers passed between them.
Therefore it may not be possible to capture these semantics within
a Valgrind door call or door return wrapper.

Nevertheless, for system or well-known door services it would be beneficial
to have a door call and a door return wrapper. Writing such wrapper is pretty
much the same as writing ioctl wrappers. Please take a few moments to study
the following picture depicting how a door client and a door server interact
through the kernel interface in a typical scenario:

```
door client thread          kernel       door server thread
invokes door_call()                       invokes door_return()
------------------------------------------------------------------
                             <----  PRE(sys_door, DOOR_RETURN)
PRE(sys_door, DOOR_CALL)  --->
                             ---->  POST(sys_door, DOOR_RETURN)
                                         ----> server_procedure()
                                         <----
                             <----  PRE(sys_door, DOOR_RETURN)
POST(sys_door, DOOR_CALL) <---
```

The first PRE(sys_door, DOOR_RETURN) is invoked with data_ptr=NULL
and data_size=0. That's because it has not received any data from
a door call, yet.

Semantics are described by the following functions
in coregring/m_syswrap/syswrap-solaris.c module:
o For a door call wrapper the following attributes of 'params' argument:
  - data_ptr (and associated data_size) as input buffer (request);
      described in door_call_pre_mem_params_data()
  - rbuf (and associated rsize) as output buffer (response);
      described in door_call_post_mem_params_rbuf()
o For a door return wrapper the following parameters:
  - data_ptr (and associated data_size) as input buffer (request);
      described in door_return_post_mem_data()
  - data_ptr (and associated data_size) as output buffer (response);
      described in door_return_pre_mem_data()

There's a default case which may not be correct and you have to write a
more specific case to get the right behaviour. Unless Valgrind's option
'--sim-hints=lax-doors' is specified, the default case also spits a warning.

As above, please create a bug report and attach the patch as described
on http://www.valgrind.org.

6. README_DEVELOPERS

Building and not installing it
~~~~~~~~~~~~~~~~~~~~~~~~~~~~~~
To run Valgrind without having to install it, run coregrind/valgrind
with the VALGRIND_LIB environment variable set, where <dir> is the root
of the source tree (and must be an absolute path). Eg:

  VALGRIND_LIB=~/grind/head4/.in_place ~/grind/head4/coregrind/valgrind

This allows you to compile and run with "make" instead of "make install",
saving you time.

Or, you can use the 'vg-in-place' script which does that for you.

I recommend compiling with "make --quiet" to further reduce the amount of
output spewed out during compilation, letting you actually see any errors,
warnings, etc.

Building a distribution tarball
~~~~~~~~~~~~~~~~~~~~~~~~~~~~~~~~~
To build a distribution tarball from the valgrind sources:

  make dist

In addition to compiling, linking and packaging everything up, the command
will also attempt to build the documentation.

If you only want to test whether the generated tarball is complete and runs
regression tests successfully, building documentation is not needed.

  make dist BUILD_ALL_DOCS=no

If you insist on building documentation some embarrassing instructions
can be found in docs/README.

Running the regression tests
~~~~~~~~~~~~~~~~~~~~~~~~~~~~~~
To build and run all the regression tests, run "make [--quiet] regtest".

To run a subset of the regression tests, execute:

  perl tests/vg_regtest <name>

where <name> is a directory (all tests within will be run) or a single
.vgtest test file, or the name of a program which has a like-named .vgtest
file. Eg:

  perl tests/vg_regtest memcheck

```
perl tests/vg_regtest memcheck/tests/badfree.vgtest
perl tests/vg_regtest memcheck/tests/badfree
```

Running the performance tests
~~~~~~~~~~~~~~~~~~~~~~~~~~~~~~~
To build and run all the performance tests, run "make [--quiet] perf".

To run a subset of the performance suite, execute:

```
perl perf/vg_perf <name>
```

where <name> is a directory (all tests within will be run) or a single
.vgperf test file, or the name of a program which has a like-named .vgperf
file. Eg:

```
perl perf/vg_perf perf/
perl perf/vg_perf perf/bz2.vgperf
perl perf/vg_perf perf/bz2
```

To compare multiple versions of Valgrind, use the --vg= option multiple
times. For example, if you have two Valgrinds next to each other, one in
trunk1/ and one in trunk2/, from within either trunk1/ or trunk2/ do this to
compare them on all the performance tests:

```
perl perf/vg_perf --vg=../trunk1 --vg=../trunk2 perf/
```

Debugging Valgrind with GDB
~~~~~~~~~~~~~~~~~~~~~~~~~~~~~
To debug the valgrind launcher program (<prefix>/bin/valgrind) just
run it under gdb in the normal way.

Debugging the main body of the valgrind code (and/or the code for
a particular tool) requires a bit more trickery but can be achieved
without too much problem by following these steps:

(1) Set VALGRIND_LAUNCHER to point to the valgrind executable. Eg:

```
export VALGRIND_LAUNCHER=/usr/local/bin/valgrind
```

   or for an uninstalled version in a source directory $DIR:

```
export VALGRIND_LAUNCHER=$DIR/coregrind/valgrind
```

(2) Run gdb on the tool executable. Eg:

```
gdb /usr/local/lib/valgrind/ppc32-linux/lackey
```

   or

```
gdb $DIR/.in_place/x86-linux/memcheck
```

(3) Do "handle SIGSEGV SIGILL nostop noprint" in GDB to prevent GDB from

stopping on a SIGSEGV or SIGILL:

(gdb) handle SIGILL SIGSEGV nostop noprint

(4) Set any breakpoints you want and proceed as normal for gdb. The
macro VG_(FUNC) is expanded to vgPlain_FUNC, so If you want to set
a breakpoint VG_(do_exec), you could do like this in GDB:

(gdb) b vgPlain_do_exec

(5) Run the tool with required options (the --tool option is required
for correct setup), e.g.

(gdb) run --tool=lackey pwd

Steps (1)--(3) can be put in a .gdbinit file, but any directory names must
be fully expanded (ie. not an environment variable).

A different and possibly easier way is as follows:

(1) Run Valgrind as normal, but add the flag --wait-for-gdb=yes. This
puts the tool executable into a wait loop soon after it gains
control. This delays startup for a few seconds.

(2) In a different shell, do "gdb /proc/<pid>/exe <pid>", where
<pid> you read from the output printed by (1). This attaches
GDB to the tool executable, which should be in the abovementioned
wait loop.

(3) Do "cont" to continue. After the loop finishes spinning, startup
will continue as normal. Note that comment (3) above re passing
signals applies here too.

Self-hosting
~~~~~~~~~~~~
This section explains :
    (A) How to configure Valgrind to run under Valgrind.
        Such a setup is called self hosting, or outer/inner setup.
    (B) How to run Valgrind regression tests in a 'self-hosting' mode,
        e.g. to verify Valgrind has no bugs such as memory leaks.
    (C) How to run Valgrind performance tests in a 'self-hosting' mode,
        to analyse and optimise the performance of Valgrind and its tools.

(A) How to configure Valgrind to run under Valgrind:

(1) Check out 2 trees, "Inner" and "Outer". Inner runs the app
    directly. Outer runs Inner.

(2) Configure inner with --enable-inner and build/install as usual.

(3) Configure Outer normally and build/install as usual.

(4) Choose a very simple program (date) and try

```
outer/.../bin/valgrind --sim-hints=enable-outer --trace-children=yes  \
    --smc-check=all-non-file \
    --run-libc-freeres=no --tool=cachegrind -v \
    inner/.../bin/valgrind --vgdb-prefix=./inner --tool=none -v prog
```

Note: You must use a "make install"-ed valgrind.
Do *not* use vg-in-place for the outer valgrind.

If you omit the --trace-children=yes, you'll only monitor Inner's launcher
program, not its stage2. Outer needs --run-libc-freeres=no, as otherwise
it will try to find and run __libc_freeres in the inner, while libc is not
used by the inner. Inner needs --vgdb-prefix=./inner to avoid inner
gdbserver colliding with outer gdbserver.
Currently, inner does *not* use the client request
VALGRIND_DISCARD_TRANSLATIONS for the JITted code or the code patched for
translation chaining. So the outer needs --smc-check=all-non-file to
detect the modified code.

Debugging the whole thing might imply to use up to 3 GDB:
    * a GDB attached to the Outer valgrind, allowing
      to examine the state of Outer.
    * a GDB using Outer gdbserver, allowing to
      examine the state of Inner.
    * a GDB using Inner gdbserver, allowing to
      examine the state of prog.

The whole thing is fragile, confusing and slow, but it does work well enough
for you to get some useful performance data. Inner has most of
its output (ie. those lines beginning with "==<pid>==") prefixed with a '>',
which helps a lot. However, when running regression tests in an Outer/Inner
setup, this prefix causes the reg test diff to fail. Give
--sim-hints=no-inner-prefix to the Inner to disable the production
of the prefix in the stdout/stderr output of Inner.

The allocator (coregrind/m_mallocfree.c) is annotated with client requests
so Memcheck can be used to find leaks and use after free in an Inner
Valgrind.

The Valgrind "big lock" is annotated with helgrind client requests
so helgrind and drd can be used to find race conditions in an Inner
Valgrind.

All this has not been tested much, so don't be surprised if you hit problems.

When using self-hosting with an outer Callgrind tool, use '--pop-on-jump'
(on the outer). Otherwise, Callgrind has much higher memory requirements.

(B) Regression tests in an outer/inner setup:

 To run all the regression tests with an outer memcheck, do :
   perl tests/vg_regtest --outer-valgrind=../outer/.../bin/valgrind \
                --all

To run a specific regression tests with an outer memcheck, do:
    perl tests/vg_regtest --outer-valgrind=../outer/.../bin/valgrind \
                    none/tests/args.vgtest

To run regression tests with another outer tool:
    perl tests/vg_regtest --outer-valgrind=../outer/.../bin/valgrind \
                    --outer-tool=helgrind --all

--outer-args allows to give specific arguments to the outer tool,
replacing the default one provided by vg_regtest.

Note: --outer-valgrind must be a "make install"-ed valgrind.
Do *not* use vg-in-place.

When an outer valgrind runs an inner valgrind, a regression test
produces one additional file <testname>.outer.log which contains the
errors detected by the outer valgrind. E.g. for an outer memcheck, it
contains the leaks found in the inner, for an outer helgrind or drd,
it contains the detected race conditions.

The file tests/outer_inner.supp contains suppressions for
the irrelevant or benign errors found in the inner.

(C) Performance tests in an outer/inner setup:

To run all the performance tests with an outer cachegrind, do :
    perl perf/vg_perf --outer-valgrind=../outer/.../bin/valgrind perf

To run a specific perf test (e.g. bz2) in this setup, do :
    perl perf/vg_perf --outer-valgrind=../outer/.../bin/valgrind perf/bz2

To run all the performance tests with an outer callgrind, do :
    perl perf/vg_perf --outer-valgrind=../outer/.../bin/valgrind \
                    --outer-tool=callgrind perf

Note: --outer-valgrind must be a "make install"-ed valgrind.
Do *not* use vg-in-place.

To compare the performance of multiple Valgrind versions, do :
    perl perf/vg_perf --outer-valgrind=../outer/.../bin/valgrind \
        --outer-tool=callgrind \
        --vg=../inner_xxxx --vg=../inner_yyyy perf
    (where inner_xxxx and inner_yyyy are the toplevel directories of
    the versions to compare).
    Cachegrind and cg_diff are particularly handy to obtain a delta
    between the two versions.

When the outer tool is callgrind or cachegrind, the following
output files will be created for each test:
        <outertoolname>.out.<inner_valgrind_dir>.<tt>.<perftestname>.<pid>
        <outertoolname>.outer.log.<inner_valgrind_dir>.<tt>.<perftestname>.<pid>
    (where tt is the two letters abbreviation for the inner tool(s) run).

For example, the command

```
perl perf/vg_perf \
   --outer-valgrind=../outer_trunk/install/bin/valgrind \
   --outer-tool=callgrind \
   --vg=../inner_tchain --vg=../inner_trunk perf/many-loss-records
```

produces the files
```
callgrind.out.inner_tchain.no.many-loss-records.18465
callgrind.outer.log.inner_tchain.no.many-loss-records.18465
callgrind.out.inner_tchain.me.many-loss-records.21899
callgrind.outer.log.inner_tchain.me.many-loss-records.21899
callgrind.out.inner_trunk.no.many-loss-records.21224
callgrind.outer.log.inner_trunk.no.many-loss-records.21224
callgrind.out.inner_trunk.me.many-loss-records.22916
callgrind.outer.log.inner_trunk.me.many-loss-records.22916
```

Printing out problematic blocks
~~~~~~~~~~~~~~~~~~~~~~~~~~~~~~~~
If you want to print out a disassembly of a particular block that
causes a crash, do the following.

Try running with "--vex-guest-chase-thresh=0 --trace-flags=10000000
--trace-notbelow=999999". This should print one line for each block
translated, and that includes the address.

Then re-run with 999999 changed to the highest bb number shown.
This will print the one line per block, and also will print a
disassembly of the block in which the fault occurred.

7. README_PACKAGERS

Greetings, packaging person! This information is aimed at people building binary distributions of Valgrind.

Thanks for taking the time and effort to make a binary distribution of Valgrind. The following notes may save you some trouble.

-- Do not ship your Linux distro with a completely stripped /lib/ld.so. At least leave the debugging symbol names on -- line number info isn't necessary. If you don't want to leave symbols on ld.so, alternatively you can have your distro install ld.so's debuginfo package by default, or make ld.so.debuginfo be a requirement of your Valgrind RPM/DEB/whatever.

Reason for this is that Valgrind's Memcheck tool needs to intercept calls to, and provide replacements for, some symbols in ld.so at startup (most importantly strlen). If it cannot do that, Memcheck shows a large number of false positives due to the highly optimised strlen (etc) routines in ld.so. This has caused some trouble in the past. As of version 3.3.0, on some targets (ppc32-linux, ppc64-linux), Memcheck will simply stop at startup (and print an error message) if such symbols are not present, because it is infeasible to continue.

It's not like this is going to cost you much space. We only need the symbols for ld.so (a few K at most). Not the debug info and not any debuginfo or extra symbols for any other libraries.

-- (Unfortunate but true) When you configure to build with the --prefix=/foo/bar/xyzzy option, the prefix /foo/bar/xyzzy gets baked into valgrind. The consequence is that you _must_ install valgrind at the location specified in the prefix. If you don't, it may appear to work, but will break doing some obscure things, particularly doing fork() and exec().

So you can't build a relocatable RPM / whatever from Valgrind.

-- Don't strip the debug info off lib/valgrind/$platform/vgpreload*.so in the installation tree. Either Valgrind won't work at all, or it will still work if you do, but will generate less helpful error messages. Here's an example:

Mismatched free() / delete / delete []
   at 0x40043249: free (vg_clientfuncs.c:171)
   by 0x4102BB4E: QGArray::~QGArray(void) (tools/qgarray.cpp:149)
   by 0x4C261C41: PptDoc::~PptDoc(void) (include/qmemarray.h:60)
   by 0x4C261F0E: PptXml::~PptXml(void) (pptxml.cc:44)

```
    Address 0x4BB292A8 is 0 bytes inside a block of size 64 alloc'd
    at 0x4004318C: __builtin_vec_new (vg_clientfuncs.c:152)
    by 0x4C21BC15: KLaola::readSBStream(int) const (klaola.cc:314)
    by 0x4C21C155: KLaola::stream(KLaola::OLENode const *) (klaola.cc:416)
    by 0x4C21788F: OLEFilter::convert(QCString const &) (olefilter.cc:272)
```

This tells you that some memory allocated with new[] was freed with free().

```
Mismatched free() / delete / delete []
    at 0x40043249: (inside vgpreload_memcheck.so)
    by 0x4102BB4E: QGArray::~QGArray(void) (tools/qgarray.cpp:149)
    by 0x4C261C41: PptDoc::~PptDoc(void) (include/qmemarray.h:60)
    by 0x4C261F0E: PptXml::~PptXml(void) (pptxml.cc:44)
    Address 0x4BB292A8 is 0 bytes inside a block of size 64 alloc'd
    at 0x4004318C: (inside vgpreload_memcheck.so)
    by 0x4C21BC15: KLaola::readSBStream(int) const (klaola.cc:314)
    by 0x4C21C155: KLaola::stream(KLaola::OLENode const *) (klaola.cc:416)
    by 0x4C21788F: OLEFilter::convert(QCString const &) (olefilter.cc:272)
```

This isn't so helpful. Although you can tell there is a mismatch, the names of the allocating and deallocating functions are no longer visible. The same kind of thing occurs in various other messages from valgrind.

-- Don't strip symbols from lib/valgrind/* in the installation tree.
   Doing so will likely cause problems. Removing the line number info is
   probably OK (at least for some of the files in that directory), although
   that has not been tested by the Valgrind developers.

-- Please test the final installation works by running it on something
   huge. I suggest checking that it can start and exit successfully
   both Firefox and OpenOffice.org. I use these as test programs, and I
   know they fairly thoroughly exercise Valgrind. The command lines to use
   are:

   valgrind -v --trace-children=yes firefox

   valgrind -v --trace-children=yes soffice

If you find any more hints/tips for packaging, please report
it as a bugreport. See http://www.valgrind.org for details.

8. README.S390

Requirements

- You need GCC 3.4 or later to compile the s390 port.
- To run valgrind a z10 machine or any later model is recommended.
  Older machine models down to and including z990 may work but have
  not been tested extensively.

Limitations

- 31-bit client programs are not supported.
- Hexadecimal floating point is not supported.
- Transactional memory is not supported.
- Instructions operating on vector registers are not supported.
- memcheck, cachegrind, drd, helgrind, massif, lackey, and none are
  supported.
- On machine models predating z10, cachegrind will assume a z10 cache
  architecture. Otherwise, cachegrind will query the hosts cache system
  and use those parameters.
- callgrind and all experimental tools are currently not supported.
- Some gcc versions use mvc to copy 4/8 byte values. This will affect
  certain debug messages. For example, memcheck will complain about
  4 one-byte reads/writes instead of just a single read/write.

Hardware facilities

Valgrind does not require that the host machine has the same hardware
facilities as the machine for which the client program was compiled.
This is convenient. If possible, the JIT compiler will translate the
client instructions according to the facilities available on the host.
This means, though, that probing for hardware facilities by issuing
instructions from that facility and observing whether SIGILL is thrown
may not work. As a consequence, programs that attempt to do so may
behave differently. It is believed that this is a rare use case.

Recommendations

Applications should be compiled with -fno-builtin to avoid
false positives due to builtin string operations when running memcheck.

Reading Material
----

(1) Linux for zSeries ELF ABI Supplement
    http://refspecs.linuxfoundation.org/ELF/zSeries/index.html
(2) z/Architecture Principles of Operation
    http://publibfi.boulder.ibm.com/epubs/pdf/dz9zr010.pdf

(3) z/Architecture Reference Summary
http://publibfi.boulder.ibm.com/epubs/pdf/dz9zs008.pdf

9. README.android

How to cross-compile and run on Android. Please read to the end, since there are important details further down regarding crash avoidance and GPU support.

These notes were last updated on 4 Nov 2014, for Valgrind SVN revision 14689/2987.

These instructions are known to work, or have worked at some time in the past, for:

arm:
    Android 4.0.3 running on a (rooted, AOSP build) Nexus S.
    Android 4.0.3 running on Motorola Xoom.
    Android 4.0.3 running on android arm emulator.
    Android 4.1   running on android emulator.
    Android 2.3.4 on Nexus S worked at some time in the past.

x86:
    Android 4.0.3 running on android x86 emulator.

mips32:
    Android 4.1.2 running on android mips emulator.
    Android 4.2.2 running on android mips emulator.
    Android 4.3   running on android mips emulator.
    Android 4.0.4 running on BROADCOM bcm7425

arm64:
    Android 4.5 (?) running on ARM Juno

On android-arm, GDBserver might insert breaks at wrong addresses. Feedback on this welcome.

Other configurations and toolchains might work, but haven't been tested. Feedback is welcome.

Toolchain:

  For arm32, x86 and mips32 you need the android ndk r6 native
    development kit. r6b and r7 give a non-completely-working build;
    see http://code.google.com/p/android/issues/detail?id=23203
    For the android emulator, the versions needed and how to install
    them are described in README.android_emulator.

    You can get android-ndk-r6 from
    http://dl.google.com/android/ndk/android-ndk-r6-linux-x86.tar.bz2

  For arm64 (aarch64) you need the android-ndk-r10c NDK, from
    http://dl.google.com/android/ndk/android-ndk-r10c-linux-x86_64.bin

Install the NDK somewhere. Doesn't matter where. Then:


```
# Modify this (obviously).  Note, this "export" command is only done
# so as to reduce the amount of typing required.  None of the commands
# below read it as part of their operation.
#
export NDKROOT=/path/to/android-ndk-r<version>
```


```
# Then cd to the root of your Valgrind source tree.
#
cd /path/to/valgrind/source/tree
```


```
# After this point, you don't need to modify anything.  Just copy and
# paste the commands below.
```


```
# Set up toolchain paths.
#
# For ARM
export AR=$NDKROOT/toolchains/arm-linux-androideabi-4.4.3/prebuilt/linux-x86/bin/arm-linux-androideabi-ar
export LD=$NDKROOT/toolchains/arm-linux-androideabi-4.4.3/prebuilt/linux-x86/bin/arm-linux-androideabi-ld
export CC=$NDKROOT/toolchains/arm-linux-androideabi-4.4.3/prebuilt/linux-x86/bin/arm-linux-androideabi-gcc
```


```
# For x86
export AR=$NDKROOT/toolchains/x86-4.4.3/prebuilt/linux-x86/bin/i686-android-linux-ar
export LD=$NDKROOT/toolchains/x86-4.4.3/prebuilt/linux-x86/bin/i686-android-linux-ld
export CC=$NDKROOT/toolchains/x86-4.4.3/prebuilt/linux-x86/bin/i686-android-linux-gcc
```


```
# For MIPS32
export AR=$NDKROOT/toolchains/mipsel-linux-android-4.8/prebuilt/linux-x86_64/bin/mipsel-linux-android-ar
export LD=$NDKROOT/toolchains/mipsel-linux-android-4.8/prebuilt/linux-x86_64/bin/mipsel-linux-android-ld
export CC=$NDKROOT/toolchains/mipsel-linux-android-4.8/prebuilt/linux-x86_64/bin/mipsel-linux-android-gcc
```


```
# For ARM64 (AArch64)
export AR=$NDKROOT/toolchains/aarch64-linux-android-4.9/prebuilt/linux-x86_64/bin/aarch64-linux-android-ar
export LD=$NDKROOT/toolchains/aarch64-linux-android-4.9/prebuilt/linux-x86_64/bin/aarch64-linux-android-ld
export CC=$NDKROOT/toolchains/aarch64-linux-android-4.9/prebuilt/linux-x86_64/bin/aarch64-linux-android-gcc
```


```
# Do configuration stuff.  Don't mess with the --prefix in the
# configure command below, even if you think it's wrong.
# You may need to set the --with-tmpdir path to something
# different if /sdcard doesn't work on the device -- this is
# a known cause of difficulties.

# The below re-generates configure, Makefiles, ...
# This is not needed if you start from a release tarball.
./autogen.sh

# for ARM
CPPFLAGS="--sysroot=$NDKROOT/platforms/android-3/arch-arm" \
```

```
    CFLAGS="--sysroot=$NDKROOT/platforms/android-3/arch-arm" \
    ./configure --prefix=/data/local/Inst \
    --host=armv7-unknown-linux --target=armv7-unknown-linux \
    --with-tmpdir=/sdcard
# note: on android emulator, android-14 platform was also tested and works.
# It is not clear what this platform nr really is.

# for x86
CPPFLAGS="--sysroot=$NDKROOT/platforms/android-9/arch-x86" \
    CFLAGS="--sysroot=$NDKROOT/platforms/android-9/arch-x86 -fno-pic" \
    ./configure --prefix=/data/local/Inst \
    --host=i686-android-linux --target=i686-android-linux \
    --with-tmpdir=/sdcard

# for MIPS32
CPPFLAGS="--sysroot=$NDKROOT/platforms/android-18/arch-mips" \
    CFLAGS="--sysroot=$NDKROOT/platforms/android-18/arch-mips" \
    ./configure --prefix=/data/local/Inst \
    --host=mipsel-linux-android --target=mipsel-linux-android \
    --with-tmpdir=/sdcard

# for ARM64 (AArch64)
CPPFLAGS="--sysroot=$NDKROOT/platforms/android-21/arch-arm64" \
    CFLAGS="--sysroot=$NDKROOT/platforms/android-21/arch-arm64" \
    ./configure --prefix=/data/local/Inst \
    --host=aarch64-unknown-linux --target=aarch64-unknown-linux \
    --with-tmpdir=/sdcard


# At the end of the configure run, a few lines of details
# are printed.  Make sure that you see these two lines:
#
# For ARM:
#          Platform variant: android
#      Primary -DVGPV string: -DVGPV_arm_linux_android=1
#
# For x86:
#          Platform variant: android
#      Primary -DVGPV string: -DVGPV_x86_linux_android=1
#
# For mips32:
#          Platform variant: android
#      Primary -DVGPV string: -DVGPV_mips32_linux_android=1
#
# For ARM64 (AArch64):
#          Platform variant: android
#      Primary -DVGPV string: -DVGPV_arm64_linux_android=1
#
# If you see anything else at this point, something is wrong, and
# either the build will fail, or will succeed but you'll get something
# which won't work.


# Build, and park the install tree in 'pwd'/Inst
```

```
#
make -j4
make -j4 install DESTDIR=`pwd`/Inst


# To get the install tree onto the device:
# (I don't know why it's not "adb push Inst /data/local", but this
# formulation does appear to put the result in /data/local/Inst.)
#
adb push Inst /


# To run (on the device).  There are two things you need to consider:
#
# (1) if you are running on the Android emulator, Valgrind may crash
#     at startup.  This is because the emulator (for ARM) may not be
#     simulating a hardware TLS register.  To get around this, run
#     Valgrind with:
#        --kernel-variant=android-emulator-no-hw-tls
#
# (2) if you are running a real device, you need to tell Valgrind
#     what GPU it has, so Valgrind knows how to handle custom GPU
#     ioctls.  You can choose one of the following:
#        --kernel-variant=android-gpu-sgx5xx      # PowerVR SGX 5XX series
#        --kernel-variant=android-gpu-adreno3xx   # Qualcomm Adreno 3XX series
#     If you don't choose one, the program will still run, but Memcheck
#     may report false errors after the program performs GPU-specific ioctls.
#
# Anyway: to run on the device:
#
/data/local/Inst/bin/valgrind [kernel variant args] [the usual args etc]


# Once you're up and running, a handy modify-V-rebuild-reinstall
# command line (on the host, of course) is
#
mq -j2 && mq -j2 install DESTDIR=`pwd`/Inst && adb push Inst /
#
# where 'mq' is an alias for 'make --quiet'.


# One common cause of runs failing at startup is the inability of
# Valgrind to find a suitable temporary directory.  On the device,
# there doesn't seem to be any one location which we always have
# permission to write to.  The instructions above use /sdcard.  If
# that doesn't work for you, and you're Valgrinding one specific
# application which is already installed, you could try using its
# temporary directory, in /data/data, for example
# /data/data/org.mozilla.firefox_beta.
#
# Using /system/bin/logcat on the device is helpful for diagnosing
# these kinds of problems.
```

10. README.android_emulator

How to install and run an android emulator.

mkdir android # or any other place you prefer
cd android

download java JDK
http://www.oracle.com/technetwork/java/javase/downloads/index.html
download android SDK
http://developer.android.com/sdk/index.html
download android NDK
http://developer.android.com/sdk/ndk/index.html

versions I used:
jdk-7u4-linux-i586.tar.gz
android-ndk-r8-linux-x86.tar.bz2
android-sdk_r18-linux.tgz

install jdk
tar xzf jdk-7u4-linux-i586.tar.gz

install sdk
tar xzf android-sdk_r18-linux.tgz

install ndk
tar xjf android-ndk-r8-linux-x86.tar.bz2

setup PATH to use the installed software:
export SDKROOT=$HOME/android/android-sdk-linux
export PATH=$PATH:$SDKROOT/tools:$SDKROOT/platform-tools
export NDKROOT=$HOME/android/android-ndk-r8

install android platforms you want by starting:
android
(from $SDKROOT/tools)

select the platforms you need
I selected and installed:
Android 4.0.3 (API 15)
Upgraded then to the newer version available:
Android sdk 20
Android platform tools 12

then define a virtual device:
Tools -> Manage AVDs...
I define an AVD Name with 64 Mb SD Card, (4.0.3, api 15)
rest is default

compile and make install Valgrind, following README.android

Start your android emulator (it takes some time).
You can use adb shell to get a shell on the device
and see it is working. Note that I usually get
one or two time out from adb shell before it works
adb shell

Once the emulator is ready, push your Valgrind to the emulator:
adb push Inst /

IMPORTANT: when running Valgrind, you may need give it the flag
#
--kernel-variant=android-emulator-no-hw-tls
#
since otherwise it may crash at startup.
See README.android for details.

if you need to debug:
You have on the android side a gdbserver
on the device side:
gdbserver :1234 your_exe

on the host side:
adb forward tcp:1234 tcp:1234
$HOME/android/android-ndk-r8/toolchains/arm-linux-androideabi-4.4.3/prebuilt/linux-x86/bin/arm-linux-
androideabi-gdb your_exe
target remote :1234

11. README.mips

Supported platforms

- MIPS32 and MIPS64 platforms are currently supported.
- Both little-endian and big-endian cores are supported.
- MIPS DSP ASE on MIPS32 platforms is supported.

Building V for MIPS

- Native build is available for all supported platforms. The build system
expects that native GCC is configured correctly and optimized for the platform.
Yet, this may not be the case with some Debian distributions which configure
GCC to compile to "mips1" by default. Depending on a target platform, using
CFLAGS="-mips32r2", CFLAGS="-mips32" or CFLAGS="-mips64" or
CFLAGS="-mips64 -mabi=64" will do the trick and compile Valgrind correctly.

  Use of cross toolchain is supported as well.
- Example of configure line and additional configure options:

    $ ./configure --host=mipsel-linux-gnu --prefix=<path_to_install_directory>
        [--with-pagesize=<4|16|64>]

  * --host=mips-linux-gnu is necessary only if Valgrind is built on platform
    other then MIPS, tools for building MIPS application have to be in PATH.

  * --with-pagesize option is used to set default PAGE SIZE. If option is not
    used, PAGE SIZE is set to value default for platform on which Valgrind is
    built on. Possible values are 4, 16 of 64 and represent size in kilobytes.

  * --host=mips-linux-gnu is necessary if you compile it with cross toolchain
    compiler for big endian platform.

  * --host=mipsel-linux-gnu is necessary if you compile it with cross toolchain
    compiler for little endian platform.

  * --build=mips-linux is needed if you want to build it for MIPS32 on 64-bit
    MIPS system.

  * If you are compiling Valgrind for mips32 with gcc version older then
    gcc (GCC) 4.5.1, you must specify CFLAGS="-mips32r2 -mplt", e.g.

    ./configure --prefix=<path_to_install_directory>
    CFLAGS="-mips32r2 -mplt"

Limitations

- Some gdb tests will fail when gdb (GDB) older than 7.5 is used and gdb is
  not compiled with '--with-expat=yes'.

- You can not compile tests for DSP ASE if you are using gcc (GCC) older
  then 4.6.1 due to a bug in the toolchain.
- Older GCC may have issues with some inline assembly blocks. Get a toolchain
  based on newer GCC versions, if possible.

12. README.solaris

Requirements

- You need a recent Solaris-like OS to compile this port. Solaris 11 or
  any illumos-based distribution should work, Solaris 10 is not supported.
  Running 'uname -r' has to print '5.11'.
- Recent GCC tools are required, GCC 3 will probably not work. GCC version
  4.5 (or higher) is recommended.
- Solaris ld has to be the first linker in the PATH. GNU ld cannot be used.
  There is currently no linker check in the configure script but the linking
  phase fails if GNU ld is used. Recent Solaris/illumos distributions are ok.
- A working combination of autotools is required: aclocal, autoheader,
  automake and autoconf have to be found in the PATH. You should be able to
  install pkg:/developer/build/automake and pkg:/developer/build/autoconf
  packages to fullfil this requirement.
- System header files and GNU make is also required.
- For remote debugging support, working GDB is required (see below).

Compilation

Please follow the generic instructions in the README file.

The configure script detects a canonical host to determine which version of
Valgrind should be built. If the system compiler by default produces 32-bit
binaries then only a 32-bit version of Valgrind will be built. To enable
compilation of both 64-bit and 32-bit versions on such a system, issue the
configure script as follows:
./configure CC='gcc -m64' CXX='g++ -m64'

Oracle Solaris and illumos support

One of the main goal of this port is to support both Oracle Solaris and
illumos kernels. This is a very hard task because Solaris kernel traditionally
does not provide a stable syscall interface and because Valgrind contains
several parts that are closely tied to the underlying kernel. For these
reasons, the port needs to detect which syscall interfaces are present. This
detection cannot be done easily at run time and is currently implemented as
a set of configure tests. This means that a binary version of this port can be
executed only on a kernel that is compatible with a kernel that was used
during the configure and compilation time.

Main currently-known incompatibilities:
- Solaris 11 (released in November 2011) removed a large set of syscalls where
  *at variant of the syscall was also present, for example, open() versus
  openat(AT_FDCWD) [1]
- syscall number for unlinkat() is 76 on Solaris 11, but 65 on illumos [2]
- illumos (in April 2013) changed interface of the accept() and pipe()
  syscalls [3]

[1] http://docs.oracle.com/cd/E26502_01/html/E28556/gkzlf.html#gkzip
[2] https://www.illumos.org/issues/521
[3] https://github.com/illumos/illumos-gate/commit/5dbfd19ad5fcc2b779f40f80fa05c1bd28fd0b4e

Limitations

- The port is Work-In-Progress, many things may not work or they can be subtly
  broken.
- Coredumps produced by Valgrind do not contain all information available,
  especially microstate accounting and processor bindings.
- Accessing contents of /proc/self/psinfo is not thread-safe. That is because
  Valgrind emulates this file on behalf of the client programs. Entire
  open() - read() - close() sequence on this file needs to be performed
  atomically.
- Fork limitations: vfork() is translated to fork(), forkall() is not
  supported.
- Valgrind does not track definedness of some eflags (OF, SF, ZF, AF, CF, PF)
  individually for each flag. After a syscall is finished, when a carry flag
  is set and defined, all other mentioned flags will be also defined even
  though they might be undefined before making the syscall.
- System call "execve" with a file descriptor which points to a hardlink
  is currently not supported. That is because from the opened file descriptor
  itself it is not possible to reverse map the intended pathname.
  Examples are fexecve(3C) and isaexec(3C).
- Program headers PT_SUNW_SYSSTAT and PT_SUNW_SYSSTAT_ZONE are not supported.
  That is, programs linked with mapfile directive RESERVE_SEGMENT and attribute
  TYPE equal to SYSSTAT or SYSSTAT_ZONE will cause Valgrind exit. It is not
  possible for Valgrind to arrange mapping of a kernel shared page at the
  address specified in the mapfile for the guest application. There is currently
  no such mechanism in Solaris. Hacky workarounds are possible, though.
- Guest programs do not contain entries for AT_SUN_SYSSTAT_ADDR and
  AT_SUN_SYSSTAT_ZONE_ADDR in their auxilliary vectors. There is no direct way
  how to obtain addresses of these pages shared with the kernel as they are
  passed in auxv and kernel does not create auxv for statically linked binaries
  (such as Valgrind analysis tools).
  Indirect methods, such as scanning 1-page mappings found at Valgrind
  startup surrounded by reservations, could be possible. But it is hard to tell
  which page is which because their contents are filled only when a system
  cyclic is started. See get_hrusec() for reference.
- When a thread has no stack then all system calls will result in Valgrind
  crash, even though such system calls use just parameters passed in registers.
  This should happen only in pathological situations when a thread is created
  with custom mmap'ed stack and this stack is then unmap'ed during thread
  execution.

Remote debugging support

Solaris port of GDB has a major flaw which prevents remote debugging from
working correctly. Fortunately this flaw has an easy fix [4]. Unfortunately
it is not present in the current GDB 7.6.2. This boils down to several
options:
- Use GDB shipped with Solaris 11.2 which has this flaw fixed.

- Wait until GDB 7.7 becomes available (there won't be other 7.6.x releases).
- Build GDB 7.6.2 with the fix by yourself using the following steps:
     # pkg install developer/gnu-binutils
     $ wget http://ftp.gnu.org/gnu/gdb/gdb-7.6.2.tar.gz
     $ gzip -dc gdb-7.6.2.tar.gz | tar xf -
     $ cd gdb-7.6.2
     $ patch -p1 -i /path/to/valgrind-solaris/solaris/gdb-sol-thread.patch
     $ export LIBS="-lncurses"
     $ export CC="gcc -m64"
     $ ./configure --with-x=no --with-curses --with-libexpat-prefix=/usr/lib
     $ gmake && gmake install

[4] https://sourceware.org/ml/gdb-patches/2013-12/msg00573.html

TODO list

- Fix few remaining failing tests.
- Add more Solaris-specific tests (especially for the door and spawn
  syscalls).
- Provide better error reporting for various subsyscalls.
- Implement storing of extra register state in signal frame.
- Performance comparison against other platforms.

- Prevent SIGPIPE when writing to a socket (coregrind/m_libcfile.c).
- Implement ticket locking for fair scheduling (--fair-sched=yes).
- Implement support in DRD and Helgrind tools for thr_join() with thread == 0.
- Add support for accessing thread-local variables via gdb (auxprogs/getoff.c).
  Requires research on internal libc TLS representation.
- VEX supports AVX, BMI and AVX2. Investigate if they can be enabled on
  Solaris/illumos.
- Investigate support for more flags in AT_SUN_AUXFLAGS.
- Fix Valgrind crash when a thread has no stack and syswrap-main.c accesses
  all possible syscall parameters. Enable helgrind/tests/stackteardown.c
  to see this in effect. Would require awareness of syscall parameter semantics.
- Correctly print arguments of DW_CFA_ORCL_arg_loc in show_CF_instruction() when
  it is implemented in libdwarf.

Contacts

Please send bug reports and any questions about the port to:
Ivo Raisr <ivosh@ivosh.net>
Petr Pavlu <setup@dagobah.cz>

GNU Licenses

Table of Contents

1. The GNU General Public License

GNU GENERAL PUBLIC LICENSE
Version 2, June 1991

Preamble

The licenses for most software are designed to take away your
freedom to share and change it. By contrast, the GNU General Public
License is intended to guarantee your freedom to share and change free
software--to make sure the software is free for all its users. This
General Public License applies to most of the Free Software
Foundation's software and to any other program whose authors commit to
using it. (Some other Free Software Foundation software is covered by
the GNU Lesser General Public License instead.) You can apply it to
your programs, too.

When we speak of free software, we are referring to freedom, not
price. Our General Public Licenses are designed to make sure that you
have the freedom to distribute copies of free software (and charge for
this service if you wish), that you receive source code or can get it
if you want it, that you can change the software or use pieces of it
in new free programs; and that you know you can do these things.

To protect your rights, we need to make restrictions that forbid
anyone to deny you these rights or to ask you to surrender the rights.
These restrictions translate to certain responsibilities for you if you
distribute copies of the software, or if you modify it.

For example, if you distribute copies of such a program, whether
gratis or for a fee, you must give the recipients all the rights that
you have. You must make sure that they, too, receive or can get the
source code. And you must show them these terms so they know their
rights.

We protect your rights with two steps: (1) copyright the software, and
(2) offer you this license which gives you legal permission to copy,
distribute and/or modify the software.

Also, for each author's protection and ours, we want to make certain
that everyone understands that there is no warranty for this free
software. If the software is modified by someone else and passed on, we
want its recipients to know that what they have is not the original, so
that any problems introduced by others will not reflect on the original
authors' reputations.

Finally, any free program is threatened constantly by software patents. We wish to avoid the danger that redistributors of a free program will individually obtain patent licenses, in effect making the program proprietary. To prevent this, we have made it clear that any patent must be licensed for everyone's free use or not licensed at all.

The precise terms and conditions for copying, distribution and modification follow.

GNU GENERAL PUBLIC LICENSE
TERMS AND CONDITIONS FOR COPYING, DISTRIBUTION AND MODIFICATION

0. This License applies to any program or other work which contains a notice placed by the copyright holder saying it may be distributed under the terms of this General Public License. The "Program", below, refers to any such program or work, and a "work based on the Program" means either the Program or any derivative work under copyright law: that is to say, a work containing the Program or a portion of it, either verbatim or with modifications and/or translated into another language. (Hereinafter, translation is included without limitation in the term "modification".) Each licensee is addressed as "you".

Activities other than copying, distribution and modification are not covered by this License; they are outside its scope. The act of running the Program is not restricted, and the output from the Program is covered only if its contents constitute a work based on the Program (independent of having been made by running the Program). Whether that is true depends on what the Program does.

1. You may copy and distribute verbatim copies of the Program's source code as you receive it, in any medium, provided that you conspicuously and appropriately publish on each copy an appropriate copyright notice and disclaimer of warranty; keep intact all the notices that refer to this License and to the absence of any warranty; and give any other recipients of the Program a copy of this License along with the Program.

You may charge a fee for the physical act of transferring a copy, and you may at your option offer warranty protection in exchange for a fee.

2. You may modify your copy or copies of the Program or any portion of it, thus forming a work based on the Program, and copy and distribute such modifications or work under the terms of Section 1 above, provided that you also meet all of these conditions:

a) You must cause the modified files to carry prominent notices stating that you changed the files and the date of any change.

b) You must cause any work that you distribute or publish, that in whole or in part contains or is derived from the Program or any part thereof, to be licensed as a whole at no charge to all third parties under the terms of this License.

c) If the modified program normally reads commands interactively when run, you must cause it, when started running for such interactive use in the most ordinary way, to print or display an announcement including an appropriate copyright notice and a notice that there is no warranty (or else, saying that you provide a warranty) and that users may redistribute the program under these conditions, and telling the user how to view a copy of this License. (Exception: if the Program itself is interactive but does not normally print such an announcement, your work based on the Program is not required to print an announcement.)

These requirements apply to the modified work as a whole. If identifiable sections of that work are not derived from the Program, and can be reasonably considered independent and separate works in themselves, then this License, and its terms, do not apply to those sections when you distribute them as separate works. But when you distribute the same sections as part of a whole which is a work based on the Program, the distribution of the whole must be on the terms of this License, whose permissions for other licensees extend to the entire whole, and thus to each and every part regardless of who wrote it.

Thus, it is not the intent of this section to claim rights or contest your rights to work written entirely by you; rather, the intent is to exercise the right to control the distribution of derivative or collective works based on the Program.

In addition, mere aggregation of another work not based on the Program with the Program (or with a work based on the Program) on a volume of a storage or distribution medium does not bring the other work under the scope of this License.

3. You may copy and distribute the Program (or a work based on it, under Section 2) in object code or executable form under the terms of Sections 1 and 2 above provided that you also do one of the following:

a) Accompany it with the complete corresponding machine-readable source code, which must be distributed under the terms of Sections 1 and 2 above on a medium customarily used for software interchange; or,

b) Accompany it with a written offer, valid for at least three years, to give any third party, for a charge no more than your cost of physically performing source distribution, a complete machine-readable copy of the corresponding source code, to be distributed under the terms of Sections 1 and 2 above on a medium customarily used for software interchange; or,

c) Accompany it with the information you received as to the offer to distribute corresponding source code. (This alternative is allowed only for noncommercial distribution and only if you received the program in object code or executable form with such an offer, in accord with Subsection b above.)

The source code for a work means the preferred form of the work for making modifications to it. For an executable work, complete source code means all the source code for all modules it contains, plus any associated interface definition files, plus the scripts used to control compilation and installation of the executable. However, as a special exception, the source code distributed need not include anything that is normally distributed (in either source or binary form) with the major components (compiler, kernel, and so on) of the operating system on which the executable runs, unless that component itself accompanies the executable.

If distribution of executable or object code is made by offering access to copy from a designated place, then offering equivalent access to copy the source code from the same place counts as distribution of the source code, even though third parties are not compelled to copy the source along with the object code.

4. You may not copy, modify, sublicense, or distribute the Program except as expressly provided under this License. Any attempt otherwise to copy, modify, sublicense or distribute the Program is void, and will automatically terminate your rights under this License. However, parties who have received copies, or rights, from you under this License will not have their licenses terminated so long as such parties remain in full compliance.

5. You are not required to accept this License, since you have not signed it. However, nothing else grants you permission to modify or distribute the Program or its derivative works. These actions are prohibited by law if you do not accept this License. Therefore, by modifying or distributing the Program (or any work based on the Program), you indicate your acceptance of this License to do so, and all its terms and conditions for copying, distributing or modifying the Program or works based on it.

6. Each time you redistribute the Program (or any work based on the Program), the recipient automatically receives a license from the original licensor to copy, distribute or modify the Program subject to these terms and conditions. You may not impose any further restrictions on the recipients' exercise of the rights granted herein. You are not responsible for enforcing compliance by third parties to this License.

7. If, as a consequence of a court judgment or allegation of patent infringement or for any other reason (not limited to patent issues), conditions are imposed on you (whether by court order, agreement or otherwise) that contradict the conditions of this License, they do not excuse you from the conditions of this License. If you cannot distribute so as to satisfy simultaneously your obligations under this License and any other pertinent obligations, then as a consequence you may not distribute the Program at all. For example, if a patent license would not permit royalty-free redistribution of the Program by all those who receive copies directly or indirectly through you, then the only way you could satisfy both it and this License would be to refrain entirely from distribution of the Program.

If any portion of this section is held invalid or unenforceable under any particular circumstance, the balance of the section is intended to apply and the section as a whole is intended to apply in other circumstances.

It is not the purpose of this section to induce you to infringe any patents or other property right claims or to contest validity of any such claims; this section has the sole purpose of protecting the integrity of the free software distribution system, which is implemented by public license practices. Many people have made generous contributions to the wide range of software distributed through that system in reliance on consistent application of that system; it is up to the author/donor to decide if he or she is willing to distribute software through any other system and a licensee cannot impose that choice.

This section is intended to make thoroughly clear what is believed to be a consequence of the rest of this License.

8. If the distribution and/or use of the Program is restricted in certain countries either by patents or by copyrighted interfaces, the original copyright holder who places the Program under this License may add an explicit geographical distribution limitation excluding those countries, so that distribution is permitted only in or among countries not thus excluded. In such case, this License incorporates the limitation as if written in the body of this License.

9. The Free Software Foundation may publish revised and/or new versions of the General Public License from time to time. Such new versions will be similar in spirit to the present version, but may differ in detail to address new problems or concerns.

Each version is given a distinguishing version number. If the Program specifies a version number of this License which applies to it and "any later version", you have the option of following the terms and conditions either of that version or of any later version published by the Free Software Foundation. If the Program does not specify a version number of this License, you may choose any version ever published by the Free Software Foundation.

10. If you wish to incorporate parts of the Program into other free programs whose distribution conditions are different, write to the author to ask for permission. For software which is copyrighted by the Free Software Foundation, write to the Free Software Foundation; we sometimes make exceptions for this. Our decision will be guided by the two goals of preserving the free status of all derivatives of our free software and of promoting the sharing and reuse of software generally.

NO WARRANTY

11. BECAUSE THE PROGRAM IS LICENSED FREE OF CHARGE, THERE IS NO WARRANTY FOR THE PROGRAM, TO THE EXTENT PERMITTED BY APPLICABLE LAW. EXCEPT WHEN OTHERWISE STATED IN WRITING THE COPYRIGHT HOLDERS AND/OR OTHER PARTIES PROVIDE THE PROGRAM "AS IS" WITHOUT WARRANTY OF ANY KIND, EITHER EXPRESSED OR IMPLIED, INCLUDING, BUT NOT LIMITED TO, THE IMPLIED WARRANTIES OF MERCHANTABILITY AND FITNESS FOR A PARTICULAR PURPOSE. THE ENTIRE RISK AS TO THE QUALITY AND PERFORMANCE OF THE PROGRAM IS WITH YOU. SHOULD THE

PROGRAM PROVE DEFECTIVE, YOU ASSUME THE COST OF ALL NECESSARY SERVICING, REPAIR OR CORRECTION.

12. IN NO EVENT UNLESS REQUIRED BY APPLICABLE LAW OR AGREED TO IN WRITING WILL ANY COPYRIGHT HOLDER, OR ANY OTHER PARTY WHO MAY MODIFY AND/OR REDISTRIBUTE THE PROGRAM AS PERMITTED ABOVE, BE LIABLE TO YOU FOR DAMAGES, INCLUDING ANY GENERAL, SPECIAL, INCIDENTAL OR CONSEQUENTIAL DAMAGES ARISING OUT OF THE USE OR INABILITY TO USE THE PROGRAM (INCLUDING BUT NOT LIMITED TO LOSS OF DATA OR DATA BEING RENDERED INACCURATE OR LOSSES SUSTAINED BY YOU OR THIRD PARTIES OR A FAILURE OF THE PROGRAM TO OPERATE WITH ANY OTHER PROGRAMS), EVEN IF SUCH HOLDER OR OTHER PARTY HAS BEEN ADVISED OF THE POSSIBILITY OF SUCH DAMAGES.

END OF TERMS AND CONDITIONS

How to Apply These Terms to Your New Programs

If you develop a new program, and you want it to be of the greatest
possible use to the public, the best way to achieve this is to make it
free software which everyone can redistribute and change under these terms.

To do so, attach the following notices to the program. It is safest
to attach them to the start of each source file to most effectively
convey the exclusion of warranty; and each file should have at least
the "copyright" line and a pointer to where the full notice is found.

    <one line to give the program's name and a brief idea of what it does.>
    Copyright (C) <year> <name of author>

    This program is free software; you can redistribute it and/or modify
    it under the terms of the GNU General Public License as published by
    the Free Software Foundation; either version 2 of the License, or
    (at your option) any later version.

    This program is distributed in the hope that it will be useful,
    but WITHOUT ANY WARRANTY; without even the implied warranty of
    MERCHANTABILITY or FITNESS FOR A PARTICULAR PURPOSE. See the
    GNU General Public License for more details.

    You should have received a copy of the GNU General Public License along
    with this program; if not, write to the Free Software Foundation, Inc.,
    51 Franklin Street, Fifth Floor, Boston, MA 02110-1301 USA.

Also add information on how to contact you by electronic and paper mail.

If the program is interactive, make it output a short notice like this
when it starts in an interactive mode:

    Gnomovision version 69, Copyright (C) year name of author
    Gnomovision comes with ABSOLUTELY NO WARRANTY; for details type 'show w'.
    This is free software, and you are welcome to redistribute it
    under certain conditions; type 'show c' for details.

The hypothetical commands 'show w' and 'show c' should show the appropriate parts of the General Public License. Of course, the commands you use may be called something other than 'show w' and 'show c'; they could even be mouse-clicks or menu items--whatever suits your program.

You should also get your employer (if you work as a programmer) or your school, if any, to sign a "copyright disclaimer" for the program, if necessary. Here is a sample; alter the names:

Yoyodyne, Inc., hereby disclaims all copyright interest in the program 'Gnomovision' (which makes passes at compilers) written by James Hacker.

<signature of Ty Coon>, 1 April 1989
Ty Coon, President of Vice

This General Public License does not permit incorporating your program into proprietary programs. If your program is a subroutine library, you may consider it more useful to permit linking proprietary applications with the library. If this is what you want to do, use the GNU Lesser General Public License instead of this License.

2. The GNU Free Documentation License

GNU Free Documentation License
Version 1.2, November 2002

0. PREAMBLE

The purpose of this License is to make a manual, textbook, or other
functional and useful document "free" in the sense of freedom: to
assure everyone the effective freedom to copy and redistribute it,
with or without modifying it, either commercially or noncommercially.
Secondarily, this License preserves for the author and publisher a way
to get credit for their work, while not being considered responsible
for modifications made by others.

This License is a kind of "copyleft", which means that derivative
works of the document must themselves be free in the same sense. It
complements the GNU General Public License, which is a copyleft
license designed for free software.

We have designed this License in order to use it for manuals for free
software, because free software needs free documentation: a free
program should come with manuals providing the same freedoms that the
software does. But this License is not limited to software manuals;
it can be used for any textual work, regardless of subject matter or
whether it is published as a printed book. We recommend this License
principally for works whose purpose is instruction or reference.

1. APPLICABILITY AND DEFINITIONS

This License applies to any manual or other work, in any medium, that
contains a notice placed by the copyright holder saying it can be
distributed under the terms of this License. Such a notice grants a
world-wide, royalty-free license, unlimited in duration, to use that
work under the conditions stated herein. The "Document", below,
refers to any such manual or work. Any member of the public is a
licensee, and is addressed as "you". You accept the license if you
copy, modify or distribute the work in a way requiring permission
under copyright law.

A "Modified Version" of the Document means any work containing the
Document or a portion of it, either copied verbatim, or with

modifications and/or translated into another language.

A "Secondary Section" is a named appendix or a front-matter section of
the Document that deals exclusively with the relationship of the
publishers or authors of the Document to the Document's overall subject
(or to related matters) and contains nothing that could fall directly
within that overall subject. (Thus, if the Document is in part a
textbook of mathematics, a Secondary Section may not explain any
mathematics.) The relationship could be a matter of historical
connection with the subject or with related matters, or of legal,
commercial, philosophical, ethical or political position regarding
them.

The "Invariant Sections" are certain Secondary Sections whose titles
are designated, as being those of Invariant Sections, in the notice
that says that the Document is released under this License. If a
section does not fit the above definition of Secondary then it is not
allowed to be designated as Invariant. The Document may contain zero
Invariant Sections. If the Document does not identify any Invariant
Sections then there are none.

The "Cover Texts" are certain short passages of text that are listed,
as Front-Cover Texts or Back-Cover Texts, in the notice that says that
the Document is released under this License. A Front-Cover Text may
be at most 5 words, and a Back-Cover Text may be at most 25 words.

A "Transparent" copy of the Document means a machine-readable copy,
represented in a format whose specification is available to the
general public, that is suitable for revising the document
straightforwardly with generic text editors or (for images composed of
pixels) generic paint programs or (for drawings) some widely available
drawing editor, and that is suitable for input to text formatters or
for automatic translation to a variety of formats suitable for input
to text formatters. A copy made in an otherwise Transparent file
format whose markup, or absence of markup, has been arranged to thwart
or discourage subsequent modification by readers is not Transparent.
An image format is not Transparent if used for any substantial amount
of text. A copy that is not "Transparent" is called "Opaque".

Examples of suitable formats for Transparent copies include plain
ASCII without markup, Texinfo input format, LaTeX input format, SGML
or XML using a publicly available DTD, and standard-conforming simple
HTML, PostScript or PDF designed for human modification. Examples of
transparent image formats include PNG, XCF and JPG. Opaque formats
include proprietary formats that can be read and edited only by
proprietary word processors, SGML or XML for which the DTD and/or
processing tools are not generally available, and the
machine-generated HTML, PostScript or PDF produced by some word
processors for output purposes only.

The "Title Page" means, for a printed book, the title page itself,
plus such following pages as are needed to hold, legibly, the material
this License requires to appear in the title page. For works in
formats which do not have any title page as such, "Title Page" means

the text near the most prominent appearance of the work's title, preceding the beginning of the body of the text.

A section "Entitled XYZ" means a named subunit of the Document whose title either is precisely XYZ or contains XYZ in parentheses following text that translates XYZ in another language. (Here XYZ stands for a specific section name mentioned below, such as "Acknowledgements", "Dedications", "Endorsements", or "History".) To "Preserve the Title" of such a section when you modify the Document means that it remains a section "Entitled XYZ" according to this definition.

The Document may include Warranty Disclaimers next to the notice which states that this License applies to the Document. These Warranty Disclaimers are considered to be included by reference in this License, but only as regards disclaiming warranties: any other implication that these Warranty Disclaimers may have is void and has no effect on the meaning of this License.

2. VERBATIM COPYING

You may copy and distribute the Document in any medium, either commercially or noncommercially, provided that this License, the copyright notices, and the license notice saying this License applies to the Document are reproduced in all copies, and that you add no other conditions whatsoever to those of this License. You may not use technical measures to obstruct or control the reading or further copying of the copies you make or distribute. However, you may accept compensation in exchange for copies. If you distribute a large enough number of copies you must also follow the conditions in section 3.

You may also lend copies, under the same conditions stated above, and you may publicly display copies.

3. COPYING IN QUANTITY

If you publish printed copies (or copies in media that commonly have printed covers) of the Document, numbering more than 100, and the Document's license notice requires Cover Texts, you must enclose the copies in covers that carry, clearly and legibly, all these Cover Texts: Front-Cover Texts on the front cover, and Back-Cover Texts on the back cover. Both covers must also clearly and legibly identify you as the publisher of these copies. The front cover must present the full title with all words of the title equally prominent and visible. You may add other material on the covers in addition. Copying with changes limited to the covers, as long as they preserve the title of the Document and satisfy these conditions, can be treated as verbatim copying in other respects.

If the required texts for either cover are too voluminous to fit legibly, you should put the first ones listed (as many as fit reasonably) on the actual cover, and continue the rest onto adjacent pages.

If you publish or distribute Opaque copies of the Document numbering more than 100, you must either include a machine-readable Transparent copy along with each Opaque copy, or state in or with each Opaque copy a computer-network location from which the general network-using public has access to download using public-standard network protocols a complete Transparent copy of the Document, free of added material. If you use the latter option, you must take reasonably prudent steps, when you begin distribution of Opaque copies in quantity, to ensure that this Transparent copy will remain thus accessible at the stated location until at least one year after the last time you distribute an Opaque copy (directly or through your agents or retailers) of that edition to the public.

It is requested, but not required, that you contact the authors of the Document well before redistributing any large number of copies, to give them a chance to provide you with an updated version of the Document.

4. MODIFICATIONS

You may copy and distribute a Modified Version of the Document under the conditions of sections 2 and 3 above, provided that you release the Modified Version under precisely this License, with the Modified Version filling the role of the Document, thus licensing distribution and modification of the Modified Version to whoever possesses a copy of it. In addition, you must do these things in the Modified Version:

A. Use in the Title Page (and on the covers, if any) a title distinct from that of the Document, and from those of previous versions (which should, if there were any, be listed in the History section of the Document). You may use the same title as a previous version if the original publisher of that version gives permission.

B. List on the Title Page, as authors, one or more persons or entities responsible for authorship of the modifications in the Modified Version, together with at least five of the principal authors of the Document (all of its principal authors, if it has fewer than five), unless they release you from this requirement.

C. State on the Title page the name of the publisher of the Modified Version, as the publisher.

D. Preserve all the copyright notices of the Document.

E. Add an appropriate copyright notice for your modifications adjacent to the other copyright notices.

F. Include, immediately after the copyright notices, a license notice giving the public permission to use the Modified Version under the terms of this License, in the form shown in the Addendum below.

G. Preserve in that license notice the full lists of Invariant Sections and required Cover Texts given in the Document's license notice.

H. Include an unaltered copy of this License.

I. Preserve the section Entitled "History", Preserve its Title, and add to it an item stating at least the title, year, new authors, and publisher of the Modified Version as given on the Title Page. If there is no section Entitled "History" in the Document, create one stating the title, year, authors, and publisher of the Document as

given on its Title Page, then add an item describing the Modified
Version as stated in the previous sentence.

J. Preserve the network location, if any, given in the Document for
public access to a Transparent copy of the Document, and likewise
the network locations given in the Document for previous versions
it was based on. These may be placed in the "History" section.
You may omit a network location for a work that was published at
least four years before the Document itself, or if the original
publisher of the version it refers to gives permission.

K. For any section Entitled "Acknowledgements" or "Dedications",
Preserve the Title of the section, and preserve in the section all
the substance and tone of each of the contributor acknowledgements
and/or dedications given therein.

L. Preserve all the Invariant Sections of the Document,
unaltered in their text and in their titles. Section numbers
or the equivalent are not considered part of the section titles.

M. Delete any section Entitled "Endorsements". Such a section
may not be included in the Modified Version.

N. Do not retitle any existing section to be Entitled "Endorsements"
or to conflict in title with any Invariant Section.

O. Preserve any Warranty Disclaimers.

If the Modified Version includes new front-matter sections or
appendices that qualify as Secondary Sections and contain no material
copied from the Document, you may at your option designate some or all
of these sections as invariant. To do this, add their titles to the
list of Invariant Sections in the Modified Version's license notice.
These titles must be distinct from any other section titles.

You may add a section Entitled "Endorsements", provided it contains
nothing but endorsements of your Modified Version by various
parties--for example, statements of peer review or that the text has
been approved by an organization as the authoritative definition of a
standard.

You may add a passage of up to five words as a Front-Cover Text, and a
passage of up to 25 words as a Back-Cover Text, to the end of the list
of Cover Texts in the Modified Version. Only one passage of
Front-Cover Text and one of Back-Cover Text may be added by (or
through arrangements made by) any one entity. If the Document already
includes a cover text for the same cover, previously added by you or
by arrangement made by the same entity you are acting on behalf of,
you may not add another; but you may replace the old one, on explicit
permission from the previous publisher that added the old one.

The author(s) and publisher(s) of the Document do not by this License
give permission to use their names for publicity for or to assert or
imply endorsement of any Modified Version.

5. COMBINING DOCUMENTS

You may combine the Document with other documents released under this
License, under the terms defined in section 4 above for modified

versions, provided that you include in the combination all of the Invariant Sections of all of the original documents, unmodified, and list them all as Invariant Sections of your combined work in its license notice, and that you preserve all their Warranty Disclaimers.

The combined work need only contain one copy of this License, and multiple identical Invariant Sections may be replaced with a single copy. If there are multiple Invariant Sections with the same name but different contents, make the title of each such section unique by adding at the end of it, in parentheses, the name of the original author or publisher of that section if known, or else a unique number. Make the same adjustment to the section titles in the list of Invariant Sections in the license notice of the combined work.

In the combination, you must combine any sections Entitled "History" in the various original documents, forming one section Entitled "History"; likewise combine any sections Entitled "Acknowledgements", and any sections Entitled "Dedications". You must delete all sections Entitled "Endorsements".

6. COLLECTIONS OF DOCUMENTS

You may make a collection consisting of the Document and other documents released under this License, and replace the individual copies of this License in the various documents with a single copy that is included in the collection, provided that you follow the rules of this License for verbatim copying of each of the documents in all other respects.

You may extract a single document from such a collection, and distribute it individually under this License, provided you insert a copy of this License into the extracted document, and follow this License in all other respects regarding verbatim copying of that document.

7. AGGREGATION WITH INDEPENDENT WORKS

A compilation of the Document or its derivatives with other separate and independent documents or works, in or on a volume of a storage or distribution medium, is called an "aggregate" if the copyright resulting from the compilation is not used to limit the legal rights of the compilation's users beyond what the individual works permit. When the Document is included in an aggregate, this License does not apply to the other works in the aggregate which are not themselves derivative works of the Document.

If the Cover Text requirement of section 3 is applicable to these copies of the Document, then if the Document is less than one half of the entire aggregate, the Document's Cover Texts may be placed on covers that bracket the Document within the aggregate, or the electronic equivalent of covers if the Document is in electronic form. Otherwise they must appear on printed covers that bracket the whole aggregate.

8. TRANSLATION

Translation is considered a kind of modification, so you may
distribute translations of the Document under the terms of section 4.
Replacing Invariant Sections with translations requires special
permission from their copyright holders, but you may include
translations of some or all Invariant Sections in addition to the
original versions of these Invariant Sections. You may include a
translation of this License, and all the license notices in the
Document, and any Warranty Disclaimers, provided that you also include
the original English version of this License and the original versions
of those notices and disclaimers. In case of a disagreement between
the translation and the original version of this License or a notice
or disclaimer, the original version will prevail.

If a section in the Document is Entitled "Acknowledgements",
"Dedications", or "History", the requirement (section 4) to Preserve
its Title (section 1) will typically require changing the actual
title.

9. TERMINATION

You may not copy, modify, sublicense, or distribute the Document except
as expressly provided for under this License. Any other attempt to
copy, modify, sublicense or distribute the Document is void, and will
automatically terminate your rights under this License. However,
parties who have received copies, or rights, from you under this
License will not have their licenses terminated so long as such
parties remain in full compliance.

10. FUTURE REVISIONS OF THIS LICENSE

The Free Software Foundation may publish new, revised versions
of the GNU Free Documentation License from time to time. Such new
versions will be similar in spirit to the present version, but may
differ in detail to address new problems or concerns. See
http://www.gnu.org/copyleft/.

Each version of the License is given a distinguishing version number.
If the Document specifies that a particular numbered version of this
License "or any later version" applies to it, you have the option of
following the terms and conditions either of that specified version or
of any later version that has been published (not as a draft) by the
Free Software Foundation. If the Document does not specify a version
number of this License, you may choose any version ever published (not
as a draft) by the Free Software Foundation.

ADDENDUM: How to use this License for your documents

To use this License in a document you have written, include a copy of

the License in the document and put the following copyright and
license notices just after the title page:

> Copyright (c) YEAR YOUR NAME.
> Permission is granted to copy, distribute and/or modify this document
> under the terms of the GNU Free Documentation License, Version 1.2
> or any later version published by the Free Software Foundation;
> with no Invariant Sections, no Front-Cover Texts, and no Back-Cover Texts.
> A copy of the license is included in the section entitled "GNU
> Free Documentation License".

If you have Invariant Sections, Front-Cover Texts and Back-Cover Texts,
replace the "with...Texts." line with this:

> with the Invariant Sections being LIST THEIR TITLES, with the
> Front-Cover Texts being LIST, and with the Back-Cover Texts being LIST.

If you have Invariant Sections without Cover Texts, or some other
combination of the three, merge those two alternatives to suit the
situation.

If your document contains nontrivial examples of program code, we
recommend releasing these examples in parallel under your choice of
free software license, such as the GNU General Public License,
to permit their use in free software.

www.ingramcontent.com/pod-product-compliance
Lightning Source LLC
La Vergne TN
LVHW060134070326
832902LV00018B/2793